Competition and Cooperation

COMPETITION
&
COOPERATION:

The Emergence
of a National
Trade Association

by Louis Galambos

THE JOHNS HOPKINS PRESS
BALTIMORE

To My Father
and Mother

Preface and
Acknowledgments

This is a book about trade associations. To be more precise, it is a study of the evolution of regional and national trade associations in the American cotton textile industry. These organizations were shaped by a variety of forces, and I have attempted to describe the relevant aspects of their economic, political, and social environments, as well as the distinctive forms of association that this context produced. The trade organizations were not merely passive agents, molded by their surroundings; since they sought to influence their political and economic settings, I have also tried to determine how they did this and how effective their programs were.

The association movement in the cotton textile industry began in the years following the Civil War and reached its peak during the first two years of the New Deal. Within these limits, I have concentrated most of my attention on developments in the twentieth century and especially on the activities of a national association, the Cotton-Textile Institute, between 1926 and 1935.

My approach to this problem in economic history has been essentially historical. While the book thus presents a study of the evolution of a certain form of institution within a particular industry, I have sought to develop some hypotheses which will be of use to students of general American history and of mature capitalistic systems in other countries. Whether I have succeeded or not is for the reader to decide.

Through a case study of the regional and national associations in a major manufacturing industry, I hope that I have been able to improve our understanding of a form of business institution which has played a very significant role in the development of

America's particular brand of mixed capitalism. Certainly the associations have not received the kind of attention from historians that they deserve. Despite the advances made in business and economic history during recent years, scholars have yet to provide an adequate historical appraisal of the trade association movement. In the 1920's and 1930's trade organizations attracted considerable academic interest, but the resulting books and articles were, for the most part, narrow in scope; they suffered from a lack of perspective and a paucity of reliable information about a contemporary subject. In subsequent years economists and economic historians have marched off to conquer new fields. Very little research has been done on trade organizations. Although associations which perform important functions have emerged in almost every American industry, this kind of organization has become a sort of white whale in our economic past. Like the whale, the associations are frequently seen, often mentioned, repeatedly attacked, but never really captured—at least not by the historian.

In the course of this study I have received more help than I can possibly acknowledge. My wife, Margaret, sacrificed many vacations and listened patiently to obscure anecdotes about obscure men. She carried us through those many gloomy days when the typewriter just would not write. Our daughter, Lisa, provided moments of comic relief and seldom complained—for very long—after her father disappeared upstairs to work.

Since this is my first book, I feel compelled to acknowledge in some way the help of all those teachers who aroused my interest in history and guided my efforts as a student. I fear, however, that I must be satisfied with a "short list." At the head of this list stands David M. Potter, who directed my work when I began this study as a doctoral dissertation at Yale University. When I was at Yale, and afterwards, Professor Potter gave unstintingly of his time and his invaluable advice. Even more decisive was the manner in which he provided for me and for his other students a model of what historical research should be and how the historian should think. Earlier in my career, guidelines to the study of history were thrown down for me by Robert H. Ferrell of Indiana University and by Samuel Flagg Bemis and John Morton Blum of Yale. Several persons at Harvard University's Graduate School of Business Administration, including Ralph W. and Muriel Hidy, Henrietta Larson, Arthur M. Johnson, Barry E. Supple, and

George S. Gibb contributed to my interest in and understanding of economic and business history. I am grateful to them and to Hilma Holton, Marian Sears and James P. Baughman for the help that they gave me while I was a Business History Fellow during the year 1959–1960, and while I was a visitor at the School in the summer of 1963.

An economic historian could hardly be expected to ignore the financial assistance he received, and I am obligated to Yale University, to the American Philosophical Society, to Rice University, and to the Harvard Graduate School of Business Administration for grants which sustained my research. This support was particularly important insofar as I had to make a number of long research trips. The final revisions on the manuscript were completed while I was a fellow at the Center for the Study of Recent American History, The Johns Hopkins University, and the Center generously subsidized the publication of this book. I am particularly indebted to the Center's Director, Alfred D. Chandler, Jr., who has created at Johns Hopkins an ideal environment for the study of modern American institutions.

Several student assistants helped me, particularly with the statistical aspects of my study. Rhueina McCullough, William T. Heyck, Lillian Lubinski, Mrs. Judy Kilgore, Raymond Needham, and Cynthia Fraser all counted spindles and people and cotton mills for me. I appreciate the enthusiastic way they went about this painstaking work. Mrs. Polly Lewis, Mrs. Louise Hull and Mrs. Mary Comerford typed various drafts of the manuscript and helped in a variety of other ways, both legal and extralegal.

Since most of my research involved manuscripts which were in private hands, I am deeply obligated to the several persons who helped me obtain these vital records. In particular, I would like to mention the kind assistance of Mrs. James R. Angell, George B. Cramer, Frank P. Graham, Frederick W. Morrison, Jessie E. Vint, Josephine A. Loughry, William F. Sullivan, Mrs. H. Bartow Farr, F. Sadler Love, Goldthwaite H. Dorr, John K. Watson, Hunter Marshall, William M. McLaurine, C. C. Dawson, T. M. Forbes, O. B. Moore, Jr., Thomas N. Ingram, W. Ray Bell, the late Cason J. Callaway, Charles A. Cannon, Mr. and Mrs. Cullom Walker, Paul B. Halstead, John K. Cauthen, James Cawthon, and the late Donald Comer. Further information about the materials these persons helped me to locate and to examine can be found in the

Bibliography at the end of the book. Some of the manuscript collections that I found useful were in libraries, and while using these records I was helped by a number of conscientious librarians and archivists. Robert W. Lovett, Laurence J. Kipp, and Donald T. Clark gave me invaluable assistance at the Baker Library, Harvard University; I am also indebted to Elizabeth B. Drewry, Mrs. Anne Morris, and Jerome Deyo of the Roosevelt Library, Hyde Park, New York; and Meyer H. Fishbein, Leo Pascal, James E. Primas, Katherine H. Davidson, and Jeanne McDonald at the Business Economics Branch of the National Archives, Washington, D. C.

A number of persons read part or all of my manuscript and offered me some excellent advice; I would like to thank Richard L. Merritt and Robin Winks of Yale University, Alfred D. Chandler, Jr., of the Johns Hopkins University, Arthur M. Johnson of the Harvard Business School, and David M. Potter of Stanford University for their labors. While they were unable to catch all of the author's mistakes, they made suggestions which I believe greatly improved the final manuscript.

I would also like to thank the editor of *Explorations in Entrepreneurial History/Second Series* for permission to use material from my article on "The Trade Association Movement in Cotton Textiles, 1900–1935" (Volume II, Number 1) and the editor of the *Business History Review* for allowing me to draw upon my article on "The Cotton-Textile Institute and the Government" (Volume XXXVIII, Number 2).

Contents

Competition and Cooperation

Fall River:
Spring 1880

Fall River, Massachusetts, was dominated by the great cotton factories that sprawled down the city's steep hillsides from Lake Watuppa to the banks of the Taunton River. There were other industries in Fall River, but they were of little importance. From year to year, from season to season, from day to day, the cotton mills paced the city. They held a mortgage on the people of Fall River; the mill hands, the grocers, the tax collectors—even the bankers. Everyone in the city was dependent upon the textile industry for their present prosperity and their prospects for the years ahead.

From this indebtedness the local residents apparently had little to fear. Since the Civil War, cotton manufacturing had experienced a tremendous expansion. Favored by an even, humid climate, by proximity to the nation's cloth markets, and by inexpensive water transportation, Fall River had taken more than its share of the new spindles and looms being added to northern mills. By 1880 the city was securely established as the leading textile center of New England.

Economic optimism was the natural offspring of Fall River's past and present success. Since the war, everything—production, income, population—had shot upward in a series of brief, chaotic bursts. In the early 1870's twenty new cotton mills had been built. Two new factories were under construction in the spring of 1880, and there was talk of more plants to be built in the next year. If the mill treasurers who guided Fall River's companies were confident about the future, this was understandable. Like the rest of Fall River's citizens they had good cause for optimism. New people, new jobs, more money, more mills—Fall River's theme song in the spring of 1880 was prosperity and growth.

Chapter I

Perspective

In Western civilization the forces of change and economic growth have waged a relentless war against the men and institutions devoted to economic stability. At times the battle has been noisy and obvious; at others it has hardly been noticeable, even to the participants. Periodically one side or the other has gained a decisive victory. Still, the contest has always gone on, and neither stability nor growth has ever been established in a secure and lasting regime.

From the perspective of America in the 1960's, the forces of change appear to be all-important. We have experienced our industrial revolution; our very nation was in large part a product of an earlier commercial revolution. Things new, things improved seem natural to us. Traditional institutions have an almost un-American appearance. Devoted as we are to progress for ourselves and for others, we are fascinated by the theory and history of economic growth. In studying economic development we optimistically focus most of our attention on the factors which we hope will bring about the desired changes.[1]

My purpose is to flip the coin over, to examine an institution which was primarily dedicated to achieving stability. This institution, the trade association, arose in the modern industrial economy, but in several ways it was similar to organizations which performed the same functions in the pre-industrial age. In looking back to that earlier time, it is apparent that a most impressive

[1] Growth theory and its impact upon economic history are discussed in a series of excellent essays in *The Experience of Economic Growth*, ed. Barry E. Supple (New York: Random House, 1963), pp. 4–46.

triumph of the agencies of stability occurred during the later
Middle Ages. Agriculture, industry, and commerce were all
encased in ideological and organizational structures which held
men to the grooves of accustomed practice. The legal system mili-
tated against change. Political particularism imposed its own
subtle but effective restraint upon innovation. The Church but-
tressed the existing social and economic order, drawing man's
attention from the shifting probabilities of the material world to
the immutable truths of religion. Throughout Europe during the
fourteenth and fifteenth centuries, the economy was heavily
burdened with customs and combines devoted to the preservation
of the status quo. Prominent among these stabilizing institutions
were the guilds of artisans and of merchants.

The guild—with its emphasis upon cooperation, its dependence
upon a network of economic controls, and its tendency to develop
an alliance with the government—cast a pattern which the stabilizing institutions, subsequently developed by businessmen, have
followed.[2] Latter-day guilds—regulated companies and trade associations—have been shaped by different politico-economic environments; the trade association's link with the Medieval guild is of
course not generic. Naturally the controls and cooperative programs of the modern institutions have been attuned to a mercantile or industrial economy. They have most often sought their
political alliance with a national, not a local, government. Fundamentally, however, the organizations which businessmen in the
modern world have employed to stabilize conditions have performed the same functions as the guilds and have developed along
similar lines.

When examining these modern institutions, it is important to
remember that although the Medieval guilds were an influential
factor in their economy, they were unable to stifle the forces that
shifted the balance in sixteenth- and seventeenth-century Europe
from stabilization to growth. The economic organizations changed,
and the entire structure of Medieval society was reshaped by a

---

[2] The best guide to the development of the guilds is Sylvia L. Thrupp's
"The Guilds," in *The Cambridge Economic History of Europe,* ed. M. M.
Postan, E. E. Rich, and Edward Miller (Cambridge: The Cambridge University Press, 1963), III, 230–281. Other relevant chapters in the same volume
are: R. de Roover, "The Organization of Trade," particularly pp. 47, 111–
114, and 117–118; A. B. Hibbert, "The Economic Policies of Towns,"
especially pp. 169–170, 176–177, 181–229.

variety of political, social, and economic forces. In the economic sphere, the most outstanding innovations were associated with international trade. New markets and new sources of raw materials and precious metals provided merchants with unusual opportunities for profit-making. There was a new emphasis upon growth. Gradually and unevenly the old network of customs and controls gave way as a dynamic, capitalistic economy emerged in northern Europe.

The rate at which these changes took place varied from nation to nation, and in some parts of Europe the Medieval system remained intact. Throughout most of Germany the guilds retained their powers until well into the nineteenth century.[3] In France during the sixteenth and seventeenth centuries a different situation led to somewhat similar results. France changed the form but not the essence of its Medieval stabilizing institutions and retained them until the Revolution.[4]

England's experience, different from that of France and Germany, had important implications for America. The English mercantile system effectively bypassed the guilds. National regulations and national standards were established without relying upon the local guilds for enforcement. As a result, the merchants looked increasingly to the central government for favorable concessions. Industry spread to the suburbs and countryside, outside of the urban centers still dominated by the guilds. Gradually the guilds died a natural death, and the merchant capitalists imbued England with an economic philosophy which rejected guild concepts and stressed competition, innovation, and material progress. These values became part of the intellectual baggage that English settlers carried to America.[5]

Even in England, of course, businessmen did not completely abandon stabilizing institutions. This has never happened. Businessmen appear to have relied frequently upon simple price agreements; as Adam Smith observed, "people of the same trade seldom

[3] Theodore S. Hamerow, *Restoration, Revolution, Reaction: Economics and Politics in Germany, 1815–1871* (Princeton: Princeton University Press, 1958), pp. 17, 21–30, 33, 228–237, 241–255.

[4] Eli F. Heckscher, *Mercantilism,* trans. Mendel Shapiro (2 vols.; London: G. Allen and Unwin, Ltd., 1934), I, 144–152, 166–178.

[5] *Ibid.,* pp. 233–245; George Unwin, *Industrial Organization in the Sixteenth and Seventeenth Centuries* (Oxford: The Clarendon Press, 1904), pp. 41–46, 55–56, 71, 83–84.

meet together, even for merriment and diversion, but the conversation ends in a conspiracy against the public, or in some
contrivance to raise prices."[6] In foreign trade the merchants used
regulated companies to perform cartel functions.[7]

The continued existence of regulated companies, price agreements, and guilds cannot mask the fact, however, that England
had experienced a decisive change in economic attitudes and in
the patterns of economic activity. This change was reflected in
English law. From the middle of the seventeenth century, English
courts sought "to enlarge the scope of individual action."[8] Part of
America's heritage from the Old World was thus a legal tradition
which gave little support to stabilizing institutions. This outlook
was the natural product of a land bustling with new ventures.
The colonies themselves were a result of England's expansion in
the age of mercantilism, an age in which stabilization and security
were no longer dominant economic values.

The guild tradition which was already crumbling in England
became even weaker in the New World. From the very beginning
the English colonies were characterized by an unusual enthusiasm
for change and growth. For the individuals who came to America,
colonization was perforce a rejection of the past, an affirmation of
the need for change. Whether they came to fish or to build a city
on a hill, the colonists were seekers. In these circumstances one
would hardly expect to find a very strong interest in stability.

The institutions that were transplanted—the artisan guilds, for
instance—failed to take hold. Guilds were established in several
of the northern cities, but they generally had an unhappy career.
Abundant land and resources, matched by a shortage of labor,
created a situation in which it was hard to maintain restrictive
controls. Even in the cities the standards of apprenticeship (thus,
control of entry to the trade) were difficult to uphold because

----

[6] Adam Smith, *The Wealth of Nations* (New York: Modern Library,
1937), p. 128.

[7] Heckscher, *Mercantilism*, I, 373–392; John P. Davis, *Corporations* (New
York: Putnam, Capricorn Edition, 1961), pp. 66–113.

[8] Hans B. Thorelli, *The Federal Antitrust Policy* (Baltimore: The Johns
Hopkins Press, 1955), pp. 23–26; also see William Hyde Price, *The English
Patents of Monopoly* (Cambridge: The Harvard University Press, 1906),
pp. 3–46.

skilled labor was in such great demand. Gradually the legal and economic positions of the artisan guilds were undermined, and by the end of the Colonial period the system had virtually disappeared.[9]

Among the Colonial merchants, guilds and regulated companies enjoyed, at best, a brief existence. Few of the American merchants' undertakings were of sufficient size to warrant incorporation, and where the colonies did experiment with regulated companies and monopoly privileges in local trade and industry, the results were unsatisfactory.[10] Grants of monopoly ran against the current of a democratic dogma that was gathering strength in America. Furthermore, the experience with monopolies hardly suggested that this was a very successful way to spur economic development; the most fruitful innovations in the Colonial economy seemed always to be a product of private, not public efforts. As a consequence, the guilds, associations, and companies that had flourished in Europe failed to take root in Colonial America.

During the century which followed the Revolutionary War, there was little demand for a system of stabilizing institutions; in fact, everything in the national experience reinforced the predilection for change and growth. First, there was America's experience with manifest destiny. The nation began its separate existence as a small country, locked to the seaboard, its eyes turned respectfully to Europe. Then began a dynamic march across the continent. The successful establishment of the nation's continental boundaries strengthened the American's confidence that there would always be a better tomorrow.

Immigration also contributed to America's unique devotion to change and growth. The nation's open frontiers and expanding economy, both mythical and real, drew to this country waves of immigrants who were determined to enjoy the opportunities of the New World. Factory and farm towns throughout the North and West were peopled with new settlers from England, Scotland, Ireland, Germany, and the Scandinavian countries. As a

[9] Richard B. Morris, *Government and Labor in Early America* (New York: Columbia University Press, 1946), pp. 136–156; Victor S. Clark *History of Manufactures in the United States, 1607–1914* (2 vols.; Washington, D.C.: Carnegie Institution, 1916–1928), I, 6, 66, 161–162.

[10] *Ibid.*, pp. 47, 50–53; Bernard Bailyn, *The New England Merchants in the Seventeenth Century* (Cambridge: Harvard University Press, 1955), pp. 34, 51–53, 62–71.

result of immigration, the American folkways could never congeal about a single, homogeneous ethnic group. As the newcomers pushed upward in American society, they jarred the established cultural patterns. Social change was normal in a land that was absorbing millions of new people.

America's rapidly growing industrial economy also provided an economic environment initially hostile to guild ideas and stability-oriented institutions. In great surges of economic activity, nineteenth-century Americans built a transportation network, established domestic manufacturing industries, and reaped a harvest of seemingly boundless natural resources. New cities grew up around new factories, providing larger and more sophisticated markets for the farmer and manufacturer alike. Although rapid growth fostered problems, it unlocked for Americans a storehouse of rare opportunities. This was a land of plenty; optimism was the American creed.

In this economy the disruptive forces of industrial growth continually overturned those organizations which looked to the past for guidance and to security as a goal. Entire industries shifted about the country in order to utilize new sources of raw materials. Iron and steel production, for instance, steadily moved westward as the railroads opened the way to new supplies of ore and coal.[11] Companies with a small but secure local market suddenly faced intense competition when new forms of transportation broke down their local monopolies.[12] Equally disturbing was the rapid pace of technological change. As steam replaced water power in the textile industry, the mills in the Blackstone Valley of Massachusetts gradually lost out in their competition with manufacturing centers which could import coal more cheaply.[13] This dynamic setting was ripe with economic opportunities, and the businessman's philosophy, a kind of modified social Darwinism, reflected these conditions.

[11] Victor S. Clark, *Manufactures, 1607–1914*, I, 351–354, 496–501; also see Pearce Davis, *The Development of the American Glass Industry* (Cambridge: Harvard University Press, 1949), pp. 74–75.

[12] Arthur H. Cole, *The American Wool Manufacture* (2 vols.; Cambridge: Harvard University Press, 1926), I, 269–285. George R. Taylor, *The Transportation Revolution* (New York: Holt, Rinehart and Winston, 1951), pp. 207–210, 215, 246.

[13] J. Herbert Burgy, *The New England Cotton Textile Industry* (Baltimore: Waverly Press, 1932), pp. 4–5, 7, 9, 10.

America's exceptional dedication to individualism, to competition, and to change was also reflected in the legal status of guild-type organizations. After the Revolution American state courts adopted the English common law's hostility toward restraint of trade and monopolistic practices. Generally, agreements which embraced these objectives were not recognized by the courts as legal contracts. The customary attitude, as stated by an Ohio court in 1880, was that "public policy, unquestionably, favors competition in trade, to the end that its commodities may be afforded to the consumer as cheaply as possible, and is opposed to monopolies, which tend to advance market prices, to the injury of the general public."[14]

A number of the states specifically prohibited monopolistic combinations and restraint of trade.[15] In several states there were constitutional provisions aimed at preventing such practices. Other states passed specific statutes outlawing, as the Nebraska law stated, "devices designed to restrain competition."[16] Although these state measures had a limited effect on the all-important field of interstate commerce, they accurately reflected the basic American hostility to institutions which interfered with the competitive process.

Among the industrial nations of the West, America's dedication to competition was unique. By contrast, German public policy in the nineteenth century fostered cooperation, not competition. In this regard, Germany, which had never experienced a long period of unregulated, uncontrolled economic activity, stood at the opposite pole from the United States. Under German law, cartel agreements were legal, enforceable contracts, and this type of combination came to dominate most sectors of German industry in the late nineteenth century.[17] Even England was less determined to maintain competition than the United States. During the second half of the nineteenth century, the English common law gradually developed a new tolerance for business associations and

[14] Thorelli, *Antitrust*, pp. 36–44. The opinion quoted by Thorelli is from *Central Ohio Salt Co.* v. *Guthrie,* 35 Ohio St., 666 (1880).

[15] Thorelli, *Antitrust*, pp. 155–156.

[16] Henry R. Seager and Charles A. Gulick, Jr., *Trust and Corporation Problems* (New York: Harper & Brothers, 1929), n. 1, p. 342.

[17] *Ibid.,* pp. 552–575; Theodore F. Marburg, "Government and Business in Germany: Public Policy Toward Cartels," *Business History Review,* XXXVIII, No. 1 (Spring, 1964), 78–80.

the types of restraining agreements that Adam Smith had stoutly condemned. By 1900 a number of the leading English industries had formed cartels aimed at controlling prices and production.[18]

Even in America, where the political and intellectual environment was hostile, stabilizing institutions began to evolve throughout the economy during the second half of the nineteenth century. The pattern of their development varied slightly from industry to industry. But in almost every case, there was a period of experimentation with loose forms of combination. Sometimes this meant simple price agreements. These were often followed by formally organized pools which controlled or attempted to control prices and production. Trade associations of various sorts played an important role in this process of experimentation. The associations sought economic stability for their members. They stressed cooperation as a means of alleviating competitive pressures; and many of the associations began to create systems of precise economic controls to achieve their objectives. Due to the basic public hostility toward guild values and means of control, the associations could not in this early stage of their evolution receive political support for their economic programs. But they sought to influence the political environment so as to maintain a favorable political setting for the economic activities of their members.

It is against this historical background that the emergence of national trade associations in American industry must be viewed. The national association was one of a long series of stabilizing institutions that have developed in Western economies. In many ways it resembled its predecessors in the Medieval or early capitalistic economies of Europe. It was shaped, however, by a particular American economic, social, and political environment. Its ideology was attuned to that environment. Its programs were adapted to the necessities of a nation dedicated to competition and hostile to the associative concepts of stabilization, cooperation, and control.

[18] Thorelli, *Antitrust,* pp. 29–35.

Chapter II

The Rise of the Dinner-
Club Associations

The predecessors of the national trade association in cotton textiles were three regional organizations which emerged during the nineteenth century. Two of these, the New England Cotton Manufacturers' Association and the Arkwright Club, were in the Northeast; the third, the Southern Cotton Spinners' Association, drew its membership principally from the textile states of the Southeast. Although these organizations differed in some respects, they were all regionally oriented, reflecting the basic economic structure of the industry. They were also influenced by their political and social environments, but the most decisive factors shaping the organizations were the contours of their economic setting—the location, number, and size of the competing firms; the patterns of competition; the industry's growth rate; and the pace of technological change.

Cotton textiles led the United States into the age of manufacturing. Following the War of 1812, a New England industry which had heretofore consisted of a scattering of small spinning mills experienced a tremendous expansion in capacity and in the size and number of competing firms.[1] This sudden growth followed upon the introduction of the power loom in 1815. When the power loom was perfected in the large "Waltham-type" factories that were built in northern New England, the cotton textile in-

[1] Caroline F. Ware, *The Early New England Cotton Manufacture* (Boston: Houghton Mifflin, 1931), pp. 19–78.

dustry entered its period of rapid growth. These new companies—well-financed by Boston capitalists—were able to spin and weave coarse goods at a cost low enough to assure them control of a growing domestic market.[2] Tariff walls helped to protect that market, but by the end of the 1820's one could hardly use the protectionists' favorite rubric, the infant industry, to describe textile manufacturing in New England.[3] In the northeastern and Middle Atlantic states there were 795 mills turning out an estimated 230,461,900 yards of cloth a year. Over forty million dollars was invested in cotton manufacturing. By this time America's take-off into sustained industrialization was well underway.[4]

In subsequent years the industry encountered problems. When the early corporations made impressive profits, a swarm of new companies moved in to share the domestic market. Between 1830 and 1850, hundreds of new plants were constructed in New England. As a result, the profit rate in cotton textiles fell off sharply, and during the 1840's and 1850's the New England industry struggled with a serious problem of excess capacity and cutthroat competition.[5] The Civil War capped a decade of difficulties; after 1861, it became almost impossible to obtain cotton from the South, and the northern mills had to compete with English buyers for the available foreign supplies. Unlike most other domestic manufactures, this industry was unable to share in the prosperity that the war created in the Northeast.[6]

[2] *Ibid.*, pp. 60–78; George S. Gibb, *The Saco-Lowell Shops* (Cambridge: Harvard University Press, 1950), pp. 7–14, 26–27, 33–34, 58–62, 171–175.

[3] Frank W. Taussig, *The Tariff History of the United States* (7th ed.; New York: The Knickerbocker Press, 1923), pp. 34–36, 136–139.

[4] Melvin T. Copeland, *The Cotton Manufacturing Industry of the United States* (Cambridge: Harvard University Press, 1912), p. 6; J. Leander Bishop, *A History of Manufactures from 1608 to 1860* (2 vols.; Philadelphia: Edward Young, 1864), II, 357. The "take-off" is described in W. W. Rostow, *The Stages of Economic Growth* (Cambridge: The Cambridge University Press, 1960), pp. 7–9, 36–58; as Robert W. Fogel, *Railroads and American Economic Growth* (Baltimore: The Johns Hopkins Press, 1964), pp. 111–146, shows, however, Rostow's periodization (1840–60) is not substantiated by the available data, and there is considerable evidence suggesting that rapid industrialization began as early as the 1820's.

[5] Ware, *Cotton Manufacture*, p. 154, Evelyn H. Knowlton, *Pepperell's Progress* (Cambridge: Harvard University Press, 1948), pp. 32–34; Victor S. Clark, *Manufactures, 1607–1914*, I, 552–553; Taylor, *The Transportation Revolution*, pp. 234–235.

[6] Victor S. Clark, *Manufactures, 1607–1914*, II, 29–30.

After the Civil War, a growing domestic market provided the necessary foundation for another era of rapid expansion. Fabrics were needed for America's burgeoning industrial system. Cotton clothing was an essential part of the wardrobe of a population which ballooned from almost forty to over seventy-six million in the last three decades of the century. To meet these demands, over seven million new spindles were added to the northern industry, and New England companies were able to record good profits and to pay substantial dividends.[7] While New Bedford, Massachusetts, became the leading producer of fine cotton yarn and cloth, Fall River securely established its dominance of the nation's print-cloth market. The great corporations of Fall River became bellwethers for the entire industry; their dividends and plans for expansion were closely scrutinized by the nation's investors.[8]

Neither dividends nor the growth rate was steady because the industry's progress was periodically interrupted by severe depressions. In the mid-seventies and mid-eighties, during the downturn in the general business cycle, cotton textiles suffered acutely.[9] The depression which began in 1893 was even more severe, and the recovery this time was somewhat slower in textiles than in other manufacturing industries. As late as 1900, Fall River and other northern textile centers had yet to resume operating at full capacity.[10] There was talk of overexpansion, but since each of the previous depressions had been followed by a new era of prosperity, management was not unduly pessimistic about the industry's economic future.[11]

[7] U. S., Bureau of the Census, *Historical Statistics of the United States, Colonial Times to 1957* (Washington, D.C.: Government Printing Office, 1960), p. 7; U. S., Bureau of the Census, *Twelfth Census (1900), Manufactures, Textiles* (1902), pp. 54–57; Thomas R. Navin, *The Whitin Machine Works Since 1831* (Cambridge: Harvard University Press, 1950), pp. 89–90; Victor S. Clark, *Manufactures, 1607–1914,* II, 105, 393–394; Melvin T. Copeland, *Cotton Manufacturing,* pp. 263–264.

[8] Thomas R. Smith, *The Cotton Textile Industry of Fall River, Massachusetts* (New York: King's Crown Press, 1944), pp. 50–79, 104–112.

[9] Victor S. Clark, *Manufactures, 1607–1914,* II, 404–405, 407–410.

[10] *Ibid.,* pp. 719–721.

[11] The New England Cotton Manufacturers' Association, *Transactions* (Boston), LXII (1897), 87–94, 98; LXIII (1897), 111; LXIV (1898), 135; LXV (1898), 77–78, 91–111; LXIX (1900), 228, 231–232, 282 (hereafter cited as NECMA, *Trans.*); Victor S. Clark, *Manufactures, 1607–1914,* II, 720–721.

If northern cotton manufacturers were pessimistic about anything during the postwar years, it was political trends in the Northeast, particularly in Massachusetts. Before the Civil War the mills had operated in a kind of manufacturer's dreamland, hampered by only the most rudimentary factory or labor regulations. After the war, however, labor and reform organizations gradually grew stronger and actually won some political battles in the Bay State. In 1869 the Bureau of Labor Statistics was created, and five years later a ten-hour law was passed for women employees.[12] After these early victories the agitation for effective legislation increased, spreading to other New England states.[13] From management's point of view, these laws and the continued activity of the labor organizations seemed to pose a real threat. Other states, the manufacturers warned, were friendlier to their businessmen; other states were attracting industry by providing a regulation-free environment, low taxes, and other economic advantages. If northern mills were to remain successful, the New England states would have to match these advantages and pay less heed to labor's voice and the laborer's vote.[14]

Although politics was causing concern, northern management could look with pleasure upon the industry's record of technological change. Indeed, these were the golden years of technical innovation in cotton textiles. Almost every step in the manufacturing process felt the impact of fundamental improvements which increased output and reduced costs. New types of spinning frames were developed; carding equipment was changed; near the end of the century a revolutionary automatic loom was placed on the market.[15] To run this machinery new sources of power were tapped as the mills gradually shifted from water to steam. By the end of the century the more progressive companies were exploring the possibilities of electric motors.[16] These major innovations were

[12] U. S., Department of Labor, *History of Labor Legislation for Women in Three States,* by Clara M. Byer (Washington: Bulletin 66 of the Women's Bureau, 1929), pp. 19–21.

[13] *Ibid.,* pp. 26–27.

[14] *Ibid.,* pp. 18, 27; *Textile Record of America,* VII, No. 2 (February, 1886), 37.

[15] Navin, *Whitin Machine Works,* pp. 114–123, 183–188, 244; Gibb, *Saco-Lowell Shops,* pp. 210–215, 260–264; Tsung-yuen Shen, "A Quantitative Study of Production in the American Textile Industry, 1840–1940" (unpublished Ph.D. dissertation, Yale University, 1956), pp. 30–31, 39, 42, 43–46, 50–53, 118, 126; NECMA, *Trans.,* LIX (1895), 89–90, 101.

[16] *Ibid.,* LVIII (1895), 216–239; LXVI (1899), 298–345.

accompanied by a myriad of minor technological changes—even the factories built to house the equipment were steadily improved—and the result was an impressive increase in productivity.[17]

As the New England industry grew, a number of fairly large companies emerged. During the first half of the nineteenth century the number of firms in the industry increased tremendously, but in subsequent years the number of companies remained fairly stable while the existing firms grew larger. One of the big corporations was the Pepperell Manufacturing Company of Biddeford, Maine. By 1900, Pepperell was capitalized at over two and a half million dollars and was producing over thirty million yards of cloth a year. Firms such as Pepperell, the Amoskeag Manufacturing Company, and the Fall River Iron Works, gave the New England industry a nucleus of fairly large companies.[18]

During the late nineties a new kind of large firm, the combine or consolidation, made its appearance in cotton textiles as in other industries. In 1897 a number of competing yarn mills were combined into the New England Cotton Yarn Company; in the following year a horizontal consolidation of thread manufacturers was achieved under the guidance of the English investors who controlled J. P. Coates, Ltd.[19] If the industry had been concentrated exclusively in New England, as it had been fifty years before, these combines and the existing large companies would have provided the foundation for an oligopolistic industrial structure. But in cotton textiles the trend toward concentration was countered by a stronger force—the spread of cotton manufacturing to the South.[20]

[17] Ibid., LV (1893), 61–77; LX (1896), 111–122; LXIII (1897), 128–137; LXIV (1898), 275–284.

[18] Knowlton, Pepperell's Progress, pp. 32–33, 435, 454. The Fall River Iron Works was initially formed to produce iron for ships and barrels; later, the company moved into cotton manufacturing and became one of Fall River's leading textile producers.

[19] Arthur S. Dewing, Corporate Promotions and Reorganizations (Cambridge: Harvard University Press, 1914), pp. 310–313, 316, 338–339; Willard L. Thorp and Grace W. Knott, "The History of Concentration in Seven Industries," The Structure of Industry, ed. Willard L. Thorp, U. S. Temporary National Economic Committee, Monograph No. 27, (Washington, D.C.: Government Printing Office, 1941), p. 253.

[20] In 1860 the four leading companies in the industry accounted for 10 per cent of the industry's total capitalization; in 1899, only 8.7 per cent. Ibid., pp. 252–253.

During the last two decades of the nineteenth century, New England's mills encountered substantial competition from the fast-growing southern wing of the industry. A variety of factors contributed to the sudden expansion of cotton manufacturing in the South during the late 1870's. The end of Reconstruction created a more settled political environment which was conducive to economic growth.[21] Transportation developments and certain technological innovations also favored industrialization. By this time the railroads had laced the Piedmont, the plateau country east of the Appalachian Mountains, into the national market. Improvements in the spinning process had made it increasingly profitable to employ the untrained southern farm hand, his wife, and their multitudes of children. In cotton textiles these innovations in spinning machinery were especially important because labor costs made up a large percentage of the total cost of production.[22]

In this favorable setting, an upswing in the nation's economy in the late 1870's precipitated rapid industrialization by opening new sources of capital to southern entrepreneurs. General economic recovery fed the stream of foreign and northern capital which had already begun to flow toward the South's undeveloped natural resources.[23] This flow of investments pumped additional money into a regional economy which badly needed capital. Furthermore, as the national economy surged ahead, existing southern mills made large profits and paid impressive dividends.[24] This had the effect of softening credit terms in the North, making

[21] Broadus Mitchell, *The Rise of Cotton Mills in the South* (Baltimore: The Johns Hopkins Press, 1921), pp. 59–76. Mitchell exaggerates the sociopolitical influences; a much better, general account is that of Jack Blicksilver, *Cotton Manufacturing in the Southeast: An Historical Analysis*, Bureau of Business and Economic Research Bulletin No. 5, School of Business Administration of the Georgia State College of Business Administration (Atlanta: 1959), pp. 2–16.

[22] *Ibid.*, p. 4; Chen-Han Chen, "The Location of the Cotton-Manufacturing Industry in the United States, 1880–1910" (unpublished Ph.D. dissertation, Harvard University, 1940), pp. 145–148. For a different opinion on the influence of the new spinning frames see Seth Hammond's, "The Cotton Industry of This Century" (unpublished Ph.D. dissertation, Harvard University, 1941), p. 522.

[23] C. Vann Woodward, *Origins of the New South, 1877–1913* (Baton Rouge: Louisiana State University Press, 1951), p. 113.

[24] Gustavus G. Williamson, "Cotton Manufacturing in South Carolina, 1865–1892" (unpublished Ph.D. dissertation, Johns Hopkins University, 1954), pp. 83–89.

it easier for southerners to buy textile machinery and to win financial support from the northern commission merchants who handled cotton goods.[25] It also encouraged cotton dealers, merchants, bankers, and railroad men throughout the South to invest in cotton textiles. With the press playing up the profits of successful mills, local investment was accelerated in an industry in which the low cost of a small but efficient plant made entry relatively easy. By the mid-eighties a regional industrial revolution was well underway in the Southeast. New factories were scattered throughout the plateau country of Virginia, the Carolinas, and northern Georgia, stirring the region's sluggish farm economy, exciting the press and populace.[26]

Part of the excitement stemmed from the strong sectional feeling that flavored southern industrial growth. Realizing that each new mill would bring the South closer to economic equality with the North, and feeling as they did about the damn yankee, southerners transformed prosaic capitalism into a kind of regional religious movement. Even from the pulpit it was firmly announced that the churchgoers' Christian duty was to support local industry.[27] The matter-of-fact economic benefits of industrialization should themselves have been persuasive. But when colored by a fierce sectional allegiance, the desire for economic growth spurred state and local governments to favor the new mills in every possible way. The result was low taxes, few regulations, and, frequently, direct government subsidies for the mills.[28]

This favorable legislation helped the southern mills, but they had other, more substantial, advantages. Power was cheaper in the South. And in the early days some of the factories were able to purchase local cotton thereby saving money on transportation. The overriding cost differential was provided, however, by the South's large supply of cheap, tractable labor. From year to year

[25] Gibb, *Saco-Lowell Shops*, pp. 241–249; Navin, *Whitin Machine Works*, pp. 206–216; Blicksilver, *Cotton Manufacturing*, pp. 6–10.

[26] *Ibid.*, pp. 4–6; Gustavus G. Williamson, "Cotton Manufacturing," p. 79.

[27] Broadus Mitchell, *The Rise of Cotton Mills*, pp. 134–136.

[28] Richard W. Griffin, "The Augusta (Georgia) Manufacturing Company in Peace, War, and Reconstruction, 1847–1877," *Business History Review*, XXXII, No. 1 (Spring, 1958), 71–72; Letter of R. A. Mitchell to J. Howard Nichols, November 2, 1901, in Dwight Manufacturing Company MSS (Baker Library, Harvard University); Herbert J. Lahne, *The Cotton Mill Worker* (New York: Farrar & Rinehart, 1944), pp. 107–108, 137–138; Knowlton, *Pepperell's Progress*, pp. 178–180, 308–309, 317.

the ratio of northern to southern wages varied considerably, but the price of labor was always lower in the South. Although new southern mill hands were not accustomed to the discipline of the factory, experience was not really very important in cotton textiles. Most of the work on coarse products could be done by women and children after a few weeks of on-the-job training. As the South discovered, tending the spinning frame was dull and monotonous work, but it demanded little strength and even less intelligence.[29]

During the 1880's and 1890's, southern management did well by these advantages. In these two decades the growth rate of the southern industry was truly phenomenal. The total number of spindles in the South jumped from 522,451 in 1880, to 4,221,855 in 1900, and, by the latter date, the southern mills had taken over the domestic market for coarse products.[30] After plowing back earnings and buying the newest machinery, many of the southern mills actually increased their advantage over their more conservative northern competitors.[31] Southern workers gradually became more skilled. By the turn of the century, southern management was beginning to explore the possibilities of making medium grades of "print cloth," heretofore the private domain of Fall River.[32]

The spread of textile manufacturing into the South had a decisive impact upon the industry at a crucial stage in its development. Just when the concentration movement was getting underway, just when a series of large, horizontal combinations were being promoted, southern expansion brought into the industry hundreds of small, low-cost firms. As a result, cotton textiles, unlike most other manufacturing industries, retained its atomistic structure. In 1900 there were 973 separate establishments making cotton products, and the 3 or 4 leading companies accounted for only a small percentage of the industry's total capitaliza-

[29] Chen-Han Chen, "The Location of the Cotton Manufacturing Industry," pp. 41, 138, 163, 211–212, 281, 312–313, 348, 407–408, 410; Seth Hammond, "Location Theory and the Cotton Industry," *The Journal of Economic History, Supplement* (December, 1942), II, 108.

[30] The National Association of Cotton Manufacturers, *Yearbook, 1927* (Boston), p. 163. The states included are Alabama, Georgia, Louisiana, Mississippi, North Carolina, South Carolina, Tennessee, Texas, and Virginia (hereafter cited as NACM, *Yearbook*).

[31] Blicksilver, *Cotton Manufacturing*, pp. 24–27.

[32] Thomas R. Smith, *Fall River*, pp. 82–85.

tion. Even the consolidations that were formed in the late 1890's could not alter the structure of an industry in which so many new firms were being established.[33]

Cotton textiles thus remained an extremely competitive industry. In the national center for buying and selling cotton products—the Worth Street district of New York City—textiles moved through a market which resembled the commodity exchanges for farm products. Both Worth Street and the exchanges had large numbers of buyers and sellers, none of whom was of sufficient size to dominate the market. Most of the yarns and cloths sent to Worth Street were, like agricultural products, standard goods, undistinguished by a trade mark or strong brand name. In these markets price competition was all-important.[34]

The only thing moderating the industry's intense price competition was the relatively small part that fixed cost played in the manufacture of cotton goods. Where fixed cost was extremely high—as it was in the iron and steel industry—management was under great pressure to keep its plants running as much as possible; even though additional production forced prices down, it was best to keep running if prices covered variable costs and paid something toward the fixed costs. This was also true for the cotton manufacturer, but in his case most of the cost was variable. Prices could not drop very far below total cost of production before it became more profitable to shut down the plant than to keep running. As a result, management in cotton textiles adjusted to the industry's seasonal and cyclical fluctuations in demand by cutting back production before prices fell disastrously low. The cotton manufacturer was thus under less pressure than the iron producer to seek cooperative means of restraining competition.[35]

All of these political and economic characteristics of the industry had a direct influence upon the trade associations which

[33] Thorp and Knott, "The History of Concentration," pp. 252–253.

[34] Reavis Cox, *The Marketing of Textiles* (Washington, D.C.: The Textile Foundation, 1938), pp. 82–96, 115–202, 261–294; Conference on Price Research, *Textile Markets, Their Structure in Relation to Price Research* (New York: National Bureau of Economic Research, 1939), pp. 75, 79, 98–100.

[35] U. S., House of Representatives, *Document No. 643, Cotton Manufactures,* 62nd Cong., 2nd Sess., 1912, II, 687–742; Jules Backman and M. R. Gainsbrugh, *Economics of the Cotton Textile Industry* (New York: National Industrial Conference Board, 1946), pp. 209–215; J. Maurice Clark, *Studies in the Economics of Overhead Costs* (Chicago: University of Chicago Press, 1923), p. 238.

emerged in the postwar years. The time when the associations were formed, their basic nature, and their evolution—all were directly affected by these environmental factors. In brief, the early associations were products of an industry that was sharply concentrated in two regions of the country, that was enjoying a high but fluctuating rate of growth, that was experiencing rapid technological change. The trade groups were also shaped by a political environment that was generally responsive to the manufacturer's demands, especially in the South, but that was becoming more difficult to control in the New England states. Finally, the associations were influenced by the nature of production costs in the industry, by its atomistic structure, and by its emphasis upon price competition.

The earliest regional organization in the industry was the New England Cotton Manufacturers' Association, which was organized in 1865 by a small group of mill agents and superintendents.[36] They were concerned about their inability to keep up with all of the available information on technological developments in their industry. Almost every department of the mill was feeling the impact of crucial inventions which the agents and superintendents had to introduce in their factories. Mill treasurers normally supervised the financial side of the company's operations, bought the raw materials, and sold the finished products. They left the technical side of manufacturing to the guidance of the agents and superintendents, who felt acutely the need for a forum at which they could discuss methods of production and hear reports on new machinery that was coming on the market.

[36] There was an association of cotton manufacturers in Hampden County, Massachusetts, as early as 1854. The association did not have a charter and it is not clear whether it remained active until 1865 when the New England Cotton Manufacturers' Association was formed. Jones S. Davis was active in the formation of both associations, and there is some possibility that the Hampden County association was the predecessor of the New England Association. The latter group dated its beginnings from 1854, but early volumes of the transactions gave the founding date as 1865, when the association was formally organized. Lacking evidence to the contrary, I decided to date the founding of the New England Association as July 19, 1865, when the proposed constitution and by-laws were formally adopted. Col. Samuel Webber, "Early Days of the New England Cotton Manufacturers' Association," NECMA, *Trans.*, LXII (1897), 341–345.

It was for this purpose that a group of over forty agents and superintendents gathered in Boston, on July 19, 1865, to organize the New England Cotton Manufacturers' Association. They elected officers and adopted by-laws which made provision for regular meetings, dues, and membership. Aside from the social objective of "promoting a more intimate acquaintance with each other, . . ." the only stated goal of the organization was that "of collecting and imparting information as to the best methods of manufacturing cotton."[37]

The organization rapidly expanded. Membership was originally restricted to agents and superintendents from New England mills, but two years later the agents decided to allow treasurers to join. After 1872, mill officers from outside New England were accepted into the group.[38] Within ten years of its founding, it had 197 members, with every state in New England represented. By 1900 there were 491 active members from 20 different states. A number of treasurers had joined, and there were also 60 members from the South. Almost every cotton mill in the Northeast, large and small, was represented in the Association.[39]

Although large in numbers the organization had a very small income and not until the 1890's did it have permanent quarters or a staff. Since the members joined as individuals, not as spokesmen for their respective firms, the admission fees and annual dues were limited to an amount (ten dollars) that the average agent or superintendent could afford to pay out of his own pocket.[40] Even in 1900, after the membership had grown, the dues and fees gave the Association an annual income of only about five thousand dollars. With this much money the group could publish its transactions and finance the annual and semiannual meetings, but that was about all. There was very little surplus for administrative expenses.[41] During its first thirty years the Association's entire staff consisted of a part-time secretary-treasurer. In 1894 the organization finally established a permanent office, began a library, and

[37] NECMA, *Statistics of Cotton Manufactures in New England, 1866; Together with the Constitution, and List of Members* (n. d.), I, 3–5.

[38] *Ibid.*, p. 5; NECMA, *Trans.*, III (1867), 3–4.

[39] *Ibid.*, XVIII (1875), 5–9; LXIX (1900), 13–50.

[40] Ten dollars was the maximum assessment, but in fact the active members had never been charged over five dollars a year. *Ibid.*, p. 5.

[41] *Ibid.*, LXVIII (1900), 111–113.

hired "an experienced stenographer and typewriter."[42] But this represented only the barest beginning of a trade association bureaucracy.

Since the Association held close to its original, narrowly defined goals, it needed neither a substantial income nor a large professional staff. The conventions gave the members an opportunity to meet over a leisurely dinner and perhaps to get away from home for a little merriment in Boston. The program focused almost exclusively on technical subjects. Questions that came up in the construction of mill buildings were studied. New machinery was described and discussed. The various techniques of manufacturing cloth and yarn were debated in exhaustive detail.[43] The Association did not itself make any sustained effort to develop new ideas or techniques; it was not trying to control technological developments in that sense.[44] Instead, the organization helped the members control a body of technical information that was constantly being enlarged by private inventors, machinery manufacturers, dye companies, and the employees of the various mills.

There was one serious effort to change the New England Association. This took place in the 1890's when some of the mill treasurers (supported by a number of agents) attempted to broaden the organization's scope, adding political and economic questions to its agenda.[45] But this challenge to tradition was promptly beaten down. Eighty per cent of the members were agents and superintendents who were still principally interested in the "results obtained inside of the cotton mills." From their point of view, the technical side of production was "the most important part, and really the life and the success of manufacturing." In the past they had seldom been directly concerned with political matters and marketing problems, so they chose to hold their association to its traditional format.[46]

Between 1865 and 1900 the New England Association grew in

[42] *Ibid.*, LVII (1894), 40–41, 45–48; LVIII (1895), 54.

[43] See the papers and discussions from the annual meeting in 1900, *ibid.*, LXVIII (1900), 293–306, 318–328.

[44] The organization did appoint committees to study particular problems, but these groups did not engage in any kind of basic research. *Ibid.*, V (1868), 4, 11–12, 22, 27; VI (1869), 44–47.

[45] *Ibid.*, LX (1896), 63–64, 71; LXI (1896), 58, 249–269; LXII (1897), 55–57, 82.

[46] *Ibid.*, LX (1896), 54, 62; LXI (1896), 266; LXIII (1897), 97.

terms of membership and income while retaining its original structure and goals. By the turn of the century it was securely established as a forum for the consideration of technical matters. The organization's dinners and conventions gave the members an opportunity to discuss their common problems. With only the barest beginnings of a professional staff, the Association was able to perform its two central functions, providing two conventions a year for the consideration of technological questions and publishing transactions which allowed the members who could not attend meetings to keep up with developments in the industry. As yet the association imposed no controls upon its members, exerted no influence upon state or national politics, and avoided even a discussion of such basic economic questions as the need for stabilization.[47] Some of the members were beginning to feel that the organization asked too little and gave too little, but the majority was still satisfied with this rudimentary form of technically-oriented association.

Those mill treasurers who were disappointed with the New England Association were forced to rely upon a second regional organization, the Arkwright Club of Boston. The Club had been holding meetings since April, 1880, when Charles H. Dalton, treasurer of the Merrimack Manufacturing Company, called together a small coterie of the leading manufacturers in Massachusetts. The purpose of the meeting was "to consider the expedience of forming a club to promote consultation among all those having charge of the important trusts involved in the management of the cotton and woolen and allied industries, to cultivate good understanding and concerted action in all matters pertaining to the general interests of those industries, and to ensure mutual protection in all cases where they are in any way endangered."[48]

Recent political events in the Bay State were the chief stimuli for organizing a club. In 1879 the legislature had passed a law

[47] On at least one occasion it was proposed that the association require members to submit certain statistics; this proposition was amended to the effect that the members should submit any data called for when it was "not incompatible with private interests." *Ibid.*, VII (1869), 3, 6–8.

[48] Arkwright Club, *By-Laws of the Arkwright Club and List of Officers and Members, Together with a Brief Account of Its Origin and a Complete List of Present and Past Members* (Boston, 1924), pp. 16–17 (hereafter cited as AC, *By-Laws*).

which strengthened an earlier regulation limiting the workday for women employees. Further regulations were established for child labor. Now a bill was before the legislature requiring payment of wages on a weekly basis. It was all very upsetting to the manufacturers who met with Dalton at the Union Club; in a second meeting that same month they formally organized the Arkwright Club.[49]

Unlike the New England Association, the Club was open only to the directing officers, usually treasurers, of manufacturing companies. Initially, only fifty members were allowed to join, but this restriction was soon dropped, along with the provision that the members had to come from Massachusetts.[50] By 1883 there were 75 members, representing some of the largest companies in the Northeast. In subsequent years the membership grew rather slowly, but by 1900 there were 114 companies represented. For the most part, these were the larger and older mills, with the heaviest concentration of members coming from northern New England.[51]

The Club had a substantial income. At the regular monthly luncheon meetings the expenses were paid by the members. But the Club's political and economic activities were financed by assessing the corporations which the treasurers represented. Each company was billed according to the size of its payroll, with the assessments varying each year as the expenses changed. This form of corporate (as opposed to individual) membership ensured that the organization would have handsome financial resources when vital matters were before the legislature.[52]

---

[49] *Ibid.*, pp. 17–18; Department of Labor, *Labor Legislation*, pp. 19–21; Letter of E. F. Balch (Agent) to M. F. Dickinson, Jr., March 17, 1880; Letter of H. D. Sullivan to George Atkinson (first secretary of the Club), April 26, 1880; both in Naumkeag Steam Cotton Manufacturing Company MSS; Letter of M. F. Dickinson, Jr. to Superintendents of Hadley Thread Co. and Lyman Mills, March 16, 1880; Letter of Samuel L. Bush to M. F. Dickinson, March 19, 1880; both in Lyman Mills MSS (both the Naumkeag and Lyman MSS are in the Baker Library, Harvard University).

[50] AC, *By-Laws*, pp. 5, 17–19.

[51] *Ibid.*, pp. 20–42.

[52] *Ibid.*, p. 8. My estimate of the income is based on the membership lists and the regular assessments paid by the Naumkeag Steam Cotton Manufacturing Co.; See Letter of H. D. Sullivan to George Atkinson, November 2, 1880; Letters of H. D. Sullivan to Alfred P. Rockwell, February 5, 1884, and November 20, 1884; all in Naumkeag MSS.

Despite its considerable financial resources, the Arkwright Club did not begin to develop a professional staff until 1891. Until that time all of the officers were mill treasurers, regular members of the Club, and the organization's functions were performed by committees which were likewise chosen from among the manufacturers. The Club's first regular staff member was Edward Stanwood, a former newspaperman and a managing editor of a magazine, who was appointed secretary-treasurer in 1891. But even after his appointment—the first step toward the creation of an association bureaucracy—most of the organization's work was done by the members, not by the staff.[53]

Originally the Club appears to have been little more than a manufacturer's lobbying organization. Although the preamble to the by-laws proclaimed that its purpose was "to cultivate social intercourse among managers of corporations or private establishments manufacturing textile fabrics and machinery, or allied industries, and to promote good understanding and united action upon affairs of general interest to those industries," this meant lobbying.[54] When legislation which would affect New England's textile industry came before the state legislatures or the Congress in Washington, the Club provided the members with a convenient meeting place. Here, over dinner, they discussed the position they should take and the tactics they should employ in the struggle against such measures as the seventy-eight-hour law that was sponsored by the Massachusetts textile unions in the early 1890's. When this particular fight was underway, the Club kept a special agent at the legislature in Boston to represent the textile interests. Their spokesmen appeared before the appropriate legislative committees. And when money was needed, the Club assessed the member companies, spreading the cost of maintaining a political environment favorable to their industry.

The Club sponsored resolutions and occasionally hired a lobbying agent, but most of the political work was left in the hands of the members. There was only occasionally a demand for the kind of elaborate briefs and statistical arguments that are commonplace in pressure-group politics today. In nineteenth-

[53] Edward Stanwood's incomplete and unpublished autobiography, available at the Massachusetts Historical Society, Boston, contains considerable information on his career before he became secretary of the Club.
[54] AC, *By-Laws*, p. 5.

century America, political jousting was not so blatantly rational
as it has become in the twentieth century; it was carried on in a
personal and aggressive but somewhat haphazard fashion. As one
cotton manufacturer said in regard to the tariff, only one thing
was "pretty certain. The man who has the best pull will get the
rate he favors."[55]

The individuals who were in the Arkwright Club normally had
plenty of "pull." In Washington they could be certain their cause
was well represented when the New England congressional delegation included men such as Jonathan Chace, a mill treasurer and a
member of the Club.[56] When their friends were in the driver's seat,
the manufacturers did not have to waste time preparing careful
briefs or gathering statistics. In the New England states the same
was true. Although labor organizations had grown much stronger,
the textile industry always had a number of stout advocates in all
branches of the state government. Periodically, of course, the
Club's opponents controlled Congress or the state legislatures, and

[55] Letter of William F. Draper to F. L. Burden, August 30, 1886, and of
William F. Draper to John D. Long, March 5, 1888, in John Davis Long
Papers (Massachusetts Historical Society, Boston); Letters of C. P. Baker to
the following: Townsend and Yale, January 11, 18 and 22, 1894, and April
28, 1894; C. F. North, June 5, 1894; A. W. Sulloway, July 9, 1894; Nelson W.
Aldrich, April 9, 1894; A. W. Sulloway, January 1 and 2, 1897, and March 22,
1897; Robert Pilling, January 9, 1897, and April 12, 1897; Henry C. Lodge,
March 23, 1897; all in Lawrence Manufacturing Company MSS (Baker
Library, Harvard University); also see: Festus P. Summers', *William L. Wilson
and Tariff Reform* (New Brunswick: Rutgers University Press, 1953), p. 81;
Department of Labor, *Labor Legislation*, pp. 29–30.

[56] Chace was a member of the Club from 1880 through 1901. In 1876 and
1877 he was a member of the Rhode Island State Senate; he served in the
United States House of Representatives from March, 1881, through January
26, 1885; he was a Senator from January 20, 1885 to April 9, 1889. U. S.,
Congress, *Biographical Directory of the American Congress, 1774–1927* (Washington, D.C.: Government Printing Office, 1928), p. 798; Chace was active in
tariff matters, arguing for protection in the early 1880's; Letters of Jonathan
Chace to Edward Atkinson, January 5, 9, and 23, 1883, and June 16, 1884, in
Edward Atkinson MSS (Massachusetts Historical Society, Boston); the Club
was almost always directly represented in Congress; other members included:
William A. Russell, who was a member of the Massachusetts House of Representatives in 1869 and the U. S. House of Representatives, 1879–1885;
William F. Draper, who was a Congressman from Massachusetts, 1893–1897;
and William C. Lovering, who was a member of the Massachusetts Senate,
1874–1875, and a Congressman, 1897–1910; Congress, *Biographical Directory*,
pp. 920, 1240–1241, 1487. Of course the Club's indirect influence was far more
important than its direct representation.

then the manufacturers wheeled out their heavy artillery. But this sort of battle came only once every few years. Even then much of the fighting was done behind the scenes.[57]

When the Arkwright Club was first organized, it apparently was not intended to be a means of stabilizing textile prices, but the metamorphosis from politics to political economy was not long in coming.[58] After the downturn of the business cycle in 1883 the cotton mills encountered a period of declining demand and falling prices. Looking for a way out of their dilemma, the mill treasurers saw that the Arkwright Club might be used to achieve concerted action that would solve their problems.[59] In an effort either to raise prices on goods or to lower prices on cotton, or both, the Club formulated a curtailment program. Under this plan all of the New England mills were asked to cut operations by one day a week for a two-month period. Since widespread support was needed to make the program effective, it was stipulated that three-quarters of the northern industry had to indicate that it would cooperate before the curtailment would go into effect.[60]

The plan never got off the ground. Too many of the treasurers were unwilling to abandon the individualistic, competitive behavior that had thus far characterized the industry. The Club was unable to get the backing of the requisite 75 per cent. Reports of the time indicate that those mills with a large supply of low-priced cotton on hand (a competitive advantage that might be lost due to delay) and the companies which felt that they had extremely low production costs refused to join.[61] In any event the low fixed

[57] In 1897 C. P. Baker opined that the manufacturers had actually filed too elaborate a brief. Baker to Samuel Townsend, April 10, 1897, Lawrence MSS.

[58] AC, By-Laws, pp. 18, 20–42; Commercial and Financial Chronicle, XXX, No. 769 (March 20, 1880), 284 and XXXII, No. 811 (January 8, 1881), 28.

[59] Apparently this was the first attempt in the New England industry to achieve concerted action through a formal organization. In the earlier days it seems likely that cooperation was possible without an association because the investors who controlled the leading mills were closely associated economically, socially, and politically. Ware, Cotton Manufacture, pp. 44–46. There was a curtailment agreement formulated in 1874 by "the treasurers and managers of the larger New England companies," but nothing seems to have resulted from the meetings except resolutions. Victor S. Clark, Manufactures, 1607–1914, II, 404.

[60] Commercial and Financial Chronicle, XXXVIII, No. 983 (April 26, 1884), 497.

[61] Ibid., XXXIX, No. 1003 (September 13, 1884), 284.

costs in cotton manufacturing made it relatively easy for the mills to ride out such depressions. As one mill treasurer commented in March, 1884: "The outlook is, if possible, more discouraging than ever. But it won't always be so. And we must run meanwhile as *snugly* as possible. . . . There is no reason why we should not do as well as any mill in our lines."[62] With management thinking in these terms, cooperative production control was impossible to implement.

In subsequent years, the association made at least one other attempt to curtail production on a region-wide basis. This came during the severe depression of the 1890's. In June, 1896, the Club sponsored an agreement under which the mills closed down for four weeks during the months of July and August. Once again it was difficult to convince many of the treasurers that they should curtail. But by July 4th, around four million northern spindles were on the reduced schedule. In terms of the amount of support the Club received, this was a relatively successful program. Unfortunately, however, decisive action had been delayed until prices were already badly depressed and stocks were piled high in the warehouses. With these inventories hanging over the market, prices remained low. Moreover, it took some time to reduce the surplus. When at last orders began to increase and prices started back up, the mills junked the program, forcing prices down again.[63]

Public policy on competition seems to have had no effect on these programs. Although in 1890 the national government translated the common law prohibitions of monopoly and restraint of trade into a federal statute, the law was poorly enforced. The Justice Department pressed only a few cases, giving the courts little opportunity to put specific meaning into such vague phrases as "monopoly" and "restraint of trade."[64] Furthermore, in the E. C. Knight decision (1895), the Supreme Court ruled that the law did

[62] Letter of J. Howard Nichols to James W. Cumnock, March 31, 1884, in Dwight MSS; Letter of L. M. Sargent to Messrs. Townsend and Yale, September 5, 1884, in Lawrence MSS.

[63] *Commercial and Financial Chronicle*, LXII, No. 1618 (June 27, 1896), 1186; LXIII, No. 1619 (July 4, 1896), 39; LXIII, No. 1629 (September 12, 1896), 434–435; LXIII, No. 1641 (December 5, 1896), 994; LXIII, No. 1644 (December 26, 1896), 1170; Victor S. Clark, *Manufactures, 1607–1914*, II, 720–721.

[64] Thorelli, *Antitrust*, pp. 587–592.

not apply to manufacturing since it was not interstate commerce.[65] In the circumstances, it is easy to understand why the Club took no heed of the antitrust law and made no effort to conceal its curtailment program in 1896.

More common than these formal plans was the casual sort of price-fixing agreement which could be reached at the Arkwright Club's monthly luncheons. This kind of informal, unregulated understanding or "gentlemen's agreement" could be (and was) set up without an association. But the Club's luncheons provided convenient and regular occasions for competitors to meet. At times the manufacturers seem merely to have compared prices; at other times they cooperated closely "to help advance prices." Indeed, this sort of price fixing was omnipresent in cotton textiles—as it was in other manufacturing industries—and the results seem everywhere to have been the same; the understandings were at best temporary. They usually lasted until one of the parties got an opportunity to shade the price list.[66]

Until the late 1890's the instability of these agreements and the failure of the curtailment programs did not cause any widespread or lasting concern among the New England manufacturers. In fact, these businessmen appear to have been rather satisfied with such temporary arrangements. They looked upon the industry's problems as temporary conditions, the product of a financial panic or of efforts to lower the tariff. Confident that recovery was inevitable and that due to the industry's low fixed costs they would be able to ride out a depression without great difficulty, the manufacturers could afford to use this kind of loose combination. They could rely upon temporary measures because they were confident of the future, sure of the fact that their problems were temporary too.

By 1900 the Arkwright Club had thus experienced several important changes. Its membership had grown, and it had become almost exclusively a cotton manufacturer's organization. Its functions had gradually changed as it began to adopt typical guild programs and values. Although the members remained competitors, the Club provided them with a means of experimenting, inter-

[65] *United States* v. *E. C. Knight Co., et al.,* 156 U. S. 1, 15 Sup. Ct. 249 (1895).

[66] Sargent to Townsend and Yale, November 20 and 25, 1882; November 8, 1887; January 23, 1891; February 4, 1891; all in Lawrence MSS.

mittently, with cooperation. The members did not develop a lasting system of economic controls, but they did create more systematic means of controlling, or attempting to control, the political
environment.

In the South during these years, several trade organizations
were formed, but none of them lasted very long. During the depression of the mid-eighties, the Southern and Western Manufacturers' Association was organized in an unsuccessful effort to
curtail production. When the Association held a convention in
August, 1885, the meeting was poorly attended, and the plans for
regional production control were abandoned.[67] A year later the
Association was revived in an attempt to combat the Knights of
Labor "before the infection could spread." But the union soon
collapsed, and the Association became dormant.[68]

There were other "loose combinations" in the South, all of
which had a short lifespan. During the eighties and nineties the
manufacturers of cotton duck experimented with various kinds of
combinations, including a pooling agreement under which the
mills were assigned shares of the market. Similar to this was the
joint selling agency formed by the southern producers of plaid
fabrics. In both cases the combines had a brief existence, although
the pool in cotton duck led to a merger in 1899 of most of the
firms making this product.[69]

Not until 1897 did the southerners organize a lasting regional
trade association. In an effort to cut back on production and to
lower commissions on sales and transportation charges, a number
of executives from the yarn mills in North Carolina called all of
the southern cotton manufacturers to a meeting at Charlotte,
North Carolina, on May 27, 1897.[70] Although it was expected that

[67] *Commercial and Financial Chronicle*, XXXIX, No. 1017 (December 20,
1884), 713; XLI, No. 1049 (August 1, 1885), 141. *The Textile Record of
America*, VI, No. 7 (July, 1885), 185, and No. 8 (August, 1885), 211; Gustavus
G. Williamson, "Cotton Manufacturing," pp. 97–101.

[68] *Ibid.*, p. 193.

[69] *Ibid.*, p. 112; *Commercial and Financial Chronicle*, XLIX, No. 1264
(September 14, 1889), 327; Dewing, *Corporate Promotions*, pp. 336–337;
Victor S. Clark, *Manufactures, 1607–1914*, II, 411.

[70] *Charlotte Observer* (North Carolina), May 12, 13, and 16, 1897. D. A.
Tompkins, editor of the *Observer*, was influential in the movement to organize an association, and his paper carried full accounts of this and subsequent
meetings.

one hundred mills would be represented, the turnout was disappointing. Only about forty executives attended the meeting. This lack of interest virtually killed any hopes of successfully curtailing production, but the manufacturers nevertheless formally organized a regional trade group. Since almost all of the executives who attended were affiliated with mills which manufactured only cotton yarn, they named the organization the Southern Cotton Spinners' Association.[71]

In structure the new association closely resembled the New England Cotton Manufacturers' Association. As in the New England Association, any mill officer—president, treasurer, agent, or manager—could join, even though each mill was given only one vote. Since the members joined as individuals (not as official spokesmen for their firms), the dues were nominal and the organization's income was small. Initially there were no regular staff members, and one of the manufacturers served as secretary-treasurer.[72]

In terms of its functions, the southern organization resembled the Arkwright Club. Like the Club, it sought through cooperative means the goals of economic stability and control. In search of stability the members at the first meeting adopted a resolution which called upon all of the mills turning out coarse cotton yarns to curtail production by 25 per cent for four months. Those who were interested could sign written pledges to do this; it was hoped that without pressure from the association the manufacturers who had not attended the meeting would cooperate.[73] This first attempt at production control was apparently no more successful than the Arkwright Club's programs, but the Southern Association was not prevented by this early failure from making further attempts at controlling prices.[74]

In addition to limiting production the Association sought to control through cooperative action the cost of transportation and the commissions charged by merchants for marketing goods. Carriers moving either cotton or finished goods forced the southern mills to pay higher rates per mile than those paid by their northern

[71] Ibid., May 16, 1897; Commercial and Financial Chronicle, LXIV, No. 1664 (May 15, 1897), 961; LXIV, No. 1665 (May 22, 1897), 1009.

[72] Charlotte Observer, June 11, 1897.

[73] Ibid., May 16, 1897.

[74] Ibid., June 10 and 11, 1897; October 1, 1897; September 15, 1899; October 7, 1899; November 3, 1899; May 11 and 12, 1900; June 8 and 26, 1900.

competitors.[75] Although this sectional freight-rate differential did
not come close to cancelling out the cost advantage that the
southern mills held, management in the South wanted to make
the most of its favorable location. One of the first committees
formed was a group to study the freight-rate problem and to
negotiate with the carriers for lower charges. The mills were also
concerned about relations with the merchants, as the manufacturers felt sales commissions were too high and the merchants were
too eager to force goods on a weak market. Furthermore, many
of the contracts that were negotiated for the sale of goods allowed
the buyer to cancel the order for any of a wide variety of reasons.
Whenever prices declined, the buyers backed out of their orders,
forcing the mills to take the loss on a declining market. These
several conditions were, of course, merely different manifestations
of the excess capacity the industry accumulated during the downturn of the business cycle. But the manufacturers looked upon
them as unfair practices that should be controlled by the Association. Consequently, they attempted to bargain collectively with
the merchants to lower commissions, while passing resolutions
which firmly announced that "orders for goods shall not be can-
celled unless agreeable to both purchaser and mill."[76]

During its first three years the Southern Cotton Spinners' Association established itself as the leading regional trade group in
the Piedmont's textile industry without, however, solving any
of the basic problems that the Association initially encountered.
Greatest success was achieved in the matter of freight rates.
Through united action the mills were able to persuade the carriers
to lower their rates. Even though the North-South rate differentials
were not substantially changed, the new rates did help the Piedmont's mills.[77] Where commission charges and production control
were concerned the Association was unable to record any success
during its first three years of operation. The commission merchants

[75] David M. Potter, "The Historical Development of Eastern-Southern
Freight Rate Relationships," *Law and Contemporary Problems* (Summer,
1947), pp. 416–448.

[76] *Charlotte Observer*, May 16, 1897.

[77] *Ibid.*, June 11, 1897; May 13, 1898; continued problems with freight rate
differentials was one of the major reasons that the North Carolina manufacturers organized a state association in 1906. David Clark, "The Organization of Cotton Manufacturers Association of North Carolina" (typewritten
manuscript, North Carolina Textile Manufacturers Association, Inc., Charlotte, N.C.), pp. 1–2.

were in a strong position and the Association's membership was limited and unable, on a declining market, to unite behind a single program.[78] Although cooperation was an appealing idea, the short-term realities of the market placed such substantial innovations out of the reach of the Southern Cotton Spinners' Association.

The Spinners' Association, like the two New England organizations, could best be characterized as a "dinner-club" association. This name seems appropriate because the most important function of the trade organization in this initial stage of its development was to provide a meeting place, a dinner, a convention, or a luncheon for the members. These meetings enabled the members to coordinate their activities; yet their activities were seldom carried on by the association itself. Indeed, the organizations had virtually no means of doing so. The Southern Association had neither an office nor staff. The New England Association did not establish permanent headquarters until 1894, and then the only full-time employee was a clerk. As late as 1900 the Arkwright Club still did not employ any staff members who devoted all of their time to the association.

The essential functions of the dinner-club associations were for the most part performed by the members. Plans for price and production controls were worked out through committees or through informal contacts. Lobbying or negotiating for favorable rail rates was also left primarily in the hands of the mill executives; they used the organization to distribute evenly the expenses of their politicking and to achieve the "leverage" that could be gained by coordinating their individual efforts. Although the technical programs of the New England Association frequently drew upon outside speakers, these activities were planned by committees of the members. On the whole then, the organization, qua organization, did little more than provide a platform from which the members could launch their efforts to control particular aspects of the political or economic environment. In these efforts the leadership and most of the administrative work was provided by the manufacturers.

The dinner-club associations seldom impinged in any significant

[78] *Charlotte Observer,* June 15, 1897; July 2, 1897; May 14 and 16, 1898; June 18 and 28, 1898; August 31, 1899.

way upon the political or economic autonomy of their members. Of the three, the New England Association asked the least of its supporters. Since the Arkwright Club and the Southern Association sought to coordinate the activities of their members for political and economic action, they did generate some pressure to conform to the organization's norms. In politics, however, there was little chance for serious disagreement about such issues as the regulation of industry, which the manufacturers agreed was an absurd invasion of the rights of private property. Similarly unanimous was the response aroused by the question of freight rates. When the problems were external, as they were in these cases, there were seldom any serious disagreements about the association's objectives. Where the problems were internal to the industry, however, the opposite was true. The attempts to stabilize the market by controlling production brought to the surface the differences between the various manufacturers. Since the associations neither had, nor apparently sought, any means of forcing these programs upon the non-cooperators, the curtailment plans generally stirred up more heat than action; only the 1897 plan of the Arkwright Club was widely supported. In any case the manufacturers were free to make their own decision as to whether they would support the associations, and in 1897 a significant number of the northern mills had not agreed to cooperate with the Club.

Another general characteristic of the dinner-club associations was the *ad hoc* nature of most of their programs. Economic and political functions were performed when they were needed, not on a permanent or continuing basis. Of course the groups held regular meetings and conventions, and the New England Association had a permanent agenda of technical subjects. But between conventions even the New England Association was normally dormant; and it was the only one of the three that did not define its programs as a result of immediate and changing pressures upon management. When tariff revision or regulatory measures appeared in a legislature, the Arkwright Club leapt into action. Otherwise, the organization remained politically inactive. Even the curtailment plans of the Club and the Southern Association were in response to short-term problems; they were clearly identified as expedient, not permanent, measures. These plans had a short "time range"; they looked no further than the end of the current business cycle. Although there were exceptions, the dinner-club associations in cotton textiles generally spawned this kind of short-range, *ad hoc* program.

Within the dinner-club associations, a fully-developed cooperative or associative ideology was never articulated. On occasion the manufacturers talked about the unity of their regional interests. They expounded the need for cooperation and control. The very existence of an association testified to their awareness of joint interests in stabilization, cooperation, and control. But they failed to work out a respectable politico-economic philosophy which would justify their position and provide guidelines for future action. Instead, they depended upon *ad hoc* rationalizations that matched their *ad hoc* programs.

This type of dinner-club association was rather common throughout American industry during the latter part of the nineteenth century. Although detailed information on other industries is sparse this sort of association seems to have developed in the iron and steel, petroleum, and lumber industries—to mention only a few.[79] Where high fixed costs or other characteristics of the industry intensified competition, the dinner-club associations quickly surrendered the economic function of stabilizing prices to tighter and more effective forms of combination; then the associations became merely adjuncts to the stability-oriented trusts or giant corporations. In any case the trade association was still valuable for its political contributions, and in those industries which failed to achieve a high degree of concentration, the dinner-club association was periodically used in an effort to prevent cutthroat competition.

[79] For information on the associations in iron and steel see the following: Charles E. Edgerton, "The Wire-Nail Association of 1895–96" in *Trusts, Pools and Corporations,* ed. William Z. Ripley (Boston: Ginn and Company, 1916), pp. 49–58, 68, 72, 75–76; William H. S. Stevens, "A Classification of Pools and Associations Based on American Experience," *American Economic Review,* III, No. 3 (September, 1913), 558–559; Victor S. Clark, *Manufactures, 1607–1914,* II, 281–283, 331–333, 622–624; in regard to petroleum, see: Ralph W. Hidy and Muriel E. Hidy, *Pioneering in Big Business, 1882–1911* (New York: Harper, 1955), p. 10; Harold F. Williamson and Arnold R. Daum, *The American Petroleum Industry: The Age of Illumination, 1859–1899* (Evanston: Northwestern University Press, 1959), pp. 351–352, 356–360, 430–433; some information on the associations in lumber can be found in: R. C. Fraunberger, "Lumber Trade Associations" (unpublished Master's thesis, Temple University, 1951), pp. 11–12, 21–22, 59; Victor S. Clark, *Manufactures, 1607–1914,* II, 776–777.

In cotton textiles all three of the regional groups were dinner-club associations. These organizations were shaped by an environment which had imposed upon management only the most elementary demands for stabilization, control, and interfirm cooperation. Certain kinds of political difficulties had called for joint action; a rapid change in technology, transportation questions, and depressed prices had all elicited associative action. But most of the problems that management encountered could still be solved by individualistic, competitive behavior. As a result, the instruments for facilitating interfirm cooperation—the dinner-club associations—were rudimentary organizations. Their income was very limited. Their programs were sporadic, their ideology weak. A bureaucratic structure had barely begun to take shape.

Fall River: Summer 1900

The city was uneasy. For the mill hands there was a smallpox epidemic to keep their minds busy when they were not worrying about their jobs. Work had been irregular of late. In the hard times of the 1890's the entire city had suffered. This had happened before, but this time the recovery was unusually slow. It seemed that the day of the full pay check would never come. Some of the workers were supporting the drive to establish a cooperative mill, owned and operated by the union. Most of the people just waited and worried.

Management was also upset. While the industry as a whole was growing, far too little of the expansion was taking place in Fall River. For several years no new mills had been constructed. Three were being built in 1900, but in comparison with what was happening in the South, Fall River was slipping behind. Depressions were more frequent than they had been in the past. Despite all their efforts the treasurers were unable to get their businesses running on an even keel.

In search of stability, the city's mills had joined together in a print-cloth pool or selling agency. All of their products were sold through a single agent. Since prices were set by the selling agency, price competition was entirely eliminated among the member mills. But even this extreme measure failed to solve their problems. Although the agency could hold prices rigid, there was nothing to prevent other mills— particularly those in the South—from taking the sales. Prices were depressed. Inventories were piling up. And nobody knew exactly what could be done to stabilize prices and restore profitable conditions. Fall River had good cause to be nervous in the summer of 1900.

Chapter III

New Forces

During the early years of the twentieth century, the world of the cotton manufacturer began to change—change with a speed that was bewildering—change in the most fundamental ways. No longer did the traditional forms of individual and collective action produce satisfactory results. New concepts, new values seemed to be called for. If the manufacturer were to cope with this new environment, more collective action seemed to be necessary. Cooperation, not competition, was apparently the key to this twentieth-century puzzle. Under the new conditions, stability became a more popular goal. At the same time both the means and desirability of controlling the political and economic environment were increased significantly.

Four major developments impinged directly upon the cotton manufacturers. Of the four, the most threatening and difficult challenge to meet came from within the industry itself. At first this was not evident; during the years 1901–1910, the industry appeared to follow the patterns of growth and competitive behavior established in the previous century. Periods of sharp depression alternated with years of rapid growth and high profits. In New England, the industry's total capacity was increased by a significant measure.[1] In the South, management ran up against a

---

[1] Bureau of the Census, *Twelfth Census, Manufactures, Textiles*, pp. 54–57; Bureau of the Census, *Fourteenth Census (1920), Manufactures, 1919, Reports for Selected Industries* (1923), X, 176.

labor shortage, but this placed only a temporary restraint upon southern expansion.[2]

Although aggregate figures on growth (1900–1910) do not indicate any important changes, the New England mills were feeling—more and more acutely—the effects of southern competition.[3] Finally, in 1911, the northern wing of the industry entered the first stage of a depression that was to last for several decades—to last, with only a brief interruption, until most of New England's mills had liquidated or gone into bankruptcy.[4] As profits declined, the growth rate in the North quickly tapered off. In 1914, in fact, the total number of spindles in New England mills actually declined. No longer could northern firms escape the worst effects of low-cost competition by shifting to products which unskilled southern mill hands could not make. By 1911 the South was making almost all of the nation's coarse goods; northern and southern mills were struggling over the market for medium grades of cloth; too many New England mills were already squeezed into fine cottons. The results were cutthroat competition and an intense interest in finding some means of stabilizing the cotton textile market.[5]

[2] Richard A. Lester, "Trends in Southern Wage Differentials since 1890," *The Southern Economic Journal,* XI, No. 4 (April, 1945), 318–320, 339; American Cotton Manufacturers Association, *Proceedings* (Charlotte, N.C.), X (1906), 277–278, 300 (hereafter cited as ACMA, *Proc.*).

[3] Hammond, "The Cotton Industry," pp. 15–21, 114, 122, 128–130, 135–137, 139, 145, 149, 574–577, 593–594, 789; Thomas R. Smith, *Fall River,* pp. 109–110; Knowlton, *Pepperell's Progress,* pp. 173–175.

[4] The most thorough study of profits in cotton textiles indicates that the industry's period of subnormal earnings began before World War I. U. S., Bureau of Internal Revenue, Excess Profits Tax Council, *The Cotton Textile Industry: An Economic Analysis of the Industry with Reference to the Investigation of Claims for Relief under Section 722 of the Internal Revenue Code* (Washington, D.C.: Government Printing Office, 1948), p. 38; also see: Stephen J. Kennedy, *Profits and Losses in Textiles* (New York: Harper & Brothers, 1936), pp. 9–10, 126–128; Gordon Donald, Jr., "The Depression in Cotton Textiles, 1924 to 1940" (unpublished Ph.D. dissertation, University of Chicago, 1951), p. 6; in my discussion of the industry's bout with excess capacity, I am following (with some minor modifications) the analysis and terminology of Lloyd G. Reynolds', "Cutthroat Competition," *American Economic Review,* XXX, No. 4 (December, 1940), 736–747.

[5] NACM, *Year Book, 1926* (Boston), p. 154; National Association of Cotton Manufacturers, *Transactions* (Boston), XCI (1911), 282; XCIV (1913), 112, 243–250; XCVI (1914), 143, 158, 410; XCVII (1914), 40–41 (hereafter cited as NACM, *Trans.*); NACM, Records of the Conference of Officers of Cotton

While this was happening, the southern industry continued to expand. Although the Piedmont's mills were not by any means isolated from the difficulties besetting New England, the long-term outlook in the South was favorable. Low production costs and local support encouraged further entry and growth even though the entire industry had undoubtedly already outgrown the domestic market.[6]

Cotton textiles was given a temporary reprieve by the First World War, and after the European conflict ended, the industry experienced several more years of unusual conditions.[7] Time was nevertheless running out, especially for New England. During the immediate postwar years many northern companies were unable to make adequate profits despite a rising market. In some cases the companies paid dividends out of surplus left over from the war; in others they simply failed to make allowances for depreciation. Of course this sort of expedient could only temporarily conceal the vulnerable position of these high-cost firms in an industry that already had excess capacity.[8]

The situation facing the entire industry was serious indeed. There was very little chance that demand for cotton textiles would expand enough to keep the industry's enlarged capacity running

Manufacturing Associations, Washington, February 2, 1911, in the library of the American Textile Manufacturers Institute, Charlotte, N.C., pp. 74–75, 77; ACMA, *Proc.,* XX (1916), 94.

[6] NACM, *Year Book, 1926,* p. 155; ACMA, *Proc.,* XV (1911), 90; XVIII (1914), 94–96; XIX (1915), 96, 100, 174; XX (1916), 94; NACM, "Conference of Officers," pp. 74–75.

[7] Bureau of the Census, *Bulletin 134, Cotton Production and Distribution* (1916), pp. 33–34; Bureau of the Census, *Statistical Abstract of the United States, 1920* (1921), pp. 262–263, 805; Bert G. Hickman, Jr., "Cyclical Fluctuations in the Cotton Textile Industry" (unpublished Ph.D. dissertation, University of California, 1947), pp. 54, 116, 147, 152, 158–159, 162; Navin, *Whitin Machine Works,* pp. 338–339; NACM, *Year Book, 1925,* p. 212; Kennedy, *Profits and Losses,* pp. 128, 245–246; George Soule, *Prosperity Decade: From War to Depression, 1917–1929* (New York: Holt, Rinehart & Winston, 1947), pp. 107, 110–114.

[8] Edward G. Keith, "Financial History of Two Textile Towns: A Study of Lowell and Fall River" (unpublished Ph.D. dissertation, Harvard University, 1936), pp. 402–408; Knowlton, *Pepperell's Progress,* p. 222; Kennedy, *Profits and Losses,* p. 149; as might be expected, Fall River's print-cloth mills faced the crisis before the New Bedford fine-yarn mills. Sanford & Kelly, *Fall River, Mass: Statistics Relating to its Cotton Manufacturing Corporations for the Year 1923* (Fall River, Massachusetts, 1924).

at profitable prices. Synthetic fibers were now available to satisfy the new customers who might otherwise have used cotton.[9] With the export markets dominated by the English and by the new producers of the Far East, the American mills were left to struggle over a relatively static domestic market.[10] Unless the excess spindles and looms could be driven out of production very quickly, both wings of the industry could look forward to a long siege of cutthroat competition.

The problem was particularly acute because cotton textiles had failed to develop the kind of oligopolistic structure which exerted a stabilizing influence upon other industries. Two of the three major consolidations (in yarn, duck, and thread) which had taken place at the turn of the century had failed. Both the yarn and duck combinations ran aground on the rock of southern competition. When the combines attempted to hold prices above a competitive level, new southern mills were built to manufacture sales yarn and cotton duck. Other companies shifted from less profitable products and took customers away from the combinations. As a result of this competition and of the failure to realize any significant economies of scale, both companies were forced to undergo reorganization; neither was a financial success.[11]

The difficulties experienced by these combines had the important effect of discouraging the promotion of similar horizontal combinations in subsequent years.[12] Between 1899 and 1920, in fact, the percentage of the industry's total capitalization accounted for by the four leading companies actually declined.[13] In other consumer-goods industries, such as sugar, leather, and whiskey, horizontal combination provided a foundation upon which management built giant, vertically integrated corporations; these companies enjoyed considerable success in avoiding severe price

[9] Backman and Gainsbrugh, *Economics of the Cotton Textile Industry,* p. 178.

[10] Bureau of the Census, *Statistical Abstract of the United States, 1934* (1935), p. 437.

[11] Dewing, *Corporate Promotions,* pp. 320–322, 332, 356, 367, 411.

[12] Kennedy, *Profits and Losses,* p. 44. I am using the term "horizontal" to refer to combinations of competing units which perform the same function, e.g., spinning cotton yarn. The term "vertical" refers to combinations which encompass several successive functions in the process of manufacturing and marketing, e.g., mining ore, transporting ore, processing ore, and marketing the product.

[13] Thorp and Knott, "The History of Concentration," pp. 253, 254.

competition.[14] But in cotton textiles, during the years 1900–24, the trend toward industrial consolidation was reversed by the stronger trend of industrial expansion in the low-cost South.

The industry was thus in a difficult position when the large cotton crop of 1924 precipitated a rapid decline in the prices of cotton and cotton products. Accompanying this was a mild national recession which cut down the demand for cotton textiles.[15] As prices skidded downward, management in many southern firms faced serious losses and sought new ways to reduce unit costs. Many of them began to use a second shift. If fixed cost had been more important in cotton textiles, the mills would certainly have done this much earlier. As it was, however, the conditions of 1924 persuaded many southern executives to adopt two-shift operations and in some cases even to allow automatic machinery to run during the noon hour.[16]

Use of the second shift reduced unit costs, but it greatly expanded total capacity. On this new basis of operations the industry could quickly reach a high level of output; buyers, realizing this, were very cautious about placing future orders for goods since they knew that so-called spot goods were available when they were needed. As the competition for orders increased, northern firms, many of them already weakened, began to leave the industry through liquidation or bankruptcy. Despite their low cost of production a majority of the southern firms also found it impossible to make adequate profits. By 1924 the entire industry was in serious trouble.[17]

The beginnings of this problem of excess capacity during the years 1911 to 1923 forced management to look for some means of

[14] Alfred D. Chandler, Jr., "The Beginnings of 'Big Business' in American Industry," *Business History Review*, XXXIII, No. 1 (Spring, 1959), 6.

[15] NACM, *Year Book, 1926*, pp. 49–51, 121–131; Hickman, "Cyclical Fluctuations," pp. 162–163; Soule, *Prosperity Decade*, p. 114; Hammond, "The Cotton Industry," pp. 110–112, 153–154.

[16] Southern spindles operated an average of 3100 hours per annum for the years 1921–1924; during the 1925–1928 period, the average was 3475 hours per annum. Averages were calculated from the figures in: NACM, *Year Book, 1924*, p. 227; NACM, *Year Book, 1927*, p. 164; NACM, *Year Book, 1929*, p. 195. Also see: Donald, "The Depression in Cotton Textiles," pp. 104–105, 237–238; Lahne, *The Cotton Mill Worker*, p. 144.

[17] Hickman, "Cyclical Fluctuations," p. 172; Bureau of the Census, *Statistical Abstract, 1929* (1930), p. 828; Internal Revenue Service, *Statistics of Income, 1924* (1926), p. 135.

stabilizing the industry. The concentration movement had failed. So it was necessary to create an alternative form of stabilizing institution, some type of loose combination which would be acceptable to the manufacturers and to the federal government's Justice Department. The government's opinion was important because progressive reformers were putting new life into the antitrust law, particularly insofar as the law applied to pools and price agreements.[18] Obviously mill treasurers in the North were most interested in solving this problem. But they were supported by many southern executives who sensed that continued growth of their wing of the industry could only lead to a ruinous competitive struggle. In their search for an alternative to oligopoly, these manufacturers experimented with their trade associations as a means of achieving stability through cooperative control of production and prices.

Although cotton textiles remained a stronghold of the small firm, the concentration movement was one of the new forces that changed the cotton manufacturer's world. The influence in this case was indirect, but it was nonetheless extremely important. The various modes of competition and the techniques of rational control, developed under conditions of oligopoly, provided models for the cotton manufacturers. They saw what was being done by the successful firms in industries such as iron and steel. They were particularly impressed by the activities of the United States Steel Company.

Nothing was more appealing than the new style of competition that developed in oligopolistic industries. Where control was concentrated, market behavior was characterized by "administered" prices and non-price competition.[19] The giant firms stressed quality or style and relied heavily upon aggressive marketing,

---

[18] Thorelli, *Antitrust*, p. 597; Milton Handler, *A Study of the Construction and Enforcement of the Federal Antitrust Laws*, Temporary National Economic Committee, Monograph No. 38 (1941), pp. 8, 17, 45–46; Martin L. Lindahl and William A. Carter, *Corporate Concentration and Public Policy* (3rd ed.; Englewood Cliffs, N. J.: Prentice-Hall, 1959), pp. 453–454; Arthur R. Burns, *The Decline of Competition* (New York: McGraw-Hill, 1936), pp. 17–21.

[19] *Ibid.*, pp. 76–371.

often through advertising. In most oligopolistic industries, big business developed brand names and trade-marks to identify its products and to shelter its market from competition. Many of the large companies also competed on the basis of service and effective repair work.[20] Another weapon in this new brand of competition was research and development. Whether the growth of large firms "caused" the increased outlays for research is, for our purposes, beside the point; the cotton manufacturers clearly associated the new emphasis upon research and development with the highly concentrated industries that they sought to emulate.[21]

Another aspect of the concentration movement which affected cotton manufacturers was the vigorous search for rational techniques of control, a search that went on primarily within the industrial giants. Due to the size of the companies and the number of personnel involved, management found it necessary to develop orderly, efficient, and impersonal forms of control.[22] One of the offspring of this desire for rational control was scientific or systematic management.[23] Similar techniques included the standardization of parts and products, the development of uniform methods of testing, and the improvement of accounting techniques, especially through unit-cost accounting.

The cotton manufacturer saw what was happening, recognized that better control might mean better profits, and periodically became excited about the possibilities of introducing such systems in cotton textiles. Why, he began to ask, should his industry lag so far behind? Standardization could be achieved through the trade association, as could research and development, advertising, and perhaps even price stability. They would need to cooperate more than they had in the past, but that seemed to many to be a small

[20] *Ibid.*, pp. 372–417.

[21] Jacob Schmookler, "Technological Progress and the Modern American Corporation," *The Corporation in Modern Society,* ed. Edward S. Mason (Cambridge: Harvard University Press, 1959), pp. 141–165.

[22] Alfred D. Chandler, Jr., *Strategy and Structure: Chapters in the History of the Industrial Enterprise* (Cambridge: Massachusetts Institute of Technology Press, 1962), pp. 14–17, 24–41.

[23] *Ibid.*, pp. 36–49, 52–113, 283–323; Joseph A. Litterer, "Systematic Management," *Business History Review,* XXXV, No. 4 (Winter, 1961), 461–476; Ernest Dale and Charles Meloy, "Hamilton MacFarland Barksdale and the DuPont Contributions to Systematic Management," *ibid.*, XXXVI, No. 2 (Summer, 1962), 127–152.

price to pay if they could stabilize their market and rationalize their operations.[24]

In addition to providing a model for the textile manufacturer to follow, the concentration movement changed the intellectual environment in which he operated. In place of a nineteenth-century outlook, which stressed competition and unrestrained growth, big business substituted a new value system which stressed stability, teamwork, and systematic controls. This new business ideology was also characterized by a long-range viewpoint. When Standard Oil invested millions of dollars in an oil field, the firm was planning ahead for several decades.[25] Similarly, with many industrial research projects, management thought in terms of investments and returns extending over a number of years. In this new world of corporate giants, businessmen normally looked far into the future, seeking stable, long-range patterns of profit-making and growth. This was a new intellectual climate—one that "taught" the cotton manufacturer to accept new values and to seek new modes of behavior.[26] Complementing, as it did, the internal changes within the cotton textile industry, the new ideology led management to experiment extensively with its trade associations.

A third "new force" that influenced management was a product of the changes which took place in the political process in twentieth-century America. This was a complex phenomenon, one which had a variety of effects, some of which were contradictory. Initially the cotton manufacturers recognized merely the threatening changes that middle-class reformers were bringing about in the state and national legislatures. In state after state, the progressives challenged the laissez faire tradition and the businessman's domi-

---

[24] ACMA, *Proc.*, IX (1905), 70; XIII (1909), 167–177; NACM, *Trans.*, LXXXIV (1908), 136–151; LXXXVI (1909), 249, 324–325, 327; XCII (1912), 303–304, 312–313, 422; C (1916), 309–361, 402–407, 416; CI (1916), 83–84; CXVII (1924), 436–441, 444–445, 449; Letter of C. P. Baker to A. N. Mayo & Co., April 16, 1906, in Lawrence MSS.

[25] R. W. Hidy and M. E. Hidy, *Pioneering*, pp. 155–168.

[26] *Ibid.*, pp. 33–39; Chandler, *Strategy and Structure*, pp. 393–395; Francis X. Sutton *et al.*, *The American Business Creed* (Cambridge: Harvard University Press, 1956), pp. 33–36, 57–66, 176–177, 218–220, 246, 387–388.

nant influence upon the government. What was needed, the reformers said, was a new order that would set things right by strengthening the government's power to regulate business practices and by breaking the businessman's hold on the government.[27]

The progressives mounted a strong, well-organized campaign against laissez faire and business dominance of public policy.[28] At first these middle-class reformers had to overcome their own aversion to organization, but once this was accomplished, they were able to build a series of effective political combinations.[29] Under their guidance a number of the industrial states established ten hours as the maximum working day for women and children. Night work was prohibited in some states. Safety conditions were regulated in an effort to reduce the hazards of industrial employment, and child labor and workmen's compensation laws were passed.[30]

In New England the manufacturers resented regulations which placed them at a disadvantage vis-a-vis their southern competitors. As the president of the New England Association pointed out in 1905, northern legislatures should consider "the solid and masterful advance of the manufacture of cotton in the southern states . . ." before they drafted labor legislation.[31] A few years later the members were urged to be patient in the face of an attack "which appears to have its foundations in meddling legislation, and to have derived its impulse from political machinations."[32] Such patience as they did possess was sorely tried when the Wilson Administration took office in 1913; then, northern manufacturers lamented the fact that "the last few years of national and state legislation has witnessed a development of commissions never

[27] Eric Goldman, *Rendezvous with Destiny* (New York: Random House, 1952), pp. 85–160; George E. Mowry, *The Era of Theodore Roosevelt* (New York: Harper, 1958), pp. 17–105.

[28] *Ibid.*, pp. 85–105.

[29] Richard Hofstadter, *The Age of Reform* (New York: Random House [Vintage], 1955), pp. 215–227.

[30] Don D. Lescohier, *Working Conditions*, Vol. III of *History of Labor in the United States, 1896–1932,* ed. John R. Commons (4 vols.; New York: MacMillan, 1935), pp. 359–370; Elizabeth Brandeis, *Labor Legislation, ibid.,* IV, 405–437, 466–495, 570–581.

[31] NECMA, *Trans.,* LXXVIII (1905), 95.

[32] NACM, *Trans.,* LXXXVIII (1910), 128–129.

before dreamed of in any country under a republican form of government."[33]

Until tariff revision became a hot issue, the southern mill executives were considerably less worried about progressivism than were the northern treasurers. Most of the mill villages of the southern Piedmont were untouched by this urban reform movement, and the states of the Southeast were still too happy about having industry to begin thinking very seriously about regulating it.[34] Around 1909, however, the pressure for tariff revision mounted, and the southerners began to petition Congress "to place such duties on cotton goods as will serve to encourage the production of all classes of these within the limits of our country."[35] Two years later when a lower tariff was stopped at the last moment by President Taft's veto, the southerners were aroused to vigorous, although relatively disorganized, action.[36] By 1914 the president of the southern association, Stuart W. Cramer of North Carolina, was commenting upon the "mad race for progressiveness . . ." and the "many kinds of legislation recently passed and pending. . . ." These new laws, he said, "contribute largely to the present unsatisfactory conditions of business. . . ." By this time the southerners were almost

[33] NACM, *Trans.*, XCVII (1914), 40. My research into the political activities of this industry suggests that the reform historian's treatment of business opposition to progressive legislation is basically accurate; by the same token, Robert H. Wiebe, *Businessmen and Reform: A Study of the Progressive Movement* (Cambridge: Harvard University Press, 1962), especially pp. 206–224, is undoubtedly correct insofar as he demonstrates that businessmen disagreed about many fundamental issues and that many businessmen supported the reform movements. Wiebe has offered a healthy corrective to the rigid, black and white categories of the earlier reform historians. His emendation of the earlier interpretation should not, however, be turned into a wholesale reversal, in the style of Gabriel Kolko, *The Triumph of Conservatism: A Reinterpretation of American History, 1900–1916* (New York: The Free Press of Glencoe, 1963). My study of the political activities of the associations in cotton textiles indicates that Kolko's central thesis is inaccurate insofar as this industry's experience during the progessive era is concerned.

[34] The southern manufacturers were occasionally disturbed by agitation for reform. R. M. Miller, "Address Before the Cotton Manufacturers Association of North Carolina," June, 1909 (MS in the Association's office, Charlotte, N.C.); Cotton Manufacturers Association of Georgia, *Report* (Atlanta), XXX (1930), 45–47, 58 (hereafter cited as CMAG, *Report*); Lahne, *The Cotton Mill Worker*, pp. 137–139, 143–144.

[35] ACMA, *Proc.*, XIII (1909), 196, 201.

[36] ACMA, *Tariff Bulletin No. 2* (Charlotte, N.C.); ACMA, *Proc.*, XVI (1912), 91.

as perturbed as the New England executives were about reform measures.[37]

In addition to regulating business the progressives pushed through a number of measures designed to curb the business lobby. Included among these reform policies were the direct election of senators and the use of public hearings in Congress. Other measures aimed at giving control of government back to the people—as opposed to the interests—were the initiative, the referendum, and the recall. Even though many of these innovations fell far short of their goals, the total effect of the progressive movement was to break up the business lobby which had dominated American politics since the Civil War. In its place there developed a new style of pressure-group politics which was more open, more responsive to public pressure. Personal influence became somewhat less important; well-organized group action and the appearance if not the reality of broad support became essential to political success.[38]

When this happened, the cotton manufacturers and many other businessmen found their old forms of political action outmoded, their dinner-club associations ill-equipped to play ball in the new league. In 1911 the chairman of the southern association's committee on legislation had to admit that they had not really been prepared to deal with the tariff bill that was under consideration. They were, he said, inexperienced in such matters; "because of the difficulty in collecting and properly presenting information relating thereto in so short a time, we are forced to open a campaign of education among ourselves with the expectation that whatever ideas occur to our many members will be presented in person by them. . . ."[39] In the past, such haphazard techniques had sufficed, but as the manufacturers recognized, the old lobby was gone. They must, a northern producer said, "associate for national legislative action, if our voices are to be heard in favor of sanity and safety. . . ."[40]

---

[37] ACMA, *Proc.*, XVIII (1914), 99–100.

[38] E. Pendleton Herring, *Group Representation Before Congress* (Baltimore: The Johns Hopkins Press, 1929), pp. 31–46; Preliminary Report from the Joint Meeting held in New York City, January 17, 1917, in Northern Textile Association MSS (Boston); hereafter cited as Joint Meeting, NTA MSS.

[39] ACMA, *Tariff Bulletin No. 2.*

[40] NACM, *Trans.*, CI (1916), 33–34.

In this new context the businessman's need for a political spokesman did not end when reform measures became law. Much of the regulatory legislation was entrusted to government commissions, both state and national. On the national level, there was a Food and Drug Administration, a Federal Trade Commission, and a Federal Tariff Commission. The ICC was strengthened. In the states there were numerous commissions and agencies created to enforce and improve labor and factory regulations. This complex and vigorous governmental system called for more complex and vigorous forms of organized activity on the part of the manufacturer. If he was to make his voice heard, he had to have organizations which could operate effectively in this different context. He needed technically competent representatives to argue his case before the commissions. He needed organizations that would be ever watchful for some new administrative ruling that might affect his interests. He needed trade groups that provided more services on a more continuous basis than did the older dinner-club associations.[41]

While the progressive movement thus seemed to pose a threat to the cotton manufacturers, seen in a broader perspective, the new governmental environment that the reform movement helped to produce actually contributed to the spread of the associative concepts of stability, cooperation, and control. With the decided exception of the antitrust laws, progressive public policy implemented these associative values. Instead of allowing tariffs to be set by the free play of political forces, for instance, a Tariff Commission was charged with the task of devising a rational means of controlling tariff policies.[42] Cooperation among competing farmers was one goal of the Clayton Act, and the Webb-Pomerane Act of 1918 even extended this privilege to businessmen who were engaged in foreign trade.[43] There were a number of progressive policies which sought to achieve by regulation some form of economic stability. One of the objectives of the Federal Reserve System was greater stability in the money market and in the

[41] Letter of C. P. Baker to E. M. Townsend & Co., October 8, 1906, in Lawrence MSS; NACM, *Trans.*, XCVIII (1915), 120e; CI (1916), 34; Cotton Manufacturers Association of North Carolina, *Proc.*, XI (1917), 65–69 (hereafter cited as CMANC, *Proc.*); ACMA, *Proc.*, XXIV (1920), 141–142.

[42] Taussig, *Tariff History*, pp. 481–487; Wiebe, *Businessmen and Reform*, pp. 61, 90–97, 105, 116, 148–149, describes business support for the commission.

[43] Burns, *The Decline of Competition*, pp. 21–22.

nation's banking system. In the field of labor relations the state and federal governments began hesitantly to control certain aspects of the labor contract for special classes of workers such as railroad employees. This was a way of stabilizing working conditions which heretofore had been subject to the play of the market.[44]

These economic policies must, of course, be seen against the background of a general cultural environment which was beginning to reflect increasing interest in all forms of stability. There was in America a new interest in stabilizing the population. Whereas the United States had previously absorbed millions of diverse peoples, the nation decided in the twentieth century that large-scale immigration had to stop; the flow of immigrants had to be controlled in a manner that would preserve the existing ethnic balance. During these same years, America's territorial expansion came to a halt. After a brief flirtation with imperialism, Americans decided to be happy with their existing frontiers. Manifest destiny had been fulfilled. America still talked the language of the nineteenth century, but in business, in government, and in society in general there was a growing interest in security. Progressive government contributed to that accommodation, partly by creating a political environment conducive to the acceptance of these values. This new political and cultural milieu was the third force which challenged the cotton manufacturer in the twentieth century.

Closely associated with the progressive movement and with the rise of big business was the general organizational revolution which took place in modern America. Revolutionary changes in the size and activity of organizations occurred in almost every sector of American society.[45] This was the fourth "new force" with which the cotton manufacturer had to contend.

The labor movement was one aspect of this general organizational revolution; in industry after industry, labor unions became

[44] Seymour E. Harris, *Twenty Years of Federal Reserve Policy* (2 vols.; Cambridge: Harvard University Press, 1933), I, 79–111; Leonard A. Lecht, *Experience Under Railway Labor Legislation* (New York: Columbia University Press, 1954), pp. 14–30.

[45] Kenneth E. Boulding, *The Organizational Revolution* (New York: Harper, 1953).

larger and much stronger.[46] In New England, management in cotton textiles felt hard pressed by the growing strength of organized labor. When the reality was unimpressive, businessmen in the textile industry (as in others) never found it difficult to conjure up a frightening myth about socialism and union power. The power the unions did have was still centered primarily in New England's well-entrenched craft unions.[47] In 1901 these groups joined hands to form the United Textile Workers of America, an affiliate of the AF of L. In the South the UTW was never able to secure a good foothold, but the union periodically conducted organization drives and participated—in 1902, 1914, and 1921—in a series of bitter, violent strikes. Each time, southern management broke the union. But the UTW continued to send organizers into the South and each new wave of union activity was somewhat stronger than the last.[48]

To counter the real and imagined threat of unionism, businessmen in cotton textiles and other industries formed a variety of new business associations and rejuvenated or reorganized many of their existing groups. New employers' associations were established in a number of industries; in some cases these associations bargained with the unions, in others they fought bitterly to destroy the labor organizations.[49] To combat the political attack of the unions and reformers, businessmen also organized new lobbying groups, some of which brought together businessmen or business associations from a number of different trades.[50]

In addition to the unions and associations, there were new farm organizations interested in controlling the price and standards

---

[46] Leo Wolman, *The Growth of American Trade Unions, 1880–1923* (New York: National Bureau of Economic Research, 1924), pp. 29, 33–41, 62–64.

[47] Lahne, *The Cotton Mill Worker*, pp. 138–139, 184–201.

[48] *Ibid.*, pp. 137–139, 189, 200–206; George S. Mitchell, *Textile Unionism in the South* (Chapel Hill: University of North Carolina Press, 1931), pp. 26–56.

[49] Clarence E. Bonnett, *Employers' Associations in the United States* (New York: MacMillan, 1922); Bonnett, *History of Employers' Associations in the United States* (New York: Vantage Press, 1956).

[50] Albert K. Steigerwalt, *The National Association of Manufacturers, 1895–1914* (Grand Rapids, Michigan: The University of Michigan, Bureau of Business Research, Graduate School of Business Administration, 1964), pp. 103–165; Wiebe, *Businessmen and Reform*, pp. 32–33, 36–40; Bonnett, *Employers' Associations*, pp. 291–495; Thomas C. Cochran and William Miller, *The Age of Enterprise* (New York: MacMillan, 1942), pp. 238–241.

of raw cotton.[51] The cotton shippers formed new alliances.[52] In 1918 the commission merchants who handled mill products came together to organize the Association of Cotton Textile Merchants of New York.[53] There were also technical groups such as the American Society for Testing Materials, the Board of Safety and Sanitation, and a special interassociational conference committee on apprentices.

The total effect was revolutionary. This new world was characterized by group, not individual action. Whether the new organizations were friendly or hostile, they complicated the cotton manufacturer's heretofore simple universe. As the manufacturer soon discovered, it was desirable to keep in touch with the National Industrial Conference Board, even to keep representatives on the Board. In this way he could learn what other trade organizations were doing and could ensure that the interests of his industry were protected whenever the Board took action.[54] In order to take maximum advantage of the potentiality offered by these various groups, in order to block any hostile action, it was necessary to maintain an effective liaison organization. The individual manufacturer had neither the time nor the money to affiliate with all of these organizations; he needed an alert associational middleman. As soon as the cotton manufacturer set up a new association to protect his interests, it was necessary for his friends and foes to establish contacts with this organization or perhaps even to form additional associations to defend their own position. Thus, as the institutional environment became more complex, the movement fed upon itself—with new organizations creating the need for new organizations and for an elaborate network of interassociational committees and councils. There was a kind of bureaucratic acceleration principle at work. It drove the organizational revolution ahead at a faster and faster pace, transforming almost every facet of the cotton manufacturer's political, social, and economic environment.

[51] Theodore Saloutos, *Farmer Movements in the South, 1865–1933* (Berkeley: University of California Press, 1960), pp. 153–166, 184–212, 254–278.

[52] Letter of C. P. Baker to Edward Stanwood, July 3, 1902; Letter of C. P. Baker to C. B. Howard, Jr., July 7, 1902; both in Lawrence MSS; ACMA, *Proc.*, IX (1905), 241.

[53] *25 Years: The Association of Cotton Textile Merchants of New York, 1918–1943* (New York, 1944), pp. 13–14.

[54] NACM, *Trans.*, CI (1916), 87–88, 92; Joint Meeting, NTA MSS.

Little wonder that in the years 1900 to 1924, management found reasons to change the industry's trade associations. No longer could the old style of association supply the kind of representation and political action that the manufacturers needed. There was new interest within the industry and new support from without for cooperative methods of solving problems. Organizational skills, the techniques of controlling political and economic activity, were developing rapidly, and only through effective trade associations could the manufacturers hope to profit from these developments. More and more of the industry's executives began to accept the need for stability, for rationalization, and for cooperation; as they did, they turned a critical eye on the rudimentary dinner-club associations.

Chapter IV

The Service Associations, 1900 to 1924

To the cotton manufacturer, the new forces creating modern America and transforming his own industry posed a serious threat. They were changing the political and economic world with which he was familiar and in which he had been able to achieve some success. Ideas that had seemed perfectly reasonable in an earlier context now seemed out of date. Institutions that had solved his problems before now proved to be weak and unreliable.

Responding to these difficulties the cotton manufacturers created a new type of trade group, the "service association." It was distinguished from its predecessor, the dinner-club association, in a number of ways. In the first place, it had a substantial income and a group of full-time, professional staff members—a bureaucracy. These men, selected for their administrative, political, or technical skills, worked for the organization on a continuing basis; no longer was the association allowed to lapse into an inactive state between meetings or sessions of the state legislature. The service association was constantly in touch with the political scene, constantly surveying the industry's economic situation, constantly watching the actions of other associations. With its staff the service association could perform functions *for* its members instead of letting the members, through their committees, do all of the work.

The series of organizational changes which resulted in the transformation of the Arkwright Club into a service association began during the early 1900's. In 1907 a New England Cotton Freight Claim Bureau was created under the Club's direction.[1]

[1] Charles Storrow *et al.*, Circular Letter, September 30, 1907, in NTA MSS.

Later the Club organized a Cotton Bureau, a Cotton Classification Committee, and a Board of Appeal to handle disputes arising between the mills and the cotton merchants.[2] To perform the detailed work of these new departments, the Club employed a special staff member, Mr. W. F. Garcelon; by 1920, he had a full-time assistant, and Edward Stanwood was still serving the Club as secretary and treasurer.[3] These various activities aroused new support for the Club, and larger membership (which was still on a corporate basis) meant that the Club's financial resources were much greater.[4] In 1920 the Club's total expenses for all activities amounted to $51,318.52, and a husky balance was carried over to the following year. On the basis of this income, its staff, and its functions, the Arkwright Club was by this time a fully developed, regional service association.[5]

It took considerably more effort to change the New England Cotton Manufacturers' Association, but that organization soon followed in the footsteps of the Club.[6] First, the Association began to study such problems as potential export markets and the need for textile education; almost effortlessly, these questions led the members to consider political matters.[7] In 1906 the name was changed to National Association of Cotton Manufacturers.[8] Ten years later the Association was completely reorganized. Provision was made for "sustaining" or corporate members who paid dues on the basis of their firm's size; several new committees and departments were established; and the Association began to build up

[2] NACM, *Trans.*, XCIII (1912), 370–380; CXXX (1931), 31; NACM, *New England Terms for Buying and Selling Cotton* (1st ed.; Boston, 1911), p. 12; also see NACM, *New England Terms for Buying and Selling American Cotton (except Sea Island)* (4th ed.; Boston, 1917), p. 11.

[3] Letter of T. F. Leavitt to Nashua Mfg. Co., January 15, 1915; Letter of W. F. Garcelon to Frederic Amory, May 13, 1915; both in Nashua Manufacturing Company MSS (Baker Library, Harvard University); AC, Yearly Account Book, 1920–1930, in NTA MSS.

[4] AC, *By-Laws*, pp. 20–42.

[5] AC, Yearly Account Book, 1920–1930, NTA MSS.

[6] For the resistance to change (primarily from mill agents and superintendents) see: NECMA, *Trans.*, LXXII (1902), 115–118; LXXIII (1902), 89, 114; LXXIV (1903), 98–106.

[7] *Ibid.*, LXXII (1902), 83–86, 88; LXXIII (1902), 25, 367–373; LXXIV (1903), 22, 73–78, 326–366, 422–425; LXXV (1903), 73, 79–81, 84–85; LXXVI (1904), 102, 109, 111; LXXVII (1904), 80–89.

[8] *Ibid.*, LXXVIII (1905), 81–82, 131–133; LXXIX (1905), 83; LXXX (1906), 93–97, 159–172; LXXXI (1906), 99, 343.

a professional staff. As reorganized in 1916/17, NACM was a service association with provision for a substantial income, for a staff, and for an agenda which involved continuous associative action.[9]

In general the Southern Cotton Spinners' Association evolved along the same lines as the National Association. After a number of New England executives and officers from the southern cloth mills had joined, the organization was renamed the American Cotton Manufacturers Association (1903).[10] During the following years, the American Association gradually developed new interests and more committees.[11] When the National Association began to reorganize in 1916, ACMA followed suit, and the plans adopted by the two organizations were almost identical. ACMA created a new class of "active corporate" members who paid dues in proportion to their company's size. As a result, the Association's annual income from dues jumped from $1,000 in 1916/17 to $20,000 in 1917/18. This money enabled the members to form a number of new standing or permanent committees to take care of the Association's business on a continuing basis. By 1918 the American Association was well on its way to becoming a regional service association.[12]

In 1913 the cotton manufacturers also created an interregional group which could represent the entire industry. A number of previous attempts to merge the regional associations had failed, but during the early 1900's, several national problems developed to provide a solid foundation for North-South cooperation.[13] The

[9] NACM, *Trans.*, XCVIII (1915), 113; CI (1916), 28, 34, 82–112; CII (1917), 417–421; NACM, Outline of Enlarged Activities, July 12, 1917, in Nashua MSS; Joint Meeting, NTA MSS. It was suggested in 1916 that an additional ten to fifteen thousand dollars a year would be needed to undertake all of the activities projected in the reorganization plan. (NACM's income was $12,663.30 during the year April, 1914, to April, 1915.) Due to the provision for assessment of the sustaining members, the association was easily able to get the necessary additional money.

[10] Southern Cotton Spinners' Association, *Proceedings* (Charlotte, N.C.), VII (1903), 54–55, 163 (hereafter cited as SCSA, *Proc.*).

[11] ACMA, *Proc.*, IX (1905), 247–248; XII (1908), 147–151; XIII (1909), 204; XVII (1913), 163–175; XVIII (1914), 162–168; XIX (1915), 94–95.

[12] *Ibid.*, XXI (1917), 56–63, 101; XXII (1918), 57; XXIII (1919), 117, 132–137.

[13] For discussion of the need for national cooperation, see: NECMA, *Trans.*, LXII (1897), 56, 58; LXIII (1897), 84–85; LXVII (1899), 97–98; Joint Meeting, NTA MSS.

problems arising out of the cotton trade supplied one such national issue;[14] and after the panic of 1907, NACM and the American Association began to collaborate in an effort to prevent the kind of widespread cancellation of contracts for finished goods which always followed a sharp decline in prices.[15] In October, 1910, a joint conference of the officers of the two organizations was held, and during 1911/12, the tariff committees of NACM and ACMA worked together very closely.[16] Finally, in the fall of 1912, the manufacturers drafted plans for a National Council of American Cotton Manufacturers. After cautiously providing that the organization could take no action which might "impair the respective autonomy of either association," the two groups formally organized the Council in 1913.[17]

In addition to the Council, the regional associations "spun off" a number of small organizations designed to handle special problems. These included the Textile Alliance and the Textile Bureau (both organized in 1913). The Alliance was organized in an effort to prevent "frauds in connection with mill supplies," and the Bureau was set up to "protect the interests of the domestic manufacturer in all customs matters, and particularly to assist in preventing undervaluations and the fradulent practices of some importers."[18] Another form of special association was the "open-price" group. In textiles as in other industries, open-price associa-

[14] NECMA, *Trans.*, LXXIX (1905), 122, 126, 128–129; LXXX (1906), 380; ACMA, *Proc.*, X (1906), 305–306; Reports of the Conference of Growers and Manufacturers of Cotton, held at Washington, D.C., May 1–2, 1906, and the Second International Conference of Cotton Growers and Manufacturers' Associations, Atlanta, Georgia, October 7–9, 1907, NTA MSS.

[15] ACMA, *Proc.*, XII (1908), 147–152, 166–167; XIII (1909), 167–177; XIV (1910), 168–169; XV (1911), 204–205. NACM, *Trans.*, LXXXV (1908), 48–63, 351; LXXXVI (1909), 249, 324–325, 327; LXXXVII (1909), 48–49, 180; LXXXVIII (1910), 175–176.

[16] *Ibid.*, XC (1911), 106–107, 136–138, 320; XCI (1911), 46–47; XCII (1912), 127–128, 422–423; CXXI (1926), 246; ACMA, *Proc.*, XV (1911), 87–88, 95–96, 138–141, 206, 212; XVI (1912), 90–91; XXXI (1927), 143; Minutes of the Conference of Officers of Cotton Manufacturing Associations, Washington [D. C.], February 2, 1911, NTA MSS; National Council, Minutes, April 30, 1918, NTA MSS.

[17] NACM, *Trans.*, XCIV (1913), 87–89, 140–142. ACMA, *Proc.*, XVII (1913), 160–162, 201–202; XVIII (1914), 173–174.

[18] NACM, *Trans.*, XCVI (1914), 115–116, 209; XCVII (1914), 228; C (1916), 409–410, 413–414; ACMA, *Proc.*, XVIII (1914), 176–181; XIX (1915), 157–158; XX (1916), 139–141.

tions were a product of management's attempt to stabilize prices
while staying within (or at least near) the limits set by the
Sherman Anti-Trust Act. The first experiment along these lines in
cotton textiles was conducted by the National Association of
Finishers of Cotton Fabrics (1914).[19] In 1915, open-price or statistical exchange was discussed at the annual conventions of the
American and National Associations and at a special meeting of
the Council; afterward, separate open-price groups were established by the manufacturers of cotton blankets, gingham, duck,
yarns, print cloth, and fine goods.[20] These statistical associations,
the Textile Bureau and the Textile Alliance were all part of the
substantial framework of new and reorganized trade associations
created during the years between 1900 and 1924.

As most businessmen and a number of college presidents have
discovered, however, organizations which look good on paper often
fail. This was just as true for the service associations as it has been
for other kinds of business institutions. Unexpected political
difficulties arose; conflict between the two sections made it hard
to coordinate activities on a national basis; tension between the
old values and the new, between the realities of the marketplace
and the economic objectives of the associations continued to upset
the industry's cooperative programs. There were significant accomplishments. But the record of the service associations and their
supporting groups is not the kind of success story that business
history frequently provides.

During the years from 1900 through 1924, the new structure of
associations was used most successfully in dealing with problems
that were external to the industry. The service associations were

[19] Statement of H. E. Danner, Secretary, re National Association of
Finishers of Cotton Fabrics, March 17, 1921; Memo of C. Stanley Thompson
to Colonel Goff, March 2, 1917; both in Record Group (RG) 60, File 60–147,
National Archives (NA); Joint Meeting, NTA MSS.

[20] NACM, *Trans.*, XCVIII (1915), 176–185; CXI (1921), 378; ACMA, *Proc.*,
XX (1916), 94; XXI (1917), 39–40; *New York Journal of Commerce and
Commercial Bulletin,* November 11, 1915, and March 19, 1920; Letter of
Amory, Browne & Co. to Frederic Amory, December 9, 1918, with enclosed
copy of the Minutes of the Meeting of Certain Selling Representatives of
Manufacturers of Cotton Blankets, December 4, 1918; Blanket Association,
Report to Members, February 5, 1919; both in Nashua MSS; Milton N.
Nelson, *Open Price Associations* (Urbana: University of Illinois Press, 1923),
pp. 16–17.

able, for instance, to handle the industry's political difficulties with considerable ease. Their greatest success was in negotiating with government agencies, departments, and commissions. In this work they could make best use of their natural advantages: money, technical skills, administrative ability, and personal influence. When their work involved the legislature, their position was not so strong, their record not so good. Here they were at a disadvantage because they could not influence a large block of voters or offer a program with broad, humanitarian objectives. They nevertheless substantially improved their lobbying techniques. This was not a result of merely pouring more money into political action, although this was done; the improvements were, for the most part, a product of a more methodical, well-organized approach to political questions.

Nationally the central issue was the tariff. When the Underwood Act was passed in 1913, the associations were just beginning to adjust to the new political environment.[21] By 1921, when the tariff question next arose, the associations had made the transition from the old to the new style of lobbying. As a result, they were able to organize a very systematic political campaign. The First World War was barely over before the associations began to prepare for the inevitable battle for a higher tariff. A special consolidated tariff committee was formed in order to line up the various trade organizations behind a single proposal. The Association of Cotton Textile Merchants of New York, the three regional groups, and the National Council supported this committee. The merchants gave the committee extra financial help, but more significant was the appearance of wider support for the industry's proposals. In the national game of pressure-group politics, this was important; under the new conditions it was necessary to show how many were behind your proposal, how many organizations if not how many votes.[22]

---

[21] NACM, *Trans.*, XCIV (1913), 177–179; XCVI (1914), 90–91; XCIX (1915), 202–203; Letter of Thomas C. Thacher to Frederic Amory, October 3, 1913; Letter of Walter C. Baylies to Hon. Charles S. Hamlin, September 11, 1913; both in Nashua MSS; ACMA, *Proc.*, XVII (1913), 87–88, 93, 126–127, 136–138, 177–192; XVIII (1914), 181–182.

[22] NACM, *Trans.*, CV (1918), 175–176; CVI (1919), 216; Letter of Rufus R. Wilson to Members of NACM, June 16, 1919, in Nashua MSS; National Council, Minutes, December 14, 1920, and March 11, 1920; NACM, *Bulletin No. 9* (January 15, 1921); both in NTA MSS.

To achieve maximum effectiveness it was absolutely essential to keep everyone lined up behind a single proposal. On at least one occasion, when sectional animosities flared, this proved to be a difficult task.[23] But the Council managed to smooth over the differences, and the two sections continued to cooperate.[24]

The Consolidated Committee ran a very methodical campaign. A series of subcommittees prepared the essential schedules, charts, and briefs that were presented at the formal conferences and hearings. Several meetings were held in Washington, and spokesmen were sent to the hearings before the Committee on Ways and Means. After the public hearings, more private meetings were held with members of the House Committee. New schedules and demonstrations were prepared. Finally, a satisfactory cotton schedule was guided through the House of Representatives. But this was only half of the job. The whole process had to be repeated in the Senate. When at last President Harding signed the Fordney-McCumber Tariff Act on September 21, 1922, the members of the Consolidated Committee could be satisfied that they had conducted the kind of tightly organized, systematic campaign that was essential to success in the new legislative environment.[25] The liaison between North and South had been maintained. There had been no surprises because the various subcommittees had been constantly in contact with the situation in Congress. If the manufacturers had good cause to be satisfied with the tariff rates, they had even better reason to be pleased with the performance of their service associations and supporting groups.

When it came to the manufacturer's relations with the state legislatures there was less cause for confidence, particularly in New England. Here the coalition of unions and reformers exerted a growing pressure to strengthen labor legislation. In 1907 the

[23] ACMA, *Proc.*, XXV (1921), 178–181, 184–185; Letter of the Chairman, Consolidated Tariff Committee, to Allen T. Treadway, May 31, [1921]; Letter of W. R. Green to S. W. Cramer, July 16, 1921; Letter of S. W. Cramer to W. F. Garcelon, August 18, 1921; Letter of S. W. Cramer to John E. Rousmaniere, August 27, 1921; ACMA, Pending Tariff Legislation, Dissenting Opinion of American Cotton Manufacturers Association; all in Stuart W. Cramer MSS (North Carolina).

[24] Cramer to Garcelon, August 18, 1921, Cramer MSS; ACMA, *Proc.*, XXV (1921), 181.

[25] The work of the Consolidated Committee is described in NACM, *Trans.*, CXII (1922), 207–218; CXIV (1923), 208.

Massachusetts legislature passed a law which barred women and children from the mills between 6:00 P.M. and 6:00 A.M. This, along with the forty-eight-hour law passed in 1919, gave Massachusetts the most progressive set of regulations in all of the textile-producing states. Despite their financial resources, personal influence, and well-organized political campaigns, the manufacturers were unable to prevent these laws from passing. Their laments about intersectional competition with southern mills which were unhampered by labor legislation found few sympathetic ears. Although the Arkwright Club and NACM both kept the industry alerted to these legislative challenges and the Club kept its special lobbyist at work, they fought a losing battle against the forces pressing for labor legislation. After 1920 there were no new laws passed in New England for a number of years, but by that time, northern mill workers were already protected by a substantial framework of effective regulations.[26]

In the South the manufacturers had less difficulty with the state legislatures. Where they did have problems, they used their state trade associations to coordinate their lobbying efforts, with the American Association acting as a regional "clearing-house" in political matters. National labor legislation such as the child labor law posed a greater threat to the southern mills, and the manufacturers seem to have devoted more energy to defeating this measure than they did to any corresponding acts in the state legislatures.[27] After the Supreme Court ruled against the child labor law in 1922, there was little to fear from this quarter either; so southern executives were left to operate a sixty-hour week—on two shifts if they could get enough orders to keep their machines busy.[28]

In general, the service associations that had developed in this industry by the mid-1920's appear to have enabled the manufac-

[26] Letter of Arkwright Club to Nashua Manufacturing Company, March 7, 1913; Garcelon to Amory, March 23, 1917; Letter of W. F. Garcelon to Members of the Arkwright Club, February 24, 1919; all three in Nashua MSS; AC, Bulletin No. 8 (February 21, 1914); AC, Yearly Account Book, 1920–1930; both in NTA MSS; NACM, Trans., CVI (1919), 196, 199, 302; Department of Labor, Labor Legislation, pp. 36, 39–42, 58–60.

[27] ACMA, Proc., XXI (1917), 102, 115–116; XXVI (1922), 137; XXVII (1923), 119–120; XXVIII (1924), 162–163, 169–171; CMAG, Report, XXIV (1924), 4; XXV (1925), 67–68; CMANC, Proc., Winter Meeting (1917), 3–4; XI (1917), 73; XII (1918), 16, 18, 77; XIII (1919), 56–57; XIX (1925), 89–90.

[28] Lahne, The Cotton Mill Worker, pp. 109, 112–115, 118–120, 138–139.

turers to deal efficiently, if not always successfully, with their legislative problems. The organizations provided necessary funds and technical information and kept a watchful eye on state and national political developments. Most of the actual work of lobbying was still in the hands of the members, but the association staffs provided the extensive supporting services that were needed in the modern style of pressure-group politics.

The association bureaucracy played a more important role in the industry's relations with regulatory commissions and other agencies of the government. The Arkwright Club's Cotton Freight Claim Bureau began to represent the mills in their negotiations with the Interstate Commerce Commission. By employing lawyers experienced in transportation work, the Bureau took a great responsibility off the shoulders of the manufacturers. Acting individually they could not afford to be constantly represented before the Commission and could seldom bargain effectively with the railroad companies. Especially handicapped were the smaller mills which did not have sufficient transportation business to warrant large expenditures for ICC hearings and other action concerning the railroads. Through the Bureau they could employ "an expert freight man" and they soon discovered that he could save them money.[29] Later, the American Association and several of the state associations in the South established similar transportation departments; NACM also formed a transportation committee which cooperated with the Arkwright Club's Freight Bureau in major conflicts over rates.[30]

Through their respective transportation agencies the mills within each region were able to cooperate, but there was a fierce and relentless struggle between North and South over sectional rate differentials. Generally, the rates favored the North, which fought a holding action against southern demands for new sched-

[29] Baker to E. M. Townsend & Co., October 8 and 22, 1906, and June 25, 1908, in Lawrence MSS; Leavitt to Nashua Mfg. Co., January 15, 1915; Garcelon to Amory, May 13, 1915; both in Nashua MSS; NACM, *Trans.*, CXXX (1931), 31–32; Knowlton, *Pepperell's Progress*, p. 217.

[30] ACMA, *Proc.*, XXIV (1920), 141–142, 155; XXV (1921), 159, 161; Hunter Marshall, Jr., and George W. Forrester, *Carolina Mill Rules, Outline of the Traffic Department, Etc.* (CMANC pamphlet, ca. 1920); CMANC, *Proc.*, X (1916), 90, 96–97; XI (1917), 58, 62–63, 65–69; XIII (1919), 50–54; XIX (1925), 86–87; NACM, *Trans.*, CVI (1919), 217; CVIII (1920), 57–60; CIX (1920), 357–359, 507.

ules. Until the 1930's, New England's legal mercenaries won most of their skirmishes with the troops sent to the ICC by the southern Traffic Department. Although the several transportation agencies were unable to resolve these sectional conflicts peacefully, they were able to provide the manufacturers with the kind of continuous technical and legal representation that was needed in dealing with a federal regulatory commission.[31]

The ICC was only one of the several governmental organizations with which the associations kept in close contact; the Department of Agriculture was another. After the government began to establish standard grades of cotton (in 1909), the Department became the scene of prolonged negotiations between government officials and representatives of the manufacturers, growers, and cotton merchants. In this and other matters that came before the Department of Agriculture, management was able through the service associations to protect the manufacturers' interests insofar as their vital supply of raw material was concerned.[32]

The service associations were especially valuable to management when the United States became involved in the First World War. During the war new government agencies sprouted up overnight. The web of controls became more and more complex; as it did, effective association work became increasingly important. At first the industry was as confused as the government was by the problems of organizing the economy for a war effort. Lines of authority between the several associations and the new committees that they formed soon became tangled. When the government set up its

[31] For a narrative of the intricate maneuvers of northern and southern traffic experts, 1920 through 1925, the following sources should be consulted: ACMA, *Proc.*, XXIV (1920), 157; XXV (1921), 167–169; XXVI (1922), 52, 98–99, 123–125, 136; XXVII (1923), 63–64, 134–135; XXVIII (1924), 172–175; XXIX (1925), 122, 128–130; XXX (1926), 135, 156–160, 163; XXXII (1928), 129; CMANC, *Proc.*, XV (1921), 30–31; XVI (1922), 22–23, 38–40; XVII (1923), 46, 49, 50; XIX (1925), 35–36; a view from the New England trenches is presented in: NACM, *Bulletin No. 2* (May 15, 1920), *Special Bulletin* (June 1, 1920), *No. 4* (August 15, 1920), *No. 12*, (April 15, 1921), *No. 59* (March 16, 1925), and *No. 60* (April 15, 1925), all in NTA MSS; NACM, *Trans.*, CVIII (1920), 57–60, 286, 331–335; CIX (1920), 357–359, 507; CX (1921), 42, 264–265, 267; CXII (1922), 115, 117; CXIV (1923), 68–70; CXVII (1924), 277–279; CXIX (1925), 157–159.

[32] *Ibid.*, LXXXVII (1909), 35–36; XC (1911), 242–260; XCVII (1914), 215–222; XCVIII (1915), 87–106, 224–239; NACM, *Bulletin No. 36* (April 16, 1923), in NTA MSS.

Advisory Commission of the Council of National Defense, the industry formed a Committee on Cotton Goods Production Engineering to work with the Commission.[33] In January, 1918, the industry organized another group, the War Services Committee.[34] To confuse the issue even more, the National Council, which was trying to coordinate the work of these various committees, began to appoint its own sub-committees to handle questions of foreign trade, transportation, and related matters.[35]

Gradually, however, the government and the industry worked their way out of this organizational maze. Most of the government controls were centered in the War Industries Board, which was under the leadership of Bernard Baruch after the spring of 1918. The industry gathered its various groups into a new War Services Committee of the National Council, with the Council assuming general direction of the war effort from an office in Washington, D. C.[36] In arranging for priorities, in handling transportation problems, and in blocking various kinds of hostile government action, the Council proved itself to be a valuable representative for the industry.[37] The associations encountered no real problems in working within the framework of government bureaucracy. In fact they seemed to be well-suited to this environment.

Price-fixing was undoubtedly the most complex issue that arose during the war. And the business-government negotiations over prices clearly reveal why the service associations were generally successful in relations with the Executive Department. When the government decided to stabilize prices on certain basic products such as cotton textiles, a special Price-Fixing Committee of the War Industries Board was established under the chairmanship of Robert Brookings. Chairman Brookings knew in a rather vague way that his objective was to stabilize prices. He knew that he was armed with President Wilson's wartime powers and a general appeal to support the war effort. He did not know, however, what prices he should set for the different products, and he lacked the detailed knowledge of the industry that was needed to determine

33 NACM, Trans., CIII (1917), 27–28; ACMA, Proc., XXI (1917), 35, 79–80.
34 NACM, Trans., CIV (1918), 446, 471–472; National Council, Minutes, January 11, 1918, in NTA MSS.
35 NACM, Trans., CIII (1917), 48–51; CIV (1918), 270–271; ACMA, Proc., XXII (1918), 74–81.
36 National Council, Minutes, January 11 and May 3, 1918, in NTA MSS.
37 ACMA, Proc., XXIII (1919), 120.

these prices. In the rush of mobilization he did not have time to acquire that knowledge or to hire the men who had it. He had to turn to the industry.[38]

At first there was considerable confusion as to who would speak for the industry. Brookings was satisfied if he could work with representatives from the largest firms. But this stirred up some rumblings of complaint from within the industry, especially from the South.[39] Finally, the National Council took over the job, appointing representatives from both sections. By having a large committee of over thirty members the Council assured itself of widespread support; by then turning the negotiations over to a small subcommittee, it could be certain that the meetings would not bog down in endless discussions.[40]

In the ensuing negotiations the Price-Fixing Committee finally let the manufacturers set up a price for one standard commodity; then the Committee shaved off a few cents, apparently on the assumption that any price the manufacturers liked must be too high. There was never an agreement as to how that base price was determined. There was never a consensus as to what constituted a fair profit. Lacking information, the government had to depend upon the industry to fix its own base price and to set differentials for the various products. By dint of their monopoly on technical information about the industry, the service associations and their members were thus able to control the manner in which these government regulations were implemented.[41]

One should not, however, stress unduly the element of conflict between the associations and the government. During the war it became apparent that there were many issues on which the trade groups and the government were in basic agreement. When NACM's Labor Committee saw how the War Labor Board was standardizing and classifying wages and jobs in the metals trade, it indicated its strong support of this work.[42] From every side the

---

[38] War Industries Board, Price-Fixing Committee, Minutes, March 26, April 23, and May 29, 1918, in RG 61, National Archives.

[39] *Ibid.*, March 26 and April 23, 1918.

[40] *Ibid.*, April 10, May 29, and June 8, 1918.

[41] *Ibid.*, May 29, June 8, and July 1, 1918; the industry's committee based its price list on its estimate of a fair "return on invested capital." National Council, Statement from the War Service Committee, July 30, 1918, in NTA MSS.

[42] NACM, *Trans.*, CV (1918), 67.

manufacturers heard official voices urging them to cooperate. In the meetings with the Price-Fixing Committee, Chairman Brookings repeatedly urged the manufacturers to seek stability, to cooperate, to standardize their industry's products in order to operate more efficiently. At a meeting in July, 1918, at which he spoke for the government, he explained that "when we get behind you in this matter we think we offer opportunities for stabilizing the industry, not only as to price, but probably in getting rid of some wasteful habits you have made through excessive competition."[43] Throughout 1917 and 1918 these themes were repeated again and again: cooperation was necessary; stabilization was desirable; systematic and standardized controls were needed on an industry-wide basis. There developed an intellectual and institutional environment which favored the trade organizations and a continuing alliance between the associations and the government. The effects of that environment continued to be felt long after the Armistice in 1918.

During the early twenties the service associations found it profitable to continue their cooperation with the government, despite the fact that there were far fewer government regulations to worry about. The Department of Commerce, under the direction of Herbert Hoover, encouraged trade associations to standardize products, to improve cost-accounting techniques, to promote commercial arbitration, and in general, to eliminate what Hoover felt was waste and inefficiency in industry. Hoover's position was very similar to the ideas that Brookings had earlier expressed. In both cases these government officials strongly advocated the development of cooperative controls through trade associations; both came perilously close to suggesting that competition itself was inefficient.[44]

In all of the programs sponsored by the Department of Commerce, the service associations gave the industry effective repre-

[43] *Ibid.*, CII (1917), 257; War Industries Board, Price-Fixing Committee, Minutes, June 8, July 1, September 6, and December 12, 1918, in RG 61, NA.

[44] The following reports clearly state Hoover's position on trade associations: U. S., Department of Commerce, *Tenth Annual Report of the Secretary of Commerce, 1922* (Washington, D.C.: Government Printing Office, 1922), pp. 29–32; *Twelfth Annual Report, 1924,* pp. 22–24; *Thirteenth Annual Report, 1925,* pp. 10–27; and *Fourteenth Annual Report, 1926,* pp. 11–27; also see, NACM, *Bulletin No. 14* (June 15, 1921), in NTA MSS; NACM, *Trans.,* CXI (1921), 366.

sentation. Staff members from the regional associations and the Council cooperated with the Department's Bureau of Standards and the Federal Specifications Board (established in 1921) in devising government specifications for textile products. Whenever the government decided to draw up specifications on a new product and the Federal Board did not have sufficient data, the associations submitted samples to the Board for analysis. After the tests were finished, tentative specifications were drafted and were in all cases submitted to the associations for consideration. The trade groups then ran their own tests, studied the specifications, redrafted them, and sent them back to the Federal Board. There were apparently no substantial disagreements over this procedure or its results; and on almost all questions of standardization and simplification the associations worked closely and effectively with Secretary Hoover and the Department of Commerce.[45]

By the mid-twenties the cotton manufacturers had made a fairly successful accommodation to the new political environment of the twentieth century. The presence of a friendly Republican Administration in Washington obviously eased that accommodation; but the new structure of associations and the new techniques of cooperative action were essential to political success, whatever party was in power. Through the regional service associations and the Council, the cotton manufacturers had greatly improved their lobbying techniques. On many political issues they were able to cooperate on a national basis. Their greatest success, however, was in shaping the execution, not the formulation, of public policy. In dealing with federal commissions and executive agencies or departments, the associations were able to capitalize on their knowledge of the industry, their effective organization, and their continuous attention to the detailed aspects of business-government relations. As the federal government grew stronger, these services became more essential to the industry. Gradually a permanent working relationship, if not alliance, began to develop between the associations and particular government organizations.

The industry also carried on negotiations with a variety of nongovernment organizations. A southern manufacturer observed in

[45] NACM, *Bulletin No. 39* (July 16, 1923); *Bulletin No. 52* (August 15, 1924); *Bulletin No. 60;* Letter of Russell T. Fisher to E. T. Pickard, March 11, 1925; all in NTA MSS; NACM, *Trans.,* CXII (1922), 49–54; CXV (1923), 33–35, 43; CXIX (1925), 147–148; ACMA, *Proc.,* XXVIII (1924), 183–184.

1922 that "it is a day of associations. There is hardly a business of any importance in this country today that does not have its association, and that means that men are getting together more and more; they are doing business together more and more. . . . There never was a time when men co-operated as they do today, when they did so much for each other. . . ."[46] If he had added "and to each other" this conclusion might have stood the test of time, because no one could deny that the 1920's brought the association movement in industry to full flower.

In cotton textiles, management was able to use the service associations—fully developed by this time—to protect its interests in this new world of organizations. It was desirable to maintain contacts with the recently organized Association of Cotton Textile Merchants of New York. This was done through the National Council. Under the Council's auspices regular meetings were also held with representatives from the Cotton Yarn Merchants' Association and the Middle States Textile Manufacturers Association.[47] In the South where there were several strong state organizations, ACMA and these groups began to coordinate their activities, particularly in lobbying.[48]

Business organizations outside the cotton industry received similar attention. Both NACM and the American Association supported the work of the National Industrial Conference Board. By uncovering "facts" which showed that, in 1920, the wage increases in cotton textiles were 15 per cent above those in other industries and by studying in a "scientific" manner the need to repeal the excess profits tax (1921), the Board helped to propagate the kind of information and opinions that the manufacturers approved.[49]

Even a business organization like the Conference Board could, however, cause trouble for the manufacturers because their interests were not always the same. When the Board published a wage study in 1924, it became obvious that even the "facts" could be dangerous. In this study northern and southern wages were listed separately instead of being presented as a national average, and the southern producers objected. This made the southern mills look bad and supported the demand for national legislation to

46 ACMA, *Proc.*, XXVI (1922), 98–99.

47 National Council, Minutes, October 5, 1922, and November 18, 1925, in NTA MSS; ACMA, *Proc.*, XXVIII (1924), 167–168.

48 *Ibid.*, XXVII (1923), 120; XXVIII (1924), 162–163.

49 NACM, *Trans.*, CVIII (1920), 270–271; NACM, *Bulletin No. 9*, in NTA MSS.

equalize conditions throughout the country. In this case ACMA's representatives on the Board were able to work out a "correct" method of comparison, one which took into consideration the low rent and cheap utilities which the southern mill owners felt compensated for their lower wages. As this incident illustrated, it was important to be represented, even when the organizations involved were friendly to the businessman.[50]

The service associations maintained contacts with a number of other business organizations. Included among these were the National Association of Manufacturers, which collaborated with the Council on tax matters, the National Retail Dry Goods Association, the American Society for Testing Materials, and the American Marine Standards Committee. Since the liaison work often involved technical matters, the new staff members of ACMA, NACM, and the Arkwright Club were kept busy. In the 1920's, an age of association, such representation was essential.[51]

Less successful were the efforts to counter union activity through the regional service associations. The southern mills refused to work through a regional organization on labor matters since they felt that "conditions in different States were just as widely separated between . . . North Carolina, South Carolina, Georgia and Alabama as they are between some of the Northern and some of the Southern States." The fight against unionization continued to be a local matter or at best a subject for the state associations to handle. For a time, in 1920/21, it appeared that the United Textile Workers might organize enough southern mill hands to force a region-wide response from their employers; but in 1921 management again crushed the unions, and for the next ten years the UTW was unable to make a strong foray into the Piedmont.[52]

Employers in New England also left most of their dealings with the unions in the hands of state or local associations. This was primarily a reflection of the fact that in each of the large mill centers there was a textile council which combined the various craft unions in the city and organized strikes on a local basis. There were national unions—the United Textile Workers of America and, after 1916, the National Amalgamation of Textile Operatives

[50] ACMA, Proc., XXVIII (1924), 168–169, 194–195.

[51] Ibid., XXX (1926), 137–139; XXXI (1927), 32; NACM, Trans., CX (1921), 115; CXVI (1924), 120; CXVII (1924), 259–260, 436–441, 444–445, 449; NACM, Bulletin No. 37 (May 15, 1923), in NTA MSS.

[52] ACMA, Proc., XXXIII (1929), 127; Lahne, The Cotton Mill Worker, pp. 203–208.

—but they had little influence over the locals.[53] During World War I the national unions became stronger, and NACM began to concern itself with labor problems; but after an unsuccessful experience with regional cooperation in the early 1920's, the association abandoned this policy. In later years NACM conducted wage surveys, but most labor matters reverted to the hands of local trade organizations.[54]

Despite this unsuccessful effort in labor-management relations, the regional service associations did enable the cotton manufacturers to adjust successfully to most aspects of the organizational revolution. The trade groups provided technical assistance where it was needed. They kept intact the communication lines between the cotton manufacturers and businessmen in other trades. They kept their members alerted to any sort of group action which threatened to harm or promised to help the cotton manufacturer's interests. This was a vital service in a nation in which all forms of action were increasingly characterized by systematic, group efforts.

Although relatively successful as organizational middlemen and political spokesmen, the service associations failed in most of their efforts to provide the atomistic cotton textile industry with a reasonable alternative to oligopoly. They experimented with almost every form of economic activity that we normally identify with the giant firm, but voluntary associations proved to be weak platforms from which to launch these programs. In only one area were they partially successful; through the associations, the manufacturers were able to subject to rational control certain activities (such as the purchase of raw cotton) which heretofore had not involved any sort of systematic planning. By standardizing or rationalizing terms and products, the cotton manufacturers reduced risks and increased the efficiency of their operations. They were unable to carry rationalization as far as big business did, but they did nonetheless record some significant accomplishments.

Both the southern and northern mills were able to devise and introduce standard rules and specifications for the cotton trade. The "Carolina Mill Rules" were worked out in 1904, and the "New England Terms for Buying and Selling Cotton" were estab-

[53] *Ibid.*, pp. 190–196.
[54] NACM, *Trans.*, CVIII (1920), 42; CXIV (1923), 55, 65; CXIX (1925), 160; NACM, *Bulletin No. 2* and *Bulletin No. 8* (December 15, 1920), in NTA MSS; Hammond, "The Cotton Industry," pp. 498–499, 501.

lished in 1911. These rules imposed order on a market which heretofore had been controlled only by the traditions of the trade. After the buyers and sellers accepted the rules, they could be certain that both parties to a contract understood exactly what standards were to be used in classifying their cotton. There was no longer any room for differences of opinion as to when excess bagging and ties had been added to the cotton bales. Specific procedures were enumerated for filing claims based upon substandard shipments. Indeed, almost every aspect of the contract between cotton buyer and cotton merchant was explicitly defined, with provision made for arbitration in case there were any disputes over the quality of the cotton.[55]

During these same years, the cotton manufacturers attempted to impose standard rules on the market for finished products. Jarred by the panic of 1907 and the wave of contract cancellations which followed the decline in prices, ACMA set out to introduce to the trade a uniform sales note. A standard form of contract, ACMA felt, should be supported by "rules which should govern the rights of buyer and seller in sales of cloth and yarn, and which should clearly define the remedies of either in the event of default on the part of the other, and which should furthermore clearly define the rights when either may have to cancel or declare void contracts made." Arbitration, the manufacturers felt, was "the natural and just method" for settling differences between buyers and sellers; the courts were too slow, too costly, and too likely to favor local buyers over the distant mills. If the standard contract could also include a stipulation that all sales would be f.o.b. at the mill, that, too, would be helpful since the manufacturers would avoid paying freight charges on their finished products.[56]

After ACMA started to work on a standard contract or sales note, the National Association decided to cooperate by preparing stand-

[55] ACMA, *Proc.*, VIII (1904), 161–162; IX (1905), 241; XII (1908), 150–154; XXIX (1925), 137–138; CMANC, *Proc.*, XI (1917), 95; XVI (1922), 69–73; XIX (1925), 81–82, 86, 98; NACM, *New England Terms for Buying and Selling Cotton* (1911); Baker to A. N. Mayo & Co., April 16, 1906, Lawrence MSS; NACM, *Trans.*, XCI (1911), 47; XCIII (1912), 370–380; CXXX (1931), 31; R. T. F[isher] to R. M. Baker, Jr., February 5, 1948; Report of Conference of Growers and Manufacturers of Cotton, pp. 85–86, 117, 143, 220–238; Report of the Second International Conference of Cotton Growers and Manufacturers' Associations, pp. 162, 203, 208, 273–282; all three in NTA MSS.

[56] ACMA, *Proc.*, XI (1907), 330–336; XII (1908), 147–152.

ard specifications for the industry's major products. This would help to prevent buyers from canceling contracts on the grounds that the goods involved were of inferior quality. If successful, it would eliminate that "indefiniteness, or lack of detail, that exists today in the ordinary cloth specifications used by the trade. . . ."[57]

In 1909, however, when the associations completed their standard contract form, they were unable to persuade the merchants to use the new type of sales note. The commission merchants were anything but enthusiastic about this novel set of regulations. Buyers objected, and were able to make their objections felt. In an industry that was beginning to develop excess capacity the producers were in a weak position; as one of the manufacturers put it: "any sale note today looks good to me, I don't care what form it is written on."[58]

In the cotton market where they were buyers, the manufacturers had been able to rationalize conditions; but in the market for dry goods, where they were sellers, they failed. Vis-à-vis the cotton shippers and brokers, the mills were able to achieve enough power through the service associations to force acceptance of the New England Terms and Carolina Mill Rules. But where they were sellers, they lacked the unity that was needed to compensate for their weak position in the market. They passed unanimous resolutions approving the uniform sales note and specifications. In their day-to-day operations, however, they were unwilling to sacrifice their short-term self-interest in the hope of achieving a long-term cooperative goal. Their failure to develop "countervailing power" was quickly revealed in the market place.

Somewhat more successful were the attempts to standardize products, and the government was partially responsible for this. Much of the impetus for standardizing goods and equipment came from government agencies. When the National Association was working on standard specifications, the members became aware of the "splendid tests" being conducted by the U. S. Bureau of

[57] NACM, *Trans.*, LXXXV (1908), 48–63; ACMA, *Proc.*, XII (1908), 166–167; XIII (1909), 167–177; XIV (1910), 169.

[58] NACM, *Trans.*, LXXXVI (1909), 48–49, 108, 249–259, 324–325, 327; LXXXVII (1909), 48; LXXXVIII (1910), 175–176; XCII (1912), 303; ACMA, *Proc.*, XIV (1910), 168–169, 173; XV (1911), 204–205; XVI (1912), 93; XIX (1915), 138. The Association of Cotton Textile Merchants of New York, *Twenty-Five Years, 1918–1943* (New York, 1944), p. 38 (hereafter cited as ACTMNY).

Standards. After discovering that the government had well-equipped laboratories and a trained staff, NACM began to co-operate with the Bureau.[59] In subsequent years government officials repeatedly joined their voices with those of the engineers who were urging the associations to standardize everything from the fuel they burned to the lumber they used in mill construction.[60] Even President Woodrow Wilson pointed out in 1916 "that materials, methods, and products in industry should be standardized upon the basis of specifications drawn up in friendly cooperation with engineering societies, industrial experts, and trade associations."[61] In 1917/18 there was intense pressure from the government to standardize everything from products to job classifications. Efficiency was the keynote. Government officials, including Robert Brookings of the War Industries Board, frequently reminded the manufacturers that they must cooperate in order to eliminate "unnecessary" products and to concentrate their attention on a smaller number of standard goods.[62]

During the 1920's, when the service associations finally began to formulate effective programs aimed at standardization, most of this work was done in close collaboration with the government. Herbert Hoover—the St. Paul of the Association Movement—led the Department of Commerce into a number of cooperative efforts to eliminate waste in cotton manufacturing by cutting down the number of products. A Textile Division was established within the Department. Edward T. Pickard, Chief of the Textile Division, worked with a special Standardization Committee of the National Council and stayed in close contact with staff members of the regional associations.[63] In 1922 the associations and the govern-

[59] NACM, *Trans.*, XCIII (1912), 303–304, 312–313.

[60] *Ibid.*, XCIV (1913), 158–163; XCV (1913), 314–327; XCVI (1914), 168–178, 270–290; XCVIII (1915), 210–211; C (1916), 309–361, 402–407, 416; ACMA, *Proc.*, XVII (1913), 163–175; XVIII (1914), 104–116; XX (1916), 115–116, 119–120.

[61] Letter of Woodrow Wilson to Edward N. Hurley, May 12, 1916, as quoted in A. J. Eddy and M. M. Dickinson, "Statement of National Association of Finishers of Cotton Fabrics," in RG 60, File 60–147, NA.

[62] War Industries Board, Price-Fixing Committee, Minutes, June 8, July 1, September 6, and December 12, 1918, in RG 61, NA. NACM, *Trans.*, CIV (1918), 476–479; CV (1918), 67; National Council, Minutes, May 3 and November 13, 1918, in NTA MSS.

[63] NACM, *Trans.*, CIX (1920), 498–499; CXI (1921), 365–372; NACM, *Bulletin No. 14* and *Bulletin No. 19* (November 15, 1921); National

ment set out to eliminate the "unnecessary" sizes of various textile products, including cotton blankets. Management, the association staff, and the government officials all agreed that it was wasteful to manufacture so many different varieties of cotton blankets merely "to meet competition."[64] By the fall of 1924 the manufacturers had decided that they could eliminate about 75 per cent of the different sizes of blankets made in the past.[65] The manufacturers were also amenable to the idea of standard specifications for government contracts so long as they—working through their trade organizations—were able to assure that the specifications were fair (i.e., that the tolerances were not too exacting and the goods specified were standard, commercial products).[66] Before the rise of the service associations and of the Department of Commerce, it had been assumed that the market would automatically make these decisions. But in the 1920's the new concepts of cooperation and control were gradually supplanting the older ideals of competition and laissez faire.

Through the service associations management also attempted to improve and standardize cost-accounting techniques in the industry. As early as 1893 the National Association had undertaken a study of unit-cost accounting.[67] One year later a special committee had produced a simple guide for the New England mills to follow in determining costs. But apparently the guide did not bring about any uniformity of accounting practice among the members.[68] In subsequent years both NACM and the southern association sponsored discussions of accounting and in 1920 the New Englanders again brought out a set of instructions on unit-cost accounting.[69] By

Council, Minutes, September 14, 1921, and July 19, 1922; all four in NTA MSS. The cooperation was evidently very close; in 1922 the National Council decided to pay the head of the Department's Textile Division part of his expenses for a trip to Europe to investigate the textile situation.

[64] NACM, *Bulletin No. 29* (September 15, 1922), in NTA MSS.

[65] NACM, *Trans.*, CXVII (1924), 260; CXVIII (1925), 57–59.

[66] *Ibid.*, CXVI (1924), 167; CXIX (1925), 147–148; ACMA, *Proc.*, XXVIII (1924), 181–184; Fisher to Pickard, March 11, 1925; NACM, *Bulletin No. 52* and *Bulletin No. 60;* all three in NTA MSS.

[67] NECMA, *Proc.*, LV (1893), 22–25, 36.

[68] *Ibid.*, LVI (1894), 50–73.

[69] NECMA, *Trans.*, LXIV (1898), 250–266; LXV (1898), 128–129; LXXIII (1902), 116; LXXVII (1904), 23, 143; NACM, *Trans.*, XCIV (1913), 288–299; XCV (1913), 234–254; CII (1917), 115; CIV (1918), 481; SCSA, *Proc.*, VII (1903), 154–155; ACMA, *Proc.*, VIII (1904), 67.

this time the northern industry was hard pressed by southern competition. It was hoped that improved accounting techniques would help prevent price cutting by assuring that management would not unwittingly sell goods at prices below their average cost of production. Unfortunately, New England's dilemma was not a result of northern mills unintentionally selling below costs; it was due simply to southern costs being so low. Better accounting in the North could not alter the regional cost differential, and this no doubt explains the fact that NACM's program produced a great deal of talk and very little action.[70] The cost-accounting program ran aground on the hard economic fact that cotton textiles was an atomistic, intensely competitive industry; each firm could do little to influence market prices and had little incentive to support and little margin to finance improved systems of control.

Seen as an alternative to the combines which rationalized economic activity in other manufacturing industries, the service associations were not very successful in the years 1900 through 1924. Some progress was made. In the cotton trade the New England Terms and Carolina Mills Rules were adopted; some products were standardized; a few mills apparently improved their cost-accounting techniques as a result of NACM's work. But when measured against the systems of control developed by such industrial giants as DuPont or General Motors, it is apparent that the corporation was a strong, the association a weak, platform from which to systematize business functions. Without the iron hand of centralized authority, controls were frequently discussed but only occasionally imposed.[71]

Even less impressive were the service associations' experiments with advertising and research—two kinds of non-price competition already popular among many large firms in the 1920's. The first associative advertising program in cotton textiles was introduced by NACM in 1924, and the National Association also sponsored a textile exhibit which it hoped would "increase the demands for modern cottons. . . ." Since many southern products did not go into clothing, the American Association failed to support either of

[70] NACM, *Trans.*, CVIII (1920), 199–209; CX (1921), 36–39; CXI (1921), 333–348, 400; CXII (1922), 58–113, 270–271; CXIII (1922), 46; CXIV (1923), 67, 209; NACM, *Bulletin No. 10* (February 15, 1921), in NTA MSS.

[71] It was hard enough to impose such systems when ownership and control were centralized; see Chandler, *Strategy and Structure*, pp. 120–128.

these programs, and for that matter NACM's financial commitment was small. After a brief trial, the National Association abandoned its advertising campaign.[72]

Although the regional associations gave cooperative research somewhat more attention than advertising, the results were similar. When the American Association and NACM were jointly reorganized in 1916/17, there was considerable enthusiasm for research, especially in New England.[73] Most of this enthusiasm, however, was merely vocal. When the northern association's program got underway, it became obvious that the professional staff was more interested in the work than the members were.[74]

The advertising and research ventures foundered for much the same reasons. Management in New England was conservative. It was difficult, furthermore, to see how a particular mill would significantly strengthen its own position through cooperative advertising or research. Finally, it was hard to justify new expenditures when the pressure of intersectional competition was so great. All of these factors combined to undermine the brief experiments with research and advertising.

The service associations also failed in their efforts to provide cotton textiles with an alternative to the giant firm as a stabilizing institution. In part this failure can be traced to the inherent limitations of the voluntary associations. They lacked authority over their members. In cotton textiles the associations were particularly handicapped because of the industry's structure and the strong interregional competition that existed. Under these conditions management naturally thought in terms of the individual firm or, at best, the region. It was necessary and at the same time necessarily difficult for the associations to persuade management to think of the entire industry when framing price and production policies.

For a number of years after 1900, the associations continued to

[72] NACM, *Trans.*, CXVI (1924), 39–42, 120; CXVII (1924), 270–272, 436–441, 444–445, 449.

[73] *Ibid.*, CIX (1920), 452.

[74] *Ibid.*, CVIII (1920), 64; CIX (1920), 458–459, 482–500; CX (1921), 33; CXI (1921), 351–353, 429–431, 443–444; CXII (1922), 55; CXIV (1923), 53, 71; CXV (1923), 43–44; CXVI (1924), 55, 166; NACM, *Bulletin No. 22* (February 15, 1922), *Bulletin No. 25* (May 15, 1922), *Bulletin No. 27* (July 15, 1922), *Bulletin No. 33* (January 15, 1923), *Bulletin No. 43* (November 15, 1923), and *Bulletin No. 45* (January 15, 1924), in NTA MSS.

experiment with the kind of curtailment program that had been tried in the 1880's and 1890's. The only difference was that the demands for curtailment arose more frequently as the industry approached a condition of excess capacity. In 1907 the Arkwright Club sponsored a curtailment agreement, and in 1909 the Club and the American Association mounted a similar campaign together.[75] In the North the program of 1909/10 won considerable support from the mills. Edward Stanwood, secretary of the Arkwright Club, felt that it was the most successful effort that the Club had made. In the South, ACMA's secretary sent letters to all of the members asking them to sign the following agreement:

> We, the undersigned, agree to curtail operations of our mills one day or more each week until goods advance to a parity with the price of cotton.
>
> This agreement is conditional upon signatures by manufacturers representing 60 per cent of the spindles of the association, and will become operative upon statement by the committee to this effect.

ACMA's action was endorsed by the South Carolina Association, and it appeared at first that the agreement might be signed by as much as 75 per cent of ACMA's membership. But the results in the South were disappointing. ACMA was unable to obtain enough signatures to put the plan into effect. Although many of the mills seem to have cut back their production, this was apparently a response to burdensome inventories, not to the regional association's program.[76]

After 1911 the interest in stabilization became more intense and widespread; it was focused now primarily on the open-price groups. Under the open-price plan, manufacturers or their selling agents submitted regular reports on production, stocks on hand, unfilled orders and, in many cases, prices (hence the name) to

[75] Statement of Edward Stanwood before the Committee on Expenditures in the Department of Justice, June 28, 1911, in NTA MSS, pp. 5–9, 11–12, 21–23, 46–47; also see, *United States* v. *Patten,* 226 U. S. 525 (1913).

[76] Statement of Edward Stanwood, in NTA MSS, pp. 10–11, 23–28, 40, 58; ACMA, *Proc.,* XIV (1910), 200–201; XV (1911), 87; *Textile Manufacturers Journal,* October 16, 1909; Mr. McKercher, Report on Cotton Pool Investigation, April 25, 1910; V. N. Roadstrum, Memorandum for Mr. Kenyon, May 2, 1910; W. B. Tanner, Notarized Statement, May 7, 1910; Letter of Assistant to the Attorney-General [William S. Kenyon] to Lewis W. Parker, June 23, 1910; all four in RG 60, File 60–147, NA.

their trade association. The association's staff processed the data and sent general reports back to the contributing members. By using these reports, each participant had an intimate knowledge of what was happening in his particular branch of the market and of what his competitors (though the general reports usually avoided naming them specifically) were doing. He knew, for instance, when a large stock of goods was hanging over the market or when other mills were increasing their sales. In most cases the open-price associations had regular meetings at which the members discussed the statistics. The participants thus had some understanding of what their competitors felt about past trends and future possibilities.[77]

In theory, the exchange of information might have created a more competitive market by removing frictions. In fact, the plan was designed and introduced for the specific purpose of preventing, not improving, competition. The goal was price stability. It was intended that participating companies, guided by the figures, would avoid price cuts and would not try to change their customary percentages of the market. When orders fell off and prices began to sag, the members were expected to cut production, maintaining a fairly stable share of the market. By not forcing goods on a slow market and by not piling up unwieldy inventories, prices could be held at a level that would enable most of the mills to make a profit. This, at least, was the objective of the open-price system.[78]

In effect the open-price group was an attempt to create artificially the conditions that were conducive to price stability in highly concentrated industries. Where two or three firms dominated an industry, each company usually knew what its competitors were doing and understood that price competition would normally reduce everyone's total revenue without compensating advantages to any of the producers. In an atomistic industry such as cotton textiles this was not the case. Consequently, the open-

[77] Milton N. Nelson, *Open Price Associations;* Nelson, "Effect of Open Price Associations on Competition and Prices," *American Economic Review,* XIII, No. 2 (June, 1923), 258–275; H. R. Tosdal, "Open-Price Associations," *ibid.,* VII, No. 2 (June, 1917), 331–352; Leverett S. Lyon and Victor Abramson, *The Economics of Open Price Systems* (Washington, 1936); also see, Arthur J. Eddy, *The New Competition* (New York: D. Appleton & Co., 1912).

[78] See the explanation of open-price work in NACM, *Trans.,* XCVIII (1915), 176–185.

price associations were developed in an effort to persuade management, despite the industry's structure, to behave like oligopolists.[79] It was hoped that this could be done on a more or less permanent basis. The older style of production or price agreement was a temporary affair. With the industry developing excess capacity, what was needed after 1911 was a semipermanent type of loose combination that would enable the manufacturers to stabilize prices on a continuing basis. This change in the nature of the industry's problem, along with a new threat of antitrust action, accounts for the interest in open-price work after 1911.

The open-price plan was specifically designed to provide a legal means of achieving price stability. After the Supreme Court decisions in the Standard Oil (1911) and American Tobacco (1911) cases, the antitrust policy became a real concern to the service associations. These two decisions left no doubt that the Sherman Act applied to manufacturing. The secretary of the Arkwright Club was questioned in Washington about the industry's various attempts to control production, and the examining committee made it rather clear that it considered these plans illegal restraints of trade.[80] The open-price concept was, however, tailored to provide a restraint upon competition which the courts and the Justice Department would be likely to consider "reasonable." According to Arthur Jerome Eddy, a lawyer whose book *The New Competition* (1912) did much to popularize the plan, businessmen could not be condemned for wanting full information on market conditions; nor could discussion of *past* conditions be considered an illegal restraint of trade. So long as competitors did not actually agree to fix prices or to curtail production, the open-price plan was a legal means of fostering cooperation and achieving economic stability. Eddy was so certain that his plan was acceptable that he kept the Justice Department informed about the various open-price associations that he helped to organize.[81]

For a time, the Justice Department seemed to approve of this

[79] George W. Stocking and Myron W. Watkins, *Monopoly and Free Enterprise* (New York: The Twentieth Century Fund, 1951), p. 242.

[80] Statement of Edward Stanwood, in NTA MSS, pp. 33–35, 41–42, 44–45, 55–70; also see the comments upon antitrust in the following: ACMA, *Proc.*, XVIII (1914), 94–96; NACM, *Trans.*, XCIV (1913), 243–250; XCVIII (1915), 172–175; XCIX (1915), 34–39.

[81] Arthur J. Eddy and M. M. Dickinson, "Statement of National Association of Finishers of Cotton Fabrics," in RG 60, File 60–147, NA.

new form of cooperation among competitors. One of the original open-price groups, the Steel Founders' Society of America, was investigated and no action was taken. As other statistical associations were formed, the government was kept informed, and for several years there was not even a test case to determine the legality of the open-price plan.[82]

Initially there was a great deal of enthusiasm among cotton manufacturers for the open-price concept. Several of the groups were organized shortly after war broke out in Europe, and as foreign demand for textile products increased, the industry began to pull out of a depression that had lasted for several years. With prices rising, the manufacturers and selling agents were inclined to be happy about the so-called new competition. As one member of an open-price association explained in 1918:

> The one outstanding feature in my mind of the Gingham Association has been the mutual confidence that has resulted from the members sitting down and laying the cards on the table; perfect frankness that has been shown at all times has increased the mutual confidence and respect that we all have for each other. I believe it has been the means of largely increasing the profits of the mills represented by the various selling houses, . . . and what is perhaps equally as important, it has certainly had a very steadying effect on the trade as a whole. It has obviated these sudden fluctuations which are of course the most disturbing thing to all of our customers, even perhaps more than to ourselves.[83]

In the next few years, however, several of the groups collapsed.[84] When prices were at wartime levels statistical exchange seemed unnecessary, and after the government and the associations began to fix prices it was obviously superfluous. At the end of the war competition became more intense; this raised the price of "perfect

[82] *Ibid.;* the government's inaction is carefully discussed in Goldthwaite H. Dorr's Letter to Walker D. Hines, October 10, 1927, in Goldthwaite H. Dorr MSS. Also see: NACM, *Trans.,* C (1916), 194–195; ACMA, *Proc.,* XX (1916), 119.

[83] Minutes from the Meeting of Certain Selling Representatives of Manufacturers of Cotton Blankets, December 4, 1918, Nashua MSS.

[84] U. S., Federal Trade Commission, *Open-Price Trade Associations,* 70th Cong., 2nd Sess., 1929, Senate Doc. 226, pp. 381–382, lists only the National Association of Finishers of Cotton Fabrics and the Southern Yarn Spinners' Association among the open-price groups active in the mid-twenties; also see, *Textile World,* LXVII, No. 16 (April 18, 1925), 43.

frankness" and left "mutual confidence" in short supply. Then, too, the government struck a hard blow against the open-price groups when in February, 1920, the Justice Department brought suit against the American Hardwood Manufacturers Association. This organization of southern lumber manufacturers was operating an open-price plan similar to the ones used in textiles. After a lower court condemned this plan as an illegal restraint, the Justice Department threatened (March, 1920) to take legal action against the statistical groups in other industries, including cotton textiles.[85] In 1921 the Supreme Court strengthened this threat by supporting the lower court. The open-price plan of the Hardwood Association was denounced as "an old evil in a new dress and with a new name."[86]

Unfortunately for the manufacturers, the open-price groups in cotton textiles turned out to be about as unstable as the earlier price agreements. An adverse court decision, a change in market conditions, or a breakdown in confidence among the members was all that was needed to destroy this kind of organization's *raison d'être*. The pure and simple open-price groups, in cotton textiles as in other industries, normally had a short life.[87]

During the early 1920's, manufacturers in both regions were concerned about the industry's excess capacity and the need for some means of stabilizing prices and profits.[88] But they were unable to work out a satisfactory solution for their problems; a variety of cooperative programs were considered but not implemented.[89] By 1924 the entire industry, North and South, was operating at a net loss.

[85] James W. Silver, "The Hardwood Producers Come of Age," *Journal of Southern History*, XXIII, No. 4 (November, 1957), 439, 443; *New York Journal of Commerce and Commercial Bulletin*, March 19, 1920.

[86] *American Column & Lumber Company* v. *United States*, 257 U. S. 410 (1921).

[87] FTC, *Open-Price Trade Asssociations*, pp. 40–41.

[88] ACMA, *Proc.*, XXV (1921), 176–177; NACM, *Trans.*, CXI (1921), 330; NACM, *Bulletin No. 3* (July 15, 1920) and *Bulletin No. 15* (July 15, 1921); Y. P. Yoder [secretary, FTC] to National Council of American Cotton Manufacturers, November 3, 1920; National Council, Minutes, July 13 and September 16, 1920; all in NTA MSS.

[89] Letter of H. C. Meserve to Herbert Hoover, October 20, 1921; Herbert Hoover to H. C. Meserve, October 25, 1921; both in RG 40, 81288, Box 505, NA; National Council, Minutes, September 5, 1923, in NTA MSS; NACM, *Trans.*, CXII (1922), 50.

Clearly, the new structure of service associations and supporting groups had failed to provide a satisfactory alternative to oligopoly. Management in cotton textiles had tried to follow the organizational strategy of such giant firms as DuPont and General Motors, but the voluntary association had provided a weak structure for introducing these policies.

During the same years the type of association that emerged in cotton textiles also developed in most other manufacturing industries. Open-price work was extremely popular, both as an adjunct to, and substitute for, oligopoly. Standardization and similar activities were carried on by numerous trade groups which now functioned on a continuous basis. In industry after industry service associations began to take shape. They carried a growing burden of interfirm relations and encouraged manufacturers to increase that burden by experimenting with new forms of cooperative action. They developed programs for training apprentices, for reducing accidents, for providing representation, and for advertising products. With their professional staffs, their relatively large incomes, and their new techniques of cooperative action, these service groups provided the backbone of the trade association movement in cotton textiles and in other American industries.[90]

By the mid-twenties the service organizations in cotton textiles had been thoroughly tested. As political representatives and organizational middlemen, they had been fairly successful. Even though New England manufacturers found it difficult to block the passage of labor legislation and other restrictive measures, the service associations enabled their members to make the most of their natural advantages by approaching political problems in a systematic fashion. In national politics, the Council effectively coordinated the efforts of the northern and southern industrialists. In handling economic problems within the industry, however, the service organizations were generally unsuccessful. Aside from the standardization programs and the rules and arbitration procedures

[90] National Industrial Conference Board, *Trade Associations, Their Economic Significance and Legal Status* (New York, 1925), pp. 11–30, 179–190, 211–225, 235–296; Stocking and Watkins, *Monopoly*, pp. 123–124, 151, 153, 201–203; Nelson, *Open Price Associations;* Thomas G. Gies, "The Effect of Trade Associations upon Competition in Selected Industries" (unpublished Ph.D. dissertation, University of Michigan, 1952), pp. 266–288.

for the cotton trade, there were no significant accomplishments to record.

As was revealed when prices suddenly dropped in 1923/24, the service associations had certain inherent weaknesses. They had not anticipated this problem; they could only react after difficulties had become obvious to almost all of their members. Strong action before the fact would incur the opposition of a significant portion of the membership. Since participation was voluntary, the organization could expect to lose a number of members and their financial support if it moved too quickly. In effect, any substantial group of members could exercise a veto over the associations' policies. The principle of the concurrent majority—John C. Calhoun's famous concept—was applied within the associations, and the necessary result was a kind of organizational inertia or conservatism. Rather than risk the withdrawal of any substantial group of members, the associations normally held to the center of the road, avoiding any action that would arouse discontent within the organization.

The staff members of the service associations were unable to exert much influence upon the members. Although the associations were able to hire men with sound technical training and administrative experience the staff members were not the equals of the cotton manufacturers themselves. It was clear that the staff consisted of employees of manufacturers who told them what to do. This was a special problem in New England because management was tradition bound and hesitant to take decisive action either in the mill or the association.

Another weakness stemmed from the industry's failure to form a single national organization. There was a National Council, but it was merely an interassociational committee with no powers or income of its own. When the mills, North and South, confronted severe losses in 1924, there was no strong central agency to which they could turn. Continued dependence on the regional organizations was also expensive since it resulted in duplication of efforts, particularly in New England where there were two regional groups.

In addition to these structural problems, the service associations were weak in terms of ideology. Although there was much discussion of the organizations and their new role, the service associations did not produce articulate spokesmen for the basic values of cooperation, control, and stability. The leaders of the service associations were technicians, not philosophers. While they administered the various programs with considerable skill, they did not work out a sound economic or legal theory to explain or justify what they were doing. As a result, they did not provide the manufacturers with an appealing alternative to the traditional or classical economic dogma.

Why, then, did the manufacturers not create stronger, more effective trade organizations? A major reason was the lack of unanimity in the industry; the fundamental differences in operating conditions and in political situations, and the large number of competitors involved, made more aggressive association work impossible. Northern and southern producers still could not agree on many basic points. Even within each region the producers were often in sharp disagreement about joint programs. Cooperation might be the keynote in other industries, but the cotton manufacturer was constantly reminded by the Worth Street market that the day of competition had not passed—at least not for him. Throughout the economy, stabilization was an increasingly popular goal, but many southern mill executives continued to add new spindles and promote new mills; they were unwilling to admit that the old days of rapid expansion had ended. Support for the associative philosophy was stronger than it had been in the nineteenth century, but it took the severe losses of the mid-twenties to create a broad foundation of common concerns and to convince most of the manufacturers that they had to abandon some of their traditional values. When this happened, they organized a new form of trade association, one which had greater resources and better leadership than the service associations.

Fall River: Autumn 1925

Fall River was afraid of the future. It was a city desperately clinging to the symbols of its past success. The great mills with their thick granite walls and lofty smokestacks stood ready to serve the market, but all too often the yarn that they might have spun and the cloth that they were built to weave were manufactured elsewhere—someplace in the South. Thousands were idle. The chances that they would find work in the mills were very slim; so they waited at the Portuguese American Citizens Club or on their porches, talking about the past and worrying about the future.

The city's mayor threatened to take over the mills and to overhaul their antiquated corporate structures. He would combine all of the mills which made a similar product. He would weed out about eighty of the high-salaried officers who were lacking in courage and concern. With new machinery and new management the city's mills, he said, would be able to meet the competition of the southern producers.

The mill owners could do little to assuage the city's fears. They disagreed with the mayor. As they pointed out, the mayor's idea had been seriously considered about forty years ago and then discarded. They had no counterproposal; they merely rejected this new proposition in the same way that many of them had rejected new machinery or new ideas. As they watched and waited, more liquidations were being planned for the months ahead. Fall River's theme song was depression and despair.

Chapter V

Formation of the Cotton-Textile Institute:

A Policy-Shaping Association

"This business of running along on the idea of 'to hell with your neighbor,' won't get you anywhere now," said the president of the Cotton Manufacturers' Association of Georgia. That had worked in the past, but in 1925 it was "about time for us to look at it, and figure what we can do for each other."[1] From Georgia to Maine, cotton manufacturers were forced "to look at it, and figure. . . ." In New England Ward Thoron told the members of NACM: "Perhaps the only cure for such a situation is to be found in some form of cooperation; although admittedly cooperation is apt to develop evils of its own. . . . Human nature being such as it is, we must admit that such a possibility is in reality a probability; yet we think that such evils as it would probably develop can be controlled by some better method than the present one of forbidding cooperation, which begets the destructive evil of unlimited competition in a limited market."[2]

These strong remarks were stirred up by an industry-wide depression that had reached major proportions by 1925. In the previous year the corporations in cotton textiles had recorded a net loss of over thirty-nine million dollars. As more and more

[1] CMAG, *Report* (1925), p. 23.
[2] NACM, *Trans.*, CXIX (1925), 170.

southern firms attempted to cut costs by adopting two-shift operations, the problem of excess capacity became more severe. During
1924 and 1925, over 8 per cent of the spindles in the Northeast
were inactive. Southern mills maintained a high rate of production, but prices fell and the manufacturing margin became tighter.
Many southern producers had piled up large supplies of unsold
goods. These stocks hung over the market and kept prices depressed long after the mills had been forced to shut down. The
effects of excess capacity were felt most acutely in New England,
but heavy financial losses were also experienced throughout the
South.[3] As Tables 1–4 indicate, the industry was facing an extremely difficult situation.

One of the products of this depression and of the new interest
in stabilization, cooperation, and control was a new form of trade
association, the Cotton-Textile Institute. Unlike the service associations, the Institute was a national organization. Its financial
resources were much greater than those of the earlier groups; its
staff was larger and far more talented; its guiding philosophy was
fully and forcefully articulated by the association's leaders. The
Institute was the first association in the industry that really
emerged as an entity. Correspondingly, it was the first association
that could impinge in any decisive manner upon the individual
managers in the industry, whether they were members or not. It
was an organization that on occasions effectively influenced the
decisions of the manufacturers. This particular form of trade
group can best be described as a "policy-shaping association."

Table 1

CAPACITY, COTTON TEXTILES, 1923–1926

	1923	*1924*	*1925*	*1926*
Active Spindles				
U.S.............	36,260,001	35,849,338	35,032,246	34,750,266
New England.......	18,053,716	17,066,036	15,975,442	15,525,672
South.............	16,310,360	16,944,178	17,292,042	17,574,450
All other........	1,895,925	1,839,124	1,764,762	1,650,144

NOTE: The figures on capacity are from NACM, *Year Book, 1928*, p. 171; the figures
for the South include data from all of the cotton-growing states.

[3] Bureau of Internal Revenue, *Statistics of Income, 1924*, p. 135; NACM,
Yearbook, 1926, pp. 150, 152; Bureau of Internal Revenue, Excess Profits Tax
Council, *The Cotton Textile Industry*, p. 149.

Table 2

PRODUCTION AND SALES, COTTON TEXTILES, 1923–1926

	1923	1924	1925	1926
Cotton consumed (bales)				
U.S..........	6,666,092	5,680,554	6,193,417	6,455,852
New England.	2,049,580	1,534,777	1,636,774	1,627,997
South........	4,247,748	3,858,317	4,224,362	4,500,243
All other.....	368,764	287,460	332,281	327,612
Spindle Hours				
U.S..........	101,931,101,448	84,359,693,047	91,054,615,317	93,941,080,761
New England.	41,271,277,895	30,102,266,868	31,201,214,868	31,541,427,911
South........	55,776,192,120	50,598,557,682	55,912,066,688	58,517,714,390
All woven goods (sq. yd.)				
U.S..........	8,264,219,579		7,741,568,028	
New England.	3,143,580,641		2,607,368,068	
South........	4,767,309,272		4,842,005,472	
New Bedford fine goods produc- tion..........	5,265,132	4,246,217		
New Bedford fine goods sales....	4,127,392	3,359,785		
Excess, produc- tion over sales.......	1,137,740	886,432		

NOTE: The figures on production in terms of cotton (bales) consumed are from NACM, *Year Book, 1928,* p. 80; the years are cotton years, which end on July 31; again, the South includes all cotton-growing states. The figures on production in terms of spindle hours (that is, the total number of hours all active spindles were in operation) for 1923 (again, the cotton year was used) are from NACM, *Year Book, 1924,* p. 227; the same figures for 1924–1926 are from NACM, *Year Book, 1928,* p. 164. Information on the production of woven goods (over 12 inches wide) is from *ibid.,* p. 97. The material on New Bedford fine goods production and sales (in pieces) is from NACM, *Year Book, 1926,* p. 134; as the excess indicates, production tended to remain at a high level long after sales had fallen off.

Table 3

PRICES AND MARGINS, COTTON TEXTILES, 1923–1926

	1923	1924	1925	1926
Average cotton goods prices ($\cent$/yd.)........	17.145	16.084	15.097	12.858
Average manufacturers' margin ($\cent$/lb.)......	23.9	18.8	22.8	20.6

NOTE: The average cotton goods prices are from NACM, *Year Book, 1927,* p. 142. The average yearly manufacturers' margin is from Stephen J. Kennedy, *Profits and Losses,* p. 247; this margin is the difference between the average price of cloth and the average price of the cotton used to produce the cloth.

Table 4

PROFITS, COTTON TEXTILES, 1923–1926

	1923	1924	1925	1926
Net Income.........	$90,772,000	−$43,169,000	n.a.	−$36,216,000
Profits (selected firms)				
North............	$25,815,000	$2,474,000	$11,105,000	$3,504,000
South............	$49,754,000	$8,809,000	$24,260,000	$16,451,000
Ratio of profits to receipts				
North............	10.84%	1.16%	4.62%	1.56%
South............	10.82%	2.13%	5.30%	4.08%
Ratio of profits to net worth				
North............	11.70%	1.15%	5.11%	1.64%
South............	14.25%	2.58%	6.95%	4.76%

NOTE: The information on net income of all cotton textile manufacturing corporations after payment of income taxes is from the following: U. S., Bureau of Internal Revenue, *Statistics of Income, 1923*, p. 81; *Statistics of Income, 1924*, p. 135; *Statistics of Income, 1926*, p. 331. The remaining data is from U. S., Bureau of Internal Revenue, Excess Profits Tax Council, *The Cotton Textile Industry*, pp. 148–149; the 51 northern corporations and 178 southern corporations included in this study were relatively strong companies, as they remained in business throughout the period 1922–1940. Net worth at the end of the year includes the value of common stock, preferred stock, and surplus and undivided profits, less deficit.

The movement to establish a new form of association began in the South. While New England had a longer history of associative action and had a more immediate need for stabilization, it is not too surprising that the southerners took the initiative. Management in the South was more aggressive. Although the southern executives lived in a conservative, tradition-oriented society, they were seldom restrained by tradition and were quick to seek new modes of action to meet a new challenge. One of the northern manufacturers later observed that the southerners were "much more active in looking after their affairs than the eastern manufacturers have been in the habit of being. . . ."[4] And I believe that he was right. In 1924 when the industry's problems became acute, it was the southern manufacturers who started the search for some means of achieving production control and the stabilization of prices and profits. To the southerners, statistical exchange along

[4] NACM, *Trans.*, CXXX (1931), 33–34.

the lines already tried in several branches of the industry was appealing, but the antitrust policy seemed to stand in the way. The Hardwood decision (1920) was the Supreme Court's major ruling on an open-price plan, and in this case the decision had gone against the trade association. With an eye to avoiding a similar fate, the industrialists journeyed to Washington to discuss the problem with their good friend Herbert Hoover. In a series of informal conferences during the winter of 1924/25 Hoover assured the manufacturers that he was sympathetic. He himself was encouraging the nation's businessmen to solve problems through joint action. He offered to use the facilities of the Department of Commerce to collect and distribute statistics on production, stock on hand, and sales of cotton goods.[5]

Hoover had been fighting to liberalize the federal government's position on antitrust since he had taken office. He felt that the Justice Department should not discourage cooperation while his Department of Commerce was urging businessmen to use their associations to standardize products, to improve cost-accounting techniques, to promote commercial arbitration, and, in general, to eliminate inefficiency through cooperative programs. Hoover had an engineer's affection for order, for symmetry. While he tried to go no further than the law allowed, he was always sympathetic when businessmen talked about friendly cooperation, about efficiency through rational controls, and about industrial stability.

In an effort to prod the Executive branch into a new position on antitrust, Hoover had, in 1922, inaugurated a formal correspondence with Attorney-General Harry N. Daugherty. He had attempted to get Daugherty to say that the open-price plan, so long as it involved nothing more than the exchange of statistics, was not itself illegal. But the Attorney-General had been stubborn. He had refused to announce that this or that program would be legal. While he had enumerated certain activities which were unlikely to result in a restraint of trade, he had clearly stated that his department was always suspicious of "trade associations, whose members are vitally interested in advancing or, as they term it, stabilizing prices. . . ." Not until 1923 did the Attorney-General

<hr>

[5] ACMA, *Gazette No. 7* (July, 1925), a newsletter in the private papers of William M. McLaurine (Charlotte, N.C.); ACMA, *Proc.*, XXIX (1925), 110; CMANC, *Proc.*, XIX (1925), 88; CMAG, *Report*, XXV (1925), 23, 50.

go so far as to admit that a program conducted by the Department of Commerce would be legal.[6]

Concerned about this situation, Hoover had encouraged trade associations to work through the Department of Commerce, thereby preventing any conflict with public policy. Under his form of open-price plan, statistics were gathered by the Department and released to buyers and sellers alike, so they could hardly occasion a restraint of trade. In 1921 he had suggested that cotton textiles adopt this plan. On that occasion, the manufacturers had rejected his offer.[7] By 1925, however, the industry's situation was so perilous that even a government-sponsored plan was acceptable to some of the manufacturers.

Stuart W. Cramer, one of the leading figures in the American Association, preferred a plan operated by the industry, but under the circumstances he was willing to collaborate with the Department of Commerce. After taking part in the Washington meetings, Cramer went to the American Association's spring convention in 1925 and supported Hoover's proposition. The mills, Cramer said, must end the cycle of overproduction and subsequent curtailment by stopping speculative production for stock, by individually balancing production with demand, and by cooperating with the Department of Commerce "in any effort it may make to collect and publish complete statistics of production and ultimate distribution of the various types of textiles."[8]

While this plan was being launched, another member of ACMA was proposing an organization which would achieve the same objectives without government assistance. This was the proposition of Lee Rodman, president and treasurer of the Indiana Cotton Mills. Rodman came to the 1925 convention of ACMA armed with pamphlets explaining how an institute would develop the comprehensive program needed to restore profitable operations

---

[6] The correspondence in 1922 between Secretary Hoover and Attorney-General Harry M. Daugherty is reprinted in Franklin D. Jones, *Trade Association Activities and the Law* (New York: McGraw-Hill, 1922), Appendix J, pp. 324–335; FTC, *Open-Price Trade Associations*, pp. 20–22; Hoover's defense of the associations gradually pushed the Justice Department into a new position; compare the U. S. Department of Justice's *Annual Report of the Attorney General, 1923* (Washington, D.C.: Government Printing Office, 1923), p. 23, with the *Annual Report of the Attorney General, 1924*, pp. 15–16.

[7] F. D. Jones, *Trade Association Activities*, Chapter IV, nn. 88–89.

[8] ACMA, *Proc.*, XXIX (1925), 111.

in cotton textiles. Rodman's plan envisioned a national organization with an annual income of over three hundred thousand dollars. In this association the member mills would be grouped according to products (for the purposes of carrying on a statistical program). In addition to open-price work, the institute would direct research, encourage the development of new markets and new uses for textiles, and undertake a large-scale advertising campaign to make cotton goods more popular. A national association under the guidance of "one of the outstanding organizers of the country of the type of Judge Gary or Mr. Hoover," Rodman said, would be able to stabilize the entire industry. At the convention this proposal was thoroughly discussed. It was given further publicity in an article in *Textile World,* a trade journal.[9]

Rodman (assisted by conditions in the market place) gained a number of converts at ACMA's convention. One of them was George Harris, president of the Exposition Cotton Mills in Atlanta, Georgia. A month after ACMA's meeting, Harris gave a speech in which he enthusiastically supported the institute idea. He told the state association in Georgia that he was very familiar with the kind of manufacturer who felt that he had to drive his major competitor into the ground by selling goods at or below cost. This sort of businessman, Harris said, was going to discover that after he had forced his competitor to liquidate, the company would be reorganized and the conflict renewed. The industry's cutthroat competition, Harris suggested, was an illness which the competitive process could not cure. Instead of fruitless competition on an individualistic basis, Harris said they should cooperate. Then they would be able to see a new picture, one with

> . . . every mill radiating from a central point, which we will call the American Cotton Textile Institute. At this central point, we will find the greatest outstanding American manufacturer, whose personal interest is divorced entirely from any mill or group of mills. . . . With this man is one of the greatest of American statisticians, surrounded by [the] necessary force to gather and disseminate complete statistics covering stocks, past sales, unfilled orders, and any data required to enable American cotton manufacturers to intelligently shape their policy at all times.
>
> From this central point will radiate all of the American mills,

[9] *Textile World,* LXVII, No. 16 (April 18, 1925), 43–44, 63; CMAG, *Report,* XXVII (1927), 43–44.

irrespective of section, grouped according to various classes of constructions. . . . With every mill reporting fully to the institute, and receiving in return full and complete data, we will have an industry pitched on broad and sound principles. This naturally is predicated upon the complete elimination of the ignorance, jealousy, and lack of confidence, that appear to thoroughly permeate the industry as a whole today. We have reached the point where something has to happen.[10]

Harris and Rodman clearly had in mind a type of trade organization that had never before existed in cotton textiles. Unlike the earlier price and production agreements, the institute would be a permanent form of industrial organization. Although it would utilize statistics, the institute would also be different from the open-price associations. In the first place it would be a large national organization that would encompass all of the mills. Then, too, the new plan involved a measure of central authority that the small open-price groups had not possessed; why else would the project include an industrial czar, a man of the stature of Gary or Hoover, "the greatest outstanding American manufacturer . . ."? Such a man was needed because the supporters of the Rodman plan wanted to replace decentralized market control of prices and production with centralized control by a disinterested expert. The czar would be supported by a substantial bureaucracy, including "the greatest of American statisticians," so the members could be certain that they were adopting wise policies based upon full information. Like many other Americans, these manufacturers wanted to eliminate the risk and uncertainty of a competitive system. Through cooperation and central control they hoped to achieve stability.[11]

Several of the leading southern manufacturers snapped at the bait that Rodman and Harris offered. William Vereen, president of the American Association, was so enthusiastic about the plan that he spent ten days in New York discussing the matter with

[10] *Ibid.*, XXV (1925), 32–36.

[11] Rodman did not stress the need for centralized authority so much as Harris and others did. Rodman felt that once full and current information was available, the mills would naturally adopt policies that would stabilize conditions: "no agreement will be necessary, as common sense will dictate to each unit the proper course to pursue." Letter of Lee Rodman to H. S. Meserve, April 14, 1925, in NTA MSS.

various commission houses. Vereen decided, however, that the commission merchants should first set up the statistical organizations because the manufacturers were not yet prepared to organize an institute.[12] Vereen's suggestions fell on fertile ground, and President John E. Rousmaniere of the Association of Cotton Textile Merchants of New York asked the National Council to meet and consider the need for such a program.[13]

At the Council's meeting on May 13, 1925, representatives from all three of the regional organizations and from the merchants' association debated what specific course the industry should follow. Speaking for the merchants, Rousmaniere said that he wanted a statistical plan. He had decided that the best proposal was the one Stuart W. Cramer had made at ACMA's convention; they should operate an open-price plan through the Department of Commerce. Rodman argued that they really needed a separate manufacturers' institute that could conduct its own program. In the long discussion that followed, many of the representatives expressed the view that it would be virtually impossible at that time to persuade the hundreds of mills scattered throughout the country to support a national association. The managers were too individualistic; the habit of working through regional associations was firmly planted; the task of administering a national organization which included so many mills was too formidable. At present, they said, it might be better to undertake a less ambitious program. Little support materialized for the idea of working through the Department of Commerce. Even Cramer had been lukewarm about government sponsorship, and the representatives decided that it would be better to take a chance with antitrust than to get involved with the Department of Commerce. They wanted Hoover's support, but a public program would be too slow and too open to suit their purposes. South Carolinian James P. Gossett proposed that the mills adopt the plan which Vereen had already suggested. They should merely authorize their selling agents to form statistical associations. Since each selling agent usually handled accounts for several mills, the job of organization would be simpler. After much discussion the Council approved this proposition but decided to withhold any formal action until a test group

[12] ACMA, *Proc.*, XXX (1926), 59, 90.
[13] Letter of John E. Rousmaniere to Morgan Butler, April 21, 1925, in NTA MSS; ACMA, *Gazette No. 7.*

had been established and the plan had been tried for a short time.[14]

Although northern executives participated in these discussions, the drive for a new experiment with statistical reporting still came from the South.[15] In part this was due to the fact that many northern mills had little to gain from a national association. At New Bedford, for instance, there was already a local open-price group; also, those northern mills which manufactured specialties would receive little benefit from comparative statistics. Even the companies which produced standard goods, however, failed to get excited about the institute. One can hardly avoid the conclusion that their executives were as conservative about new associations as they were about new machinery. After the National Council's meeting, Morgan Butler, president of NACM, expressed his opinion that concerted action should be held to a very narrow and well-defined sphere. He said: "We are necessarily individualists. Each of us is accustomed to minding and conducting his own business. Each of us is capable of determining his own course of action." While "unity of interest" could be achieved under special circumstances, he felt that this would be the exception, not the rule. Apparently many New Englanders agreed with Butler. They were concerned about the depression, but when NACM polled its members as to whether the association should begin to collect and disseminate statistics, the results were discouraging. Most of the mills failed even to reply to the questionnaire. New England was cautious. And while the northern executives waited, the southerners pushed ahead with their plans to organize the industry.[16]

As a first step the leaders of the southern association formed a trial "product group." Under the supervision of William Vereen, all of the commission houses which handled one of the standard

[14] *Ibid.;* ACMA, *Gazette No. 4* (May, 1925), in McLaurine Papers; National Council, Minutes and Notes on the Meeting, May 13, 1925, in NTA MSS; ACMA, *Proc.,* XXX (1926), 137; even though Cramer was publicly espousing the Department of Commerce's plan, he was privately advocating that the manufacturers start their own program: Letter of [Morgan Butler] to Stuart W. Cramer, April 3, 1925, in NTA MSS.

[15] In his Letter to the President of NACM, Cramer proposed that the two regional associations pass the same resolution supporting the new attack upon the problems of overproduction; but NACM failed to act. *Ibid.;* NACM, *Trans.,* CXVIII (1925), 71, 94; CXIX (1925), 212–215.

[16] *Ibid.,* pp. 147, 183–184; CXXI (1926), 157; CXXX (1931), 33–34.

southern products began to submit statistics. Weekly reports were gathered from each selling house, and after the figures were totaled, general reports on sales and unfilled orders were sent back to the participants. In this program the mills depended upon the selling agents to keep them informed about conditions in the market.[17]

When this first group was organized there was a chance that the Justice Department might bring an antitrust suit against the members. Instead of working through the Department of Commerce, the manufacturers were running their own program. Furthermore, the general reports were not issued to the public; they were released only to the participating companies. As the Supreme Court had pointed out in 1923, this was reasonable grounds for the suspicion that the open-price work was in reality an illegal price-fixing scheme.[18]

Any fears that the manufacturers or selling agents had were quieted, however, when the Supreme Court announced its decisions in the Maple Flooring and First Cement cases.[19] These two decisions in June, 1925, drastically changed the federal government's position on open-price work. In both cases the majority ruled that statistical programs conducted by trade associations were not in themselves unreasonable restraints on interstate commerce. Even though the programs at hand might have contributed to stability and to uniformity of prices, they were not illegal. Justice Stone, speaking for the majority in the Maple Flooring case, said:

> It is the consensus of opinion of economists and of many of the most important agencies of Government that the public interest is served by the gathering and dissemination, in the widest possible manner, of information with respect to the production and distribution, cost and prices in actual sales, of market commodities, because the making available of such information tends to stabilize trade and industry, to produce fairer price levels, and to avoid the

[17] ACMA, *Gazette No. 6* (June, 1925), *Gazette No. 7*, and *Gazette No. 10* (December, 1925), in McLaurine Papers; ACMA, *Proc.*, XXX (1926), 91, 98, 130–131; CMANC, *Proc.*, XIX (1925), 95–96; NACM, *Trans.*, CXIX (1925), 187–189; Interview with William M. McLaurine, October 24, 1958.

[18] *United States* v. *American Linseed Oil Co.*, 262 U. S. 390 (1923).

[19] *Maple Flooring Manufacturers' Association* v. *United States,* 268 U. S. 563 (1925); *Cement Manufacturers' Protective Association* v. *United States,* 268 U. S. 588 (1925).

waste which inevitably attends the unintelligent conduct of economic enterprise. . . . Competition does not become less free
merely because the conduct of commercial operations becomes
more intelligent through the free distribution of knowledge of all
the essential factors entering into the commercial transaction. . . .[20]

While the earlier Hardwood decision was not overruled, the Court
definitely revealed a new attitude toward the open-price concept
and associations in general. By expanding the area of permissible
associative action, the judiciary was in effect accepting an interpretation of antitrust that was very similar to the viewpoint
Herbert Hoover was expounding. After these decisions, the Justice
Department lined up with Hoover, accepting the fact that associations should be given wider latitude in which to experiment
with new means of achieving economic stability.[21]

The Maple Flooring and First Cement decisions brought a
quick response from the textile industry. In June, 1925, the
American Association's newsletter, the Gazette, explained the
"gist" of the decisions; an association could now "proceed to
gather and disseminate pertinent intratrade information on costs,
sales, prices realized, stocks, production, credits, [and] freight
rates from arbitrary price-basing points. . . ." Meetings could be
held, the Gazette added, to discuss these statistics.[22] At the annual
convention of the state association in North Carolina, James A.
Emery of the National Association of Manufacturers elaborated
on this explanation; according to Emery's lengthy exposition, the
day was fast approaching when industry would be able to substitute "regulated co-operation for the absurd compulsion of cutthroat competition."[23]

Although the dawn of "regulated co-operation" had barely
arrived, the southerners were inspired; they pushed ahead even
faster with their plans to stabilize the industry. By July 1, 1925,
four product groups were functioning.[24] The American Association and the state associations throughout the Piedmont pledged

[20] Maple Flooring Manufacturers' Association v. United States, 268 U. S.
582–583.

[21] Department of Justice, Annual Report of the Attorney General, 1925
(1925), p. 20.

[22] ACMA, Gazette No. 6 and Gazette No. 10.

[23] CMANC, Proc., XX (1926), 47–48, 53, 55, 57.

[24] ACMA, Gazette No. 7. At first the economic results of the plan also
seemed encouraging. In regard to the first trial group one of the merchants
explained that "before long the price stiffened and showed a margin over
cost." ACMA, Proc., XXX (1926), 98.

the program their unconditional support and encouraged all of the mills and selling agents to cooperate. By the fall of 1925, fourteen groups were operating. President Vereen of ACMA looked forward to a future day when the entire industry would be organized and would share the benefits of "complete and representative data."[25]

Despite the early success in organizing statistical groups, the manufacturers soon became dissatisfied with the plan. At the base of this discontent lay the industry's continued financial difficulties. After a slight improvement in prices in 1925, the mills encountered narrower manufacturing margins and more profitless sales in 1926.[26] Interest in an industry-wide plan to cut back production mounted; management had only to look at its income reports to set that, for whatever reason, the existing statistical program was not solving their problems.[27] Uneasy about their losses, they looked with suspicion at the program the merchants were running. Since the selling houses worked for a commission on sales, their profits depended upon doing a large volume of business. They were naturally not as interested in curtailing production as the mills were. This worried the manufacturers. When there were rumors that the statistical information gathered in New York leaked out to the buyers on Worth Street before it got back to the mills, the manufacturers' dissatisfaction became even more intense.[28]

[25] ACMA, *Gazette No. 10;* John E. Rousmaniere told NACM's annual meeting in October, 1925, that sixteen classes of goods were now covered by reports. NACM, *Trans.,* CXIX (1925), 188–189.

[26] This problem was discussed at a special meeting of southern manufacturers and commission merchants in Spartanburg, South Carolina (April 16, 1926). As a result of that meeting, a curtailment plan similar to the earlier programs of ACMA was set in motion, but this was clearly recognized as a stopgap measure. CMAG, *Report,* XXVI (1926), 55; ACMA, *Gazette No. 13* (April, 1926), in McLaurine Papers; ACMA, *Proc.,* XXX (1926), 126–128.

[27] Bureau of Internal Revenue, Excess Profits Tax Council, *The Cotton Textile Industry,* pp. 148–149; Kennedy, *Profits and Losses,* pp. 125, 128–129.

[28] My sources on this particular point are not very strong. For the most part I have deduced these motivations from contemporary statements which were made in regard to other matters. See the following: NACM, *Trans.,* CXIX (1925), 187; ACMA, *Proc.,* XXX (1926), 105, 161; CMAG, *Report,* XXVI (1926), 29–36; CMANC, *Proc.,* XX (1926), 91, 93; my analysis has been confirmed by two men who were closely associated with ACMA and the Cotton-Textile Institute: Interview with Charles A. Cannon, March 6, 1959; Interview with Goldthwaite H. Dorr, July 20, 1959.

Capitalizing on this ill humor, George Harris launched a new campaign to organize the type of institute Rodman had outlined the year before. By the spring of 1926 the officers of ACMA agreed with Harris that a new association was needed; they built the program at ACMA's convention around Harris' proposal for a "central organization" that would prevent cutthroat competition.[29] After this "radical, new step" had been thoroughly discussed, the American Association set up a special committee of fifteen leading manufacturers "to take under advisement the various suggestions advanced and draft a comprehensive and constructive plan for *permanent relief....*"[30]

As soon as the special committee decided to push ahead, negotiations with Secretary Hoover were opened.[31] His support would provide additional insurance against antitrust action. After the Maple Flooring and First Cement decisions, it was not very likely that the Justice Department would interfere, but the manufacturers wanted to be entirely safe. They were also angling to get Hoover to accept the presidency of the institute. Even if this were impossible, his support would help the committee persuade the manufacturers to join the new association. Businessmen in cotton textiles had a deep and warm respect for the Secretary of Commerce; he was their kind of government official. His blessings would help the committee "sell" the open-price plan and the institute's concept of stability.[32]

Hoover and the manufacturers got together for a dinner meeting at the Willard Hotel in Washington on June 1, 1926. The Secretary was very pleased with the idea that cotton textiles should have an institute of the sort that already existed in steel and cement. His own efforts to improve conditions in cotton textiles had failed, he said, because the industry was poorly organized. Since he was already formulating some rather important political objectives, he would be unable to head the institute. But he gave the plan his strong support; in the words of one of the manufacturers: "that big man patted us on the back and said 'go to it.'"

[29] ACMA, *Proc.*, XXX (1926), 58–63, 82–105, 161; Interview with Hunter Marshall, August 15, 1958.

[30] ACMA, *Gazette No. 14* (May, 1926), in McLaurine Papers.

[31] *Ibid.*; ACMA, *Proc.*, XXXI (1927), 21.

[32] CMANC, *Proc.*, XIX (1925), 88; *Textile World*, LXVII, No. 16 (April 18, 1925), 43–44; CMAG, *Report*, XXVI (1926), 63; Interviews with Hunter Marshall, August 15 and October 27, 1958; Interview with Cason J. Callaway, November 6, 1958.

At this meeting Hoover also settled the question of whether the institute would be a southern or a nation-wide association. After he insisted that the Department of Commerce would only support a national organization, the southern mills quickly made a bid for northern support.[33]

Committees from the North and South met in New York later in June. After lengthy arguments over the nature of the industry's problems and the alternatives that were open, the two committees agreed that the northern and southern mills should coordinate their "efforts in stabilizing the industry along the lines of work done in other industries, particularly steel." They appointed sub-committees, directing them to "meet as soon as possible to study the existing successful trade associations, formulate a definite plan for an organization of cotton manufacturers and decide on the membership thereof." Those executives who attended the conference agreed that they would personally support this preliminary work. Since these men were representing many of the largest companies in cotton textiles, this meant that about one-third of the industry (in terms of capacity) had already put its money behind the institute.[34]

In June the subcommittees designed an associative structure to fit their strategy of industrial stabilization. They drafted a constitution, formulated a participation agreement, and made provisions for a public meeting at which the association could be formally organized. Their institute was to be a non-profit, membership corporation (organized in New York) whose member companies would pay dues and receive votes in proportion to their size. At the head of the association there was to be a president who would receive his general instructions from the board of directors. Since the board would be a large, bulky group that would meet infrequently, provision was made for an executive committee which included the chairman of the board, the president, two vice-presidents, and sixteen of the board members. This committee was to control the association when the board was not in session. According to the participation agreements, companies operating at least eighteen million spindles (one-half of the industry) would have to agree to support the institute for three years

[33] CMAG, *Report*, XXVI (1926), 65–66; CMANC *Proc.*, XX (1926), 87; ACMA, *Proc.*, XXXI (1927), 21–22; Interview with Hunter Marshall, October 27, 1958.

[34] National Council, Minutes and Notes from the Meeting, June 10, 1926, in NTA MSS.

and to be liable for a maximum annual assessment of two cents per spindle before the association could be formally organized.[35]

As originally planned the institute was to be barred from any kind of political activity. It was neither to consider nor take action "in any legislative questions, either local or national." The regional groups were to remain active. It was understood that they (and the state associations) would continue to handle the industry's political problems. Thus there would be no chance for the institute to lobby for national legislation that would change sectional differences in hours or wages. This was apparently a concession to the South. The southern manufacturers seem to have wanted stability but not at any price; as yet they were unwilling to sacrifice or even endanger their sectional advantages.[36]

In July this plan was approved by the main committee, which by now had been increased to seventy-five members. The reasons for having a large, carefully selected committee were fairly obvious. For the same reasons, the institute ultimately had seventy-five members, drawn primarily from the larger mills, on its board of directors. Membership on the committee or board would probably influence the manufacturers to support its policies, and the institute was vitally interested in cultivating this sort of group feeling. Also, by simply polling the board or committee, the association could find out what one-half of the industry wanted to do. This was illustrated at the meeting of the main committee when executives representing five-sixths of the eighteen million spindles necessary to set the plan in motion signed participation agreements. With this kind of support in pocket, the committee proceeded to elect a temporary board of directors, executive committee, and officers.[37]

[35] ACMA, *Gazette No. 16* (November, 1926), in McLaurine Papers; NACM, *Trans.*, CXXI (1926), 156, 161; Cotton-Textile Institute, Participation Agreement, in Donald Comer MSS (Baker Library, Harvard University); hereafter the Institute will be cited as CTI; National Council, Minutes, June 29, 1926; CTI, Minutes, Executive Committee, October 4, 1926; CTI, Minutes, Organization Meeting, October 20, 1926; all three in NTA MSS. Apportionment of the votes caused considerable discussion, but it was finally decided that the members would receive one vote for each 25,000 spindles in their mills.
[36] National Council, Minutes, June 29, 1926, NTA MSS.
[37] CTI, Minutes, Executive Committee, July 21, 1926, NTA MSS; ACMA, *Gazette No. 15* (August, 1926), in McLaurine Papers; ACMA, *Proc.*, XXXI (1927), 21.

During the next few months the temporary officers stumped the industry for members. In several areas they ran into stout resistance. At New Bedford, Massachusetts, the mill treasurers explained that their Fine Goods Exchange already gave them all of the statistical data they needed.[38] Why, they asked, should they incur the added expense of supporting the institute? For less obvious reasons, the managers of the print-cloth mills in Fall River were also hesitant to join. In an effort to break this resistance, speakers were sent to all of the mill centers. They made personal appeals for subscriptions and argued forcefully that New England had very little to lose by supporting an experiment that might stabilize the entire industry and prevent more of the mills from moving South.[39] In the Piedmont many of the small mills totally ignored the campaign to form an institute. They were joined in their opposition by such large producers as Cannon Mills in North Carolina, the Bibb Manufacturing Company in Georgia, and Avondale Mills of Alabama. The leaders of the state associations and ACMA bore down hard on the executives of these companies, using the same kind of personal, regional, and economic arguments that were employed in the North.[40]

By the fall of 1926 the temporary officers had persuaded a significant percentage of the industry to support the institute. Almost 21,000,000 spindles (North and South) had been committed by the middle of October, and the acting treasurer had collected $160,625.35 in dues.[41] Support was far from unanimous in either the North or South, but it was assumed that the association could operate successfully even though some of the mills failed to join.

---

[38] The New Bedford association had apparently abandoned open-price work temporarily during the early twenties, resuming statistical exchange after the political and legal situations had become more favorable.

[39] NACM, *Trans.*, CXXI (1926), 157–158, 211–212, 235–236, 238; CTI, Minutes, Organization Meeting, October 20, 1926, NTA MSS.

[40] Letter of [B. B. Comer to Donald Comer], June 5, 1926, in Comer MSS; ACMA, *Proc.*, XXXI (1927), 130; ACMA, *Gazette No. 15*; CMANC, *Proc.*, XX (1926), 99; CMAG, *Report*, XXVI (1926), 66–67; Interview with Hunter Marshall, August 15, 1958; Interview with Cason J. Callaway, November 6, 1958.

[41] ACMA, *Gazette No. 16;* CTI, Minutes, Executive Committee, October 4 and 19, 1926; CTI, Minutes, Organization Meeting; both in NTA MSS. By October 4, 1926, 19,000,000 spindles were actually covered by participation agreements; at this time the treasurer was authorized to assess the subscribing companies at a rate of one cent per spindle.

There was the hope, too, that once the program was in operation the non-members would recognize its advantages and begin to cooperate.

When the Cotton-Textile Institute was formally organized on October 20, 1926, the question of how the new structure would be used was briefly debated. Some of the manufacturers wanted the association to become a central agency that would set production and price policies for its members. Why couldn't the Institute issue "price indices"? one manufacturer had asked; then the producers would know what the association felt to be a good price for future sales.[42] Since excess capacity was a problem, another executive proposed that the Institute purchase and destroy machinery so as "to reduce production to the point of consumption."[43] These extreme proposals were given short shrift, however, and the officers quickly focused the discussion on the open-price plan, on a program aimed at developing uniform cost accounting, and on the possibility of increasing demand by finding new uses for cotton products.[44]

The heart of the program was the open-price plan. As the officers explained, they needed to organize product groups within the Institute along the lines tried by the merchants' association. Once the mills were exchanging full information and discussing the statistical reports, the worst effects of excess capacity could be avoided. In 1926 the theory of the open-price plan was the same as it had been in 1916; after exchanging information and discussing the statistics, management would maintain fairly stable shares of the market, would avoid piling up large inventories, and would keep prices relatively stable. Stuart W. Cramer, one of the Institute's vice-presidents, explained that this sort of association was already working effectively among the yarn spinners in Gastonia, North Carolina. The mills reported complete information on their operations and received weekly reports from the organization. So long as the statistics were sufficiently detailed, Cramer suggested that they could expect "that a man will naturally do the

[42] CMAG, *Report*, XXVI (1926), 29–36.

[43] CTI, Minutes, Organization Meeting, NTA MSS.

[44] *Ibid.;* also see: CTI, Minutes, Board of Directors, October 20, 1926; CTI, Minutes, Executive Committee, October 20, 1926; both in NTA MSS.

reasonable and sensible thing under given circumstances." That is, he would avoid debilitating competition.[45]

Closely allied to the open-price plan was the program for improving and standardizing cost-accounting techniques. Since the statistics sent to the association had to be accurate and comparable in value for general reports to be useful, the cost-accounting program would supplement the open-price work. When the mills began to use uniform accounting systems, they could also compare costs; this, it was hoped, would stop management from cutting prices. Once the various mills saw that their production costs were about the same as those of their competitors (and it was assumed that they would be), they would naturally avoid senseless price wars. Then, too, a sound system of unit-cost accounting would assure that management would not unwittingly cut prices below costs. In short, the basic premise was that if each member had a better system of rational control within his firm, prices would almost automatically be stabilized.[46]

Under the so-called new uses program, the Institute was to attack the demand side of the market. Many of the manufacturers felt that this was the key to the industry's problems. Competition from the new synthetic fibers had to be met. Paper was being used to replace textiles. Through a national association they hoped to start a research and development program comparable to those employed in oligopolistic industries. Although previous attempts along this line had failed, the Institute's founders felt that the new form of organization, with its greater resources, would be able to overcome the difficulties of performing this function. Consequently, they projected a New Uses Division that would "study plans for the expansion of our domestic and foreign markets."[47] When the organization meeting closed, it was clearly understood by all of the members that the Cotton-Textile Institute would mount a three-pronged attack upon the industry's problems. Statistical exchange, uniform cost accounting, and the new uses plan were the core of CTI's program.

[45] CTI, Minutes, Organization Meeting, NTA MSS; the leaders' interest in open-price work is clearly reflected in the *Certificate of Incorporation and By-Laws of the Cotton-Textile Institute, Inc.* (1926 ed.), in NTA MSS.

[46] NACM, *Trans.*, CXXXI (1926), 146–151; ACMA, *Proc.*, XXXI (1927), 106–107.

[47] CTI, Minutes, Organization Meeting; CTI, Minutes, Executive Committee, October 20, 1926; both in NTA MSS.

Before anything could be done, the Institute's staff and central office had to be organized. An undertaking of this magnitude called for a substantial administration, and CTI's founders spent considerable time searching for the right men to fill these posts.[48] The manufacturers were well armed during this quest. With 447 mills supporting the organization, CTI had an income of over $300,000 during its first year of operations. A substantial portion of this was designated for the key officers in the professional staff— the president, secretary, and legal adviser.[49]

The first president of the Institute was Walker D. Hines. A leading New York corporation lawyer, Hines had logged years of experience as a counsel to some of the nation's largest railroad empires. For a time he had been an officer in the Atchison, Topeka, and Santa Fe Railway Company. From January, 1919, through March, 1920, Hines had served as director-general of the railroads (which were under government control), and after completing this job, he had arbitrated questions of river shipping that arose under the Versailles settlement.[50] In 1921 he had returned to private law practice. Four years later he went back to Europe to investigate for the League of Nations problems arising over the navigation of the Rhine and Danube Rivers. When Hines became president of CTI, the organization thus acquired a number of important assets: the prestige of a public figure identified with wartime service to his country and peacetime service to the agencies of international cooperation; the talents of a top-flight lawyer who had worked for years in the railroad industry; the experience of an administrator who had dealt extensively with government officials and businessmen. Little wonder that Secretary of Commerce Hoover had recommended Hines for the job.[51]

Although Hines was obviously well prepared to head CTI,

[48] As one of the manufacturers explained, "we had no idea of what the experiment was going to cost, but we had a general feeling that its success would depend largely on getting very expert and able executives, and that it might be a matter of considerable expense to induce persons of the necessary ability to abandon other enterprises . . . ;" NACM, *Trans.*, CXXI (1926), 156.

[49] *Ibid.*, CXXIII (1927), 179; Letter of Walter D. Hines to G. H. Dorr, August 7, 1929, in Dorr MSS.

[50] Hines later wrote a *War History of American Railroads* (New Haven: Yale University Press, 1928).

[51] Jackson E. Reynolds and C. H. Hand, "Memorial of Walker Downer Hines," in Dorr MSS; ACMA, *Gazette No. 17* (January, 1927), in McLaurine Papers.

neither his personality nor his appearance fitted the stereotype of the organization man. He was short and slight in build, neat in appearance, precise in expression. He was an austere man who looked very much as if he had come from Boston instead of from Russelville, Kentucky. With a dark bowler on his head and a pince-nez perched rather delicately on his nose, he had the appearance of a retiring college professor; he looked ever so much like one of those quiet men who work at Harvard and then journey forth to teach at one of the small colleges that dot the landscape in northern New England.

Naturally reserved, Hines was not the type of man one would slap on the back at a convention. But he quickly won the respect of the cotton manufacturers. His careful, penetrating analyses of the industry's plight and his sense for the equities involved in any conflict within or without the industry captured their confidence. It was essential that the Institute's president hold the respect of executives from all of the mills, large and small, southern and northern. If CTI were to succeed, sectional conflict had to be replaced by national accord, individualism had to give way to industry-wide cooperation. Even with good leadership, this new order would be difficult to introduce; without it, the association had no chance of stabilizing the industry. Hines' leadership gave the Institute a strong hand for the difficult game ahead.

Assisting Hines was the Institute's secretary, George A. Sloan, a young man with previous experience in trade association work. After graduating from the School of Law at Vanderbilt, Sloan had served during the war as an army officer. From 1920 through 1925, he had been executive-secretary of the Copper and Brass Research Association, a trade group which attempted to find new markets for the industry's products.[52]

In addition to his experience with another association, Sloan brought to his job at the Institute a youthful enthusiasm and sincere dedication to the association's ideology. He fitted well the role that he was to play. He was a tall and handsome man. An impeccable dresser, he looked exactly like a top manager from a large industrial firm or a large association should look. Unlike Hines, who left the impression of depth and quiet finesse, Sloan was an exuberant, hard-driving administrator, a tireless spokesman for the Institute's cooperative programs. Where Hines was inclined

[52] *Nashville Tennessean,* September 9, 1934; *New York Times,* September 12, 1924; ACMA, *Gazette No. 15.*

to wait, Sloan would push ahead. When a full and elaborate definition of the association's position was needed, Sloan was at a disadvantage; when a program had to be organized and forceful leadership provided, he was at his best.

Both Sloan and Hines frequently turned to the Institute's counsel, Goldthwaite H. Dorr, for advice. Dorr was a careful, reflective person who expressed his ideas in that precise manner characteristic of the upper reaches of the legal profession. He was tall and rather stately in appearance, his face adorned with a small goatee. His specialty was antitrust law, and he had lectured on this subject at both Columbia University and Harvard. Like Hines, he had had considerable experience with the government. On several occasions he had been a special assistant to the U. S. Attorney-General and during 1917/18 had worked in the War Department. This experience, his far-ranging contacts, and his recognized legal ability all were extremely valuable to the Institute. Although his particular job would be to keep the Institute out of trouble with the Justice Department, Dorr was the type of attorney who could be a valuable adviser on a wide range of problems.

Dorr, Hines, and Sloan differed in background and personality, but it was their similarities that were most outstanding. All three had attended college and held advanced degrees. This presented a contrast to the staff of the dinner-club and service associations. The former had few if any full-time staff members; those persons who did serve as secretaries or treasurers were not trained in a profession such as law. In the service associations there were full-time staff members, but their training and orientation were primarily technical or administrative in nature. With the emergence of the policy-shaping association, the staff was led by men such as Hines, Dorr, and Sloan, who were equipped by training and talent to navigate in the upper levels of our society. They could hold their own with the kind of men who dominated the pinnacles of industry and politics in modern America.

The fact that all three of these association leaders held law degrees and that Hines and Dorr continued to practice law as their primary profession is significant for another reason. This new type of economic institution was recruiting its leaders from a profession which inculcated in its practitioners an economic philosophy similar to that of the trade association. The legal point of view and the associative ideology blended together very well. Each favored constructive cooperation over seemingly destructure competition. Far better, the lawyer says, to settle out of court than to engage in a long battle that merely weakens both contestants. Far better, the association leader said, to settle out of the market place, avoiding a long siege of destructive competition. Another similarity can be found in their attitude toward rational systems of control. The law was built around the concept of systematic judicial procedures while the association was dedicated to the further extension of rational controls over all forms of economic activity. Finally, both the law and the association tended to frame their conclusions primarily in terms of the status quo. The association programs were created to preserve an existing industrial structure which included, most prominently, the organization's members. Similarly, the legal profession emphasized existing rights and equities, looked to the principles of the past and not the probabilities of the future, and stressed the importance of preserving intact the fabric of the law.[53] Among business executives, the philosophical counterpart of the lawyer and association leader was the professional manager, not the entrepreneur.

The association leader must be carefully distinguished from the business leader. Hines, Sloan, and Dorr directed the affairs of an interfirm organization, not of a firm. Their performance was measured against the income report of the entire industry. They were not businessmen. Of the three, only Hines had been involved in the direct operation of a business firm. And his experience had been in railroads, an industry which labored under a complex system of government controls. The association leader was a new and special type of bureaucrat called into existence by the policy-shaping association.

A number of other industries seem to have developed similar leaders and similar policy-shaping associations during the 1920's and early 1930's. Until more thorough studies are made, it will be difficult to ascertain whether a particular group was a service or a policy-shaping association; nevertheless, the available evidence suggests that the Wool Institute, the Institute of Carpet Manufacturers, the Rubber Institute, and for a brief time, the Iron and Steel Institute fitted the new mold. In the lumber industry one

---

[53] Or, in the words of de Tocqueville: "I do not, then, assert that *all* the members of the legal profession are, at *all* times, the friends of order and the opponents of innovation, but merely that most of them are usually so." Alexis de Tocqueville, *Democracy in America* (Phillips Bradley ed., 2 vols.; New York: Alfred A. Knopf, 1945), I, 274.

might classify the West Coast Lumber Manufacturers Association as a policy-shaping organization. In 1928 the latter group appointed as its chief executive Colonel W. B. Greeley, who had been Chief Forester of the U. S. Forest Service. A similar type of leadership was obtained for the Iron and Steel Institute when Thomas Lamont became its president.[54]

Policy-shaping groups were never as widespread as the service associations. Many industries found their leaders in the chief executives of the major firms. Others experimented with high-powered associations and quickly abandoned them. It is clear that the service associations provided the backbone of the association movement, even though the various institutes attracted far more than their share of attention. One of the most important contributions of the institutes was in fact the discussion they provoked, particularly insofar as this dialogue influenced public policy. CTI itself excited considerable public comment, if only because Walker D. Hines was its first president.

With a professional staff headed by Hines, Sloan, and Dorr, the Cotton-Textile Institute was well armed for the battle it faced—a battle which was unavoidable. An entire industry had to be organized. A group of men accustomed to thinking in individual or, at best, in regional terms had to be convinced to adopt an industry-wide viewpoint. Entrenched concepts of competition had to be modified with cooperative programs—programs tailored to avoid conflict with the federal antitrust policy. It was a formidable task that faced the Institute and its leaders in 1927.

[54] The best account of the various institutes is in Simon N. Whitney, *Trade Associations and Industrial Control* (New York: Central Book Company, 1938), especially pp. 78–84, 103–111, 121–127, 138–141; also see Fraunberger, "Lumber Trade Associations," pp. 27, 35; Burns, *The Decline of Competition,* pp. 214–216.

Chapter VI

Testing the Institute, 1927 to 1929

During the three years which followed the Cotton-Textile Institute's successful organization, the staff and the manufacturers most closely associated with CTI's operations—the founders—preached the new cooperative gospel to the rest of the industry. Some of this missionary work was directed at the members, but the principal target was the business executives who had refused to join. CTI needed converts. It was not very clear how many were needed to make the plan successful. But it was certain that the failure of about one-third of the industry to join weakened the resolution of the members.

Hines and Sloan spent a considerable amount of their time appealing for support. They appeared frequently at the meetings of the regional and state associations. In their addresses they analyzed the industry's basic problems and carefully described the Institute's program.[1] Personal appeals were directed to some of the executives.[2] Sloan also circulated elaborate memoranda expounding CTI's philosophy.[3]

[1] ACMA, *Proc.*, XXXI (1927), 104–113; XXXII (1928), 62–69; NACM, *Trans.*, CXXII (1927), 114–129; CXXIII (1927), 171–179; CXXIV (1928), 153–158; CXXV (1928), 182–186; CXXVI (1929), 107–112; CMAG, *Report*, XXIX (1929), 57; ACMA, *Gazette No. 18* (June, 1927), in McLaurine Papers; *Atlanta Constitution*, March 12, 1927.

[2] See, for instance, the correspondence with Donald Comer, Birmingham, Alabama; Telegram of G. A. Sloan to D. Comer, September 3, 1927; Telegram of Avondale Mills to G. A. Sloan, September 6, 1927; and Letter of the President and Treasurer of Avondale Mills to G. A. Sloan, November 2, 1927; all in Comer MSS.

[3] Memorandum of G. A. Sloan, March 26, 1929, in George A. Sloan MSS (Wisconsin Historical Society).

The founders provided the heavy artillery to back up this verbal assault. They joined voices with the association leaders, made personal appeals to any of their colleagues who had yet to subscribe, and pulled the state and regional groups into CTI's vanguard.[4] Resolutions approving the Institute's work were passed; the *Bulletin* of NACM and the *Gazette* published by ACMA urged the mills to cooperate: "The day of the individual has passed [ACMA announced]. By this is meant that individuals must agree on fundamental policies and principles. . . . Individualism has failed to solve the problem. Co-operation has solved the problem for others. Are you willing to try it?"[5]

All of the mills, whether they paid dues or not, were invited to participate in CTI's programs. It was assumed that this would also increase the membership. After the executives attended a few meetings, began to receive statistical reports, and discussed the reports with their competitors, they would probably be prepared to join the organization. If not, they would at least be contributing data from their own company, making the reports more complete, and (hopefully) following the policies adhered to by the group.[6]

In their efforts to sell the Institute to the non-members, the association leaders and founders were actually assisted by the federal government. The helping hand was that of Herbert Hoover. While the association was being organized, the founders and the first staff members had stayed in close contact with the Department of Commerce. In February, 1927, they were rewarded with a strong public announcement by Hoover. In a message to the readers of *Textile World,* Hoover said:

> The textile industry has been suffering from many difficulties— hangovers from the war, changes in styles, shifts in location, and lack of cooperation within itself for the many purposes which can be undertaken in the interest both of the public and the industry.
>
> The organization during the past year of The Cotton-Textile Institute with a membership of three-quarters of the industry has

[4] ACMA, *Proc.,* XXXI (1927), 22, 115, 143–144; XXXII (1928), 37–38; XXXIII (1929), 92, 132, 144–145; NACM, *Trans.,* CXXII (1927), 129–139; CXXIII (1927), 168–169, 170–171; CXXIV (1928), 160–161; CXXV (1928), 181, 327–332; CTI, Minutes, Carded Yarn Group Meeting, July 7, 1927, in Comer MSS; CMAG, *Report,* XXVII (1927), 43–44; CMANC, *Proc.,* XXII (1928), 89, 101–102; XXIII (1929), 93.

[5] ACMA, *Gazette No. 29* (September, 1929), in McLaurine Papers.

[6] CTI, Minutes, Print Cloth Group Meeting, May 11, 1927, in Comer MSS.

great promise of fundamental assistance toward stability. An industry with so great a number of people dependent upon it, with so large a volume of capital and savings invested in it, cannot long remain in distress without great hardship in its own ranks and without infection to other industries.

The fact that the industry has organized itself to exhaust every effort that scientific and economic investigation can indicate for the elimination of waste and irregularity to production is itself a mark of our industrial progress from the old notions of trade restraint as the basis of cure for economic ills and is also a mark of the initiative and courage within the industry.[7]

The subjects of all this attention—let us call them the nonconformers—remained outside of the Institute for a variety of reasons. Some of them were simply uncertain. As William D. Anderson of Macon, Georgia, observed, the previous president of his own company had been convinced,

> . . . that the final and probably the best solution of all the ills from which we are suffering in the Textile Trade was to be found in the operation of the law of the survival of the fittest. Theoretically that is right. It is a doctrine to which I can heartily subscribe in theory. The difficulty about it is that when you put it into practice, the time involved is so long and the amount of "hide" that is taken off the very best of us is so large in quantity and so painful in its abstraction, that I wonder if there is not a better way.
>
> Certainly, the movement of all business with which I am familiar is more along the lines of co-operation, during the past decade, than it has been along the other line. The time was when the able, hard-headed, two-fisted man could go out and win over his weaker competitors, but it does not seem so easy to do that today. Maybe we are short of the type of men to which I have referred.
>
> The Steel Industry used to be operated by a lot of hard-boiled, two-fisted men who went to the mat with each other every day. Today all that has disappeared and the Steel Industry is run along a co-operative line, with the Steel Institute administering things.
>
> The same thing has occurred in the railroad business, although that change has been brought about largely by Government supervision. Still, the result has been the same. . . .

[7] *Textile World,* LXXI, No. 1 (February 5, 1927), 130.

My personal preference would be to stay out of the Institute. My choice always will be to have a free hand to run our own business as we see fit to run it, and regardless of what anybody else does.

However, as I intimated above, the question in my mind is whether or not we have not come on to a different day, whether or not we are facing conditions that call for a different type of treatment from that to which difficulties have heretofore yielded.[8]

Anderson and others could not decide whether the new day had dawned. They worried. They talked and watched and waited.

Other nonconformers were confident that their best interests were still served by competition and further expansion. In some cases these mills were in a particularly strong competitive position; they manufactured specialties or their production costs were relatively low. At least they felt this to be true. Among southern executives there was still considerable confidence that growth and competition—the guiding values of their past success—should not be abandoned. New mills were still being constructed in the South. So long as management felt that the industry was merely experiencing one of its "periodical inflations and deflations," there was little cause to embrace the new association or its ideology.[9]

A number of mill presidents and treasurers explained that they could not join the Institute because they disagreed with specific aspects of the program. One of the sources of disagreement was the publicity that CTI gave to certain of the statistical reports.[10] A more formidable source of discontent was CTI's failure to undertake a program aimed at eliminating night work. By 1929 Walker D. Hines estimated that night operations accounted for a

[8] Letter of W. D. Anderson to D. Comer, January 16, 1928, in Comer MSS; ACMA, *Proc.*, XXXII (1928), 68–69.

[9] *Ibid.*, pp. 62–63; ACMA, *Gazette No. 26* (December, 1928), in McLaurine Papers; B. B. Gossett, Address to the Students and Faculty of the North Carolina A. and E. College, Raleigh, N. C., December 12, 1929 (Copy in the library of the American Textile Manufacturers Institute, Charlotte, N. C.); CMAG, *Report*, XXIX (1929), 54–55.

[10] Anderson to D. Comer, January 3, 1929; Letter of C. A. Cannon to W. D. Anderson, February 11, 1929; both in Comer MSS; CTI, Minutes, Executive Committee, December 13, 1927, in Dorr MSS; NACM, *Trans.*, CXXVIII (1930), 99–100.

substantial portion of the goods produced by the industry.[11] Unquestionably, the adoption of the night shift had greatly increased the industry's excess capacity, accentuating the cutthroat competition that already existed. To many of the manufacturers it seemed obvious that prices could not be stabilized so long as part of the mills continued to operate two shifts. Donald Comer of Birmingham, Alabama, felt that he could not bring Avondale Mills into the Institute until it attacked the problem of the night shift.[12]

Opposition to night operations had once been a New England monopoly, but in the late twenties Comer and many other southern executives began to advocate the elimination of night work throughout the industry. They did this despite the fact that they would lose one of their sectional advantages. Mills in Massachusetts were handicapped by a state law prohibiting the employment of women and children at night; they could only operate a second shift by paying higher wages and putting men on the night run. In the South there were no such laws, but still some southern executives felt that night work for women and children should be eliminated. The southern position reveals a delicate blend of humanitarian and economic motives. Some southern industrialists —Donald Comer, for instance—opposed night work so strongly on humanitarian grounds that they refused to employ a second shift despite financial difficulties. Others were solely interested in the question of excess capacity. Whatever their motives, the opponents of night work grew steadily more vocal in their demands for action.[13] In late 1928 a poll indicated that at least 50 per cent of

[11] W. D. Hines, Memorandum relative to night running, March 2, 1929, in Dorr MSS.

[12] Comer's motivations were—like those of any man—complex: at first he refused to join because his father had rejected such cooperative programs and because of a number of specific features of CTI's plan; gradually, however, the night-work issue became his major concern. Letters of D. Comer to W. D. Anderson, January 11, 1928, April 11, 12, and 23, 1928, and January 4, 1929, in Comer MSS.

[13] ACMA, *Proc.*, XXXII (1928), 70–71, 74–80; Letter of W. D. Anderson to W. J. Vereen, March 29, 1928; Letter of H. R. Fitzgerald to the Cotton Manufacturers of the South, June 28, 1928; Letter of William M. McLaurine to D. Comer, August 30, 1928; T. M. Marchant, Annual Address, President, Cotton Manufacturers Association of South Carolina, June 29, 1929; all four in Comer MSS; Letter of Lanier Branson to W. D. Hines, April 26, 1929; Letter of W. D. Hines to W. J. Vereen, August 24, 1928; Letter of W. D. Hines to Flint River Cotton Mills, August 31, 1928; Letter of W. D. Hines to W. K. Moore, July 10, 1929; all four in Sloan MSS.

the southern industry was against night work and would not oppose the passage of uniform state regulations to prevent women
and children from working at night.[14]

Nevertheless, CTI had to wait. Balanced against the gain in
membership and effectiveness that would result from a program
to eliminate night work was the threat that some of CTI's largest
members in the South would drop out. Like the service associations, CTI could not take action until an overwhelming majority
of its members approved.[15] Something more than a simple majority was needed before a trade association, whether regional or
national, could move.[16] Hines attempted in 1928 to sustain the
members' interest in balancing production with demand, while
"leaving the matter of elimination of night operation to develop
as rapidly as its supporters can make possible." His Executive
Committee agreed that CTI should avoid such a "controversial
and sectional question. . . ."[17] In 1929 the Institute again refused
to attack the night work problem.[18] A proposal to override this
decision was taken before the annual convention, but the proposition was defeated by a substantial majority.[19] As a result, the night-
work issue continued to weaken the resolution of the members
and to keep a number of mills outside of the Institute.

Under these circumstances, the efforts to increase the membership were not very successful. During the first year, 932,084
spindles were brought into the association; between October, 1927,
and the summer of 1928, 127,758 new spindles joined; in the

[14] Letter of George Harris to D. Comer, April 30, 1928; Anderson to
D. Comer, May 21, 1928; McLaurine to D. Comer, November 12, 1928 and
January 12, 1929; Letter of H. R. Fitzgerald to the Members of the American
Cotton Manufacturers Association, February 23, 1929; all in Comer MSS.

[15] Hines to Vereen, August 24 and 31, 1928, in Sloan MSS.

[16] W. D. Anderson to H. R. Fitzgerald, March 25, 1929; D. Comer to
Anderson, April 8, 1929; both in Comer MSS.

[17] Hines to Flint River Cotton Mills, August 31, 1928; Hines to Moore,
July 10, 1929; both in Sloan MSS; CTI, Minutes, Executive Committee,
December 11, 1928, in Dorr MSS.

[18] Letter of Eben E. Whitman to G. A. Sloan, February 15, 1929; Letter of
W. D. Hines to Robert Amory et al., September 16, 1929; both in Dorr MSS.

[19] W. D. Hines, Memorandum for File, February 7, 1929 and Memorandum
relative to night running, March 2, 1929; CTI, Extract from Minutes of
Executive Committee Meeting, March 7, 1929; all three in Dorr MSS; *Textile
World, LXXXI*, No. 16 (October 19, 1929), 38.

following year only 83,242 were added.[20] This meant that by 1929 there were still about 13 million spindles—37 per cent of the total spindleage in the nation—outside of CTI. The non-members were a minority but a very strong minority.

Despite the failure of about one-third of the industry to join, CTI's staff and the founders pushed ahead with the task of organizing an effective program. As soon as the central office was in operation, they set out to form "product groups" through which the open-price and cost-accounting programs could be implemented. By May, 1927, four of these groups were functioning; they included mills making some of the industry's most basic products: wide sheeting, narrow sheeting, carded yarn and print cloth.[21] In a few cases, the mills were getting satisfactory results from the plan controlled by the Merchants' Association, and CTI left these groups undisturbed. Hines and Sloan merely tried to persuade more of the mills to support the open-price plan whether it was operated by CTI, the Merchants' Association or one of the smaller statistical associations.[22] Gradually, however, the number of groups operating under CTI increased: by 1929 the manufacturers of some eleven different products had organized under the Institute's auspices.[23]

Each of the organization meetings followed the same general pattern. After a discussion of the problems being encountered by the mills, a series of resolutions was presented and passed. These resolutions formally authorized the group to organize, set up

[20] Letter of G. A. Sloan to D. Comer, November 3, 1927, in Comer MSS; CMANC, *Proc.*, XXII (1928), 47; XXIII (1929), 49. While CTI was adding new members, the association was also losing some supporters, as mills left the industry due to liquidation or bankruptcy. Consequently, in 1929 the organization's total membership was slightly over 21,800,000 spindles of the 32,417,036 active spindles and 34,819,534 spindles in place in the entire nation.

[21] G. A. Sloan, Memorandum to Craig Smith, March 27, 1933; CTI, Minutes, Print Cloth Group Meeting, May 11, 1927; both in Comer MSS; ACMA, *Gazette No. 18;* ACMA, *Proc.*, XXXI (1927), 112.

[22] W. D. Hines, *First Annual Report of the President* (1927), in Dorr MSS, pp. 5, 9–11; NACM, *Trans.*, CXXIV (1928), 157–158; W. D. Hines, Memorandum for File, May 6, 1929, Dorr MSS.

[23] W. D. Hines, *Third Annual Report of the President* (1929), in Dorr MSS, pp. 13–14; CMANC, *Proc.*, XXIII (1929), 51.

an Advisory Committee, and asked the Committee to study the possibilities of collecting and disseminating trade statistics, of developing better cost systems, and of finding new markets for the group's product. The members of the Advisory Committee were appointed and a "captain" was selected to supervise each of the group's major activities. Where the manufacturers were interested in special programs not included in the basic format, each group was allowed to proceed on its own. But all of the groups adopted the three basic programs: statistical reporting, cost accounting, and new uses.[24]

Each group set up just about the same type of open-price plan. The reports generally covered the amount produced, the stock that the mill was carrying, and the unfilled orders that the manufacturer had on hand. The participants sent in their data at the end of each week to CTI's New York office and received in return an aggregate report covering these categories for the entire group.[25] Meetings were held in order to discuss the statistics. As might be expected, the leitmotiv of these gatherings was the need to cut back production in order to prevent further price declines. Within one of the groups, prices were exchanged, but only part of the mills in the group took part in this aspect of the program. In CTI the emphasis was upon production, not price; the staff and the founders realized that any effort to stabilize prices without controlling production would be fruitless.[26]

[24] CTI, Minutes, Carded Yarn Group Meeting, July 7, 1927; CTI, Minutes, Osnaburg Group Meeting, August 30, 1927; CTI, Minutes, Chambray Group Meeting, October 20, 1927; all three in Comer MSS; CTI, Proposed News Release, July 22, 1927, and Draft of Minutes of the Chambray Group Meeting, October 20, 1927, in Dorr MSS.

[25] Letter of W. D. Hines to B. B. Comer, June 16, 1927; Letter of Paul B. Halstead, to All Manufacturers of Narrow Sheetings, September 1, 1927; Letter of P. B. Halstead to D. Comer, December 5, 1928; all three in Comer MSS; Hines, *First Annual Report,* pp. 9–11; W. D. Hines, *Second Annual Report of the President* (1928), in Dorr MSS, pp. 2–3; NACM, *Trans.,* CXXIII (1927), 188–189.

[26] [G. H. Dorr], Letter to be sent to Members of Wide Sheeting Group, November 29, 1927; Letter enclosed in Letter of G. A. Sloan to G. H. Dorr, December 12, 1927; CTI, Minutes, Bedspread Group Meeting, July 12, 1928; CTI, *Senate Investigation: Steps taken by the industry . . . to bring the production of cotton into line with the demand therefor;* all four in Dorr MSS; Hines to D. Comer, December 1, 1927; Letter of A. H. Bahnson to D. Comer, January 12, 1928; Sloan to D. Comer, February 11, 1928; all three in Comer MSS.

By the summer of 1927 the open-price work was well underway, but the cost-accounting program was just getting launched.
Although each group had a cost-accounting captain, most of the
work remained in the hands of CTI's cost engineer, George W.
Duncan. Duncan's program started with a meeting of the accountants from each of the mills in the group. He and the representatives went over all of the factors which were normally included in costs; they discussed in detail any items which the
members or Duncan considered as essential to a thorough cost
system. Certain issues came up at almost every meeting, occasionally stirring up disagreement. For instance, Duncan always argued
forcefully that the mills had to include adequate depreciation
allowances and to make provision for interest on investment as
a normal element in total costs. Some of the accountants disagreed
about the latter element. They felt that this was really profit, not
cost. CTI was interested, however, in developing an accounting
system which would ensure that a mill did not use too low a figure
for total costs and thus cut prices below prevailing market levels.
Duncan fought hard for this and other interpretations, and normally he was backed up when the accountants voted on various
methods of figuring costs. As each of the groups adopted certain
rules, CTI gradually developed an accepted body of cost-
accounting principles.[27]

During 1927 the program made steady progress, but it took
some time to develop a consensus about the basic format for a
standard cost-accounting system. It was the fall of 1928 before
CTI was prepared to issue its cost-accounting guide. This pamphlet was entitled *An Outline of Bases to be Used in Predetermining Costs for Guidance as to Sales Policies.* Using the guide, any
mill could work out a sound, unit-cost system based upon principles widely accepted in the industry.

The third phase of the program, new uses, depended very little
upon the product groups. It was guided and operated almost
entirely by CTI's central office. There was a director for the New
Uses Division (formally established in April, 1927), and there were
several staff members who assisted him; for a time the Division

[27] CTI, Minutes, Carded Yarn Group Meeting, July 7, 1927; CTI, Minutes,
Narrow Sheetings' Cost Accountants' Meeting, August 9, 1927; CTI, Minutes,
Chambray Group's Cost Accountants' Meeting, February 7, 1928, all in Comer
MSS; Hines, *First Annual Report,* p. 16.

also sponsored a research associate who worked at the laboratories of the U. S. Bureau of Standards in Washington.[28]

As a combination research and advertising program, new uses surpassed anything that the service associations had tried. In terms of the amount of money invested or personnel involved, it still fell far short of the work being done by most of America's giant firms. Nevertheless, the New Uses Division logged some significant accomplishments during its first two years of operation. Over 130 separate studies were conducted on new markets for cotton products. CTI sponsored a large-scale advertising campaign centered around styled, cotton fabrics for dresses. In 1929 the Institute spent almost $150,000 for the advertising of cotton fabrics, distributed millions of pamphlets, and began to issue a special report, "Flashes of Fashion," to buyers in department stores and other retail establishments.[29]

New uses, cost accounting, and statistical exchange—all three phases of CTI's program were organized and operating by the summer of 1927. Despite the handicap of having only two-thirds of the industry as members, the Institute had successfully created that central organization which the founders had envisioned in 1925 and 1926. This had been achieved, furthermore, without any conflict with public policy.

One of the main reasons that conflict was avoided was that the association leaders, particularly Hines and Dorr, exerted considerable influence upon the specific characteristics of CTI's program. Both men realized that unless CTI was able to encourage each of the manufacturers to control production with the industry-wide objective of stability in mind, the Institute's plan would fail. Outright price and production agreements—obvious and illegal restraints of trade—would not strengthen the program. Lacking a consensus about stability, they would collapse as had the earlier attempts to fix prices. In the meantime CTI might be charged with a violation of the antitrust laws, and neither Hines nor Dorr

[28] *Ibid.,* pp. 1–2; NACM, *Trans.,* CXXIII (1927), 192–200.
[29] G. A. Sloan, Memorandum to Members, March 29, 1929, and Memorandum to Mills, January 22, 1930, in Comer MSS; CMANC, *Proc.,* XXII (1928), 49–54; XXIII (1929), 50, 71–72; NACM, *Trans.,* CXXV (1928), 192–194; Hines, *Second Annual Report,* pp. 17–18; ACMA, *Proc.,* XXXIII (1929), 63–64.

wanted to be affiliated with an organization that was deliberately charting a collision course with the federal government.

If the founders had been willing to employ men of less stature, the staff would not have exerted so much influence upon the program; then the Executive Committee would have easily dominated the Institute. Instead, the founders had elected Hines as president, and the association could certainly not afford to lose him. His departure would tarnish the Institute's image, weaken its support from within the industry, and disrupt relations with the government.

Under the direction of Hines and Dorr, the product groups were designed so that they emphasized individual decision-making within an industry-wide organization. Special care was taken to assure that the Institute would collect data and supply reports without telling any particular mill how to use the information.[30] CTI's staff was extremely careful to stay within the limits set by the most recent Supreme Court decisions on open-price activities. This was why reports were mailed to the Department of Commerce and the FTC. This was why a monthly statistical summary was given to the press.[31] In its cost-accounting work CTI concentrated upon general principles of bookkeeping, leaving to the members the responsibility for applying these concepts.[32]

As might be expected by any student of Adam Smith, the association leaders were not able to prevent some of the members from experimenting with agreements to fix prices or to share the market. To some extent the groups were autonomous. Once they were formed, the central office could not direct all of their actions. Where conditions favored direct means of restraining competition, such means were tried. In wide sheeting, for instance, the number of competitors was relatively small; a few large companies dominated a field in which brand names were fairly important. The

[30] Letter of G. A. Sloan to G. H. Dorr, October 29, 1927; [G. H. Dorr], Memorandum re Meetings of Wide Sheetings Group, June 23, 1927; Letter of Sidney P. Simpson to W. D. Hines, July 25, 1927; all in Dorr MSS; ACMA, *Proc.*, XXXI (1927), 107.

[31] Letter of W. D. Hines to W. D. Anderson, June 25, 1929, in Comer MSS; Hines, *Second Annual Report*, p. 4; the Association of Cotton Textile Merchants of New York had begun the practice of releasing statistics; the merchants' association apparently gave more publicity to this data than CTI did. NACM, *Trans.*, CXXXI (1926), 147; CTI, Minutes, Executive Committee, December 13, 1927, Dorr MSS.

[32] Hines, *First Annual Report*, p. 20.

product group in this branch of the industry soon developed a means of controlling or "pegging" prices—a system which remained intact until late 1929 when the entire group collapsed, a victim of the forces that had always destroyed such efforts in the past.[33] After the members began to shade the accepted prices, the group became demoralized. Soon the entire association program in this branch of the industry broke down.[34] Among the small number of mills making heavy industrial fabrics, a similar arrangement was made, only this time quotas were assigned to the various producers. The fate of this particular agreement is unknown, but it seems unlikely that it survived the bitter competition of the early thirties.[35]

Neither of these agreements was sponsored by CTI's association leaders. In fact, Hines and Dorr seem not to have known that they existed. Unquestionably the formation of CTI facilitated such violations of the antitrust law by bringing competitors together at group meetings. But under Hines' and Dorr's direction, CTI's general policy was to avoid illegal actions.[36] One of the New England manufacturers resigned from the Executive Committee over this issue. In his opinion, "any Institute, that is run by a series of officials who are afraid of going to jail, is not worth the paper its circulars are written on or the money that is being put into it. The whole object of an Institute is to make one worthy of jail and try to avoid getting in it. But if you are going to be so nice and call in counsel, and do everything under the sun to make it certain that you will not go to jail, you are not going to do a darn thing for the industry."[37] Despite such opposition, Hines and Dorr were for the most part able to guide the association in accordance with their convictions.[38]

While attempting to hold CTI within the boundaries of legal

[33] Robert S. Smith, *Mill on the Dan: A History of Dan River Mills, 1882–1950* (Durham, N. C.: Duke University Press, 1960), pp. 215–219. According to Smith, similar action was taken by the producers of chambray and gingham.

[34] *Ibid.*, pp. 217–219; NACM, *Trans.*, CXXVIII (1930), pp. 124, 247.

[35] Interview with Cason J. Callaway, November 6, 1958.

[36] CTI, Minutes, Executive Committee, December 13, 1927; letter of W. D. Hines to G. H. Dorr, October 12, 1928; both in Dorr MSS; Hines to Anderson, June 25, 1929, Comer MSS.

[37] NACM, *Trans.*, CXXVIII (1930), 100.

[38] Anderson to D. Comer, January 3, 1929, Comer MSS.

associative activity, the staff and officers tried to shape the public image of their program. This was purely a defensive maneuver. There was no effort at this time to change public policy by changing public opinion. CTI merely wanted to ensure that there would not be any widespread demand for government action against the organization. To prevent such action, a public relations agency was employed to advise the association in "publicity matters."[39] Communications that might reach the press, directly or indirectly, were channeled through the New York office and carefully censored. Certain generally desirable aspects of the Institute's operations were stressed while all references to production control were carefully worded. No attempt was made to conceal the Institute's fundamental goal: stability. Stabilization, as such, was not illegal and was in fact an increasingly attractive concept to many Americans within and without the government. It was the means of achieving that goal, the particular technique of control, the form that cooperation took, that was dangerous. Consequently CTI's staff took pains to assure that the public would distinguish between the Institute's program and the more familiar kinds of price and production agreements in restraint of trade.[40]

As a final defense the Institute stayed in close contact with its friend within the government, Herbert Hoover. He and his department were kept fully informed as the Institute's program was organized and set in motion. Of course Hoover's support was no absolute guarantee that another branch or official of the government would not attack CTI for illegally restraining trade; but the publicly announced good wishes of one of the strongest cabinet members made such an attack far less likely.[41]

The strategy dictated by the association leaders succeeded. No attack came from the government. During the first crucial months when the program was taking shape, CTI was able to organize two-thirds of the producers in one of the nation's basic manufac-

[39] CTI, Minutes, Executive Committee, October 18, 1927, Dorr MSS.

[40] Letter of S. P. Simpson to G. A. Sloan, August 4, 1927; CTI, Minutes of Narrow Sheetings' Cost Accountants' Meeting, August 9, 1927; Hines to Dorr, December 19, 1927; Dorr to Hines, June 25, 1928; all in Dorr MSS.

[41] *Textile World*, LXXI, No. 1 (February 5, 1927), 130; [W. D. Hines], Suggested Letter to Wide Sheetings Mills, October 31, 1927, in Dorr MSS; NACM, *Trans.*, CXXIII (1927), 194–195; ACMA, *Proc.*, XXXI (1927), 109–110; CMANC, *Proc.*, XXII (1928), 48–49.

turing industries without stirring up any unfavorable response from the Justice Department.[42]

As CTI's leaders soon discovered, however, all that begins well can very quickly fail. It shortly became apparent that even the members were only partially dedicated to stability and self-regulation. They were willing to join the association, to pay dues, to submit and receive statistical reports, and to participate in the cost-accounting program. But they were unwilling to adopt an industry-wide viewpoint when shaping their production and price policies. Although fully informed as a result of the statistical reports, they continued to behave as they had in the past. Instead of adopting the oligopolist's attitude, they continued to run their mills as if they were competitors in an atomistic industry—which of course they were. Although the association leaders, the Executive Committee, and the Board of Directors fiercely preached the doctrines of stability, cooperation, and control, the producers ignored CTI's dogma when they made their vital business decisions.

By the fall of 1927 CTI's plan for production control was in trouble. During the late summer, demand began to drop off, but the members failed to cut production. The statistical reports clearly indicated what was happening. Cotton textiles was following its customary pattern of seasonal changes in demand. As the members kept producing, inventories built up, and prices began to sag. Apparently something more than knowledge of the industry's situation was needed.[43]

Before CTI's central office could respond to the situation, two of the product groups started their own curtailment programs. In the narrow-sheeting organization, one of the group's officers took it upon himself to encourage all of the members to cut production by 20 per cent until prices were stabilized.[44] The manu-

[42] Whitney, *Trade Associations*, p. 143, says that CTI's proposed program "resulted . . . in adverse comment by government officials. . . ." I have, however, been unable to find any evidence to substantiate this—at least insofar as CTI's basic, three-phased program was concerned.

[43] W. D. Hines, Draft of Speech, November 16, 1927; Sloan to Dorr, November 28 and December 2, 1927; CTI, Report of the Situation in Print Cloths, April, 1928; all in Dorr MSS; ACMA, *Proc.*, XXXII (1928), 29; XXXIII (1929), 86–87.

[44] Sloan to Dorr, November 28, 1927, Dorr MSS.

facturers of wide sheeting passed a formal resolution declaring it "an unsound trade practice" to carry stocks in excess of ten weeks' production.[45] Both of these steps greatly increased the association's role in shaping the policies of the mills. Both provided specific guidelines for production policies. Both whetted the demands from within the industry for more forceful and effective measures aimed at controlling production.

When prices continued downward and the demands for action became intense, CTI responded with a new program of "emergency curtailments" similar to the plans adopted by the Arkwright Club in the early 1900's. The first step was taken at a meeting of the narrow-sheeting group in December, 1927. President Hines opened this conference with an analysis of the industry's dire situation. After a general discussion of the problems, "one of the substantial members of the group said that he felt that the situation was a serious one and he thought that production ought to be slowed down under existing conditions and that he proposed to take that action himself irrespective of whether or not the others in the industry did likewise." Following this announcement, the formal meeting was closed. Informally, the members continued in session. Once again they studied their situation, coming to the general conclusion that a common curtailment policy was absolutely essential: "It was the view of substantially all of the mills represented that the sound course was, for a time, to close Friday noon for the rest of the week." Most of those present indicated that they would follow this policy, and after the meeting all of the mills producing this kind of fabric were informed of the action taken. All were asked to let the group secretary know what their own policies would be. The secretary then sent each mill a circular which described the production schedule of each of the cooperating companies. By December 9 about 90 per cent of the spindleage in this group was operating on a restricted schedule, with most of the mills closing down each Friday at noon.[46]

From the association's point of view, this new experiment in production control was economically desirable but politically dangerous. It edged CTI over the hazy line of legality drawn by

[45] [G. H. Dorr], Letter to be sent to Members of Wide Sheeting Group, November 29, 1927, Dorr MSS.

[46] Memorandum of Conference with the Assistant to the Attorney-General, Colonel Donovan, December 5, 1927; Letters of W. J. Vereen to Narrow Sheetings Manufacturers, December 9 and 14, 1927; all in Dorr MSS.

the Supreme Court's most recent decisions. Assuming that the program and the Institute should not be abandoned, the association's officers were faced with the possibility of conflict with the Justice Department. Of course they could simply proceed with the program, taking the chance that the government would not bring suit, or if it did, would not be able to win its case. This was the way the legal boundaries of associative action had been established in the past. They might, on the other hand, seek to change those boundaries by pressing for new legislation. Or, being less ambitious, they might try to arrange a *modus vivendi* with the Justice Department, an "accommodation" that would change the government's antitrust policy in their case without really establishing a legal precedent. The choice was obvious. Legislative action was ruled out by the association's by-laws. An antitrust suit would scare members away from the association. What was needed was an understanding with the antitrust division of the Justice Department.

With this in mind, Dorr and Hines visited the assistant to the Attorney-General, Colonel William ("Wild Bill") Donovan, in December, 1927.[47] Dorr opened the conference by carefully outlining the industry's general condition and the difficulties that the Institute had experienced in organizing the mills. Echoing Hoover's recent remarks, Dorr pointed out that cutthroat competition in cotton textiles had important effects both within and without the industry. The mills were faced, he said, with "the development of a situation where with the slackening of demand and continuation of production at peak level the orders on hand were now rapidly diminishing and in some branches of the industry, the excess of such orders over stocks on hand had entirely disappeared. . . ." There was "an inevitable *violent* adjustment of production to demand confronting the industry if no *orderly* adjustment were made."

Then Hines took over. He described in some detail the Institute's basic program and the new curtailment plan. It was likely, he said, that other branches of the industry facing the same problem would take similar action in the near future. Hines also made use of Hoover's support. Before this new plan had been inaugu-

---

[47] Unless otherwise noted, the following account of this confrontation is taken from: Memorandum of Conference with the Assistant to the Attorney-General, Colonel Donovan, December 5, 1927, Dorr MSS.

rated, one of the manufacturers had met with Hoover and discussed "the importance of slackening of production to correspond to the slackening in demand if a violent adjustment was to be avoided. . . ." That very day, Dorr and Hines had talked over their new program with Hoover, who had assured them "that . . . that Department regarded what was being done as sound economics. . . ." Hoover had even told them that he would be happy to talk to Donovan about the matter.

For a moment "Wild Bill" Donovan was sympathetic but cautious. Although he represented an administration which felt that the business of America was business, he was, after all, specifically entrusted with the enforcement of the antitrust laws. He sparred lightly, searching for an opening more favorable to the antitrust division. He recognized "that industry was going through processes of change and that its changing needs were not without effect upon the interpretation of the law. . . ." Even the courts had on occasion recognized that "emergency measures taken to relieve an industry and secure results which tended toward its stabilization and the avoidance of disaster" were different from "action taken in another spirit." He would like to see the law clarified on this point. Would it not be possible to use the Institute's program as a test case, under circumstances that would be favorable to the association?

No. This was not what Dorr and Hines wanted, and they deftly parried Donovan's offer. CTI's authority within the industry was too weak to withstand court action, Dorr said. He agreed that the law needed to be clarified, but he explained that they were faced with "a situation where those engaged in the industry ought not to feel that to accomplish results which were not only for the protection of the industry but for the protection of the public there was occasion to resort to furtive and secret means: it was the desire to put the situation very frankly before the Department." In the present emergency, Hines added, any government action against the association would be a "serious matter."

Donovan considered their rebuttal and apparently decided that he had given adequate expression to his role as antitrust enforcer. He promptly gave Hines and Dorr the assurance they sought. He could not, he said, guarantee that the antitrust division would not take action in the future. On the other hand, he could not see "any necessity for making a test case of the general questions on the basis of what was being done. . . ." There was, he felt, no need "to restrain what it had been outlined was being done in the emergency which apparently did not conflict with the public interest." Despite his qualifying phrases, Donovan had created with the Institute an executive agreement which in this specific instance adjusted public policy on industrial self-regulation.

Several things favored this conclusion. The Coolidge Administration's general attitude toward business was important, as was the specific support that CTI had received from Hoover. Even Donovan felt that stabilization was a desirable goal; he was predisposed to favor what he felt was the business point of view. Equally significant, however, was the effective representation that Hines and Dorr provided the Institute. The administration's friendly attitude was a natural advantage for CTI, but such advantages are seldom exploited naturally. They are exploited by men with special training, experience, and skill—men like the association leaders serving CTI. Hines and Dorr were able to keep their organization out of trouble by nudging the Justice Department into a new position on antitrust. During the following two years, CTI regularly used "emergency curtailments" to supplement its basic, threefold program.[48]

The "emergency curtailments" were merely one part of a gradual and general metamorphosis within CTI. Failing to achieve its goal of stability, the Institute kept experimenting with new policies and adjusting its old plans. The cumulative effect was to shift the emphasis of the entire program. Instead of stressing individual decision-making within a relatively weak associational framework, CTI began to emphasize the need for cooperative decision-making guided by a central coordinating agency.

In its cost-accounting work, for instance, CTI began to circulate average or representative cost figures. After a survey of actual cost data in one of the product groups, the Institute announced that at current prices (1928), the mills in that group were losing from

[48] Telegram of John A. Law to G. A. Sloan, January 3, 1928; A. H. Bahnson, Letter sent out to Chambray and Cheviot Mills, January 6, 1928; CTI, Draft of Report on Fine Goods Meeting, March 5, 1928; CTI, *Senate Investigation: Steps taken by the industry;* all four in Dorr MSS; Sloan to D. Comer, February 11, 1928, Comer MSS; other industries were able to achieve similar understandings with Donovan: see, Robert F. Himmelberg, "Relaxation of the Federal Anti-Trust Policy as a Goal of the Business Community During the Period 1918–1933" (unpublished Ph.D. dissertation, Pennsylvania State University, 1963), pp. 133–148.

1.01 cents to 5.95 cents per pound on one of their standard fabrics. Similar investigations were conducted in other groups, and by October, 1929, CTI was making regular weekly analyses of average costs for a number of the product groups.[49] Ever more forcefully the Institute's officers began to suggest to management how these figures should be interpreted. Through their circulars and speeches they hummed a steady refrain: continued production when prices were so low could only bring further losses.[50]

As the program developed, it became very clear that merely publishing a manual of accounting principles was not going to change the cost systems in many of the mills. More direct action was needed. Consequently, in 1929 CTI began to send field representatives to the mills to install better cost systems at a minimal charge. Originally this had been left to the individual mills, but when they failed to act the association moved in with its own personnel.[51]

By 1929 the Institute was repeatedly and intensely proclaiming its position on prices and production. Whenever inventories built up, the association circularized the members, urging them to cut production in order to prevent further price declines. In a typical memorandum sent out in 1929, Hines pointed out that if stocks continued to pile up, prices would break again. The mills, Hines said, had to hold down their production or they could never expect to sell their products at profitable prices.[52] Whenever a favorable position on inventories and incoming orders was achieved, CTI advised the mills to hold firm for better prices.

---

[49] Hines to D. Comer (with enclosure), February 23, 1928; Letter of W. D. Hines to Executives of Chambray Mills, January 30, 1929; both in Comer MSS; Hines, *First Annual Report*, pp. 18–19; Hines, *Second Annual Report*, pp. 8–9; Hines, *Third Annual Report*, pp. 15–16.

[50] Letter of George W. Duncan to D. Comer, March 2, 1928, in Comer MSS; Letter of G. W. Duncan to Mr. Dorr, March 5, 1928; CTI, *Print Cloth Group, Relationship of Present Prices to Costs as of July 12, 1928;* CTI, *Carded Yarn Group, Relationship of Present Prices to Costs as of July 13, 1928;* CTI, *Narrow Sheetings Group, Relationship of Present Prices to Costs as of July 14, 1928;* Letter of W. D. Hines to Malcolm D. Whitman (with enclosure), December 19, 1928; W. D. Hines, Draft of Letter to Members of Advisory Committee of Carded Yarn Group, May 30, 1929; all six in Dorr MSS; ACMA, *Proc.,* XXXIII (1929), 97.

[51] Hines, *Third Annual Report,* pp. 15–16; CMANC, *Proc.,* XXIII (1929), 73.

[52] W. D. Hines, Memorandum for Executives of Print Cloth and Narrow Sheetings Mills, December 31, 1929, in Comer MSS.

Another manifestation of the association's changing role was the industrial codes that were drafted and adopted by two of the product groups. Each of these codes stipulated certain forms of market behavior which would thereafter be considered unethical. Each attempted to remove certain elements of the contract between buyer and seller from the control of either party by setting up standard terms of sale. Through the carded-yard code, CTI also sought to curb speculation by preventing commission merchants from selling for the mills while dealing in the same products on their own behalf. This latter provision was apparently approved by a vast majority of the merchants themselves. It nevertheless represented an additional attempt to modulate by rational planning the patterns of market behavior that had developed naturally under conditions of competition.[53] The same can be said for CTI's efforts to prevent piracy of design among the manufacturers of bedspreads; associative self-regulation was to replace the traditional legal or economic recourses open to injured parties.[54]

The bureaucratic process was at work here, slowly but relentlessly pressing the Institute forward in search of stability. Although the members were unwilling or unable to give their full support to the programs implementing the associative values, they nevertheless approved of the manner in which CTI was developing. They could see no alternative to this course. In fact, most of the changes in CTI's role as a coordinating or central agency were first suggested by the manufacturers in their product group meetings.

Some of the changes in CTI during its first three years of operations were, however, the work of the professional staff—particularly the innovations that gradually turned the association into a spokesman and organizational middleman for the entire industry. Initially these functions had been left to the regional

[53] Mary G. Conner, Memorandum re Carded Yarn Trade Practices Code, June 21, 1927; Letter of William J. Donovan to G. W. [sic] Dorr, June 21, 1927; both in RG 60, File 60–147, NA; [G. A. Sloan], Draft of Letter, December 6, 1927; W. D. Anderson et al., "Code of Trade Practices for the Cotton Wrapping Twine Industry," November 20, 1928; both in Dorr MSS.

[54] CTI, Draft of Minutes of Bedspread Advisory Committee Meeting, May 7, 1928; G. A. Sloan, Draft of Letter to Bedspread Mills, November 2, 1928; both in Dorr MSS; CTI, Letter of Information, December 11, 1928, in Comer MSS.

groups, but the need for a single, national organization that could speak for the industry was great. By dint of its larger income and superior staff, the Institute was able to provide more forceful representation than any of the existing regional groups. Furthermore, CTI, like the service associations, was better able to handle this sort of problem than to cope with the economic difficulties that had been staked out as the Institute's sole concern.

In the new uses program the Institute quickly showed its ability as an organizational middleman. One of its typical campaigns involved cooperation with about twenty trade organizations. The groups with which CTI worked included the National Association of Purchasing Agents, the Architectural League of New York, Associated Business Papers, and the American Wholesale Grocer's Association, to mention only a few.[55] Seldom did the association have contacts with individuals who were not representing some organization. By working through other trade groups, CTI was able to achieve maximum efficiency and maximum coverage for its programs. Besides, it was easy for the various association representatives to work together. They spoke the same language, cherished similar values, and grappled with almost identical problems. They even had their own trade group, the Association of American Trade Association Executives.[56]

CTI also began to cooperate with various governmental agencies and departments, carrying forward the work already begun by the service associations. In 1927 and 1928 the Institute, the Department of Commerce, and the Department of Agriculture joined in the search for new markets for cotton goods. Using money appropriated for this purpose by the Sixty-ninth Congress, a new uses committee was formed to facilitate business-government cooperation and "to allocate the different phases of proposed investigations in order to prevent duplication."[57] The Institute and the Department of Commerce also collaborated on standardization; in December, 1927, the National Council formally turned

[55] NACM, *Trans.*, CXXIII (1927), 195–196; CMANC, *Proc.*, XXII (1928), 50–54, 56–57, 86–87; CMAG, *Report*, XXIX (1929), 27.

[56] C. J. Judkins, *Trade and Professional Associations of the United States* (Washington: U. S. Department of Commerce, Industrial Series No. 3, 1942), p. 33. This group was established in 1920.

[57] ACMA, *Gazette No. 20* (September, 1927), in McLaurine Papers; ACMA, *Proc.*, XXXIII (1929), 44–45, 63–64; NACM, *Trans.*, CXXIII (1927), 194–195; CXXV (1928), 204–207; CMANC, *Proc.*, XXII (1928), 48–49, 60–63.

this job over to CTI.[58] Similarly, the industry's negotiations with the Internal Revenue Bureau over the problem of depreciation rates were left in CTI's hands.[59] In effect, by 1929, the Institute had become spokesman for the entire industry in all non-legislative matters involving the federal government.[60]

On October 16, 1929, the Institute held its annual convention in New York. It was not a very cheerful gathering. Everyone in America seemed to be making money except the cotton manufacturers. The stock market was booming; on October 15, a learned professor at Yale University had confidently predicted that the market would go even higher in the next few months. President Hoover, the manufacturer's friend, had sagely announced that "the final triumph over poverty" was at hand. Unfortunately the cotton mills seemed unable to share in that great victory. Their industry was still "sick."

Walker D. Hines, who addressed the convention, was resigning as president; he agreed to accept the position of Chairman of the Board so that he could continue to advise CTI and to help shape the association's policies. But he was turning the presidency over to George Sloan. Hines' remarks were thus a final evaluation of his own work as head of the organization.

Although he tried to sound an optimistic note, Hines had to admit that the basic difficulties he had described in 1927 still beset the industry in 1929. Overproduction was, he said, "a fundamental element of weakness." Prices still did not cover the full cost of production, even when inventories were low. Periodically the mills allowed stocks to pile up, causing further depression in prices. CTI's educational and statistical programs had made some progress, he felt, but the major objective, stability, had yet to be achieved.[61]

[58] [W. D. Hines], Suggested Letter to Wide Sheetings Mills, October 31, 1927, Dorr MSS; ACMA, *Proc.*, XXXI (1927), 109–110; National Council, Minutes, December 14, 1927, in NTA MSS.

[59] CTI, Minutes, Executive Committee, December 13, 1927; Draft of Letter to Directors [*ca.* February 6, 1928]; both in Dorr MSS; Letter of W. D. Hines to Cotton Mill Executives, November 13, 1930, in Comer MSS; G. A. Sloan, *Fourth Annual Report of the Cotton-Textile Institute, Inc.* (1930), pp. 22–24.

[60] ACMA, *Proc.*, XXXI (1927), 110; Hines, *Second Annual Report*, pp. 19–20; CTI, Material in Preparation for Senate Inquiry, November 28, 1929, in Dorr MSS; NACM, *Trans.*, CXXIX (1930), 325.

[61] Hines, *Third Annual Report*, pp. 2–14.

Hines was right. Measured against its goal, CTI had failed. As yet, about one-third of the industry was unwilling to join the association. Even the members were not fully committed to the Institute's values. They found it extremely difficult to follow the production policies dictated by the association. They found it impossible to hold firm for prices that would cover costs and would ensure even normal profits. As a stabilizing institution, CTI was a failure. It was not that the association had been entirely unable to influence the policies of the member mills. The accounting program had met with some success; a number of the firms had already improved their accounting systems. Through the open-price plan and the "emergency curtailments," CTI had undoubtedly been able to influence production policies, cutting down somewhat on burdensome inventories that demoralized the market.[62] But any total effect on prices or profits was impossible to find. As the data in Tables 5–8 indicates, excess capacity was still being driven out of the industry by subnormal earnings and by a shrinking manufacturing margin that enabled only the strongest mills to earn normal profits.[63] That was why the Institute had gradually altered its policies, shifting the emphasis of its programs from individual to cooperative decision-making. The clearest sign of CTI's failure was the continuous effort that was exerted to strengthen the central organization and to tighten its control over the members.

TABLE 5

CAPACITY, COTTON TEXTILES, 1927–1929

	1927	1928	1929
Active spindles			
U.S............	34,409,910	33,569,792	32,417,036
New England....	14,995,460	13,815,242	12,537,512
South..........	17,893,908	18,281,754	18,540,634
all other........	1,520,542	1,472,796	1,338,890

NOTE: The data on capacity is from NACM, *Yearbook, 1930*, p. 145; the years are cotton years ending on July 31; the South refers to all of the cotton-growing states.

[62] See, for instance, the following: [CTI], Report of the Situation in Print Cloths, April, 1928, Dorr MSS; Hines to Executives of Chambray Mills, February 14, 1929, Comer MSS.

[63] NACM, *Yearbook, 1931*, pp. 168–169; Kennedy, *Profits and Losses*, pp. 248–249.

TABLE 6

PRODUCTION, COTTON TEXTILES, 1927–1929

	1927	1928	1929
Cotton consumed (bales)			
U.S.	7,189,585	6,834,063	7,091,065
New England	1,674,772	1,438,431	1,447,451
South	5,193,500	5,113,842	5,392,265
all other	321,313	281,790	251,349
Spindle hours			
U.S.	102,605,403,478	96,451,049,937	99,604,009,191
New England	33,052,209,769	27,862,204,584	28,252,638,733
South	65,864,979,698	65,272,570,540	68,360,570,750
all other	3,688,214,011	3,316,274,813	2,990,799,708

NOTE: The figures on production in terms of cotton (bales) consumed refer to running bales, exclusive of linters; the years are cotton years; and the South includes all cotton-growing states; the source is NACM, *Yearbook, 1930*, p. 46. Information on spindle hours is from *ibid.*, p. 149; the figures refer to total hours of operation for the region's spindles; the years are cotton years and, again, the South encompasses all cotton-growing states.

TABLE 7

PRICES AND MARGINS, COTTON TEXTILES, 1927–1929

	1927	1928	1929
Average cloth prices (¢/yd.)	12.663	13.141	12.938
Average manufacturers' margin (¢/lb.)	21.8	19.7	18.1

NOTE: The average cloth prices are taken from NACM, *Yearbook, 1930*, p. 132. The manufacturers' margin (the difference between the price of a pound of gray goods and the price of the cotton used to make the cloth) is from Kennedy, *Profits and Losses*, p. 248.

Although unable to achieve stability, CTI was successfully established as the industry's national association. The very fact that a stable, well-financed national organization had been formed could be seen as a considerable accomplishment. About two-thirds of the industry had been brought into a single association; an open-price plan was operating; the product groups were well organized and most of them were continuing to function despite the industry's economic plight. Due to the success in organizing a stable association, there had at least been "a very pronounced improvement in the *opportunities* for the industry to deal with its problem in an effective way."[64]

[64] Hines, *Third Annual Report*, p. 1 (italics mine).

TABLE 8

PROFITS, COTTON TEXTILES, 1927–1929

	1927	1928	1929
Net income.....................	$64,384,000	$5,024,000	$16,249,000
Profits (selected firms)			
51 northern corporations.........	$18,353,000	$6,843,000	$9,587,000
178 southern corporations.........	$40,949,000	$17,146,000	$20,028,000
Ratio of profits to receipts			
51 northern corporations.........	8.44%	3.36%	4.55%
178 southern corporations.........	9.67%	4.11%	4.46%
Ratio of profits to net worth			
51 northern corporations.........	8.34%	3.13%	4.35%
178 southern corporations........	11.09%	4.56%	5.29%
Average dividends			
New Bedford...................	3.50%	2.08%	2.11%
Fall River....................	3.51%	2.94%	3.83%

NOTE: The income data is for all cotton manufacturing corporations and the figures are for net income after taxes; the sources of this data are: U. S., Bureau of Internal Revenue, *Statistics of Income, 1927*, p. 327; *Statistics of Income, 1928*, p. 335; *Statistics of Income, 1929*, p. 289. The figures on profits are from U. S , Bureau of Internal Revenue, Excess Profits Tax Council, *The Cotton Textile Industry*, pp. 148–149; the term "profits" and the ratios are explained in Chapter V, Tables 1–4. The dividends are average cash dividends as a percentage of total capital for the mills in New Bedford and Fall River, Massachusetts; the data is from NACM, *Yearbook, 1930*, p. 140.

One of the by-products of CTI's establishment was the emergence of the association leader in cotton textiles. The industry was increasingly identified with the names, Hines, Sloan, and Dorr. These three association leaders were primarily responsible for the fact that CTI had begun to act frequently and effectively as a spokesman for the industry. In their relations with other organizations, whether governmental agencies or trade groups, CTI's officers had been extremely successful.

The association leaders formulated and articulated a new cooperative ideology. For the first time a trade association in the cotton textile industry had a philosophy with which to justify its actions. Framed in terms of the traditional guild objectives of stabilization, cooperation, and control, the associative philosophy stood in sharp contrast to the laissez faire, competitive concepts that had held an unchallenged dominion in the nineteenth century. The new ideology was only beginning to make an impression, but the association leaders channeled much of their energy into the definition and promulgation of this new outlook.

It was the association leaders, too, who guided CTI into an alliance with the federal government. This sort of working arrangement had begun to take shape under the service associations; it was more pronounced, however, after CTI was organized. While the association still had problems with the Justice Department, compromise—not conflict—was the keynote of CTI's business-government relations. In working with Herbert Hoover, with the Bureau of Standards, and with the Department of Agriculture, the association leaders were building an alliance that was to become much stronger and more meaningful in the years ahead. That, however, carries our story forward into CTI's experiences of the next three years—into a period when the policies of the association and the government would be shaped by the depression which struck a few short days after the Institute's convention in October, 1929.

Chapter VII

The Institute and
the Great Depression,
1930 to 1932

Black Thursday: eight days after CTI's meeting the stock market collapsed. At first the troubles on Wall Street seemed to be little more than a frightening but temporary chastisement for speculators. The economy, Americans were told, was fundamentally sound. That theme echoed and re-echoed through the business offices of Wall Street, through the government offices in Washington—while the depression deepened. Prices and wages bumped their way down, lower and lower. Soon an army of unemployed workers stood as witnesses against the old order; the economy, they said, was not fundamentally sound.

For the manufacturers of cotton textiles, little joy could be squeezed from the fact that other industries were now facing the same problem they had been struggling with for several years. As the depression tightened its hold on the economy, demand for cotton products fell off. Industrial customers needed less, and the nation's unemployed workers had little money to spend on cotton clothing.[1] Prices dropped and the manufacturer's margin shrank.[2] During 1929 about 55 per cent of the firms in the industry had reported some net income, but in 1930, over three-quarters of the companies had net deficits. After paying federal income taxes in

[1] Backman and Gainsbrugh, *Economics of the Cotton Textile Industry*, p. 179.
[2] Kennedy, *Profits and Losses*, p. 249.

139

1930, the entire industry showed a net loss of over ninety-two million dollars.[3]

The depression wore away the confidence that had held many of the manufacturers outside the Institute. They had placed their faith in the competitive process. After weathering five years of intense competition, they found things getting worse, not better. Disenchanted with the traditional concepts of competition and growth, many of them now embraced the Institute's values: stability, cooperation, and control. Between October, 1929, and October, 1930, CTI gathered in new members controlling almost three million spindles, about one-tenth of the industry's capacity.[4]

Those manufacturers who had already joined CTI were also affected by the depression. More acceptable now were the various forms of self-regulation which impinged to a considerable degree upon the individual mill's production or price policies. With the manufacturers' very existence threatened, they became somewhat less protective about individual advantages, slightly less suspicious of industry-wide programs.[5] After all, they had nursed their advantages for several years and what had been gained? They had refused to participate whole-heartedly in industry-wide programs, and now they faced disaster.

A similar kind of ideological chemistry was at work throughout the nation. The mood and mentality of American society as a whole was altered by the depression. Traditional values were questioned; new ideas found easy entrance where before the way had been barred. As the depression ground on, stability became more and more attractive to more and more Americans. To the average citizen economic stability now was a precisely defined and desirable goal. Stability meant that he would have a job. His savings would be secure, his status in society protected or restored. Competition? He had just about had enough of that. If it meant competition for his job, if it meant still lower prices and wages,

[3] U. S., Bureau of Internal Revenue, *Statistics of Income, 1929*, p. 289; U. S., Bureau of Internal Revenue, *Statistics of Income, 1930*, p. 232.

[4] CTI, Minutes, Annual Meeting, October 15, 1930, in Comer MSS. This brought into the Institute about 23 per cent of the capacity which had been outside of the association in 1929.

[5] The new programs undertaken also encouraged some manufacturers to join; D. Comer to Anderson, May 20, 1930; Anderson to D. Comer, May 21, 1930; both in Comer MSS.

he was ready for a change; cooperation, he began to feel, was the only course open to a depression-ridden country.

As unemployment increased, as wages, prices, and production spiraled downward, the values expressed in public policy also changed. To the Congress, to the judiciary, to the executive branch, economic stability became a prime objective. President Hoover had been interested in this long before 1929. Once he realized the seriousness of the depression he was even more convinced that the government could best help the country by helping business institutions, like CTI, which were trying to achieve stability in their respective industries.[6] The Congress and the courts came to this conclusion more slowly, but public pressure and the nation's plight finally convinced all three branches of the federal government of the need for stability.

For Hoover, as for most congressmen and judges, the depression did not, however, provide convincing evidence that the traditional antitrust policy should be abandoned. In his inaugural address in 1929, Hoover had pointed out that cooperative institutions in the business world could continue their record of progress "only so long as business manifests its respect for law."[7] This clearly meant antitrust, and Hoover attempted to stand by this conviction.[8] With ambivalence characteristic of his entire term in office, he wanted to squeeze his solutions into a rigid framework of traditional values. For a time, the other two branches of the government concurred; while the antitrust policy tottered, it was not allowed to fall.

Although antitrust was still a threat, CTI responded to the new situation by extending its program and by again attempting to elaborate and tighten its system of controls. In South Carolina the manufacturers started things moving. S. M. Beattie, a prominent member of the print-cloth and narrow-sheeting groups, devised a

[6] Herbert Hoover, *The Memoirs of Herbert Hoover* (2 vols.; New York: Macmillan, 1952), II, 301; Whitney, *Trade Associations*, pp. 126–127; Ray L. Wilbur and Arthur M. Hyde, *The Hoover Policies* (New York: C. Scribner's Sons, 1937), pp. 297, 301–305, 309.

[7] Davis N. Lott (ed.), *The Inaugural Addresses of the American Presidents* (New York: Holt, Rinehart and Winston, 1961), p. 226.

[8] Whitney, *Trade Associations*, pp. 55–56.

plan under which the mills would limit their running time on the day shift to fifty-five hours a week; they would use the night shift only when it was necessary to produce additional goods needed to satisfy immediate demand. If they followed the Beattie Plan, the mills would also stop operating machinery at noon time or at other hours outside the regular shifts. This would cut production and would set up uniform limits on the work week, providing a foundation for further curtailment when it was necessary. It would help CTI eliminate the complaint that curtailment was impossible because all of the southern mills did not follow the same, basic production schedule.[9]

At first, however, it appeared that the mills were not yet ready to accept even this mild restraint. Early in January, 1930, the state association in South Carolina approved Beattie's suggestions; but the print-cloth and narrow-sheeting groups endorsed only that part of the provisions that referred to overtime. There the policy stopped. Only South Carolina had a law limiting the work week to fifty-five hours. In the other southern states the limit was sixty hours, and their state associations were unwilling to sacrifice that five-hour advantage by endorsing Beattie's plan. CTI's other product groups ignored the proposal. Even Beattie's print-cloth and narrow-sheeting groups refused to support the fifty-five-hour week.[10]

While Beattie's plan was being discussed in the Piedmont, a similar movement started in the North under the leadership of Henry P. Kendall, a Bostonian with heavy interests in textile mills in both sections of the country. He carried the industry's problems directly to Washington and dumped them in Hoover's lap. Kendall wrote to President Hoover and described to him the industry's situation. He asked Hoover to call a conference of manufacturers so that they could "meet this situation frankly by a permanent curtailment of output." Kendall recommended that the entire industry adopt a maximum operating schedule of fifty hours a week on both the day and night shifts, without cutting wages. This program, he added, should be accompanied by "an agreement looking to the gradual elimination of women and minors from

[9] Cotton Manufacturers Association of South Carolina, Minutes, Executive Committee, January 2, 1930 (a book of minutes is available at the office of the association, Columbia, S. C.); hereafter cited as CMASC.

[10] Hines to D. Comer (with enclosure), January 25, 1930, Comer MSS.

the night run."[11] Hoover and Secretary of Commerce Lamont were interested in Kendall's proposal. In January, 1930, they invited CTI's officers and about fifteen of the country's leading cotton manufacturers to the White House to discuss the idea.[12]

Before the manufacturers saw Hoover, George Sloan brought them together for a short, informal meeting. He tried to persuade them to adopt a definite program which they could present to the chief executive. The manufacturers could not agree. Everyone wanted something to be done, but there were several different ideas as to what that something should be.[13]

With the manufacturers disorganized, what could Hoover do? He encouraged them to work together until they could concur upon some practical answers to the industry's problems. Neither he nor Lamont was prepared to supply the industry with a ready-made solution.[14]

Six of the businessmen decided that they would push ahead on their own. Before leaving the meeting, they prepared a statement announcing that "the industry should voluntarily take steps to shorten the hours of employment in many localities which are now operating their mills long hours, that women and young people should be gradually eliminated from night work and night work in general discouraged." This declaration (which was signed by Robert Amory, C. A. Cannon, Malcolm G. Chace, Donald Comer, B. B. Gossett, and H. P. Kendall) also proposed certain immediate steps to put these principles into effect.[15]

From the point of view of CTI's staff and officers, the night-work proposal was obviously the most attractive part of the petition. By eliminating night work for women and children, the association would impose a considerable restraint upon those mills that were using a second shift; this, they felt, would bring a significant cut in production. Under any circumstances, it was more promising as a means of reducing output than the Beattie Plan's fifty-five-hour shift. Equally important to CTI was the humanitarian aspect of the night-work plan. It would help them "sell" the program to the industry. As Hines, Sloan, and Dorr knew, it would also have a significant effect upon their rela-

---

[11] NACM, *Trans.*, CXXVIII (1930), 258, 264.
[12] *Ibid.*, p. 265; Sloan to D. Comer, January 28, 1930, Comer MSS.
[13] NACM, *Trans.*, CXXVIII (1930), 264.   [14] *Ibid.*
[15] Hines to D. Comer (with enclosure), January 25, 1930, Comer MSS.

tions with the federal government. The night-work proposal linked production control with humanitarian objectives which could not help but be attractive to government officials and the general public. In effect, the proposal would marshal the cotton textile industry's forces behind an idea that had in the past aroused vigorous opposition throughout the industry, especially in the South. For years reformers had been pressing for child labor legislation and for laws limiting the work week for women. In New England such legislation had been passed despite the stout opposition of the manufacturers, but the southern states had not followed suit. Past attempts to deal with the problem through national legislation had failed. It would be a truly significant event if the industry, North and South, dramatically altered its course by voluntarily promoting the popular idea of improving working conditions for women and children. After this sort of compromise, CTI would probably have little to fear from the Justice Department and could, no doubt, expect the Hoover Administration's active support.[16]

With these happy thoughts in mind, CTI's officers quickly pushed ahead. First they got the approval of the Board of Directors.[17] Then they carried the declaration that had been signed at the Hoover conference to a special meeting of southern mill executives. At this gathering, held in Atlanta, Donald Comer and other prominent southern manufacturers argued that the industry should indeed try the night-work plan on a two-year trial basis. If it proved to be economically unsuccessful, Comer said, they could always abandon it, although he personally favored the elimination of night work for women and children whether it affected production or not.[18]

Many of the representatives at the meeting were, however, unenthusiastic about the plan. Of course they wanted to cut production. They realized how serious the situation was. But was it necessary to sacrifice so much of their regional advantage? Look what had happened to New England's mills, they said. It was better to wait, to accept a less drastic measure than the one Comer had proposed. Like most men who stand before the jaws of economic

[16] *Ibid.*   [17] *Ibid.*

[18] Letter of D. Comer to W. D. Hines, January 27, 1930; Telegram of Hines to D. Comer, January 28, 1930; Anderson to D. Comer, February 8, 1930; all in Comer MSS.

disaster, they chose to wait until it was absolutely certain that they were to be devoured.[19]

The Beattie Plan was less radical. After some discussion they agreed upon an adaptation of this program: for the day shift, fifty-five hours would be the self-imposed limit, with a fifty-hour maximum on night operations; overtime (including noontime work) would be completely eliminated. The only concession to the opponents of night work was the five-hour difference between the day and night shifts, a difference which would impose at best only a slight handicap on the mills that ran at night.[20]

In New England the manufacturers were not overjoyed when they heard about the "55–50" plan. At their regional conference they exposed 55–50's many weaknesses. It failed to provide the drastic curtailment that northern management felt was obviously needed; it side-stepped the vital question of night operations; it set limits which were less restrictive than state laws in most parts of New England. The manufacturers admitted, however, that 55–50 was a small step forward; the Institute's officers were apparently able to persuade them that it was "an entering wedge which will result in further improvement later on, to the great benefit of the industry." With a guarantee of strong support from both sections, CTI formally introduced the new program in February, 1930.[21]

Several aspects of 55–50 were extremely risky insofar as CTI's relations with the Justice Department were concerned. When a company's management accepted the program they were asked to sign a subscription blank. All of CTI's previous curtailment plans had been handled informally through conversation or correspondence, but with 55–50 the association was using a subscription form that looked suspiciously like a binding, legal contract. Furthermore, there was no time limit, either explicit or implied. The subscribers were apparently accepting a permanent reduction in operating time. Except for an allowance made for northern mills, there was no provision for minor differences in production schedules. There was an escape clause in the contract—the subscriptions would not become effective until 80 per cent of the capacity in the

[19] D. Comer to Hines, February 6, 1930; Hines, Memorandum for File, February 7, 1930; Hines to D. Comer, February 10, 1930; all in Comer MSS.
[20] Hines, Memorandum for File, February 7, 1930, Comer MSS.
[21] NACM, *Trans.*, CXXVIII (1930), 115–116; Hines to D. Comer, February 10, 1930, Comer MSS.

subscriber's particular branch of the industry had signed. But on the whole, 55–50 looked very much like the kind of association agreement that would cut production, influence prices, and result in an unreasonable, hence illegal, restraint of trade.[22]

From the association's viewpoint all of these innovations in the technique of cooperative production control were essential. They were needed if the Institute were to persuade the manufacturers to behave like oligopolists. CTI had to give its members a strong assurance that their competitors were adopting the new production schedule. What better assurance could they have than a signed subscription blank? They could be certain, furthermore, that 80 per cent of their competitors were following the association's plan. This, it was hoped, would strengthen the manufacturers' confidence in CTI's policies; it would re-enforce their acceptance of the Institute's cooperative methods of achieving stability.

Helpful as it might be to CTI, the 55–50 plan involved a real danger of antitrust action; consequently, the association became concerned about its public image. Dorr cautioned all of the staff and officers to be careful to put the situation in its "true light before the public." Their publicity, he explained, should reflect the fact that "it is not a question of the industry taking steps to bring about a curtailment of what under the circumstances is normal production, but rather an effort on the part of the industry to avoid the evils of a wholesale shutdown. . . ." Following his advice, the association emphasized the manner in which 55–50 would improve working conditions in cotton textiles. Eliminating noontime operations would give the employees the rest time that they needed during the day. A fifty-five-hour week would make that workday shorter. If the plan cured the industry's ailments, it would soon bring back the days of full employment.[23]

As a further safeguard, CTI wove a delicate fabric of executive acquiescence to cover its vulnerable legal position.[24] The asso-

[22] Sloan to D. Comer, February 28, 1930; G. A. Sloan, Letter to Narrow Sheeting Mills, February 27, 1930; P. B. Halstead, Memorandum to Narrow Sheetings Group, February 28, 1930; all in Comer MSS; CMANC, *Proc.,* XXIV (1930), 50; G. A. Sloan, *Sixth Annual Report of the Cotton-Textile Institute, Inc.* (1932), p. 25.

[23] G. H. Dorr, Memorandum for Mr. Sloan, January 6, 1930, in Dorr MSS.

[24] In the U. S. Steel case the informal approval given to the combination by President Theodore Roosevelt was considered by the Court to be a factor substantiating the legality of a particular acquisition. *United States* v. *United States Steel Corporation, et al.,* 251 U. S. 446, 447 (1920), as cited in Henry R. Seager and Charles A. Gulick, Jr., *Trust and Corporation Problems,* p. 260.

ciation had worked with President Hoover and Secretary of Commerce Lamont when 55–50 was in its formative stage. Subsequently, the Institute kept the Department of Commerce fully informed about the program's development and took every opportunity to stress the social aspects of the plan. Lamont and his assistant secretary, Julius Klein, would obviously have been happier if the industry had made an effort to eliminate night work for women and minors. As they made clear, they were worried about the antitrust question and afraid to get deeply involved in CTI's maneuverings. About all that they could do was to keep CTI apprised of the administration's attitude toward the program, and they faithfully performed this service. The Institute's activities were discussed at a Cabinet meeting where it was finally agreed that "the stress was really on relieving the night shift . . ."; afterwards, Klein carried the news to Walker D. Hines. Klein also indicated that "he thought this was too far from any restraint of trade to cause trouble." CTI's officers obviously wanted more positive support than this, but they settled for the same sort of *modus vivendi* or accommodation in public policy that they had received in 1927.[25] With this informal agreement in hand they could at least push ahead without any immediate fears of hostile government action.[26]

The campaign for subscriptions to 55–50 marked an important stage in the evolution of the association. For the first time the organization exerted strong pressure on the manufacturers. Mem-

[25] Hines, Memorandum for File, February 7, 1930, Comer MSS; Letter of G. A. Sloan to Robert P. Lamont (with enclosures), February 28, 1930; Memo of William L. Cooper to Mr. Kerlin, March 8, 1930; Memo of Edward T. Pickard to Mr. Cooper, March 6, 1930; Letter to W. D. Hines and G. A. Sloan to R. P. Lamont, March 25, 1930; Letter of Julius Klein to H. Lauten, June 5, 1930; all in RG 40, File 87481, Box 675, NA.

[26] Although CTI's officers probably did not know it, the Department of Justice investigated the Institute early in 1930; the following report was filed: "The investigation . . . regarding the operations of the Cotton Textile Institute discloses no evidence of an agreement on prices or of an agreement to curtail production. The industry is in a wretched condition, and Mr. Walker D. Hines, Chairman of the Institute, has impressed upon the various members the necessity for their curtailing production, but in no case do the activities approach the point of agreement. . . . On the whole, I think it would be a very difficult matter for this industry to get together for any effective restraints of trade"; Memorandum of James L. Fly to Mr. O'Brian, February 15, 1930, in RG 60, File 60–147, NA.

bers and non-members alike were pressed to conform to the industry-wide program. Having emerged as an entity separate from the members, CTI was now beginning to act upon the manufacturers in a forceful manner.

CTI launched the new program at a group meeting of the narrow-sheeting executives and by February 28, 1930, had signed up about 80 per cent of the spindles in that group.[27] The association's staff members then held meetings with each of the groups, and by March 13, 1930, they had the subscriptions of from 50 per cent to 100 per cent of all the product groups.[28] Shortly after these meetings, the association corresponded directly with each of the non-subscribers, carefully explaining the plan's merits. If this failed to bring results, the Institute's field agents visited the firm and gave the executives a sales talk on the advantages of 55–50.[29]

To bolster these efforts CTI focused considerable social pressure on the non-subscribers. The pressure came from their peers, the manufacturers who had already signed. Special meetings were arranged so that enthusiastic supporters of 55–50 would have a chance to buttonhole the non-subscribers. At these meetings the association leaders gave formal addresses extolling cooperation and production control. The regional and state associations joined the demand for support of 55–50.[30] Members of the Institute's Board of Directors were given lists of non-subscribers in their state or product group so that they could appeal personally to these men to back the plan.[31] Apparently no economic pressure was applied. But the manufacturer who stood outside the program was placed under intense social pressure; friends and fellow manufacturers made it impossible for him to ignore, extremely difficult for him to resist, the call for cooperation.

By April 1, 1930, over nineteen million spindles were pledged;

[27] Sloan, Letter to Narrow Sheetings Mills, February 27, 1930; CTI, Press Release, February 27, 1930; Sloan to D. Comer, February 28, 1930; all in Comer MSS.

[28] Sloan to D. Comer, March 13 and 24, 1930, Comer MSS.

[29] *Ibid.;* CTI had five field agents working on the program. CMAG, *Report,* XXX (1930), 78.

[30] ACMA, *Proc.,* XXXIV (1930), 14–15, 101; CMAG, *Report,* XXX (1930), 41, 82, 85; CMASC, Minutes, June 20, 1930; CMANC, *Proc.,* XXIV (1930), 50, 92.

[31] Sloan to D. Comer (with enclosure), January 3, 1931, Comer MSS.

when CTI held its annual meeting in October, 1930, subscriptions had been received from mills operating a total of 22,971,800 spindles. About two-thirds of the spindles in place or three-fourths of the active equipment in the industry was thus adhering to the new program. Of the equipment not covered by the agreement, 2,250,000 spindles were in Massachusetts, where state laws effectively prevented mills from operating any shift longer than forty-eight hours. Another 1,500,000 spindles were in other New England states where most of the mills were already operating fewer hours than 55–50.[32] By January, 1931, over 80 per cent of the capacity of the mills making such major products as fine goods, print cloths, sheeting (wide and narrow), and carded yarn had subscribed.[33]

Still, 55–50 was at best a stopgap measure. In the North, 57 mills (4,443,097 spindles), and in the South, 224 mills (4,522,914 spindles) still rejected CTI's argument that stability could best be achieved through the 55–50 plan. Furthermore, New England management complained that even if all of the mills subscribed, the program would not cut production enough to be of any help.[34] Another argument against 55–50 came from Worth Street. As inventories began to pile up in the fall of 1930, prices again dipped lower. The telegrams from commission merchants and the market reports in the *Daily News Record* told the same story: more restrictive measures were needed before prices could be stabilized.[35]

Elimination of night work for women and children was obviously the answer.[36] In September, 1930, CTI's Executive Committee approved a program seeking to "eliminate, as soon as

[32] Halstead to D. Comer, April 1, 1930, Comer MSS; Sloan, *Fourth Annual Report,* pp. 14–15.

[33] Sloan to D. Comer, January 3, 1931, Comer MSS.

[34] *Ibid.;* NACM, *Trans.,* CXXVIII (1930), 86–96, 123–125.

[35] Letter of C. A. Cannon to G. A. Sloan, July 18, 1930; Letter of G. A. Sloan to C. A. Cannon, July 21, 1930; both in Sloan MSS; Anderson to Sloan, August 29, 1930; Letter of W. D. Anderson to C. A. Cannon, September 1, 1930; Letter of W. D. Anderson to T. M. Marchant, September 2, 1930; Letter of [W. D. Hines?] to J. R. Millar, November 6, 1930; all four in Comer MSS.

[36] Letter of Comer to Cotton-Textile Institute, May 28, 1930, in Comer MSS.

possible and not later than March 1, 1931, the employment of women and minors under 18 years of age between the hours of 9 p.m. and 6 a.m." After sounding out the Board of Directors, CTI was able to push ahead, assured of the support of one-third of the industry.[37]

Like 55–50, the night-work program was built around subscription agreements which were carefully designed to assure each subscriber that a significant and growing number of his competitors were joining the movement. According to the subscription blanks, the plan would go into effect only if 75 per cent of the industry's spindles and 75 per cent of the night runners (defined as mills "that have run at night at any time during the last two years or are now equipped to run at night") had signed by March 1, 1931. By the following year 80 per cent must have subscribed; 85 per cent was the target for March 1, 1933. If an individual executive chose to—and most did—he could be even more cautious. He could make his signature contingent upon CTI's receiving support from these same percentages of the spindleage within his particular product group. Thus, it would be necessary for the Institute to sign 75 per cent of the spindles and 75 per cent of the night runners in, say, the carded-yarn group before the agreement in that group would become effective.[38]

Sloan and Hines argued against these restrictions. They feared that the entire plan might capsize if they were unable to win enough subscriptions in merely one of the groups. But the manufacturers on the Board and Executive Committee insisted that the restrictions be kept; they were unwilling to get entangled in such a formidable program unless they were assured that most of their competitors would follow suit.[39]

When the night-work proposal was introduced at the annual meeting in 1930, CTI began at once to play a numbers game that was to dominate the Institute's activities for the next two years. The members in attendance voted overwhelmingly in favor of the proposal. That meant that 14,067,734 spindles were behind the

[37] P. B. Halstead, Letter to Members of the Board of Directors, September 13, 1930; CTI, Minutes, Board of Directors, September 24, 1930; W. D. Hines, Letter to Members of the Board of Directors, October 1, 1930; all in Comer MSS.

[38] CTI, Minutes, Executive Committee, October 14, 1930; CTI, Minutes, Board of Directors, October 14, 1930; Halstead to D. Comer (with enclosure), October 25, 1930, Comer MSS.

[39] CTI, Minutes, Board of Directors, September 24, 1930, Comer MSS.

plan, but many more were needed to reach the goal of 75 per cent by March 1, 1931. Before the meeting adjourned Hines announced that a number of companies not represented had assured him they were backing the plan. With their subscriptions, he said, they would have 20,975,682 spindles (5,885,843 in the night classification) enrolled.[40]

Progress toward the first bench mark, 75 per cent, was initially very swift. Sixty-five per cent of the active machinery in the industry was under agreement by the middle of November; by Christmas 70 per cent was covered.[41] Then, however, the association began to encounter the bedrock of nonconformers. In the South there were a significant number of executives who still wanted nothing to do with the Institute. A surprisingly large number of northern executives also stood aloof. Many of these manufacturers said that it would be nice to eliminate night work for women and children so long as it was done later or in some other way. For the moment, however, they were unwilling to do anything.

CTI hammered away at this resistance, using all of the techniques that had been developed for 55–50. The staff and officers spoke at meetings of the various product groups.[42] Lists of non-subscribers were circulated among the Institute's directors, who were asked to make personal appeals to their recalcitrant colleagues.[43] Once again the state and regional associations stood beside CTI; newsletters, such as the ACMA *Gazette,* lauded cooperation and condemned "unorganized communities and selfish individualism."[44] With all of its chips riding on this one hand, CTI played harder than it ever had before. There was an intensity, a

---

[40] CTI, Minutes of the Annual Meeting, October 15, 1930; G. A. Sloan, Letter to Cotton Mill Executives, October 17, 1930, in Comer MSS. On the basis of these figures, about 68 per cent of the active equipment (about 62 per cent of the equipment in place) was supporting the plan.

[41] Halstead, Letter to Cotton Mill Executives, November 18, 1930; Halstead to D. Comer, December 26, 1930; both in Comer MSS.

[42] G. A. Sloan, Memorandum for Board of Directors, October 1, 1930; Sloan to D. Comer, January 3, 1931; D. Comer to Hines, January 16, 1931; all three in Comer MSS. ACMA, *Gazette No. 34* (November, 1930), in McLaurine Papers.

[43] Sloan to D. Comer, October 29, 1930 (with enclosure), and January 3, 1931, in Comer MSS.

[44] ACMA, *Gazette No. 34;* ACMA, *Gazette No. 35* (December, 1930), in McLaurine Papers. CTI had several field agents who visited mills in an effort to persuade management to sign the subscription blanks; Letter of P. B. H[alstead] to G. A. Sloan, January 14, 1931, in Comer MSS.

fervor that had been lacking in the Institute's previous efforts. When one of the producers who had refused to sign escaped on vacation to Michigan, CTI's emissaries tracked him into the northern woods, shooting out more arguments in favor of cooperation.[45]

As the campaign became heated, the association leaders made a series of extremely significant decisions. They decided, repeatedly, to venture outside the industry for assistance in establishing their authority. This clearly marked the difference between CTI and the earlier forms of association; only a semi-autonomous or policy-shaping institution could draw heavily upon external help in disciplining its own members. This innovation was particularly revealing in light of the historical context out of which the association movement had emerged. As we saw in an earlier chapter, a major force behind the association movement in cotton textiles was the pressure exerted by political reform groups. One of the results of this pressure was a strong desire on the part of manufacturers to draw together for mutual protection; they felt the need to present a firm, united front to their enemies. Within their trade associations they worked hard to preserve a façade of unanimity, concealing within their group the dissenting opinions that might have comforted their opponents. An important break with tradition was made when CTI began repeatedly and systematically to use institutions outside the industry to force the manufacturers into line on the night-work plan.

One of the outside forces used by the association leaders was the newspaper. George Sloan wrote to a number of editors, explaining the Institute's problem and the need for additional support in the night-work campaign. He found a receptive audience. The cooperators were applauded; the non-subscribers found themselves condemned roundly in such southern newspapers as the Birmingham *Age Herald* (Alabama) and the Atlanta *Constitution* (Georgia).[46] In a typical editorial, the *Constitution* announced that it was

[45] D. Comer to G. A. Sloan, March 2, 1931; also see W. D. Hines and G. A. Sloan, Copy of Telegram, February 19, 1931; both in Comer MSS.

[46] *Atlanta Constitution*, December 4, 1930; *Birmingham Age Herald* (Alabama), February 14, 1931; northern editorial support for CTI came from the *New York Evening Telegram*, February 16, 17, 18, 19, 20, and 21, 1931; the *Boston Transcript*, March 14, 1931; and the *New Bedford Standard* (Massachusetts), March 15, 1931.

. . . unthinkable that any small group of backward, selfish and narrow-minded mill executives should by insisting upon the continuance of the system which has been a sore spot on the industry for so many years, block the full fruition of the benefits which would accrue from the complete elimination of night work for women and children.

The first step towards forcing them to come into line should come from the leaders, and the people generally, of the communities where such mills are located, and The Constitution earnestly bespeaks such co-operation for the constructive and far-sighted leaders of the industry who are liberally giving of their time and money to make the campaign a complete success.[47]

Sloan also published in various papers the names of the mills which had already subscribed.[48]

Further support from outside the industry came from the very kind of reform organization that the service associations had fought in the earlier days. The League of Women Voters endorsed the night-work program, as did the National Consumers League. CTI also won the backing of the Southern Council on Women in Industry, a group which was closely aligned with the United States Department of Labor.[49]

The association leaders turned to the federal government for aid, and President Hoover's Administration threw its weight behind the new program. The formal ties that developed between the association and the government at this stage were a natural outgrowth of the cooperative arrangements that had been taking shape since the early 1900's. Nevertheless, Hoover's policies constituted a dramatic acknowledgment and extension of the alliance that was being forged between the federal government and the business institutions dedicated to stability, cooperation, and control.

With Sloan's guidance, Hoover and the Department of Com-

[47] *Atlanta Constitution*, March 22, 1931.

[48] Sloan to D. Comer, December 24, 1930, Comer MSS.

[49] *Charlotte Observer*, October 31, 1932; Letter of D. Comer to Mrs. L. B. Tunstall, January 16, 1931; Southern Council on Women and Children in Industry, Report, Suggestions, and Bibliography of Lucy R. Mason, March 9, 1931; both in Comer MSS; the National Women's Party opposed the program on the grounds that it discriminated against women; Letter of CTI to Mr. Fred C. Croxton (with enclosure), August 17, 1931, in Comer MSS.

merce helped to whip the non-cooperators into line. CTI's leaders
stayed in close contact with the Department, and in early 1931
Sloan called for help.[50] He was having trouble persuading some of
the mills to join. Would the Administration help him? The answer
came in the form of a conference between Sloan, President
Hoover, and Secretary of Commerce Lamont. After the meeting,
Sloan announced to the press that "the President had evinced deep
interest in the type of cooperative work being done by the cotton
textile industry and was particularly impressed with the constructive efforts to stabilize employment for men and women through
the new tendency to concentrate normal operations on the day
shift. He wished for the movement every success, especially in view
of its humanitarian aspects."[51] Secretary Lamont gave even more
direct aid. He sent personal letters to leading northern and
southern manufacturers, expressing the Administration's firm support of the plan. His letters closed with an assurance that "the
President and all of us here are greatly interested in the progress
that has been made, and we wish for the plan every success."[52]

With the combined force of its own resources and the prestige
and power of its allies outside the industry, CTI bore down heavily
upon the cotton manufacturers who had not signed. By January
14, 1931, almost twenty-three million spindles (85 per cent of the
spindles in the North; 63 per cent of the spindles in the South)
had been subscribed. As the March 1 deadline approached, Sloan
was still searching for signatures.[53]

With only a day to spare, CTI filled its first quota. At the last
moment a group of mills concentrated around Gastonia, North

[50] Sloan, Memorandum for Board of Directors, October 1, 1930; Sloan to
D. Comer, October 17, 1930; Sloan to Lamont, October 31, 1930; Letter of
R. P. Lamont to G. A. Sloan, November 3, 1930; all in Comer MSS.

[51] Sloan to D. Comer, January 14 and February 10, 1931, Comer MSS;
G. A. Sloan to Herbert Hoover, February 9, 1931, in RG 40, 87481, Box 675,
NA; *Textile World,* LXXIX, No. 1 (February 21, 1931), 881.

[52] Letter of R. P. Lamont to T. M. Marchant, February 12, 1931; Letter of
R. P. Lamont to Henry F. Lippitt, February 12, 1931; Sloan to Lamont,
February 16, 1931; all in RG 40, 87481, Box 675, NA.

[53] H[alstead] to Sloan, January 14, 1931; D. Comer to Alfred Moore,
February 19, 1931; both in Comer MSS.

Carolina, pledged their support. That gave the Institute 83 per cent of the entire industry and 79 per cent of the "night runners," enough to clear the first hurdle. In at least one of the product groups, three-quarters of the night operators did not sign; but among the mills turning out most of the industry's major products at least 75 per cent of the total spindles and 75 per cent of the equipment on night work were covered by the new dispensation.[54]

There was, however, no time to rest after this final drive to meet the deadline. The Institute's staff and officers could not relax their pressure because there was a constant threat that the program's fragile authority would break down. Subscribing mills kept a wary eye on their competitors. The cooperators watched with discomfort as the remaining non-subscribers continued night operations with their regular labor force. Rumor and fancy blended with fact, spreading distrust throughout the industry.[55] In an effort to counter the rumors and to preserve the industry's confidence, CTI's field agents began to police the agreement, surveying the subscribing mills at first hand and reporting back to the association. Then CTI circularized the members, announcing that almost 100 per cent of the mills were remaining faithful to their declaration of policy. During 1931 CTI managed to hold the line and in fact was able to dredge up a few new subscriptions.[56]

As the March, 1932 deadline approached, CTI again threw its program into high gear.[57] During this phase of the campaign particular attention was focused upon two of the product groups:

[54] Telegram of W. D. Hines and G. A. Sloan to D. Comer, February 28, 1931; Sloan to D. Comer, December 4, 1931; both in Comer MSS; [G. A. Sloan], Draft of Letter to Lawrence O. Hammett, *ca.* November 14, 1931, in Dorr MSS.

[55] Sloan to D. Comer, July 29 and October 5 and 9, 1931; D. Comer to Sloan, October 7, 1931; D. Comer to Jas. C. Self, September 28 and October 2 and 7, 1931; all in Comer MSS.

[56] G. A. Sloan, Special Memorandum for Mill Executives, April 2, 1931; CTI, Minutes, Executive Committee, May 20, 1931; both in Comer MSS; G. A. Sloan, *Fifth Annual Report of the President of the Cotton-Textile Institute, Inc.* (1931), p. 5.

[57] D. Comer to Sloan, October 14, 1931; Halstead to D. Comer, February 2, 1932; Letter of D. Comer to P. B. Halstead, February 4, 1932; G. A. Sloan, Draft of Letter, *ca.* February 20, 1932; Telegram of Sloan to D. Comer, February 25, 1932; all in Comer MSS; ACMA, *Proc.,* XXXV (1931), 21–22, 31; CMAG, *Report,* XXXI (1931), 94.

print cloth and narrow sheeting.[58] Both of these groups had special problems due to the adamant opposition of a few of the major producers. Furthermore, it was necessary to achieve the 80 per cent mark in these groups because their products—particularly print cloth—were felt to have a special influence upon the level of prices in the Worth Street market.[59]

With the help of the Hoover Administration, CTI battered away at the nonconformers in these two product groups. Again and again CTI called on the executive branch for help. In November, 1931, the Department of Commerce sidestepped Sloan's request, but in early 1932, the administration once more threw its prestige behind the night-work plan.[60] In January the Secretary of Commerce called a special conference for government officials, a group of prominent bankers, and some of the nation's leading textile manufacturers. Included among the manufacturers were a few of the key non-cooperators; in fact, the entire meeting seems to have been arranged to persuade these particular executives to subscribe to the industry-wide agreement. It was helpful to have the bankers there because they might be able to convince the recalcitrant minority that the institutions which controlled the vital flow of credit to their firms were backing CTI's plan for stabilization.[61] At the meeting Lamont told his visitors that the government wanted stability; Hoover wanted the night-work plan to succeed.[62]

[58] CTI was now making full use of newspaper support. Sloan to D. Comer (with enclosures), February 11, 1932; Letter of G. A. Sloan to Colonel Wade H. Harris [editor of the *Charlotte Observer*], February 11, 1932; both in Comer MSS. In his Letter to Comer, Sloan included clippings from the following: *Gastonia Gazette* (North Carolina), October 22 and 28, 1931, November 27, 1931, and January 16, 1932; the *Concord Tribune* (North Carolina), November 2, 1931; the *Charlotte Observer*, December 3, 1931; the *Augusta Chronicle*, December 27, 1931.

[59] Sloan to D. Comer, February 11 and 20, 1932, Comer MSS.

[60] *United States Daily* (Washington, D.C.), August 14, 1931, in Comer MSS; Letter of G. A. Sloan to J. Klein, November 9, 1931; Letter of J. Klein to G. A. Sloan, November 11, 1931; both in RG 40, 87481, Box 675, NA.

[61] In regard to the influence of the bankers see the Letter of Benjamin D. Riegel to R. C.[sic] Lamont, January 27, 1932, in RG 40, 83057, Box 546, NA.

[62] Telegram of R. P. Lamont to G. A. Sloan, January 22, 1932, in Sloan MSS; G. A. Sloan, Special Memorandum, January 26, 1932; letter of D. Comer to Frederick O. Tyler, February 1, 1932; D. Comer to Sloan, March 3, 1932; all three in Comer MSS; Sloan told Herbert Hoover that Lamont "struck exactly the right note in his appeal for sound cooperation." Sloan to Hoover,

There was apparently no direct pressure applied, just a subtle hint from the President of the United States and a few of the nation's leading bankers.[63]

By March 1, 1932, the second bench mark had been reached, even though the final, crucial subscriptions had been exceptionally hard to get. In the print-cloth and narrow-sheeting groups, the percentages among the night runners were only 80.3 per cent and 80 per cent respectively, and there is some reason to believe that CTI fudged a bit to get the figures this high.[64] Nevertheless, for the moment the plan was intact.

By this time the Institute had broken the resistance of most of the lukewarm opponents of cooperation and control. CTI had gathered into the fold most of those executives who had admitted that the night-work policy was desirable but had said that it could not be adopted at that time by their particular mill. Against this sort of opposition, CTI's brand of social pressure was rather effective. Most of the temporizers had folded by early 1932.[65]

Now CTI stood nose to nose with the industry's ardent competitors. The nonconformers, the hard core of competitors, simply rejected both the ends and means of the trade association. They were still dedicated to individualism, to competition. They were not about to accept CTI's promise of industrial stability.[66] Who were these nonconformers? What were their characteristics? How long had they been in business? What size firm did they represent? To answer these and other questions we must take a closer look at this important group of manufacturers. By limiting the inquiry to southern mills, we can avoid regional differences

January 27, 1932, in RG 40, 87481, Box 675, NA; Lamont's correspondence in regard to this conference is available in RG 40, 83057, Box 546, NA.

[63] Telegram of Lamont to Sloan, February 24, 1932; Telegram of R. P. Lamont to D. Comer, February 25, 1932; Letter of Elliott Springs to R. P. Lamont, March 1, 1932; all in RG 40, 87481, Box 675, NA.

[64] G. A. Sloan, Memorandum to Cotton Mill Executives, March 1, 1932, in Comer MSS.

[65] Halstead to [D. Comer?], 1930, in Comer MSS.

[66] When asked to subscribe, one such executive refused and explained that "his idea was a further reduction of wages, to operate day and night and make goods just as cheap as he could." D. Comer to Hines, January 16, 1931, Comer MSS.

and get a more meaningful profile of the companies which refused to cooperate with CTI.

About 131 firms in the southern Piedmont can be classified as ardent nonconformers. These firms consistently rejected cooperative programs; they were not members of the Institute; they had refused to join 55–50 in 1930. Later in that same year they had turned their back on the night-work program. Although the pressure to join became intense during the following year, they refused to agree to eliminate night work for women and minors.[67]

At first glance there appear to be no distinctive characteristics for the entire group, but when median figures are determined for the nonconformers, a pattern begins to emerge. It becomes even clearer when the nonconformers are compared to another group of southern mills which consistently supported CTI—the cooperators. The cooperators were members of CTI; in 1930 they were the first mills to join the 55–50 program. Later they signed subscription blanks which pledged their support for the night-work plan. During the hard times of 1931 they continued to honor their pledges.

When the nonconformers (131 firms) and the cooperators (275 firms) are compared statistically, it quickly becomes evident that the mills in the former group are relatively small. The median firm among the nonconformers falls into the 10,001 to 15,000 spindle range, while for the cooperators the median is in the 20,001 to 25,000 range. The majority of the mills in the nonconformer group (and 44 per cent of their spindleage) comes from small companies operating 30,000 spindles or less; among the cooperators, a majority of the firms (but only 23 per cent of the

[67] All of the information on support for 55–50 and for the night-work plan came from the following: CTI, List of mills that have not signed 55–50 declaration of policy, June 9, 1930; CTI, List of mills that have signed 55–50 declaration of policy, June 9, 1930; CTI, List of mills that have signed night-work declaration of policy, October 17, 1930; CTI, Supplementary List of mills that have signed declaration of policy regarding elimination of night work for women and minors, November 3, 1930; CTI, List of mills that have not signed night-work declaration, November 3, 1930, and December 17, 1930; CTI, List of mills indicating conformity to elimination of night employment of women and of minors, February 28, 1931; all in Comer MSS. All of the data on spindles, age of the firm, management groups, age of the management, firms still in business in 1936, and location of the firm is taken from annual editions of *Davison's Textile Blue Book* (New York: Davison Publishing Co., 1916–1936).

spindleage) falls into the small-mill classification. In the entire group of nonconformers only 5 per cent of the companies (8 per cent for the cooperators) and 26 per cent of the spindleage (37 per cent for the cooperators) fits into the large mill category (over 100,000 spindles).

The contrast between the size of the nonconformers and the cooperators becomes sharper if the various firms which had interlocking directorates are grouped together. This is necessary because many southern manufacturers controlled a number of separate corporations. It seems to have been common in the South to expand operations by creating new corporations instead of merely adding to the existing companies. Thus, Elliot White Springs controlled several companies which were not consolidated into a single corporation until 1933. For the purposes of our statistical study, however, it is helpful to group all of these mills and to compare the nonconformers and cooperators again. When this is done, the median among the nonconformers still falls into the 10,001 to 15,000 spindle range, but among the cooperators the median is the mill or combine of 25,001 to 30,000 spindles. With this new classification, 57 per cent of the spindleage of the cooperators and only 41 per cent of the spindleage of the nonconformers comes from mills or combines with over 100,000 spindles; again, the contrast between the two groups is heightened by taking interlocking directorates into consideration.

The nonconformers also had been in business for a shorter period of time than the cooperators. The average age of the firm for the nonconformers was 18.8 years, while for the cooperators the figure was 25.9 years. One would anticipate that the smaller mills of the nonconformers would be younger, but almost the same pattern emerges when mills of comparable size in the two classifications are compared. The small- and medium-sized mills in the nonconformer group are, for instance, generally younger than the small- and medium-sized mills among the cooperators. Only in the large-mill category does the opposite prove true. For the most part, however, it was the newer—as well as the smaller—companies which rejected CTI's promise of stability.

In addition to the firms being younger, the management in the nonconformer class was newer. This is significant because the older firms in the cooperator group might have recently acquired new managers; in a sense they would have then become new firms

160 COMPETITION AND COOPERATION

insofar as their management was concerned. This was not the case, however. In the nonconformer class, the managers of 1931 had been operating their firms for an average of 6.8 years. The managers of the cooperator mills, on the other hand, had been in control of their mills for an average of 8.2 years. About 23 per cent of the managers in the cooperator class had been in office since 1919; the comparable figure for the nonconformers was 16 per cent.

Figures for size, age of the firm, and age of the management provide a more meaningful pattern than does the data on location within the South. One would expect to find a considerably larger percentage of the cooperators coming from the upper South, where the industry was older and production costs slightly higher than they were in the lower South. State regulations in the upper South also tended to be slightly more stringent. In both cases, however, about 65 per cent of the spindleage came from the upper South, from North and South Carolina; slightly over 14 per cent came from Georgia in each group. The only significant difference was in the number of spindles drawn from Alabama; here the industry was of much more recent vintage, and the mills apparently had a cost advantage over their competitors in the Carolinas. It is not surprising to find 13 per cent of the nonconformers' spindleage coming from Alabama, while for the cooperators, 8.3 per cent of the spindles came from this state.

The conclusions are fairly clear. The strongest support for CTI's programs and for the associative philosophy of stabilization, cooperation, and control tended to come from the older firms whose management had been in office for a relatively long time. These companies were generally larger than those in the nonconformer class. Management in the cooperator class seems to have had more to lose in the industry's competitive struggle; instead of fighting for a place in the sun, they were trying to consolidate, to protect a position they had already won—a position they had held for a number of years. Due to their firms' greater size and age, they would naturally be more inclined to accept the long-range viewpoint that CTI was promoting. Managers who had been in control of their firms for a relatively long period of time could be expected to be conservative about the risks of competition.

The bitter opponents of cooperation, on the other hand, tended to be the managers of younger and smaller firms. They had been in control of their companies for a relatively short period of time. The nonconformers had less to risk and more to gain from competition. From the vantage point of a small mill in Alabama, it was no doubt very difficult to take the industry-wide outlook that CTI was promoting. To the smaller and newer producer, a competitive struggle for a larger share of the market must have seemed more reasonable than a plan to stabilize production. Sharp price competition had been the key to past southern growth, and the nonconformers could apparently see no reason to reject the Darwinian philosophy of survival of the fittest.

Paradoxically, in terms of survival it did not seem to matter too much whether a firm cooperated or not. Five years later, in 1936, 81 per cent of the cooperators were still in business, as were 77 per cent of the nonconformers. In looking at mills of a comparable size the same is true; the survival rates for the small, medium, and large cooperators were 75 per cent, 91 per cent, and 95 per cent respectively; figures for the same groups of nonconformers were 75 per cent, 88 per cent, and 83 per cent. The latter figures suggest that at least a few of the nonconformers chose their course of action because they were under greater financial strain than the cooperators. Without supporting statistics on income, however, it is impossible to determine how many of the nonconformers were in a particularly weak or an unusually strong competitive position. Some contemporary observers felt that the latter was the case with a few of the leading nonconformers, but this conclusion remains at best tentative.[68]

A more satisfying conclusion can be reached with regard to the nonconformers' reaction to CTI's program. Most of the executives in this group resented intensely the pressures that the Institute imposed upon them.[69] Most outspoken and colorful of the nonconformers was Colonel Springs of Lancaster, South Carolina. During the First World War, Springs had been an ace combat pilot. After returning home, he had found it impossible to settle down to the business of running his father's cotton mills. He tried his hand as a writer, turning out several popular books, but much

---

[68] For a contemporary opinion that a number of the nonconformers were in a very strong competitive position see Letter of Riegel to Lamont, January 27, 1932, in RG 40, 83057, Box 546, NA. The same idea—which strikes the author as being a very reasonable interpretation—is advanced in the Memo of V. S. von Szeliski to Leon Henderson, August 4, 1934, in GR 61, Franklin D. Roosevelt Library (Hyde Park, New York); hereafter cited as RL.

[69] See, for instance, the angry Letter of L. O. Hammett to G. A. Sloan, March 30, 1932, in Comer MSS.

of his energy was devoted to the traditional escapades of the prodigal son. Finally, in the early thirties he calmed down enough to take over the family's business interests. Perhaps "calmed down" is not really the best expression; when Springs took over the mills he poured into his business the same intense energy that had thus far been channeled into his life as a southern playboy.[70]

Elliot Springs was an exciting and excitable man who flatly rejected the Institute's promise of economic stability. He was interested in growth, not stability. Some years later he described what he felt were the three kinds of cotton manufacturers:

> . . . one type attends all conventions, sits on the platforms of all banquets, and will always agree to shut down for the good of the industry. . . . [Another variety] runs his plant at capacity until his warehouse is full of cloth and his office full of bankers. Then he tries to get rid of them by selling all his goods in one day . . . [but] the market breaks right in his fancy face. Then he makes speeches about cutthroat competition and . . . greedy competitors. He clamors for everyone else to shut down. . . .
>
> Lastly, there is the Bastard, First Class. He runs his mills twenty-four hours a day, six days in the week, fifty-two weeks in the year. When he goes to New York he lunches alone at the Automat. . . . He makes the finest cloth in the market, because, if he did not, the customers would reject every yard of it. He has never curtailed for the good of the industry. . . .
>
> Join me [Springs added] at the Automat for lunch someday.[71]

Against this kind of opposition, CTI's programs were ineffective.[72] So long as the spindles and looms of the nonconformers continued to pour out yarn and cloth, heedless of the "emergency curtailments," the statistical reports, 55–50, or the night-work plan, CTI's authority in the industry was extremely tenuous. Other manufacturers joined the program, but they were constantly looking over their shoulders at men like Springs.

---

[70] *Daily News Record,* October 16, 1959; Hammond, "The Cotton Industry of This Century," pp. 222, 224.

[71] *Fortune,* XLI, No. 1 (January, 1950), 66. On March 13, 1931, Springs announced to the press that the night-work plan was "not humanity—it's bunk"; Sloan to D. Comer (with enclosure), March 16, 1931, Comer MSS.

[72] At times Springs' position was not entirely clear; it is possible that he actually subscribed for two of his mills in 1932. Springs to Lamont, March 1, 1932; Letter of R. P. Lamont to E. W. Springs, March 4, 1932; both in RG 40, 87481, Box 675, NA.

Despite the opposition of the nonconformers, CTI continued its drive to cut production, increase demand, and stabilize prices. While 55–50 and the night-work plan held center stage, the association kept plugging away at its core programs of statistical exchange, cost accounting, and new uses. Each of these programs continued to evolve, following the same general patterns of development established during the previous three years: that is, CTI's role as a central agency in the industry was gradually strengthened.

The New Uses Division threw more resources into its seemingly hopeless battle against the industry's shrinking markets. In 1929 and 1930 over a quarter of a million dollars was poured into the Institute's advertising campaign for styled cotton fabrics. This was an impressive exercise in industry-wide cooperation; it was the closest that any of the organizations in cotton textiles had come to matching the advertising campaigns of the large corporations in other industries.[73] While this was being done, the New Uses Division pressed forward with the other phases of its program, particularly the work that it was doing in collaboration with the government. Hand in hand with the Departments of Agriculture and Commerce, the association searched for new outlets for cotton fabrics; in 1930 CTI inaugurated National Cotton Week with the official blessing of the Hoover Administration. Even though money for these promotional efforts was hard to obtain, the New Uses Division strengthened its program in the early thirties.[74]

As the depression deepened, significant qualitative changes took place in the open-price and cost-accounting plans. CTI's cost-accounting program became more and more aggressive. Using its field agents, the Institute conducted frequent surveys of the mills' accounting techniques and pushed ahead with the laborious work of installing cost systems.[75] In its frequent communications with

[73] Letter of G. A. Sloan to John Holt, July 22, 1930, in Sloan MSS; ACMA, *Gazette No. 31* (March, 1930), in McLaurine Papers; ACMA, *Proc.,* XXXIV (1930), 65–66.

[74] Halstead to D. Comer, February 24, 1931; G. A. Sloan, Letter to All Members, May 9, 1931; CTI, Minutes, Board of Directors, May 20, 1931; G. A. Sloan, Letter to Board of Directors, December 8, 1931; all in Comer MSS; Letter of G. A. Sloan to J. M. Gamewell, July 22, 1930, in Sloan MSS; Sloan, *Fifth Annual Report,* pp. 35–39; ACMA, *Proc.,* XXXV (1931), 34–35; XXXVII (1933), 26; XXXVIII (1934), 55.

[75] Letter of Sydney P. Munroe to D. Comer, January 6, 1931; CTI, Minutes, Board of Directors, May 20, 1931; CTI, Minutes, Executive Committee, March 24, 1932; all in Comer MSS; Sloan, *Fourth Annual Report,* pp. 16–17; Sloan, *Fifth Annual Report,* pp. 24–26.

the mills, CTI's analyses and recommendations became ever more specific. By the summer of 1932 the Institute's cost engineer was using detailed statistics to illustrate to the mills that they would lose less money by closing down than they would by continuing to sell goods at current prices.[76] A similar emphasis upon prices began to appear in the statistical work. The association made repeated suggestions as to how present and future production policies would affect prices. And when the mills were unable to turn a favorable statistical position into better prices, CTI started to bear down on the need to resist sales at unprofitable prices. In November, 1931, a typical memorandum to one of the members pointed out that "in accepting future business mills have continued to allow buyers to dictate prices in the face of every statistical reason for a seller's market with a fair profit. Unless the mill executives and their selling agents offer a greater resistance to this constant draining of mill assets, we can see nothing ahead but continued market demoralization."[77] By the spring of 1932 Sloan was advising all of the manufacturers in one product group to "refuse to sell their present production, and particularly their future output, at present yarn prices which are lower than any which have been recorded in many years."[78] As these dispatches reveal, CTI had moved far from its original position that price stability would result from giving the mills full information, allowing each to see the wisdom of avoiding overproduction. Now the association felt compelled to advise the mills what, specifically, their price and production policies should be. CTI had moved a long way down the road leading to central control of the industry. The depression and the association's continued difficulties made further progress along that route virtually inevitable.

[76] S. P. Munroe, Letters to: the Executives of Carded Yarn Mills, October 28, 1930; Cotton Mill Executives, March 31, 1931; Carded Yarn Mill Executives, November 12, 1931 (similar letters were sent to the narrow-sheetings, print-cloth and flat-duck mills at this time); Letter of S. P. Munroe to All Carded Yarn Mill Executives, July 8, 1932; all in Comer MSS.

[77] Sloan to D. Comer, June 24, July 3, October 10, and November 13, 1931; G. A. Sloan, Press Releases, June 24, 1931, and March 21, 1932; Letter of G. A. Sloan to All Carded Yarn Mill Executives, May 7, 1932; Letter of G. A. Sloan to Wide Sheetings Group, March 11, 1932; G. A. Sloan, Confidential Memorandum to the Board of Directors, May 9, 1932; all in Comer MSS; ACMA, *Proc.*, XXXVI (1932), 94.

[78] Sloan to All Carded Yarn Mill Executives, May 7, 1932, Comer MSS.

It is hard to avoid the conclusions that CTI had fully explored the possibilities of voluntary cooperation and that, judged in terms of its own primary goal, the association had failed. From the historian's vantage point—thirty years after the event—this seems obvious. The Institute had attempted to stabilize prices and profits; but the available statistics suggest that CTI's various programs had made a negligible economic impact, if, indeed, they had had any aggregate effect at all. As Tables 9–12 (below) show, prices declined and the manufacturers' margin on cotton goods became tighter and tighter. Even more revealing are the statistics on income. During the years 1930–1932, the entire industry operated at a total net loss of over two hundred million dollars. Under these conditions, management could hardly afford to lose orders because of the cooperative programs, and many of the mills continued night work by simply using an all-male night shift. The high rate of unemployment made it unlikely that any of the mills could not find a sufficient work force to handle any available orders.[79]

With the advantage of hindsight, one can see that the association's situation was almost hopeless. The Institute could exert no influence on the nonconformers and only a slight influence on its own members. To stabilize prices it would have been necessary for the organization to exercise tight control over the production of virtually all of the mills, and without some kind of binding, government authority, that sort of control was out of CTI's reach. By 1932 the association leaders and many of the manufacturers were ready to accept this conclusion and to abandon voluntarism.

It was thus likely that the next major step would involve a political solution and that CTI would act as spokesman for the industry. Between 1929 and 1932 the Institute had quietly but steadily strengthened its role as political and organizational representative for the entire cotton textile industry. When a general arbitration council of the textile industry was organized, the Institute was given primary responsibility for protecting the manufacturer's interests.[80] When the cotton textile merchants introduced

[79] CTI, Minutes, Executive Committee, June 16, 1932, Comer MSS; Sloan, *Sixth Annual Report*, p. 4.

[80] Letter of G. A. Sloan to Our Members, June 2, 1931, in Comer MSS; ACMA, *Gazette No. 34;* ACMA, *Proc.,* XL (1936), 125–126; NACM, *Trans.,* CXXIX (1930), 288.

TABLE 9

CAPACITY, COTTON TEXTILES, 1930–1932

	1930	1931	1932
Active spindles			
U.S.............	31,245,078	28,979,646	27,271,938
New England....	11,351,290	9,655,114	8,565,978
South..........	18,585,878	18,073,208	17,629,524
all other........	1,307,910	1,251,324	1,076,436

NOTE: The data on capacity is from U. S., Bureau of the Census, *Bulletin 179, Cotton Production and Distribution, Season of 1941–42* (Washington, 1942), p. 31.

TABLE 10

PRODUCTION, COTTON TEXTILES, 1930–1932

	1930	1931	1932
Cotton consumed (bales)			
U.S...................	6,105,840	5,262,974	4,866,016
New England...........	1,142,730	936,741	677,462
South.................	4,749,179	4,147,573	4,033,351
all other..............	213,931	178,660	155,203
Spindle hours			
U.S...................	87,515,000	75,264,000	68,755,000
New England...........	23,038,000	18,757,000	13,260,000
South.................	61,878,000	54,483,000	53,613,000
all other..............	2,598,000	2,024,000	1,882,000

NOTE: All of the figures on production are for cotton years; the South includes all cotton-growing states; the bales are running bales. The figures on spindle hours are from U. S., Department of Commerce, *Statistical Abstract of the United States, 1933* (Washington, 1933), p. 742.

TABLE 11

PRICES AND MARGINS, COTTON TEXTILES, 1930–1932

	1930	1931	1932
Average cloth prices (¢/lb.)..............	29.71	22.35	15.69
Average manufacturers' margin (¢/lb.)....	13.19	12.17	9.43

NOTE: The price series and manufacturers' margin are not comparable to those given for the years 1923–1929; the figures for 1930–1932 are taken from Jules Backman and M. R. Gainsbrugh, *Economics of the Cotton Textile Industry*, p. 207.

TABLE 12

PROFITS, COTTON TEXTILES, 1930–1932

	1930	1931	1932
Net income	−$92,601,000	−$64,785,000	−$54,547,000
Profits (selected firms)			
North	−$12,258,000	−$13,084,000	−$13,336,000
South	−$13,616,000	−$5,276,000	−$3,436,000
Ratio of profits to receipts			
North	−7.58%	−9.42%	−13.87%
South	−4.15%	−1.99%	−1.63%
Ratio of profits to net worth			
North	−6.16%	−7.02%	−7.72%
South	−3.82%	−1.53%	−1.05%

NOTE: The figures on net income after taxes for all cotton manufacturing corporations are from U. S., Bureau of Internal Revenue, *Statistics of Income, 1930*, p. 232; *Statistics of Income, 1931*, p. 143; *Statistics of Income, 1932*, p. 149. In regard to the source and specific nature of the remaining data, see Chapter V, Tables 1–4.

a standard set of rules and a standard form of sales note in the Worth Street market, it was once again CTI that handled most of the negotiations for the mills.[81] Through its work with the Departments of Commerce and Agriculture and through its close contacts with President Hoover, CTI was beginning to be identified within and without the industry as the forceful voice of the nation's cotton manufacturers. By 1932, all that remained to be done was to change the by-laws so that CTI could become the official as well as the unofficial representative for the industry.[82]

By the summer of 1932 CTI had emerged as a fully developed policy-shaping association. In the three hard years of the Great Depression, a number of important changes had taken place in the association; the significant characteristics of this type of institution now stood out very clearly. They involved: (1) a new relationship between the trade association and its members; (2) a new role for the association leader; and (3) a growing dependence upon the association's ally, the federal government.

As CTI matured as a business institution, its relationship to its members had changed considerably. For one thing, the Institute

[81] ACTMNY, *Twenty-Five Years*, pp. 38–44. CMASC, Minutes, June 26 and 27, 1931.

[82] Also see Sloan, *Fifth Annual Report*, pp. 43–46.

had been forced repeatedly to tighten its program. Initially it had attempted to achieve stability by organizing the industry and by insuring that each manufacturer would be able to base his decisions on full and accurate information. But the failure of that program had forced CTI to make specific recommendations about the mills' production policies. Through 55–50 and the night-work plan the association tried to impose a uniform and reduced production schedule on all of the mills. By 1932 CTI was also giving the manufacturers specific directives as to what their price policies should be. There was a relentless logic of control at work here. It thrust the association toward the position of centralized decision-maker for the industry.

In addition to tightening its controls, the association had begun for the first time to exert considerable pressure on its own members and on the nonconformers. This was a mark of CTI's maturity as a semi-autonomous business institution with its own values, its own leaders, and its own administrative techniques. To develop the pressure, the Institute relied in part upon the manufacturers who were already cooperating; further assistance, however, came from outside the industry—from newspapers, from reform organizations, and from the federal government. By utilizing outside support, the association leaders and the cooperators in effect indicated the extent of their dedication to the Institute's values. They were willing to sacrifice the appearance of unanimity, to give up the well-established principle that differences should be settled within their camp.

As the Institute's program evolved, it also became clear that one of the association leader's most important roles was to act as an intellectual broker, a middleman who arranged compromises. Among the members, the officers had to set up compromises between the various factions: between the northern and southern producers; between the mills in the upper and lower South; between the managers who wanted very tight controls and those who wanted only minimal restraints. The association leaders also negotiated vital compromises with the government. In a sense, the night-work program was a compromise between the association's desire to cut production and the government's (and the public's) desire to eliminate women and children from night operations. Both the government and the manufacturers sacrificed something to achieve this compromise: the government surrendered some of its traditional antitrust policy while the manufacturers gave up part of their opposition to social control of working conditions. Both sides also gained something. In this instance the association leaders had engineered a successful compromise. In the course of doing this they had helped to shape the content of public policy and business behavior.

Such a compromise paved the way for a closer alliance between the association and the government. Of course this alliance had been taking shape since the days of the service associations, but during Hoover's Administration, it took on a new form. Now the government was actively seeking economic stability and forcefully supporting CTI as one of the means of achieving that objective. While the two parties continued their joint efforts to develop new markets, government officials and the association leaders were now working hand in hand to impose CTI's plan for production control upon the manufacturers. Hoover lent his prestige to the night-work plan. Secretary of Commerce Lamont frequently threw the weight of his department against the nonconformers. Although still informal, this alliance between the trade association and the government had reached formidable proportions by 1932.[83]

The compromises and the association-government alliance had enabled CTI to explore fully the possibilities of relatively noncoercive association programs. It was unlikely that more social pressure would break the resistance of the nonconformers. That hardy bunch of competitors was not going to yield to anything short of a direct, legal exercise of political power. But, under existing laws, neither CTI nor the Hoover Administration could force the nonconformers to cooperate. The antitrust laws had been virtually nullified for CTI, but that was not enough. This modern stabilizing institution needed political power to make its programs work. That was the lesson that could be drawn from the Institute's experience in the early 1930's. Before a majority of the manufacturers could accept this conclusion, however, they needed to be jarred by one more crisis.

[83] On the basis of CTI's experience, I find it difficult to accept Robert F. Himmelberg's conclusion that Herbert Hoover and Secretary Lamont "sought to maintain rather than undermine, the competitive qualities of American business." Hoover had developed a new position which placed him between the old attitude, which favored unrestrained competition, and the cartelization policy that was to emerge under the New Deal. To determine exactly where Hoover stood on this issue, one must consider both his actions and his words—frequently they were at variance. Himmelberg, "Relaxation of the Federal Anti-Trust Policy," pp. 211–212.

Fall River:
Winter 1932

For Fall River the winter of 1932 was cold and dreary. In November the presidential campaign aroused some enthusiasm as well as some bitter jokes about Republican prosperity. But after the city gave Franklin D. Roosevelt an overwhelming majority of its votes there was nothing to do but sit out the icy winter. For the unemployed that was no simple task. Private charity helped, but private funds were no longer able to meet the city's demands. Fall River itself was bankrupt; it was, in fact, in the hands of a receiver—they called it the Board of Finance, but it was the same thing. It was a committee established by the state legislature in an effort to restore the city's finances. Fall River could not meet its debts.

The cotton textile industry which had piloted the city's growth was barely able to keep its head above water. Three of the mills which had been shut down started running again in November, but by that time it would have taken a miracle to restore Fall River's fortunes. Half of the city's spindles had already been liquidated. Between the stock market crash and 1932, seventeen mills had closed their doors for the last time. An industry which a few years before had employed 30,000 now had work for slightly over 9,000 mill hands. There were short-time and frequent layoffs for those who remained on the job.

By 1932 Fall River was discouraged What did the future hold for the city and its vital industry? The depression had begun here while the rest of the country was enjoying a prosperity unequaled in American history. Now the depression was nation-wide. Even a rapid recovery promised little for the city on the Taunton; recovery would only *spur the southern mills to produce more. Recovery would do nothing for the companies which had sold their machinery, emptied their granite-walled mills, and offered their property for rent. In the winter of 1932, a cloud of despair hung over Fall River and its empty mills. The theme song of this once proud city was filled with the notes of final defeat.*

Chapter VIII

The Institute and
the National
Industrial Recovery Act

"Make the difficult strange paths plain, and give to them the sense of victory as they walk through these baffling, challenging, bewildering days." Dr. L. R. Christie opened ACMA's annual convention in 1932 with these words.[1] His plea for help from above was addressed to a sympathetic audience of southern manufacturers. They and their northern brethren in the industry were indeed baffled, challenged, and bewildered. To their eyes the strange path ahead was not plain at all. Neither competition nor cooperation seemed to provide any solution to their problems. Perhaps some entirely new approach was needed, but they were not yet certain what that approach might be.

During the summer and early fall of 1932 a crisis took place within CTI against the background of a national depression that was reaching tragic proportions; the crisis convinced a majority of the members that through their association they should seek a political solution to their problems. Some of the manufacturers and all the association leaders had reached this conclusion before 1932. But for most of the members, that path became plain only after the Institute's program received a series of sharp blows which threatened to bring about the complete collapse of industry-wide cooperation.

[1] ACMA, *Proc.*, XXXV (1931), 22.

The crisis began in the spring of 1932. Inventories in most branches of the industry began to climb as orders fell off. Despite compliance with the night-work program, output exceeded demand, and the manufacturing margin dipped to a new low.[2] By this time almost 90 per cent of the industry was supporting the night-work agreement; but as CTI discovered, the policy was being nullified by mills which ran at night with an all-male shift. A survey of 712 southern mills revealed that although two and a half million spindles had abandoned night work entirely, 43 per cent of the industry's spindleage still normally used a second shift.[3] The mills which had abandoned night work were under intense pressure to cut unit costs by adopting a second shift. As one of the manufacturers explained to George Sloan:

> This whole question of night operation is worrying us a great deal and we can easily see that our own welfare is being rapidly injured by the increased operation at night on lines that we make. The truth of the matter is that the suggestion has been strongly made to me that it is going to be necessary for us to run our sheeting mills at night if we are going to fight the competition that is robbing us of our customers. . . . [Other large mills, he continued,] produce in sufficient volume at night to be most injurious to those of us who are trying to run in a reasonable way, and large customers some of whose business we have had, seem to be drifting to the idea of getting their supplies through one source, and we are afraid that other mills will find it necessary to run at night with men in order to fight this ruinous competition. [W]e hope we are not going to be forced to fight the devil with fire.[4]

In an effort to cope with this situation the Institute made an abortive attempt to eliminate the night shift entirely. In June, 1932, the Executive Committee tentatively approved this project on a one-year experimental basis; the plan was to be organized along the same lines as the night-work program.[5] By July 7 the

[2] Sloan, *Sixth Annual Report,* pp. 14, 25–26; Kennedy, *Profits and Losses,* p. 249; G. A. Sloan, Special Memorandum to Executives of Carded Sales Yarn Mills, June 10, 1932, in Comer MSS.

[3] CTI, Minutes, Executive Committee, June 16, 1932, Comer MSS; Sloan, *Sixth Annual Report,* p. 4.

[4] Letter of K. P. Lewis to G. A. Sloan, March 3, 1932, in Sloan MSS.

[5] CTI, Minutes, Executive Committee, June 16, 1932, Comer MSS.

plan had been perfected, the Board of Directors and Executive Committee had given their final approval, and the subscription blanks had been mailed.[6] As the entire association mechanism was being thrown into gear (in August), however, the industry experienced a sudden increase in demand. The mills scrambled for new orders, and the desire for further curtailment was temporarily forgotten. The new program was, in CTI's words, "deferred." To be more realistic, it was abandoned, and with it went a portion of the Institute's authority in the industry.[7]

During these same months the association's cost-accounting program was re-evaluated; one of the original goals of the plan was dropped. A careful study of a group of mills (which were situated in the same area and made a standard product) revealed to CTI's cost engineer that after six years of educational efforts, estimates of production costs varied so greatly that average or comparative figures were useless. Conditions were so different from mill to mill that the member firms could not be expected to arrive at the same or similar figures for unit costs. One of the basic objectives of the program was uniformity of cost estimates, but CTI was now forced to acknowledge that uniformity was beyond its reach. Again, the association's authority was endangered by this acknowledgment of defeat.[8]

On the heels of this report on cost accounting came even more discouraging news. In the narrow-sheeting and print-cloth groups, compliance with the agreement to eliminate night work for women and children had fallen below the 80 per cent level. According to the "Declaration of Policy" that the mills had signed, Sloan was forced to announce that the mills in these groups were no longer obligated to honor their subscriptions. This announcement encouraged other mills to break away. By November only 74.1 per cent of the print-cloth spindles and an even smaller percentage of the sheeting group were still adhering to the night-work standards. The dike was broken. Confidence in CTI's cooperative plan

6 Sloan to D. Comer (with enclosed subscription blanks), July 7, 1932, in Comer MSS.

7 Munroe to Cotton Mill Executives, August 24, 1932; Letter of G. A. Sloan to the Board of Directors, September 19, 1932; Letter of G. A. Sloan to B. B. Comer, Jr., September 21, 1932, in Comer MSS; Sloan, *Sixth Annual Report*, pp. 25–26.

8 *Ibid.*, pp. 20–23.

fell lower and lower.[9] Even George Sloan, a professional optimist, acknowledged that there was a "general feeling of discouragement" in the industry.[10]

The cooperators were discouraged and bitter men. Is it surprising, then, that some of them decided that the minority should be forced to conform to a plan approved by the majority of the industry? Social pressure was not enough. Political force was needed. In 1930 and 1931 some of the cooperators had appealed for state laws that would support CTI's programs, but their requests had been ignored.[11] The only answer seemed to be national legislation. For some, labor legislation seemed to be the best solution, but others wanted a more thoroughgoing system of production control.[12]

[9] Letter of G. A. Sloan to Members of the Executive Committee, September 29, 1932; CTI, Minutes, Executive Committee, October 18, 1932; CTI, Minutes, Board of Directors, October 19, 1932; G. A. Sloan, Special Memorandum to Print Cloth and Narrow Sheetings Executives, November 23, 1932; all in Comer MSS; CMANC, *Proc.*, XXVI (1932), 74–75, 86.

[10] Sloan, *Sixth Annual Report,* p. 11.

[11] Donald Comer led the abortive movement to pass regulatory legislation in Alabama; Letter of George H. Lanier to Scott Roberts, January 14, 1931; D. Comer to Hines, January 16, 1931; Telegram of W. S. Nicholson to D. Comer, March 25, 1931; Telegram of D. Comer to Nicholson, March 25, 1931; Letter of D. Comer to Governor B. M. Miller, May 25 and 29, and June 23, 1931; Charles R. Townson, Memorandum, May 29, 1931; Letter of D. H. Turner to D. Comer, July 20, 1931; D. Comer to Hugo Black, December 7, 1931; all in Comer MSS. A similar movement took place in North Carolina: CMANC, *Proc.*, XXIV (1930), 92–93; XXV (1931), 127; Southern Council on Women and Children in Industry, Report, Suggestions, and Bibliography, Comer MSS. A significant number of South Carolina's manufacturers wanted such legislation, and there was interest among the Georgia producers; Sloan to D. Comer, March 27, 1931; Letter of D. Comer to W. K. Moore, April 6, 1931; both in Comer MSS; also see, ACMA, *Proc.*, XXXV (1931), 26. There was considerable opposition within the industry, and the opponents of regulation were generally successful; D. Comer to Sloan, June 11, 1931, Comer MSS; CMAG, *Report,* XXXI (1931), 23, 26, 30, 32, 55; XXXII (1932), 72.

[12] In regard to national labor legislation see the Letters of: D. Comer to Anderson, July 7, 1930; Anderson to D. Comer, July 8, 1930; W. D. Anderson to Harry Riemer, July 11, 1930; Anderson to Fitzgerald, August 20, 1930; Anderson to Marchant, September 2, 1930; D. Comer to C. A. Cannon, November 5, 1931; J. Klein to D. Comer, November 11, 1931; D. Comer to George Huddleston, November 17 and 23, 1931; C. A. Cannon to D. Comer,

While many of the businessmen talked about merely relaxing the antitrust laws so as to allow producers to act in concert, there was growing support for a program which would require the minority to adhere to majority decisions about prices and production. Often the businessmen spoke about these two policies as if they were not fundamentally different. The manufacturers probably did this because they were hesitant to acknowledge that in effect they were getting ready to abandon cooperation in favor of some form of industry-wide control with government sanctions. Whether hesitant or merely unaware of the distinction, they nevertheless pushed on toward that significant turning point when appeals for cooperation would be supplanted by appeals to force. In 1932 ACMA's president flatly stated that

> we must have some form of economic control. Such a plan would involve not only the balancing of production to demand but perhaps also reasonable price regulation and the proration of business. Unfortunately, the limitations of the present laws will not permit of the setting up of such a plan of economic control. It is therefore felt that an effort should be made to have the anti-trust laws amended to such an extent as will permit of the regulation of these matters in a reasonable way, possibly subject to Government supervision, alike in the interest of the manufacturers and their customers as well as the public in general.[13]

As the summer wore on, more and more cotton manufacturers

November 30, 1931; Hugo Black to D. Comer, December 5, 1931; D. Comer to Black, December 7, 1931; D. Comer to S. H. Hobbs, Jr., February 9, 1932; D. Comer to S. Roberts, April 6, 1932; Robert Amory to D. Comer, April 12, 1932; H. M. Carter to D. Comer and others, April 4, 1932; J. T. Stokely to D. Comer, April 19, 1932; F. O. Tyler to D. Comer, April 21, 1932; Benjamin Russell to D. Comer, April 26, 1932; D. Comer to E. Howard Bennett, September 2, 1932; Henry P. Kendall to D. Comer, October 6, 1932; all in Comer MSS. President Irving Southworth of NACM called for federal legislation setting a maximum workweek and a minimum wage and prohibiting night work by women and children; NACM, *Trans.*, CXXXII (1932), 155–156. There was, of course, no shortage of opponents to federal action, as seen in the following letters: Cason J. Callaway to D. Comer, March 23, 1932; G. S. Harris to D. Comer, April 13, 1932; H. A. Wells to D. Comer, April 18, 1932; H. G. Pratt to D. Comer, April 28, 1932; Tyler to D. Comer, October 12, 1932; D. Comer to Black, December 24, 1932; all in Comer MSS.

[13] Letter of B. B. Gossett to Our Members, June 3, 1932, in Comer MSS.

began to echo this call for strong measures of industrial control.[14]

In October, 1932, the growing desire for a political solution to the industry's problems brought about a fundamental change in CTI's by-laws. By a vote of 369 to 30, the members approved a resolution which authorized the Institute to deal with "legislative and political questions." In the words of the Executive Committee the change was "particularly helpful at this time while so much public attention is attracted to the need of revision in our business regulatory statutes."[15]

There was a real possibility that the efforts to change public policy might succeed. With America's economy tottering, thousands of businessmen and business associations were calling for a new deal from the government. In this general movement for new legislation, the Institute had a prominent and influential position. CTI's officers clearly held a strong hand. Their organization's image had been glossed by the humanitarian aspects of the night-work program. Furthermore, the Institute's officers could claim, with justice, that they had six years of experience with the sort of problem that was facing the entire nation—the problem of stabilizing an industrial system. While the trade association was only one of the means that might be used to achieve that objective, CTI's officers could argue that their type of institution would provide the government with a ready-made organization and experienced leaders. From the perspective of 1932, CTI's arguments could well be rejected, but they could not be ignored.

The possibility of changing public policy was also enhanced by the groundwork that Dorr and Hines had laid in 1931 and 1932.

[14] *King Cotton Weekly,* March 29 and June 15, 1932 (copies of this publication of the Gaston County Textile Manufacturers Association are kept at the office of the Southern Combed Yarn Spinners Association, Gastonia, N. C.); *Textile World,* LXXXI, No. 13 (March 26, 1932), 1094–1095; B. B. Gossett, Report to Board of Government of ACMA, July 1, 1932 (Library, American Cotton Manufacturers Institute); D. Comer to E. H. Bennett, September 2, 1932; D. Comer to Black, December 24, 1932; both in Comer MSS.
[15] Sloan to the Board of Directors, September 19, 1932; CTI, Minutes, Executive Committee, October 18, 1932; CTI, Minutes of the Annual Meeting of the Cotton-Textile Institute, Inc., October 19, 1932; all three in Comer MSS.

These association leaders had not waited until CTI's membership recognized the need to arm the organization with government authority. Neither man had spoken officially for the association on political matters before October, 1932; nevertheless, they had embarked on their own personal campaign to reorient the federal antitrust policy. They had been mulling over the need for a different approach to the problems of cutthroat competition since the late twenties. They had carefully watched the activities of the Federal Trade Commission and the petroleum industry's fumbling attempts to devise a legal means of production control.[16] Encouraged after 1929 by President Hoover's favorable attitude toward cooperation, they had finally decided that a serious attempt to change the antitrust policy might succeed.[17] They had not tried to campaign for broad public support. Instead, in 1931 they had begun to address their concept of associative self-regulation to a small number of leaders, an elite, in the upper levels of the business world, the legal profession, and government service.

Initially, Hines was the principal spokesman. In April, 1931, at a meeting of the Taylor Society in Philadelphia, he delivered a paper on the antitrust laws and their effect upon competition in cotton textiles.[18] His plea for "intelligent planning to keep production in balance with demand. . . ." was reported in the *New York Times* and later published as a bulletin of the Taylor Society.[19] Although this seemed to be a rather inauspicious way to launch the campaign, Hines' remarks eventually reached the right audience. A year later this bulletin was cited by Justice Brandeis of the Supreme Court in a minority opinion in which Brandeis argued for experimentation with economic planning.[20]

Brandeis also referred to a report of a Columbia University symposium on the antitrust question.[21] This symposium, held in December, 1931, had brought together a group of economists,

---

[16] W. D. Hines to G. H. Dorr, March 16, 22, and 30, 1929; April 11 and July 12, 1929; Dorr to Hines, April 1, 8, and 12, 1929; July 16, 1929; G. H. Dorr, Memorandum to Mr. Hines, March 29, 1929; G. H. Dorr to W. W. Montgomery, Jr., July 16, 1929; Sloan to Dorr, July 22, 1929; all in Dorr MSS.

[17] Dorr to Hines, January 16, 1929, Dorr MSS.

[18] W. D. Hines, *Promotion of Stabilization through Keeping Production in Balance with Demand* (pamphlet in Dorr MSS).

[19] *New York Times*, May 1, 1931.

[20] *New State Ice Co.* v. *Liebmann*, 285 U. S. 307, n. 51 (1932).

[21] *Ibid.*

businessmen, and lawyers—including Walker D. Hines—to debate
the question of modifying the antitrust laws. Hines' paper argued,
of course, for modification to allow thoroughgoing self-regulation.
This brought a sharp rebuttal from I. L. Sharfman, an economist
at the University of Michigan; but Professor Gardiner Means of
Columbia University found Hines' ideas worthy of further consideration.[22] At that time Means was working with Adolf A. Berle,
Jr. on a study of the economic and legal aspects of corporate concentration. His research had made him very suspicious of economists like Sharfman who talked about a form of competition
which Means felt existed only in the minds of economists like
Sharfman. In a long letter to Hines, Means objected to Sharfman's
rebuttal on the grounds that it was based on a concept of pure
competition that was at variance with market realities. Means
felt that by exploring this aspect of the problem Hines could get
"serious consideration for [his] plan from economists. . . ." For his
own part, Means said: "While I do not offer any opinion on the
merits of your plan I do think that it deserved more comprehend-
ing economic analysis than Sharfman gave it. Furthermore I am
inclined to agree with you that *if* its economic desirability were
well established, there is a very real possibility that it would be
found legal under existing laws." Even such backhanded encour-
agement as this indicated that Hines was making some progress.[23]

By working through the U. S. Chamber of Commerce, Hines
and Dorr attempted to spread the gospel of the trade association in
the business community. Their manner of approaching this aspect
of the campaign indicates how decisively America had been transformed by the organizational revolution. In the previous century
they would probably have approached individual businessmen.
But in the highly organized society of the twentieth century, trade
association officers normally cooperated with other associations,
not with businessmen as individuals. In this way they could get
the maximum amount of political leverage; and among other
association officers they could expect to find an audience sympathetic to the cooperative ideology that they represented. This was
certainly true of the Chamber of Commerce, which by early 1931

[22] Milton Handler (ed.), *The Federal Anti-Trust Laws: A Symposium*
(Chicago: Commerce Clearing House, 1932), pp. 75–95, 101–104.

[23] Letter of Gardiner C. Means to W. D. Hines, December 9, 1931, in Dorr
MSS.

was receiving from the member associations many proposals in regard to the antitrust question.[24]

As the Chamber's policy on antitrust took shape, Dorr and Hines gained a strong position from which to exert influence upon the organization's platform. In January, 1931, the Chamber set up the Committee on Continuity of Business and Employment, with Henry I. Harriman serving as chairman. One of the members of Harriman's committee was Stuart W. Cramer of North Carolina, a cotton textile manufacturer who had served as one of CTI's first vice-presidents.[25] Dorr and Hines could depend upon Cramer to speak out for their concept of associative self-regulation, but they were given a better means of introducing their ideas when Hines was appointed to the Chamber's Committee on Trade Relations. This latter group formulated policy on trade associations and antitrust issues. Hines was thus in a good position to exert influence on the Chamber's program.[26]

At the end of 1931 the Chamber took a firm stand in favor of stabilization through trade associations. In a referendum completed by December, the Chamber's members approved a proposal that "the anti-trust laws should be modified so as to make clear that the laws permit agreements increasing the possibilities of keeping production related to consumption."[27] According to the Chamber's new economic policy, the government needed a national economic council, supported by representative trade associations which would serve as economic councils in their respective industries. As the Harriman Committee's report stated:

> Only through a proper coordination of production and consumption can a sane, orderly, and progressive economic life be developed. A freedom of action which might have been justified in the relatively simple life of the last century cannot be tolerated

---

[24] U. S. Chamber of Commerce, Minutes, Executive Committee and Minutes, Board of Directors, January 23, 1931; these minutes and other records of the Chamber subsequently cited are at the office of the U. S. Chamber of Commerce, Washington, D. C., unless otherwise indicated.

[25] U. S. Chamber of Commerce, Minutes, Executive Committee, March 21, 1931.

[26] U. S. Chamber of Commerce, Minutes, Board of Directors, June 26, 1931; U. S. Chamber of Commerce, Report to the Committee on Trade Relations, September 28, 1931, in Dorr MSS.

[27] U. S. Chamber of Commerce, Special Bulletin, January 18, 1932, in *Referenda, Nos. 54–68, 1929–1934.*

today, because the unwise action of one individual may adversely affect the lives of thousands. We have left the period of extreme individualism and are living in a period in which national economy must be recognized as the controlling factor.[28]

Harriman's report and the referendum indicated that Dorr and Hines now had at least one strong ally in their campaign to change the antitrust policy.

Other supporters appeared as the depression spilled more and more red ink on the books of American business. Gerard Swope, president of the General Electric Company, published a plea for production control through trade associations. The Swope Plan generated considerable discussion of the antitrust problem, as did the U. S. Chamber of Commerce referendum. Throughout American industry, businessmen and association leaders began to sing the same chorus: stability could be achieved if only the trade associations were unleashed and if somehow the organizations could be given the authority necessary to make their programs work. This chorus urged Hines and Dorr to press ahead with their effort to reshape public policy.[29]

At first, CTI's leaders made only a halfhearted attempt to win government support for their proposal. Hines corresponded with Attorney-General Mitchell, and Dorr sent the Attorney-General an outline of his ideas on the antitrust question.[30] At this time, however, Hines and Dorr seem to have envisioned their task as one of gradual re-education. The Institute's rule against political activity might have given them pause. But more important was their realization that it was essential to cultivate the intellectual and legal environments very carefully before attempting to bring forth an entirely new government policy.

[28] *Ibid.*

[29] Gerard Swope, *The Swope Plan, Details, Criticisms, Analysis,* ed. J. George Frederick (New York: The Business Bourse, 1931); Broadus Mitchell, *Depression Decade* (New York: Holt, Rinehart and Winston, 1947), p. 231; Arthur M. Schlesinger, Jr., *The Coming of the New Deal* (Boston: Houghton Mifflin, 1957), pp. 88–89; Letter of W. D. Hines to Gerard Swope, September 29, 1931, in Dorr MSS.

[30] W. D. Hines, *Anti-Trust Act: Must all agreements for balancing production with demand be regarded as per se in restraint of trade?;* Letter of W. D. Hines to Attorney-General William D. Mitchell, 1931; Letter of Attorney-General W. D. Mitchell to G. H. Dorr, May 14, 1931; Memo of G. H. Dorr to Mr. Hand, August 7, 1931; Letter of G. H. Dorr to Attorney-General W. D. Mitchell, August 18, 1931; all five in Dorr MSS.

During 1932 Dorr and Hines diligently built up this essential foundation of ideas. Hines remained active in the U. S. Chamber of Commerce, and in March he began to correspond with James Emery of the National Association of Manufacturers.[31] Dorr and Hines also began to draw together a small group of influential lawyers who were interested in the antitrust laws. They began to exchange ideas with Gilbert A. Montague, a New York attorney who was chairman of the Committee on the Federal Trade Commission and the Anti-Trust Laws of the Merchants Association of New York. In April they were joined by William Church Osborn, a lawyer who was influential in New York politics. By the end of 1932, they had a veritable committee on correspondence functioning, with its attention focused squarely on the antitrust laws.[32]

In the spring of 1932 George Sloan was drawn into their effort to recast public policy. Until that time he had been concentrating his attention on the night-work plan and avoiding anything that might appear to be lobbying. He had left this task to Dorr and Hines since they were not as directly involved as he was in the administration of CTI's affairs.[33] In April, however, Sloan was called to Washington by Secretary of Commerce Lamont, who said that he and President Hoover were extremely worried about the continued downward spiral of wages. Lamont had heard that there were to be further wage cuts in cotton textiles. Did Sloan have any information on this? The Institute, Sloan replied, was not involved in the wage question; but he could give Lamont his personal opinion on this and other problems. Wages were not the key issue, Sloan said. The only path to recovery was through changes in the antitrust laws. After observing that the Institute's

[31] U. S. Chamber of Commerce, Minutes, Board of Directors, September 23, 1932. Letter of James A. Emery to W. D. Hines, March 29, 1932; Letter of Henry P. Fowler to W. D. Hines, May 19, 1932; Letter of John M. Redpath to G. H. Dorr (with enclosure), November 22, 1932; all three in Dorr MSS.

[32] Letter of Gilbert H. Montague to W. D. Hines (with enclosures), March 9, 1932; Letter of William C. Osborn to W. D. Hines, April 19, 1932; both in Dorr MSS.

[33] Hines was president of CTI from 1926–1929 and chairman of the board from 1929 to October, 1931. After 1931 he served as counsel, with Dorr, and as general adviser to the association and its officers. He continued to serve the Institute in these official and unofficial roles until June, 1933, when he went to Turkey as an economic adviser. He died on January 14, 1934; Roger R. Trask, "The United States and Turkish Nationalism," *Business History Review*, XXXVIII, No. 1 (Spring, 1964), 73.

by-laws still excluded political activity, Sloan went on to suggest that Congress begin a thorough study of the antitrust situation, meanwhile allowing associations to formulate binding agreements to control production. Lamont said that he would pass Sloan's ideas along to President Hoover, who, he felt, "would like to see some relief provided along the lines suggested." But the possibilities of action on the antitrust question, Lamont added, were poor.[34]

A few months later Sloan was again summoned to Washington, this time for a conference with the President. In their meeting, Sloan briefed Hoover on the Institute's various programs and its problems with the nonconformers. Hoover made it clear that he was sympathetic; he agreed "that some way must be found in our scheme of economic planning to strengthen cooperation among those units which are endeavoring to promote the best interest of a given industry. . . ." He agreed that they needed to devise some means of encouraging "a more reasonable attitude on the part of those who have persistently ignored all constructive plans and policies."[35]

Hoover did not, however, have any specific ideas about how this was to be accomplished. He obviously was not prepared—as many businessmen and association officers were—to talk about coercing the uncooperative minority; he was still leaning on euphemisms, talking about strengthening cooperation and encouraging "a more reasonable attitude." As Sloan discovered, his talks with the administration were like the other "no-business" conferences that the President held in 1931 and 1932: they created the appearance of great activity without requiring the President to do anything.[36] Experimentation along the lines suggested by Sloan (and others) was a radical move, too radical for Hoover; it would have required the government to reverse a time-honored policy. Hoover resisted this. He wanted solutions that stayed within, or at least appeared to stay within, America's framework of traditional values. He could give Sloan a sympathetic audience, but that was about all that he had to offer.

[34] Letter of G. A. Sloan to W. D. Hines, April 27, 1932, in Dorr MSS; CTI, Memorandum for Personal File: G. A. Sloan's Personal Folder, May 2, 1932, in Sloan MSS.

[35] Sloan to the Board of Directors, September 19, 1932, Comer MSS.

[36] John K. Galbraith, *The Great Crash, 1929* (Boston: Houghton Mifflin, 1961), pp. 144–146, gives an engaging description of this type of conference.

After the Institute's officers were given formal permission to undertake political activities (October, 1932), Hines and Dorr decided to mount a direct attack upon the Supreme Court's interpretation of the antitrust statutes. Due to the change in CTI's by-laws, they could now do this in the Institute's name. In December, 1932 they filed a brief with the Supreme Court as *amici curiae* in the Appalachian Coals case.[37] Wilson Compton, also a trade association officer, collaborated with Dorr and Hines so that they were able to submit their brief in behalf of the Window Glass Manufacturers' Association and the National Lumber Manufacturers Association, as well as the Cotton-Textile Institute.[38]

The Appalachian Coals case involved a joint marketing agency established by a group of bituminous-coal producers in the Appalachian region of Virginia, West Virginia, Kentucky, and Tennessee. Since the companies forming the agency produced only about 12 per cent of the bituminous coal mined east of the Mississippi River (and 64 per cent to 74 per cent of that mined in the Appalachian region), the district court which first heard the case had decided that the agency would "not have monopoly control of any market nor the power to fix monopoly prices"; nevertheless, the agency would effectively eliminate competition among the companies that joined. On these grounds the court had found the plan in violation of the Sherman Act. The defendants had then appealed to the Supreme Court.[39]

The brief that Dorr, Hines, and Compton submitted dealt primarily with the economic aspects of concerted action by a group of competitors. This sort of action, the brief said, did not necessarily contravene the antitrust laws. The laws were supposed to preserve "an effectively functioning competitive system in industry," and such agreements might actually support that purpose. This was possible, the brief said, because the competitive system would not function properly unless there was active competition among buyers as well as sellers. "If this duality of competition is

[37] *Appalachian Coals, Inc., et al.* v. *United States*, 288 U. S. 344 (1933).

[38] *Brief of Walker D. Hines, Goldthwaite H. Dorr and Wilson Compton, as Amici Curiae on Behalf of the Cotton Textile Institute, Inc., Window Glass Manufacturers' Association and National Lumber Manufacturers Association* (New York, n.d.).

[39] *Appalachian Coals* v. *U. S.*, 356–359.

destroyed by a monopolistic combination either among buyers or among sellers, then the competitive system, certainly so far as furnishing any protection to the public is concerned, is destroyed in that industry. . . ." The "duality of competition" could, however, be disrupted by conditions other than monopoly: "A great overplus or marked shortage as compared with the accustomed needs of the community will be quite as devastating to the protective functioning of the competitive system . . . as a monopolistic combination would be"; therefore, an effort to deal with the problems of overproduction or extreme shortage by forming a marketing agency or association might actually contribute to the smooth functioning of the competitive system. The brief maintained that the joint selling agency of the coal producers was designed to help, not hinder, the competitive process which the antitrust statutes attempted to protect.[40]

If the Supreme Court accepted this line of reasoning, the boundaries of legal association work would be greatly expanded. Agreements to limit production could well become legal contracts that would be upheld by the courts. So long as the agreements were not aimed at breaking down "a normally functioning competitive system," they would not be in conflict with public policy. This was the objective of the brief that Dorr and Hines filed with the Court in December. Since it would be several months before the decision was rendered, however, they shifted their attention to president-elect Franklin D. Roosevelt.

In their attempt to influence the future administration, CTI's officers and the business and association leaders with whom they were working first approached Roosevelt's advisers. In December George Sloan and a subcommittee from CTI met with General Hugh Johnson "of Mr. Bernard Baruch's office" to discuss the farm problem. At Johnson's request the Institute also sent a delegation to a Chicago conference on agriculture; as Sloan commented: "We feel that the request comes pretty close to being a suggestion from the new administration and consequently that we should lean over backwards to meet that request." Correctly anticipating that a cooperative attitude would pay dividends later (when

[40] *Brief . . . as Amici Curiae,* pp. 7–19, 39, 41.

they were able to raise the subject of antitrust), the association's representatives were receptive to the proposals for farm relief made by Johnson, Raymond Moley, and others.[41] In January Henry I. Harriman and Gilbert Montague got a chance to talk about antitrust with some of the brain trusters. After consulting with Hines, Montague sent a memorandum on the antitrust issue to Rexford Guy Tugwell and Adolf A. Berle, Jr.[42]

As they began to bear down on the brain trust, the group with which CTI's leaders were cooperating started to expand. Howard Coffin, who had once been president of the Hudson Motor Car Co., joined forces with the Institute. During the First World War, Coffin had been a member of the National Defense Council, and he was now convinced that the nation needed a federal planning agency like the Council. Since this proposal involved giving government authority to a system of trade associations, he and the Institute were natural allies.[43]

In February these business and association leaders were drawn into a more formal alliance when they made their first and only attempt to sell their ideas to Congress. James Emery of the National Association of Manufacturers precipitated this move by arranging a meeting with the House Judiciary Committee.[44] When they confronted the Committee on February 8, the business representatives quickly discovered that the congressmen wanted specific suggestions, not general laments.[45] Although the business group was not organized behind any specific proposal,[46] the members hastily appointed Hines to outline a recovery measure for

[41] G. A. Sloan: Memorandum to Executive Committee, December 21, 1932; Memorandum for Members of CTI, December 31, 1932; Memorandum to Members of CTI, January 4, 1933; Memo to Board of Directors of CTI, January 13, 1933; all in Comer MSS.

[42] Rexford Guy Tugwell, Notes from a New Deal Diary, January 14, 1933, in RL; G. H. Montague to Hines, January 31, 1933, Dorr MSS.

[43] Sloan to the Board of Directors, September 19, 1932; Sloan, Memo to Board of Directors, January 13, 1933; both in Comer MSS.

[44] Letters of J. A. Emery to W. D. Hines, December 22, 1932, and January 31, 1933, in Dorr MSS.

[45] W. D. Hines, Memorandum, March 16, 1933, in Dorr MSS.

[46] A preliminary meeting had been held in an effort to get the association and business leaders to agree on a single proposal, but they had been unable to reconcile their differences. G. A. Sloan, Confidential Memorandum for Board Members, February 8, 1933, in Comer MSS.

the congressmen.[47] The response to Hines' recommendations was, however, essentially negative, and the meeting concluded on an indeterminate note.[48]

From their experience at this conference, the representatives of industry drew two conclusions: First, it was useless to approach Congress since the initiative in measures of this magnitude would rest with the newly elected administration; they needed to sound out the incoming President, to explore more fully the possibility of getting his support for their proposal. Second, they decided that it was futile to talk about industrial self-regulation and stabilization in general terms; they would have to present a specific and carefully drafted bill.[49] They might also have concluded that the theoretical foundations of their ideas needed to be worked out more carefully, but they avoided this subject and pushed ahead toward their goal.

Dorr was given primary responsibility for drafting a bill. He was assisted by Walter G. Merritt, a New York attorney, and Rush C. Butler, a prominent Chicago lawyer who was chairman of the Commerce Committee of the American Bar Association. With their help Dorr was able to put together a bill by the middle of February. This proposal followed closely the economic philosophy expressed in the Appalachian Coals brief; the bill stated that the "national economic emergency" facing America was the result "of a general shrinkage in consuming power and a general over-development of the facilities of production and distribution, resulting in destructive competition, the marketing of commodities below cost and at progressively lower levels, irregular employment and underpayment of labor. . . ." To stop this downward spiral, the bill provided for an economic emergency board along

[47] Sloan, Memorandum to Members of the Board of CTI, February 18, 1933, Comer MSS.

[48] Statement of Walker D. Hines to the Conference with the House Judiciary Committee, February 8, 1933, in Dorr MSS.

[49] Letters of G. H. Dorr to Rush C. Butler, February 10 and 28, 1933; Hines, Memorandum, March 16, 1933; all three in Dorr MSS; R. F. Himmelberg, "Relaxation of the Federal Anti-Trust Policy," pp. 206–209; Himmelberg (pp. 156–184) also discusses the activities during the late 1920's of several of the men who worked closely with Dorr and Hines in 1932–1933.

the lines proposed by Howard Coffin. The board, consisting of the Secretaries of Commerce, Labor, and Agriculture, would be empowered to investigate depressed industries, "to confer with, aid and guide persons engaged therein in the formation of measures of economic planning and cooperative action designed to remedy the causes or effects of the emergency, and, as occasion arises, to investigate and pass upon the operation of such measures in their relation to the public interest." During the emergency the board would encourage associations to establish agreements in regard to production, sales, and distribution, with the antitrust laws suspended insofar as these understandings were approved by the board.[50]

At Dorr's suggestion, the proposed bill gave the emergency board authority to force the uncooperative elements in an industry to conform to an approved trade association program. This was the first time the vital distinction between voluntary cooperation and industrial control by government force was spelled out clearly. By using cease and desist orders the board could require non-cooperators to adopt policies consistent with the agreements sponsored by associations. Coercive powers were essential, Dorr and Merritt felt, because it was necessary to make "it more difficult for selfish interests to make sound planning in a national interest impossible by refusing their cooperation." Judging from CTI's experience with voluntary programs, this provision was absolutely essential; but it raised a controversial issue that was to arouse serious differences within the group for whom the bill was drafted.[51]

Before consulting with their colleagues, however, Dorr and Hines took their proposal directly to Roosevelt's assistants. On February 18 they saw Berle and discussed the matter with him at considerable length. They felt that he was appreciative of "the gravity of the problem" and willing "to consider some such method of dealing with it." They left him a copy of their bill and supporting memorandum. Berle carried their ideas to Roosevelt, who also seems to have reacted positively to the general idea of industrial self-regulation through trade associations. After discussing the bill

[50] Dorr to Butler (with enclosure), February 10, 1933; Letter of W. D. Hines to G. H. Montague (with enclosed *Memorandum on Economic Emergency and Emergency Legislation*), February 21, 1933; both in Dorr MSS.

[51] *Ibid.;* Dorr to Butler, February 10, 1933, Dorr MSS.

with Berle a second time, Dorr and Hines decided to reconvene
the industry group in order to unify it behind this specific
measure.[52]

A conference and consensus seemed essential; several members
of the group were already in contact with Roosevelt's counselors
and there was some danger that the president-elect might be given
conflicting advice. Howard Coffin had talked to Bernard Baruch,
who liked the general idea of self-regulation; Baruch felt, however,
that they would never get a change in the antitrust laws unless
they accepted the government's right to fix maximum prices.[53]
Henry I. Harriman discussed these questions with Raymond Moley
and Rexford G. Tugwell. Tugwell was interested in any plan that
would bring "business closer under general government direction . . . ," and Harriman encouraged him to believe that businessmen would be willing to accept a fair measure of control in order
to escape the threat of periodic depressions.[54]

When the group reconvened on March 8, however, it quickly
became apparent that there were strong differences of opinion
about the amount of government regulation that should be accepted. William Osborn was suspicious of the bureaucratic controls that might be spun out by Dorr's proposed emergency board.
James Emery of NAM and Robert P. Lamont, who was now
president of the American Iron and Steel Institute, were extremely
critical of the measure proposed by Dorr's subcommittee. Emery
was worried about the labor unions; they would, he thought, take
advantage of government authority to gain new power. Lamont
felt that businessmen should be more cautious about asking for
any kind of government interference. They should consider and
reconsider, he said, "what industry might lose by getting tied in
with bureaucracy." C. E. Bockus of the National Coal Association
seconded Lamont's fears. Bockus also questioned whether trade
association programs should be forced on the producers who did
not elect to join. As Bockus and the others quite correctly saw,

[52] Letters of W. D. Hines to A. A. Berle, February 21 and 24, 1933; Letter
of A. A. Berle to W. D. Hines, February 23, 1933; Dorr to Butler, February
28, 1933; all in Dorr MSS.

[53] W. D. Hines, Memorandum for Mr. Dorr, February 13, 1933, in Dorr
MSS.

[54] R. G. Tugwell, Notes from a New Deal Diary, February 12, 1933, RL.

Dorr's proposal was bold and forceful. Even in the economic crisis of March, 1933, these spokesmen of industry were hesitant, mindful that they might not be able to retreat after stepping forward into a full alliance with the government.[55]

John Redpath, who represented the Chamber of Commerce, took a different tack. He was not worried about government controls, but he did take exception to the fact that Dorr had drafted an emergency measure. Instead of a temporary experiment with associative self-regulation, Redpath wanted the government to abandon permanently the antitrust laws' prohibition of concerted action by competitors. Trade association control, he felt, should be a permanent part of our modern industrial system. Although there were several members present who strongly supported the Dorr bill—including Gilbert Montague and J. Harvey Williams (a Chicago tool manufacturer)—about the only things that the entire group could agree on were the need for unanimity (in the abstract!) and the necessity of carrying their ideas directly to F.D.R. They gave J. Harvey Williams the hopeless task of uniting the various associations and industries behind a single proposal, while Hines was commissioned to speak to Roosevelt.[56]

The path to the President became considerably smoother on March 13 when the Supreme Court handed down its decision in the Appalachian Coals case. It was impossible for Dorr and Hines to tell how effective their brief had been; but they could not help but be satisfied with the decision since it sharply altered the Supreme Court's position on the antitrust laws. Speaking for the majority, Chief Justice Hughes reversed the decision of the lower court and found that the joint selling agency of the coal producers was not in violation of the Sherman Act. In his careful inquiry into the economic structure of the industry, Hughes took special note of the "highly organized and concentrated buying power" that could be exerted against the producers. "Distress selling" and other manifestations of cutthroat competition were described as "evil conditions" which the producers had a right to correct through concerted action. In a passage that seemed to reflect Dorr's economic philosophy, Hughes observed that "the existing situation prompted defendants to make, and the statute did not preclude

[55] Letter of J. Harvey Williams to R. C. Butler, March 10, 1933; Hines, Memorandum, March 8, 1933; both in Dorr MSS.
[56] *Ibid.*

them from making an honest effort to remove abuses, to make competition fairer, and thus to promote the essential interests of commerce." He acknowledged that the selling agency might tend to stabilize prices but maintained that this did not itself constitute an unreasonable restraint of trade; under certain conditions, Hughes said, "putting an end to injurious practices, and the consequent improvement of the competitive position of a group of producers . . . may be entirely consonant with the public interest. . . ."[57] The decision armed CTI's leaders and the other advocates of trade association control with what appeared to be a strong vote of approval from the Supreme Court.

Paradoxically, the Appalachian Coals decision further complicated the task of uniting industry behind the bill drafted by Dorr's subcommittee. The Court's new attitude toward loose combinations encouraged those who wanted a permanent relaxation of the antitrust laws to strike out on their own. Gilbert Montague decided to work independently in behalf of a bill that he had drafted.[58] The Chamber of Commerce was even more determined to push for permanent relief from antitrust, and Silas H. Strawn called another meeting of the group in the hope that he could at last pull them together behind his proposal. At the meeting held on March 27, however, Strawn was unable to draw the participants into agreement. They all felt that there was a need for associative self-regulation. But these assembled representatives of the organized forces of industry seemed determined to defy the stereotyped picture of a monolithic business community. They left the conference in disarray.[59]

By the end of March the group had virtually dissolved. Although they continued to communicate with one another and continued to cooperate in a limited sense, they all descended upon the Roosevelt Administration with their own plans for industrial recovery. Robert Lund of the National Association of Manufacturers forwarded his own plans directly to F.D.R.[60] On April 1 Henry I. Harriman presented Attorney-General Homer Cum-

[57] *Appalachian Coals* v. *U. S.*, 360–364, 372–374, 377.

[58] Hines, Memorandum, March 16, 1933, Dorr MSS.

[59] Anti-Trust Conference, March 27, 1933; J. M. Redpath to Dorr, April 13, 1933; both in Dorr MSS.

[60] Letter of Robert L. Lund to Louis McHenry Howe, March 29, 1933, in President's Personal File (PP) 8246, RL.

mings with a proposal that had been hastily drafted by Chamber of Commerce officers. Harriman's bill would have enabled associations to sponsor agreements to stabilize their industries as long as these contracts were filed with and approved by the government. No provision was made for a national emergency board; and the bill would have allowed the barest minimum of government control.[61] All of these proposals had certain ideas in common, but they also included significant differences.

Despite the fact that his group had disintegrated, Hines proceeded with his plans to meet the President. He had already sent to the White House a short memorandum outlining his position. The new administration, the memorandum said, had already eliminated several of the barriers to renewed business confidence, but it had not yet tackled the antitrust problem. This problem had to be confronted because the antitrust laws prevented "the necessary concerted effort by those engaged in industries to check the downward spiral of prices below cost and increased unemployment, and to reestablish credit, buying power, and to put industry on the upgrade." If a permanent change in the laws on competition could not be passed, a temporary emergency measure was absolutely essential. The memo outlined Dorr's analysis of the "duality" of competition; it pointed out that in the Appalachian Coals decision the Supreme Court had, in a limited way, approved cooperative measures to stabilize prices. What was needed now, Hines said, was "drastic affirmative action" with strong government leadership. On the basis of his experience with the textile industry and his "contact with a group of representatives of a wide range of industries" Hines suggested that he discuss with the President the need for "the immediate leadership of the Administration in a matter vitally important to the recovery of the country."[62]

By this time the antitrust question was, according to Berle, "getting red hot."[63] Hundreds of businessmen and association

[61] Letter of Henry I. Harriman to W. D. Hines (with enclosure), April 3, 1933; Redpath to Dorr, April 13, 1933; both in Dorr MSS.

[62] Letter of W. D. Hines to M. H. McIntyre (with enclosed *Draft of Points for White House*), March 23, 1933; McIntyre to Hines, March 24, 1933; both in Official File (OF) 466, RL.

[63] Telegram of A. A. Berle to Col. McIntyre, March 30, 1933, in Alphabetical File, RL.

officers were calling for a new deal on antitrust. The Black Thirty-Hour Bill, which would have spread the available employment by limiting workers to a thirty-hour week, had been introduced in the Senate on April 3; this bill was forcing the Roosevelt Administration either to take action on industrial recovery or to lose control of the measure to Congress. Roosevelt was looking for a solution to this problem and on April 11 he and Assistant Secretary of Commerce John Dickinson met with Hines.

Hines found F.D.R. sympathetic to the idea of associative self-regulation under government leadership. This was hardly surprising since Roosevelt himself had once served as the president of a trade association. In the 1920's he had headed the American Construction Council. Still, the President did not seem to be in any hurry to experiment with this radical new approach to the nation's economic plight. Like Hoover, Roosevelt was leary of tampering with traditional values. As he explained to Hines, the antitrust question "was a highly controversial matter the consideration of which would take many weeks. . . ." The President said very emphatically "that it ought not to be brought up at the present session of Congress."[64]

Hines was discouraged; but developments in the next few days suggest that he and the other trade association devotees had successfully lodged their ideas in the President's mind. At his press conference on April 12, Roosevelt indicated that the administration might be interested in a production-control program that would spread work throughout an industry instead of allowing it to be concentrated in the hands of a few producers. He used a specific example to drive home his point. He knew of a sweater factory, he said, which had agreed with its employees to cut wages, thus getting enough orders to ensure full production: "That is bad business, in all ways," Roosevelt commented. "In the first place, it cuts the scale of wages and the scale of living. Of course, they get a good deal of cash into the community because they have got three shifts working. But the worst feature of it is that they undoubtedly, by taking these orders, put two other sweater factories completely out of business." There were, F.D.R. observed, many obstacles to a government program that would deal with this problem. But he assured the press that it was "a pretty important subject," one which his administration was "exploring."[65]

[64] Letter of W. D. Hines to H. I. Harriman, April 14, 1933, in Dorr MSS.
[65] Franklin D. Roosevelt, Press Conference No. 11, April 12, 1933, in RL.

A few days later Roosevelt was even more specific. In his press conference of April 14, he described the problem that the cotton textile industry had encountered in its cooperative programs. If the government set up minimum wage boards, he said, they would run into the same difficulty, the resistance of a small percentage of non-cooperators. "The fair employers would represent 85% or 90% of industry. You take the cotton mill owners of this country: Probably 90 or 95% will go along with some kind of fair wage proposition, but the fact that 5 or 10% of them won't sign up, makes it impossible to put the agreement through." If they could find some constitutional means of handling this problem, the President said, he would favor it.[66]

These remarks strongly suggest that by this time Roosevelt had accepted the fundamental proposition that CTI's officers and others were trying to put across. Under pressure, F.D.R., unlike his predecessor, was abandoning traditional values and accepting a new philosophy which he felt was more in accord with the realities of our political and economic system. Like the association leaders, F.D.R. now described the non-cooperators as villains and the majority, the producers who wanted stability, as heroes. Instead of looking at the competitive process as a self-correcting mechanism in which the hardest competitors played a vital role, the President—like the Supreme Court—was inclined to favor cooperative methods of eliminating cutthroat competition.

Shortly after the press conference on April 14, the administration set three teams to work writing the bill that was to become the National Industrial Recovery Act. Senator Robert Wagner headed one of the groups. Another centered around Hugh Johnson, a third around John Dickinson, the Assistant Secretary of Commerce. Out of a confusing and complex process of drafting there finally emerged a single recovery measure.[67] Although historians

[66] Franklin D. Roosevelt, Press Conference No. 12, April 14, 1933, in RL.

[67] The best treatment of the actual drafting is in Schlesinger's *The Coming of the New Deal*, pp. 96–98; for slightly different versions, the reader might consult the following: Charles F. Roos, *NRA Economic Planning* (Bloomington, Indiana: Principia Press, 1937), pp. 39–40; Hugh S. Johnson, *The Blue Eagle from Egg to Earth* (Garden City, New York: Doubleday, Doran & Co., 1935), pp. 200–201, 204; Donald Richberg, *My Hero* (New York: G. P. Putnam's Sons, 1954), p. 164; Frances Perkins, *The Roosevelt I Knew* (New York: The Viking Press, 1946), pp. 197–200.

will probably never understand the precise manner in which the final draft evolved, it is fairly clear why the measure included provisions for a temporary relaxation of the antitrust acts and government support for trade associations: the industrial and association leaders with whom Hines and Dorr had been working had successfully lodged their ideas with certain members of each of the three groups, not to mention the President. Gilbert Montague, who by this time was once more supporting Dorr's draft of an emergency measure, was actually helping Senator Wagner's group draft their version of the bill.[68] CTI's leaders had been in touch with Hugh Johnson since December 1932; they had furthermore been assured of the support of Bernard Baruch, Johnson's "patron."[69] For weeks both Montague and Harriman had been in close contact with Dickinson, who had indicated that he favored the Chamber's proposals for a permanent measure based upon the FTC's Trade Practice Conferences.[70] Whatever form the final bill took, it was thus fairly certain that it would include some provision for a close alliance between the associations and the government—an alliance that would no longer be hindered by the antitrust laws.

To Dorr, Hines, and Sloan, things were not this clear. The situation in Washington was confusing. They were obviously making some headway, but this seemed to be no time to relax their campaign. Dorr outlined his views on production control before a meeting of the American Bar Association's Committee on Commerce; on this occasion he gave special attention to the need for measures that would prevent a small percentage of individualists from breaking down cooperative programs.[71] Meanwhile, Hines stayed in touch with Harriman, Montague, Emery, Osborn, and several other members of their erstwhile group.[72] When the Na-

---

[68] Schlesinger, *The Coming of the New Deal,* p. 96; Letter of Gilbert H. Montague to John Dickinson, May 3, 1933, in RG 40, 94694, NA.

[69] Johnson later explained that the cotton textile industry's code came in so early because "we have been working with these people since last March." NRA, Press Release No. 32, July 7, 1933, RG 9, Transcript of Hearings, NA.

[70] Montague to Hines, April 20, 1933; Hines to Dorr, April 25, 1933; both in Dorr MSS.

[71] Mr. Dorr's Talk at Proceedings of the Committee on Commerce, April 12, 1933, in Dorr MSS.

[72] Letter of W. D. Hines to J. A. Emery, April 19, 1933; Letter of W. D. Hines to W. C. Osborn, April 19, 1933; Harriman to Hines, April 19, 1933; Hines to Dorr, April 25, 1933; all in Dorr MSS.

tional Association of Manufacturers held a special meeting in Washington (April 28) to discuss industrial recovery, CTI's views were presented by Howard Coffin, one of the speakers.[73]

The U. S. Chamber of Commerce met in Washington on May 3–4, and both Dorr and Sloan were on the program. Sloan was there to receive for the Institute the annual award of the American Trade Association Executives. Since the award was given, along with the customary speech, by Secretary of Commerce Roper, Sloan had a chance to talk to Roper about "self-regulation of industry backed up by Government support." Sloan also presented his views to Secretary of Agriculture Wallace and to John Dickinson, with whom he discussed the bill that was being drafted.[74] Dorr presented a paper on "The Effects of the Anti-Trust Laws under Conditions of Depression."[75]

As Dorr's remarks indicate, he was willing to compromise on certain essential issues in order to get a chance to experiment with a trade association program backed by government authority. Creating this sort of compromise was, after all, one of the association leader's most important functions. Although many businessmen were skittish about using the government to bring the recalcitrant minority into line, Dorr was eager to take this important step forward. As he explained: "You can't have self-government in industry unless you have power to govern the minority, or if you are going to have that of course you have got to have, to insure its being done fairly and in the interest of the public, some supervision, public supervision, and some public arbitrament of those measures of government. You can't have one as a practical matter without having the other." He also bowed to the administration's recently expressed interest in minimum wages, pointing out that concerted action was needed in regard to wages as well as production.[76]

Two of the following speakers made it very clear that the

[73] National Association of Manufacturers, *Governmental Control of Industry—And Industry's Alternative* (Bulletin, May 2, 1933), copy in RG 40, 94694, Box 733, NA.

[74] U. S. Chamber of Commerce, Minutes, Twenty-first Annual Meeting, May 3, 1933; Sloan to D. Comer, May 4, 1933; CTI, Minutes, Executive Committee, May 8, 1933; last two in Comer MSS.

[75] U. S. Chamber of Commerce, Minutes, Twenty-first Annual Meeting, May 4, 1933.

[76] *Ibid.*

administration was ready to act. John Dickinson assured the audience that "within the administration there is at the present time very active consideration going forward in connection with these problems, and that the point of view that has been so ably expressed by Mr. Dorr is receiving the most sympathetic consideration."[77] President Roosevelt, who addressed the Chamber that evening, reaffirmed his own support for "an orderly industrial system" in which the majority within an industry would, with government backing, bring "minorities to understand that their unfair practices are contrary to the sound public policy of the nation."[78] Roosevelt (like Hoover) was still talking about making the nonconformers "understand," but by this time it was clear that understanding would be achieved by employing the full force of the government.

Three days later in a fireside chat, Roosevelt outlined in greater detail the bill that was being drafted. To illustrate how the measure would work, F.D.R. again used one particular example:

> Take the cotton goods industry. It is probably true that ninety per cent of the cotton manufacturers would agree to eliminate starvation wages, would agree to stop long hours of employment, would agree to stop child labor, would agree to prevent an overproduction that would result in unsalable surpluses. But, what good is such an agreement if the other ten per cent of cotton manufacturers pay starvation wages, require long hours, employ children in their mills and turn out burdensome surpluses? The unfair ten per cent could produce goods so cheaply that the fair ninety would be compelled to meet the unfair conditions. Here is where government comes in. Government ought to have the right and will have the right, after surveying and planning for an industry to prevent, with the assistance of the overwhelming majority of that industry, unfair practice and to enforce this agreement by the authority of government. The so-called anti-trust laws were intended to prevent the creation of monopolies and to forbid unreasonable profits to those monopolies. That purpose of the anti-trust laws must be continued, but these laws were never intended to encourage the kind of unfair competition that results in long hours, starvation wages and overproduction.[79]

Roosevelt's remarks made it virtually certain that CTI's officers

---

[77] *Ibid.*   [78] *Ibid.*
[79] The President's Fireside Chat, Transcript, May 7, 1933, in RL.

were going to get the law they wanted. Although the fish was in the net, the Institute made one more effort to ensure that their quarry would not escape. On May 8, CTI's Executive Committee held an emergency meeting in New York City. To assure the President that their industry wanted the new deal he had described, the Committee launched a program imposing voluntary limits of two forty-hour shifts a week on all of the nation's cotton mills.[80] Two days later the association had received a large number of favorable reactions, and George Sloan wired Roosevelt that one-third of the industry had already lined up behind the plan the President had outlined in his fireside chat.[81] What better proof could there be of the practicability of self-regulation through trade associations? One of the country's leading trade organizations had already boldly launched a recovery program incorporating a drastic reduction in the work week.

When the National Industrial Recovery Bill was introduced in Congress five days later, Dorr, Hines, and Sloan had good cause to be satisfied with the bill's major provisions. Of course the measure contained many sections upon which CTI's officers had not exercised any influence whatsoever; it included several sections which they definitely opposed; but their fundamental objective of reversing the antitrust policy and winning government support for the trade association was achieved.

As should be clear, CTI's association leaders had considerable influence upon Title I of the NIRA. Hines and Dorr had labored long and hard to create the proper legal and intellectual background for this change in public policy. Through their committee on correspondence and the influential group of business and association leaders that they led, they had transformed their general concepts into a specific proposal and effectively transmitted this measure to the administration. Through the earlier night-work plan and the forty-hour-week program CTI had provided Roosevelt and his advisers with a convincing demonstration of how the trade association could benefit labor and the general public, as well as the businessman.

It should be made equally clear, however, that CTI was merely

[80] CTI, Minutes, Executive Committee, May 8, 1933, Comer MSS.
[81] Telegram of G. A. Sloan to Franklin D. Roosevelt, May 10, 1933, OF 372, RL.

one element in a broad, trade association movement which provided the vital background for this shift in public policy. The
service associations, which had developed in a wide variety of
industries, and the policy-shaping associations which had emerged
in a few, had already helped to establish a new institutional and
ideological environment in America. By early 1933 hundreds of
these trade groups were calling for a change in public policy on
competition. Within this general array of organizations, groups such
as CTI and the Chamber of Commerce played special roles, but
without the general association movement these roles would not
have existed and there would have been no change in the traditional antitrust policy.[82]

Throughout this episode in business-government relations the
association leaders held center stage. They had taken over the
major role in representing their industry. Thirty years earlier the
manufacturers had done this work themselves. Now they allowed
most of the responsibility for the shaping of public policy to rest
in the hands of their professional middlemen. It was the middlemen who negotiated the vital compromises with government
officials and other association officers. It was the association leaders
who laid most of the "educational" and organizational groundwork that paved the way to success.

In a sense the new public policy was a personal victory for these
association officers and their colleagues. All three of CTI's representatives were men with great ability and the type of background
and personality that opened the doors of America's business and
government elites. CTI's officers were able to communicate effectively with public officials, businessmen, and other trade association leaders. In 1933—when so many ideas on economic recovery
were floating about Washington—it was no small trick to make
your voice heard. Even the President of the United States listened
to Hines' ideas. This, as much as anything, was responsible for the
special role that CTI played.

It is equally true, however, that the organizations, particularly

---

[82] On the basis of my study it seems that Arthur M. Schlesinger, Jr., *The
Coming of the New Deal*, pp. 88–89, 97, and William E. Leuchtenburg,
Franklin D. Roosevelt and the New Deal, 1932–1940 (New York: Harper &
Row, 1963), p. 56, give too much credit to the Chamber for the new policy.
Title I of the NIRA bore a much closer resemblance to Dorr's proposal than
it did to either of the bills drafted by the Chamber.

the policy-shaping associations, were responsible for the new policy. The institutions created the role of association leader. Without these institutions, men of the stature of Hines, Dorr, and Sloan would not have been spokesmen for the associative philosophy. Without this strong organizational base, industries such as cotton textiles would not have experimented so fully with voluntary programs. As a result of their experience with these organizations, the association leaders had been able to work out in some detail an ideology which incorporated the values of stability, cooperation, and control. This ideology was important in 1933. It seemed to offer a path out of the Great Depression, and the Roosevelt Administration decided to follow that path, guided by the association leaders.

NIRA opened the way for a tight alliance between this form of stabilizing institution and the government. Although these two parties had been cooperating closely for a number of years, their alliance was now legal and binding—for at least two years. Although it had taken the most serious depression in American history to complete this entente, there was no reason to believe that the treaty would not be renewed and the alliance preserved as a permanent policy.[83]

With the passage of the NIRA the Cotton-Textile Institute entered a new stage in its development; voluntarism was being replaced by majority control with coercion of the recalcitrant minority. Like the guild, this modern association was to employ government power to achieve its objectives. There was still much talk about voluntary cooperation, but the Recovery Act made it very clear that the nonconformers were going to have to decide whether they wanted to follow the common policies willingly or whether they wanted to follow the common policies under duress. No longer would they have the option to ignore the general will. There were several things about the new order which were not

---

[83] Certain elements of Gabriel Kolko's thesis about the close relationship between reform measures and businessmen interested in stabilization are supported by CTI's history, particularly by the NIRA episode. It must be remembered, however, that the businessmen and association leaders worked in an environment which was far more complex than the one Kolko depicts: reform elements and their activities can not be ignored by the historian; nor can the historian afford to neglect the type of interbureaucratic alliance which slowly developed between the government and various types of business institutions; Kolko, *Conservatism.*

clear, but there was no mistaking the fact that the associations and the government did not intend to tolerate nonconformity.

This was, then, an historic turning point for America. Like Germany and Great Britain, the United States was experimenting with a cartel policy. Temporarily abandoning its dedication to competition, the nation was trying to use trade associations to stabilize and control its crippled economy. The associations were given ideal circumstances in which to prove their abilities. They needed only to lead the way to economic recovery in order to establish a primary and permanent role in the American system.

Chapter IX

Formative Days
of the Condominium

In the middle of May, 1933, Capitol Hill was a bubbling political stew of legislators, professors, secretaries, reformers, union officials, businessmen, administrators (seasoned and fresh), and the spice of a hundred thousand ideas—old and new ideas, some of them wild, some of them cautious, all of them offered with the same avowals of high purpose and selfless sacrifice. Since the master chef was F.D.R., the Institute's officers could virtually ignore Congress and assume that the National Industrial Recovery Bill that the President sent to Capitol Hill would be passed without much delay or amendment. Other recovery measures had been whipped through Congress in record time. Consequently, CTI began at once to draft a code and to establish on a firm basis the projected condominium of business and government.

Before attacking the Washington front, CTI's officers made certain that the majority of their own forces were prepared for the new campaign. They used the "40–40" proposal for this purpose. They beat the drum loudly and by May 19 had 18,500,000 spindles subscribed; in the next few days they added 2,000,000 more spindles to this total.[1] With two-thirds of the industry marshaled behind the 40–40 plan CTI's position was secure.

[1] Letter of G. A. Sloan to Fred M. Allen, May 19, 1933, in Sloan MSS; G. A. Sloan, Memo for Executive Committee of CTI, May 20, 1933, in Comer MSS; *New York Times*, May 21, 1933; CTI stayed in touch with the administration: Letter of G. A. Sloan to Marvin H. McIntyre, May 15, 1933, OF 372, RL.

Under the new dispensation proclaimed by F.D.R., the mills which were not supporting the Institute were merely labeled the "unfair" minority that had always opposed the "fair employers."

The Roosevelt Administration was also optimistic about the recovery bill: shortly after the measure went to Congress, CTI, NACM, and the American Association were asked to organize a representative committee which could draft a code for the industry. This call to duty came from Hugh Johnson and other officials who were already forming the Recovery Administration that Congress had yet to approve. Although the request was unofficial, the associations responded quickly. They appointed a special inter-associational committee which included the manufacturers—most of them from the larger firms—who had been most active in their associations. Included were six northern producers, nine southern manufacturers, and four representatives of the New York mercantile interests. George Sloan was the only association leader who was a regular member, although it was assumed that the secretaries of the National and American Associations would assist in the committee's work. By May 24 this committee was marshaled in Washington at the Mayflower Hotel, ready to draft a code that would bring their industry under the new policy.[2]

The Code Committee's position was very strong. Compared to the other forces with which it would have to contend, the Committee was extremely well organized. Among these particular manufacturers, the concept of industry-wide authority was firmly established. They recognized the need for cooperation and control. Furthermore, for a number of years they had been working together in the National Council, in the regional associations, and in CTI. They knew each other well; and they were not inclined to let personal differences prevent them from achieving their objectives. Within the nascent NRA, by contrast, personalities loomed large. Bitter disputes over power and principles kept the government off balance and gave the industry an important advantage.

The Committee also had exceptionally good leadership. All of

[2] CTI, Minutes, Cotton Textile Industry Committee, May 24, 1933, in Dorr MSS (hereafter cited as CTI, Minutes, CTIC); this group is also called the Code Committee and later the Code Authority, and I occasionally refer to the group as CTI or the association; Telegram of Sloan to D. Comer, May 21, 1933, Comer MSS.

the manufacturers had experience as officers in the national or regional associations. Several of the members were seasoned "businesscrats" with extensive experience in government bureaucracy as well as business.[3] During the First World War many of them had shared in the work of the War Service Committee and other government agencies.[4] Assisting the businessmen were Sloan and Dorr, both of whom had already shown their ability to lead the industry and to work with government officials. In 1933 when this kind of talent was in short supply in Washington, the Committee was well stocked with articulate, experienced leaders.

Moreover, the industry's leaders had a clear concept of what their goal was. The members of the Committee knew exactly what they wanted. In May, 1933, they were striving to achieve the same goal that had brought about the formation of CTI in 1926: stability of prices and profits. Among the other factions and organizations concerned with the recovery program, there was far less clarity about objectives. As the NRA took shape, the government officials in charge of its operations had frequent and frequently bitter disputes over what exactly the administration was trying to do. There was no such controversy within the Code Committee.

One of the Committee's greatest advantages was its storehouse of information about the industry. Each member had been in the business for a number of years. Each understood the terminology of the market place, the structure of the industry, the categories of labor employed, and the technical problems of production; at least they understood them better than the government or union officials with whom they were associating in NRA. When the recovery program began, the government did not have much more information than it had had during the First World War. NRA needed technically competent administrators and staff specialists—but so did a dozen other government agencies. Until these men could be found, NRA had to depend upon the Committee for technical knowledge of the industry.[5]

[3] I am indebted to Professor Gerald D. Nash for the word "businesscrats," which accurately describes a twentieth-century breed of businessman who spends a significant part of his life working as a government bureaucrat.

[4] CTI, Minutes, CTIC, May 24 and 25, 1933, Dorr MSS; ACMA, *Proc.*, XXI (1917), 35, 79–80; National Council, Minutes, January 11, 1918, NTA MSS; War Industries Board, Price Fixing Committee, Minutes, March 26 and May 29, 1918, RG 61, NA.

[5] NRA, Résumé of Testimony [by W. L. Allen?], June 28, 1933, in RG 9, 1810, NA.

Even when the government did begin to acquire a competent staff the Code Committee did not lose this advantage—at least not at first. Many of the government's top-level administrators were drawn from the business world. In some instances the cotton manufacturers found that these new officials were old friends— and whether there was a personal tie or not, the businesscrats in NRA were sympathetic with the industry's point of view. In a few cases administrators came from the cotton textile industry itself. This was the case with Nelson Slater, a cotton manufacturer who became an assistant to Hugh Johnson.[6] As long as men with his background were near the sources of power within NRA, the industry could be certain that it would have, at the very least, a fair hearing.

Another advantage that the Code Committee had was an un-tapped supply of goodwill built up during the night-work campaign and the subsequent efforts to recast public policy. As a result of CTI's close liaison with the Roosevelt Administration and the "progressive" attitude reflected in the 40–40 proposal, cotton textiles was a favorite son among American industries. Other industries (including, most prominently, the automobile manufacturers) seemed hesitant about self-regulation in alliance with the government. But cotton textiles was ready to join hands with NRA, and the Roosevelt Administration was grateful for this enthusiastic support.[7]

The industry had a strong but not a free hand. There were several constraints which limited in a significant fashion the Committee's ability to exercise its power. In May, 1933, the most de-cisive of these constraints was the need for immediate action. Whether the Committee chose to or not, it was being forced to draft an industrial code quickly. The administration needed a program that would immediately increase purchasing power and cut down on unemployment; the NRA could not afford to linger

---

[6] NACM, *Trans.*, CXXXIII (1933), 36; Letter of G. A. Sloan to T. M. Marchant, September 22, 1933, in Comer MSS; Special Industrial Recovery Board, Proceedings, June 19, 1933, RG 44, NA.

[7] See the remarks of Hugh Johnson in Special Industrial Recovery Board, Proceedings, July 17, 1933, RG 44, NA; Letter of G. A. Sloan to A. D. White-side, September 8, 1933, in Comer MSS; Sidney Fine, *The Automobile Under the Blue Eagle* (Ann Arbor: University of Michigan Press, 1963).

over the codes, especially the first one.[8] By moving fast the Committee would give the labor unions and other potentially hostile groups less time to gather their forces and to zero in on the industry's code. The sooner the Committee agreed with the government as to the precise nature of the code, the less likely it was that the industry's opponents would be able to use the new program to their own advantage. Swift action was imperative.[9]

Although the textile unions were in a relatively weak position, their presence and their demands also had to be considered by the Code Committee. Section 7(a) of the bill that was before Congress virtually guaranteed the unions a voice in NRA; the administration's general attitude toward organized labor made their presence mandatory. To the manufacturers from the northern wing of the industry this was an unpleasant but acceptable feature of the new program. To southern management the union presence was an anathema. Their mill hands were as yet unorganized, and the southern executives were loath to sit in the same room with a union official, let alone to negotiate with him. Despite these strong feelings, the Committee found it impossible either to ignore or to vanquish the unions and their influence upon the code.[10]

A third constraint upon the Code Committee's decisions was imposed by the government, or to be more precise, by the new Recovery Administration. Fortunately for the Committee, the NRA lacked the essential administrative personnel and techniques that would have made it a formidable organization. Until qualified men were appointed and effective procedures were developed, the NRA found it difficult to exert a decisive influence on the code. Initially this was not a serious handicap for the government because the administration and the industry agreed about most of the basic elements in the recovery policy. The industry had already accepted the government's concept of minimum wages;

[8] Letter of G. A. Sloan to Craig Smith, June 8, 1933; D. Comer to Sloan, June 12, 1933; both in Comer MSS; NACM, *Trans.*, CXXXIII (1933), 74.

[9] Telegram of Sloan to D. Comer, June 14, 1933, Comer MSS.

[10] Letter of D. Comer to T. Marchant, May 27, 1933, in Comer MSS; Interview with Donald Comer, November 3, 1958; Interview with Cason J. Callaway, November 6, 1958; Letter of W. L. Allen to Hugh S. Johnson, June 19, 1933, RG 9, 1802, NA; [W. L. Allen], Notes, RG 9, 1810, NA; unless otherwise cited, all of the NRA MSS (RG 9) are in The Consolidated Approved Industry File.

the only potential dispute was over how high the minimum wage would be. In regard to limiting the workweek the NRA representatives and the Committee agreed on the principle and were, in fact, very close insofar as the precise limits were concerned. CTI had already accepted the forty-hour week. For its part, the Roosevelt Administration had indicated by fighting the Black Thirty-Hour Bill that it was not inclined to seek a drastic reduction in the workweek.

About production control there was a similar consensus.[11] Perhaps the only disagreement was that the industry said that the code should eliminate cutthroat competition, while the government said that it should prevent cutthroat competition without supporting illegal price-fixing—whatever that meant. In brief, the NRA's position on production control reflected the fact that there were still misgivings about abandoning competition. This was true even though President Roosevelt's statements and the bill before Congress accepted the concept of production control that had been advanced by the trade association leaders. At first, however, this hardly provided enough substance for a real conflict between NRA and the Committee. On the fundamental principles of recovery the NRA and the Committee saw eye to eye.[12]

A more serious restraint was imposed by the industry itself. There were certain obvious limits that the Committee could not exceed so long as it wanted to present itself as a representative for the industry. The complete elimination of North-South wage differentials, for instance, would have sparked a revolt by southern management.[13] Even though the Committee had government backing, major factions within the industry had to be heard. The Com-

---

[11] In subsequent years, participants in the NRA's activities and historians have emphasized the conflict that existed over price and production controls. They have, I believe, made the mistake of assuming that the controversies which later ripped the NRA apart were of vital concern during the first days of code drafting. My research suggests that this was not the case, but for a different opinion see: Schlesinger, *The Coming of the New Deal,* pp. 110–111, 126; Roos, *NRA Economic Planning,* pp. 73–74, 364.

[12] Committee of the Special Industrial Recovery Board, Proceedings, June 19, 1933; NRA, *Bulletin No. 2,* June 19, 1933; both in RG 44, NA; also see, G. A. Sloan, Memo to Mill Executives, June 10, 1933, in Comer MSS; G. H. Dorr, *Comment on Certain Phases of the Draft of N. R. A. Textile Industry Report,* March 20, 1936, in Sloan MSS.

[13] Members of the Cotton Textile Industry Committee were considered to be representatives of either the North, the South, or New York.

mittee would of course alienate certain of the nonconformers; but at least during the first stages of code drafting it was best to avoid a major battle within the industry.[14] This consideration, the need for quick action, the presence of the unions, and the necessity of winning approval of the NRA officials all acted to limit the power that the Code Committee possessed in May, 1933. Each of these restraints became obvious when the Committee first bumped into the man who was slated to run NRA, General Hugh S. Johnson.

In the eyes of the manufacturers Johnson was a friendly but often frightening man. He was bluff and excitable, hard but occasionally maudlin, vigorous and extremely articulate—a man given to excesses of work and play, of order and chaos. He was sympathetic with business; after all, he was Baruch's man. But he was impatient with administrative details and instantly hostile, in an almost paranoid fashion, to any threat to his personal authority. To the rational, counting-house mind of the manufacturers, working with Johnson—or as they referred to him privately, Old Ironpants—was like trying to tame a whirlwind: if they succeeded, they would hold the reins on a source of tremendous power; if they failed, the whirlwind might well destroy them and all of their plans. This was a dangerous situation, and the Committee was careful to do its homework before the first session with the General.[15]

As the Committee began its work, it became apparent that two of the three major provisions that would have to go into the code were, in effect, already drafted. About 80 per cent of the industry had agreed to accept the forty-hour week for their mill hands. Along with this proposal, they had decided to limit production by operating their machinery no more than eighty hours—two forty-hour shifts—a week. These two points were settled so far as the Committee was concerned. That left them to confront the difficult problem of minimum wages. What wages should they propose to Johnson? How much difference should there be be-

[14] Sloan, Memorandum to Mill Executives, June 10, 1933, Comer MSS.
[15] Interview with Cason J. Callaway, November 6, 1958; Letter of W. D. Anderson to G. A. Sloan, May 25, 1934; Anderson to D. Comer, July 25, 1934; both in Comer MSS.

tween wages in the North and South? These were tough questions, and unfortunately the associations had virtually no experience in dealing with wages.[16]

After hours of discussion by the Committee and a special subcommittee, a minimum wage proposal was adopted. At first the full Code Committee had been unable to make any progress. All they could agree on was the general principle that they should pay about the same wages for the shorter forty-hour week that they were now paying for fifty or sixty hours of work. Finally the problem was handed to a subcommittee of southern and northern manufacturers, which worked out the following recommendation: the North-South differential should be $1.00 a week; the minimum in the South should be either $8.00 or $9.00 and in the North $9.00 or $10.00. The Committee accepted this recommendation, with the understanding that it would try to get Johnson to accept the lower figures.[17]

The manufacturers got a rude shock when they placed this proposal before the General. He had strong convictions about the textile industry. Wages, he said, should be increased substantially. He had in mind a minimum that might be as high as $15.00 a week; $12.00 might be acceptable, but it would obviously not make him very happy. At any rate, an $8.00 minimum was ridiculously low; they must, he said, raise their workers' standard of living. He was not so worried about the length of the workweek, but he was afraid that a forty-hour week would not spread the work enough. He thought in terms of a thirty or thirty-two-hour week. After a brief and fruitless discussion, he sent the businessmen back to work out another proposal that came closer to the standards he had outlined.[18]

When the Committee next confronted Johnson (on June 1), it stuck by the 40–40 schedule but suggested minimum wages of $10.00 and $11.00 a week. By this time the group had piles of statistics to support its proposal. The entire twenty-man Committee filed in to argue for this recommendation, ready to meet John-

[16] CTI, Minutes, CTIC, May 24 and 25, 1933, NTA MSS.

[17] *Ibid.;* the secretary of ACMA later recalled that the southerners went to Washington with the idea of getting wages set at about twenty-five cents an hour or $10.00 a week for forty hours; Interview with William M. McLaurine, October 28, 1958.

[18] Sloan, Memorandum to Mill Executives, June 10, 1933, Comer MSS; CTI, Minutes, CTIC, May 24 and 25, 1933, NTA MSS.

son head on. But the General brushed them aside. He could not meet with twenty men, he said. He had to negotiate with all of the nation's industries, and most of the work had to be done by small committees. They should appoint a few representatives. He would do the same, and then these subcommittees could work out an acceptable plan.[19]

That afternoon the two groups got together. Again the manufacturers hauled out their data and argued for the $10.00 and $11.00 minimum wage and the 40–40 schedule. According to the statistics, they said, two forty-hour shifts would allow the industry to produce as much as it had in 1929. If they cut the limits below 40–40, the print-cloth mills would be unable to produce enough to meet the orders that they had at that time. Although demand was obviously being stimulated by the anticipation of higher prices to come with the code's adoption, they argued that their limits were reasonable, especially in light of the periods of peak demand that the industry had experienced in the past. In truth this was a conservative proposal. It was unlikely that the 40–40 plan would impose any significant restraint upon output, even though it drastically cut the normal workweek in the southern mills. Johnson had mentioned a thirty-hour week, but he was apparently not adamant on this point. His representatives quickly accepted the industry's arguments. Alexander Sachs of NRA decided that the forty-hour week was satisfactory since it would re-employ all of those who had held jobs in the industry during its period of peak employment. Thomas McMahon, President of the United Textile Workers of America, was assisting Sachs; and McMahon stated "that organized labor was 100 per cent with the manufacturers on the question of a 40-hour work week with an 80 hour machine limitation." That virtually settled the issue.[20]

The industry also was able to push through the $10.00–$11.00 minimum wage proposal. When Sachs took the proposition back to the General, Johnson was considerably less hostile than he had been in his first encounter with the wage problem. He nevertheless sent Sachs, George Sloan, and some of the manufacturers to talk to Secretary of Labor Frances Perkins, who was, of course,

[19] CTI, Minutes, CTIC, June 1, 1933, NTA MSS.

[20] *Ibid.;* Letter of Alexander Sachs to G. A. Sloan, March 12, 1934; Dorr, *Comment on Certain Phases of the Draft of N. R. A. Textile Industry Report,* March 20, 1936; both in Sloan MSS.

interested in the minimum wage. Perkins raised no serious objections to the $10.00–$11.00 rates, and after clearing this hurdle the Committee was able to push ahead with some assurance that this level of wages would be approved. Their support on this issue still appeared a bit shaky, but the minimum wage question was ostensibly settled by June 9.[21]

Although production control was later to cause a tremendous dispute inside and outside of NRA, the 40–40 proviso was accepted by the government with hardly any resistance. Alexander Sachs and the other planners on the government staff were apparently a bit suspicious of the limitation; but the industry's arguments were persuasive, particularly the argument that 40–40 would stabilize production and employment at the level that had been reached in 1929. Stability at that level looked good from the perspective of 1933. Furthermore, the Roosevelt Administration had already abandoned the antitrust principle in the bill submitted to Congress; if the codes were not to contain provisions such as 40–40, why had the antitrust laws been relaxed for a two-year period? The answer was obvious. And the industry's representatives never budged from their strong position on limiting production.[22]

One attack upon production control came from an unexpected source—Congress. While the bill was under consideration, Senator Borah of Idaho introduced an amendment which would in effect have nullified the relaxation of antitrust proposed by the administration.[23] Speaking for the cotton textile industry, Walker D. Hines wired Roosevelt a sharp protest against the amendment. Their code, Hines said, had already been drafted; it had been worked out in consultation with government officials and representatives of organized labor. Now, the Borah Amendment made acceptance of the code doubtful. As Hines pointed out, "The language of that amendment . . . seems to make uncertain if not

[21] CTI, Minutes, CTIC, June 1 and 3, 1933, NTA MSS.

[22] As early as June 19, 1933, Rexford G. Tugwell was asking for a statement of "the general purpose of the act." But Johnson's reply was that he did not "want to get into policy. Going to treat it when I get to it. Don't want to be too specific." By this time, however, he had already established the policy of approving a production-control plan; Committee of the Special Industrial Recovery Board, Proceedings, June 19, 1933, RG 44, NA.

[23] U. S., Congressional Record, 73rd Cong., 1st Sess., 1933, LXXVII, Part 6, 5246.

entirely impossible the carrying out of the objectives of the act in dealing with overproduction and cutthroat competition and so interposes obstacles to spreading employment and increasing the purchasing power of labor. . . . My acquaintance with the cotton textile industry leaves me convinced that the Borah Amendment would largely if not wholly destroy the wholesome purposes of the bill."[24] Apparently Roosevelt agreed. The administration beat back the amendment, confirming the New Deal's acceptance of the association philosophy. With this threat out of the way, the machine-hour limitation was safely established as a basic element in the NRA's first code proposal.[25]

During the negotiations between the Committee and the NRA, another major issue, the problem of controlling entry and expansion, came up. At the suggestion of Deputy Administrator W. L. Allen, the Committee drafted a code provision which declared a two-year moratorium on the construction of new mills or the expansion of existing plants. In its original form this article flatly stated that "No person shall, during the emergency period, install any new productive machinery except for replacements"; exceptions could be made only on the approval of President Roosevelt, supported by the top officers of the three trade associations.[26] On reflection, both the NRA and the industry decided to soften this harsh edict. As amended, the code provision required registration of all existing equipment and provided a regular procedure for applying for permission to install new machinery. Even in the new version, however, the industry's representatives could delay and perhaps block any attempt at expansion or entry into the industry. This rounded out an industrial code that already embodied the principles of stable wages, stable hours, stable production and, hopefully, stable prices.[27]

By June 16, when the National Recovery Bill emerged from Congress, the industry and Hugh Johnson's staff had completed the first code. Included in the code were five central provisions:

[24] Telegram of W. D. Hines to Franklin D. Roosevelt, June 9, 1933; Telegram of G. A. Sloan to D. Comer, June 9, 1933; both in Comer MSS.

[25] Schlesinger, *The Coming of the New Deal*, pp. 100–102.

[26] CTI, Minutes, CTIC, June 9 and 16, 1933, NTA MSS. R. T. Stevens, Memorandum to Dr. Sachs, July 10, 1933, in RG 9, 1824, NA; Dorr, *Comment on Certain Phases of the Draft of N. R. A. Textile Industry Report,* March 20, 1936, Sloan MSS.

[27] NRA, Transcript of Hearing No. 1, June 30, 1933, in RG 9, 7152, NA.

a minimum wage of $10.00 per week in the South, $11.00 in the North; a forty-hour week for the workers; section 7(a) which apparently guaranteed the workers' right to organize unions; the two-shift limitation on production; and a provision for control of entry and expansion. From the Committee's standpoint, these were satisfactory terms for an alliance between their industry and the government. Section 7(a) had been a bitter pill to swallow, but the Recovery Act flatly stated that this provision had to be included in all of the codes; the manufacturers considered 7(a) as part of the price of governmental authority for their own program. Their basic objective, production control, had been accepted by the government with little resistance. By the time they had finished drafting the code, Hugh Johnson had been fully converted to the guild ideology.[28] Management, government, and even labor stood together, ready to embark on this grand experiment with industrial organization.

The big issues were settled, but the code had barely been roughed out before the Committee began a paralyzing descent into the administrative minutia of definitions and descriptions. If the minimum wage did not apply to learners, who, exactly, were the learners? How long would their apprenticeship last? Would some mills be tempted to classify large numbers of workers as learners? And what about repairmen and outside help? Did they come under the code's provisions? If not, what was their minimum wage to be? How long could they work each week?

At first the manufacturers felt that questions such as these presented no serious problems. With supreme confidence in their own ability and the ability of their peers, they simply decided that they could leave these minor difficulties to be ironed out by the associations or the managers and workers who were involved. This was what they had done in previous trade association programs. Was there any reason to change now?[29]

The answer came quickly. And the answer was "yes." It soon

[28] Judging from Johnson's remarks at the public hearing, any doubts that he had about the new order of guild government had melted away in Washington's hot summer sun. *Ibid.*, June 28, 1933.

[29] Sloan, Memorandum to Mill Executives, June 10, 1933, Comer MSS; this attitude was also reflected in the system that the Code Authority set up to handle labor problems; CTI, Minutes, CTIC, August 1, 1933, NTA MSS.

became apparent that their code and their alliance with the government had opened a pandora's box of organizational disputes. The cause of the learners was taken up by the Department of Labor. Miss Perkins was concerned about this particular question; she was determined to see that the learners were protected from exploitation. As the Committee soon learned, Miss Perkins and the Department of Labor were formidable adversaries.[30] On this and a number of other issues the Committee found itself involved in a complex series of negotiations over the details of industrial control.[31]

One of the most difficult problems was resolving differences within the industry itself. It was no mean task to impose the tight hand of centralized control over such an old and complex industry. Within each of the subindustries or product groups there were particular problems, special terms and market arrangements, unusual conditions that seemed to necessitate a separate code or special provisions in the basic code. What, for instance, was the Committee to do about finishing machinery and the finishing industry itself? In Fall River and other textile centers there were many finishing companies which did nothing but bleach and print cloth that was manufactured by other mills. The finishers had their own trade association. They felt that theirs was a separate industry; should they have a separate code? If so, what was to be done about the mills which did their own finishing? Were their finishing machinery and the workers who handled it to be excluded from the provisions of the basic code? This would leave these mills operating under two codes, sending in reports to two code authorities, with the possibility that workers in the same plant would operate on different shifts and would receive different wages.[32]

Under pressure to fragment the code or to provide detailed

[30] CTI, Minutes, CTIC, June 3, 1933, NTA MSS.
[31] Letter of John F. McNamara to Edward F. McGrady, June 26, 1933; Letter of H. H. Broach to H. S. Johnson (with enclosure), June 27, 1933; both in RG 9, 1809, NA.
[32] CTI, Minutes, CTIC, June 14, 1933, NTA MSS; also see: *King Cotton Weekly,* June 21, 1933, in files of the Southern Combed Yarn Spinners Association, Gastonia, N.C.; Telegram of Charles D. Owen to H. S. Johnson, June 26, 1933; Letter of secretary to Mr. W. L. Allen to C. D. Owen, June 29, 1933; Letter of Russell E. Watson to H. S. Johnson, June 29, 1933; all three in RG 9, 1813, NA; Letter of G. A. Sloan to W. L. Allen, June 23, 1933; Letter of G. A. Sloan to S. G. Carkhuff, June 23, 1933; both in Comer MSS.

exceptions for each subindustry, the association leaders, the Committee, and the NRA agreed that for the time they would simply
ignore the pressure, blanketing the entire industry under one set
of regulations. The administration wanted to get the recovery
program moving. The Committee was also in a hurry, impatient
about exceptions and eager to impose production controls. Exemptions might weaken the program's effect. At any rate, such
problems could be left to the association leaders to solve—after
production and prices were stabilized. In May and June of 1933
neither the government nor the Committee was really prepared
to accept and perform the detailed tasks of administration that
went with national industrial control, and requests for special
treatment met a hostile audience.[33]

All of the problems that Johnson and the Committee had been
trying to sweep under the rug became public issues when hearings
on the code were opened on June 27. This was the first NRA
code. And NRA held center stage in Roosevelt's recovery program.
Throughout the nation, eyes were focused on Washington; the
press and the people watched while Hugh Johnson unveiled the
nation's first industrial code. In the "goldfish bowl"—Johnson's
description of the public hearing—the basic problems of industrial
control had to be confronted.

Never one to avoid public attention, Johnson was on hand to
launch the hearings. "The function of the government," he said,
"is to safeguard the public to see to it that such agreements as
are presented attain the end for which they are designed, but in
attaining that end they do injustice to nobody." Those who might
feel the code was unjust could present "facts" supporting their
contention. There would be no rebuttals or arguments, however.
He stressed the point that the hearings were held merely to allow
interested parties to present information—facts—that suggested
that the code should be modified in the public interest. The suggestions, he said, must reveal no animosity; the keynote was to be
cooperation. The partnership principle, Johnson said, was in full
force.[34]

[33] Sloan to Allen, June 23, 1933, Comer MSS; NRA, Transcript of Hearing
No. 1, June 28, 1933, RG 9, 7152, NA; all subsequent references to NRA,
Hearing No. 1, refer to this record.
[34] NRA, Hearing No. 1, June 27, 1933.

Appropriately, the government's business partner presented its case first. George Sloan plodded through the code, provision by provision. He explained each of the central articles, especially the machine-hour limitation. The members of the Committee, he said, considered "the basic problem in the rehabilitation of the industry to be to check the destructive effects of over-capacity, spread employment and increase the purchasing power of employees." So they had written a code that they estimated would put 100,000 additional workers back on the job, while the minimum wage and 40–40 provisions would create more purchasing power and steadier employment. Unless they restricted production, Sloan concluded, they could not "hope to rehabilitate the industry and stabilize employment."[35]

Sloan was anticipating an attack upon the machine-hour limitation. Although Hugh Johnson and the other NRA officials had accepted the concept of production control, they still talked about eliminating cutthroat competition and destructive practices without fixing prices or restricting production. This flimsy position might collapse at any time, and Sloan and the Committee were nervous. On the eve of the hearings they had discussed the fact that, outside of NRA, opposition to the machine-hour provision seemed to be mounting. What should they do if the government now refused to back them up on production control? After a long discussion they decided that if the 40–40 proviso were eliminated they would scuttle the entire code. It would be better, they felt, to wait for the NRA to write a code and impose it on the industry than to introduce their own code without this vital provision. Production control was non-negotiable.[36]

After Sloan presented the code and defended 40–40, representatives of the northern and southern regional associations were given a chance to speak on behalf of their branches of the industry. Robert Amory, who represented New England, was brief and to the point. He hinted at northern discontent with the wage differential; but for the present, he said, he and his colleagues in New England were satisfied with the code. Then William D. Anderson of Macon, Georgia, spoke for the American Association. As he rambled through a long and tedious account of the numerous blessings of the southern mill and life in the mill village, Hugh

[35] *Ibid.*
[36] CTI, Minutes, CTIC, June 26, 1933, NTA MSS.

Johnson became impatient. Anecdote piled on anecdote. The General interrupted. Finally, after trading sharp words with Johnson, Anderson strayed to the end of his speech, leaving the floor to the opponents of the code.[37]

The opposition got precious little support from Johnson or Deputy Administrator Allen. The General had some suggestions as to how the code might be improved, but he was determined to preserve the partnership that he had established with the Committee. He was effusive in his praise of the business and association leaders with whom he had worked out this first code. Both Johnson and Allen left no doubt that they fully supported the machine-hour limitation.

It soon became clear, however, that everyone was not as pleased with the code as Johnson was. There were reform organizations which felt that an explicit regulation on child labor should be included. Labor concentrated its attack upon the relatively low minimum wage and the forty-hour week. From within the industry itself there came a bitter assault upon the 40–40 clause.

Most successful of these opponents were the reform groups. They had begun their campaign before the hearing; the New York Child Labor Committee, the Child Welfare League of America, and other kindred organizations had laid down a barrage of letters upon NRA headquarters.[38] During the hearings, Johnson suggested to Sloan that this demand should perhaps be met. CTI's president agreed but pointed out that the industry's position had been that the minimum wage would automatically eliminate child labor; manufacturers would not be willing to pay the new wages to children; nevertheless, he would be happy, Sloan said, to consider including this in the code.[39]

As Sloan knew, there was already strong support within the industry for such a proposal. The earlier night-work program had softened the resistance to the basic concept of social control of working conditions. Whereas southern manufacturers had once led the fight against regulation of child labor, many of the Piedmont's leading executives were now exponents of such laws. One of these was T. M. Marchant, President of the American Association. When the Committee met that evening to discuss the day's

[37] NRA, Hearing No. 1, June 27, 1933.

[38] Letters from the Child Welfare League of America, the Children's Service Society of Utah, the League of Women Voters, the National Child Labor Committee, etc., are in RG 9, 1814, NA.

[39] NRA, Hearing No. 1, June 27, 1933.

proceedings, Marchant said that he had been working for three years to get the industry to stop employing minors under sixteen years of age; they should not, he said, lose this opportunity to eliminate child labor from their industry. The response was immediate and enthusiastic. Within a few moments they had drafted the statement that Marchant read as the hearings entered their second day.[40] Amidst applause, Marchant announced that the industry's Code Committee was putting into the code a provision expressly prohibiting the employment of minors under sixteen years of age in any cotton textile mill covered by NRA regulations.[41]

Labor's attack on the code was less successful. One of the provisions the unions fired at was the forty-hour week. Labor representatives—including Thomas McMahon of the United Textile Workers, William E. G. Batty of the New Bedford Textile Council, and William Green of the American Federation of Labor—charged that the forty-hour week was too long; it would not spread the available work far enough. Senator Hugh Black lent the unions his support. He spoke out for a standard thirty-hour week for all of the nation's laborers.[42]

These arguments failed to move the NRA officials. In the first place McMahon had previously approved the forty-hour limit. Deputy Administrator Allen pointed out that he was "somewhat 'flabbergasted' " by this sudden reversal; McMahon had been his adviser while the code was being drafted—why had he failed to mention these objections at that time? McMahon fumbled with a weak explanation apparently designed to cover up the fact that his own union had not backed up the provisions he had agreed to in the previous negotiations. It was a poor moment for the unions. After this, their objections to the forty-hour regulation fell on deaf ears. Unable to controvert the evidence indicating that a forty-hour week would enable management to employ as many hands as had worked in cotton textiles in 1929, the union's bid for a shorter week failed.[43]

[40] CTI, Minutes, CTIC, June 27, 1933, NTA MSS.

[41] NRA, Hearing No. 1, June 28, 1933. It seems likely that this was carefully staged or at least fully anticipated by the industry's committee; the day before the Hearings the committee voted to include in its brief a letter from the Child Labor Committee of the State of New York; CTI, Minutes, CTIC, June 26, 1933, NTA MSS; Statement of Cotton Textile Industry Committee, June 27, 1933, in Comer MSS.

[42] NRA, Hearing No. 1, June 28 and 29, 1933.

[43] Ibid.; NRA, Résumé of Testimony [by W. L. Allen?], June 28, 1933, RG 9, 1810, NA.

More formidable was labor's assault upon the code's minimum wage. Each of the labor representatives pounded away at the substandard living conditions that would be necessitated by a wage this low. A minimum wage of $10.00 or $11.00 would, McMahon said, enforce "an animal existence." William Green cited F.D.R.'s promise that the NRA would establish a "living wage" and not a wage that would force the mill hands to scratch out their existence at a "bare subsistence level." Similar pleas issued from the National Consumers League and the Consumers League of Massachusetts. Senator Black drew the applause of the crowd when he expressed his hope "that we will never adopt a minimum wage of $10.00 per week for men who work in America."[44]

Speaker after speaker demanded a higher minimum wage, and their charges struck home with Johnson and some of his staff members. Initially the General had wanted a higher minimum and now he again pressed the Committee to raise the wages above $10.00 and $11.00.[45] It is likely that President Roosevelt also intervened. Among the President's advisers there was widespread discontent with this aspect of Code No. 1; there was fear that this would set too low a standard for subsequent codes.[46] At any rate, Johnson now applied pressure to the Committee to revise its proposed wage schedule.

Reluctantly the Committee rehashed the minimum wage problem. After considerable backing and hauling it decided to preserve the $1.00 differential and raise the minimum to $12.00 in the South and $13.00 for New England. By this time the southern mill executives were happy to escape with any differential, and they accepted the new wages without serious disagreement. Since these wages allowed for a 10 per cent increase in the cost of living, Hugh Johnson and the unions were both pleased with the new proposal. This was far more improvement than McMahon had earlier hoped for and certainly as much as Johnson had ever thought he could get.[47]

Least successful of the three major attacks on the code was the

[44] NRA, Hearing No. 1, June 28 and 29, 1933.

[45] Special Industrial Recovery Board, Proceedings, June 19, 1933, RG 44, NA; Letter of G. A. Sloan to A. F. Hinricks, February 4, 1935, in Comer MSS.

[46] Letter of John Dickinson to M. H. McIntyre (with enclosed Memorandum for the President), June 23, 1933, OF 466, RL; the President (through the Special Industrial Recovery Board), Memorandum (n.d.), in RG 9, 1802, NA.

[47] NRA, Hearing No. 1, June 30, 1933.

attempt to get rid of the machine-hour stipulation. Leading the forces opposed to production control was a representative from Johnson & Johnson, one of the nation's largest producers of cotton surgical supplies and bandages. Johnson & Johnson was one of the few vertically integrated firms in the industry. Its cotton mills, which had been built or purchased to supply fabrics only to the company's own plants, were set up to run on a twenty-four-hour basis. Russell E. Watson, who represented Johnson & Johnson, pointed out that his company was willing to pay wages as high as $14.00 a week; it was willing, furthermore, to accept any reasonable limits on the work week for labor. But it was unalterably opposed to the machine-hour limitation. For the consumer's sake, for the sake of the efficient plant, he said, the NRA should abandon the idea of penalizing the efficient producer.[48]

His proposition hit a brick wall of resistance. While Hugh Johnson and William Allen were sympathetic to Watson's suggestion that the minimum wage be raised, they fiercely defended the basic concept of production control. Allen brought up the problem of the small mill in a small community. Surely, he said, they did not want to drive that company out of business. Watson rebutted: you could not afford to support these inefficient manufacturers. Then Allen struck back with the information that Johnson & Johnson was running a twelve-hour shift (for men) in its Massachusetts plant; if there were no limitations, Allen said, the large companies would juggle production back and forth between their northern and southern plants, favoring the workers in one section. For that matter, he said, the 40–40 regulation would not curtail production, it would merely "stabilize" it.

With Watson already retreating, General Johnson threw a fast barrage of questions:

"A more efficient plant is one that turns out more units of production per unit of labor? Is that right?"

"Yes sir; at the higher wage and the minimum rate," Watson answered.

"If we carried that principle to its logical conclusion we would eliminate such inefficient plants throughout the United States and leave the production to the more efficient plants? Is that correct?"

"To the benefit of the consuming public," Watson said.

[48] NRA, Hearing No. 1, June 28, 1933.

"And if the more efficient plants turn out more units of production at less man hours, what happens to employment?"

"You are going to limit the man hours and raise the wages, and we are going to pay them, and we have been paying them."

But Johnson was not to be put off; he was in for the kill:

"If you limit the man hours of the inefficient as well as the efficient plants there is hardly any escape from the conclusion that you will reduce the number of jobs; isn't that so? I will say the number of man hours."

"Yes, sir; I will say that. But it is economically sound and disadvantageous to do otherwise in the long run."

"In the long run, perhaps. But in a great crisis where we are trying to put men back to work and where we are confronted by an industrial condition with the situation exactly as it is in this situation, would you suggest that we adopt during this emergency as a principle appropriate to this crisis a principle from which there is no escape from the conclusion that the result of it is to reduce jobs?"[49]

Watson could not escape the question, could not avoid the conclusion thrust upon him by Johnson's dialogue. In the short run, unrestrained competition promised no solution to the nation's unemployment problem; Johnson preferred to stabilize production and to spread the existing work among a larger number of employees. In light of the NRA cooperative philosophy Watson had "presented a strong self-serving case but not a position that is truly in accordance with the objective of the Recovery Act. . . ."[50]

More subtle and less easy to solve was the problem addressed to the hearing by the tire manufacturing companies which controlled their own cotton mills. These industrial giants were fully integrated. The tire-cord mills that they operated produced entirely for the parent companies; none of their cotton products went into the general market for tire cord. Due to the unusually large seasonal demand that the industry was then experiencing, the tire manufacturers maintained that if they ran their cord mills on the 40–40 schedule it would actually force them to cut production and to lay off some employees. They did not oppose the machine-hour limitation on principle; they merely argued that it would cause

49 Ibid.

50 NRA, Résumé of Testimony [by W. L. Allen?], June 28, 1933, RG 9, 1810, NA.

undue hardship for their cord mills and their mill hands if they were forced to abide by the code's provisions. They proposed instead to bring their captive cotton mills under the general code they were drafting for the tire industry.[51]

From the Code Committee's viewpoint the solution was obvious. The tire-cord mills were part of the cotton-textile industry; they had to be covered by the regulations of Code No. 1. If the tire companies needed more cotton cord, they could purchase it in the general market and thus spread production among a larger number of firms. If it allowed this exemption, the Committee said, its efforts to stabilize production and employment would be endangered.[52]

It was not that simple for Hugh Johnson and his staff. The tire companies' request forced the NRA to deal for the first time with one of the complex situations that inevitably arose out of an effort to impose tight controls on a heretofore uncontrolled economic system. Any decision would damage one of the parties involved. There was really only one thing to do: "season" the problem. Johnson decided to stay the code temporarily insofar as the captive mills were concerned, leaving the policy to be determined later. This hedge did not satisfy the Committee, but there was still an opportunity to influence NRA's final decision about the captive mills.[53]

Aside from the child labor clause and the higher minimum wage, the only significant amendment that was introduced during the hearings was a provision that would transform the Code Committee into a cotton textile industry committee. This group was to serve as a "planning and fair practice agency for the cotton textile industry. . . ." It was specifically empowered to make recommendations to the NRA about statistical reports that might be needed, about the vital matter of entry and expansion, about changes in or exemptions from the code's regulations and about any general problems facing the industry. Under the terms of this amendment —which was drafted by the Code Committee—the trade association

[51] NRA, Hearing No. 1, June 27, 1933; Letter of G. A. Sloan to P. W. Litchfield, May 30, 1933; Sloan to Carkhuff, June 23, 1933; Sloan to Allen, June 23, 1933; all three in Comer MSS.

[52] CTI, Minutes, CTIC, June 26, 1933, NTA MSS; Sloan to Allen, June 23, 1933, Comer MSS.

[53] NRA, Résumé of Testimony [by W. L. Allen?], June 28, 1933, RG 9, 1810, NA; Franklin D. Roosevelt, Code Approval No. 1, July 9, 1933, in RG 9, 1809, NA.

would play a vital role in the administration of the code. To Johnson and his assistants, this was perfectly acceptable. They were pleased with the performance of the Code Committee. They felt that the duties outlined for the new Industry Committee (or Code Authority) were entirely consonant with the partnership idea that everyone, from F.D.R. down to the lowest deputy administrator, had proclaimed was the guiding principle of the recovery program.[54]

When the public hearings closed on June 30, the industry had good cause to be satisfied. In comparing the old deal and the new, *King Cotton Weekly* jubilantly proclaimed that the mills around Gastonia, North Carolina, were operating the fullest schedule they had seen since 1930. With unrestrained enthusiasm, the *Weekly* assured its readers that the industry was "just getting ready for what's ahead. . . ."[55]

Some clouds developed in this bright sky when the code went to the White House for F.D.R.'s approval. On July 9 when Roosevelt approved the code, he added thirteen conditions which he said had to be met.[56] These amendments were, in fact, the suggestions of the Special Industrial Recovery Board, which had been given a chance to look at one of Johnson's products. On July 9 Roosevelt had suddenly called the Board together and read the code aloud to them. Under pressure, the Board accepted the code but insisted upon some amendments, thirteen in all; these ranged from a rather harmless provision that employees could not escape the forty-hour limit by working in two mills to an ominous amendment which limited presidential approval to a four-month trial period, after which the code would be subject to renewal or modification.[57]

The Committee was furious. The members felt that they had established a "contract," a partnership with the government—and such arrangements, they felt, could not be changed unilaterally. Roosevelt had proclaimed that the NRA was a venture in business-government cooperation. Johnson had echoed this same philosophy. And in practice, negotiation and compromise had

[54] NRA, Hearing No. 1, June 30, 1933.

[55] *King Cotton Weekly,* June 28, 1933.

[56] F. D. R., Code Approval No. 1, July 9, 1933, RG 9, 1809, NA.

[57] Special Industrial Recovery Board, Proceedings, July 10, 1933, RG 44, NA; Harold L. Ickes, *The First Thousand Days, 1933–1936* (New York: Simon Schuster, 1953), p. 60.

characterized the procedure of code drafting. Now, suddenly, the government was introducing amendments and conditions without warning and without negotiation.[58]

Swallowing their anger, the manufacturers decided to barge ahead on the simple assumption that they were equal parties in the alliance. The General encouraged them to stand by this premise; when they confronted him with the President's conditions, Johnson apologized. It was his fault, he said, that this had happened. He shunted the Committee aside into a conference with Deputy Administrator Allen, with the assurance that whatever they worked out with Allen would be acceptable to him.[59] By 2:30 the next morning the Committee and Allen had agreed; the amendment limiting the President's acceptance to a four-month trial period was dropped completely; five of the conditions were altered to suit the Committee; seven of the less important stipulations were accepted without change. After breakfast the following morning the code, as amended, was presented to Johnson and accepted without question by the General and his new right-hand man, Donald Richberg. In a sense Johnson had undercut the President's authority in order to preserve the partnership concept.[60]

A day later, on July 16, the General, the code, and the President went cruising down the Potomac on Roosevelt's yacht. While the Committee waited anxiously, Johnson and the President studied the revised draft of Code No. 1. It was a precedent-setting step. They could not be too careful with this, the first product of the Recovery Administration. At last, the yacht was back. The word came out. A swift relay carried the news from the Potomac, to Johnson's office, to New York City. Champagne corks popped and the manufacturers and association leaders celebrated their success: the Cotton Textile Code was signed and the new order proclaimed.[61]

After two months of frantic effort, the specific terms of the guild-government alliance were established. For a moment it had

[58] NACM, *Trans.*, CXXXIII (1933), 74.

[59] *Ibid.*

[60] Sloan to D. Comer, [July 15, 1933?], Comer MSS; CTI, Minutes, CTIC, July 14, 1933, NTA MSS.

[61] Sloan to D. Comer, [July 15, 1933?]; Telegram of Sloan to D. Comer, July 16, 1933; both in Comer MSS; CTI, Memorandum to Cotton Mill Executives, July 18, 1933, Dorr MSS; Interview with Goldthwaite H. Dorr, August 31, 1961.

appeared that the association would become a subordinate partner, but that threat had been beaten down. Similarly, the attempt to eliminate stability-oriented controls had been countered—NRA held true to the course that F.D.R. had outlined in his speeches on the recovery program. Neither the unions nor the dissident elements within the industry had been able to alter the NRA's goals or to disrupt the close contacts between the associations and the government.

Other industries responded to NRA more slowly; they could be arrayed along a spectrum which would range from cotton textiles at one end to the automobile manufacturers at the other. A brief look at the opposite extreme from cotton textiles suggests some reasons for the wide variance in the timing and nature of the industries' responses to NRA. In the automobile industry there had been very little trade association activity prior to 1933. The large firms were able to solve most of their economic problems without reliance upon interfirm organizations. Even where cooperation had seemed desirable it was seldom tried because of the belligerent individualism of Henry Ford and his company. Ford's resistance to associative programs, with or without government assistance, blocked most of the common efforts in the industry. Furthermore, in 1933, the major, common concern of the automobile manufacturers was the potential growth of the unions and not excess capacity; unionization could best be defeated by staying out of the NRA as long as possible, which is exactly what the industry did.[62]

By contrast, most of the cotton manufacturers were pleased with the new order; they considered the code to be an impressive victory for CTI and the industry. While forced to make concessions, they had successfully turned the vague promises of the National Industrial Recovery Act into a specific code embodying their basic values of stability, cooperation, and control. Their strategy had succeeded. And they were left in an excellent tactical position to reap the benefits of the code. Their Industry Committee was ensconced within the Recovery Administration; George Sloan was by now a close friend and personal adviser to Hugh Johnson. By moving fast and first, the associations in cotton textiles had earned the goodwill of Johnson and Roosevelt. The future looked good for the industry and the Institute.

[62] Fine, *The Automobile Under the Blue Eagle.*

Chapter X

Guild and Government, August 1933 to May 1934

President Roosevelt had barely placed his signature on Code No. 1 before the Cotton Textile Industry Committee set forth to administer the new program. Moving swiftly, the Industry Committee attempted to consolidate its position within NRA. In the swirling chaos over which Hugh Johnson reigned, that was no small task. Personnel kept changing every day. Men and issues and power all became tangled in a confusing bureaucratic battle. Bitter struggles over the philosophy and practice of economic recovery were a commonplace of NRA operation. It was frequently necessary for the Industry Committee and association leaders to defend their program in theoretical terms—a type of debate that was unusual and unpleasant for the businessmen and their representatives.

Despite these difficulties, the Committee succeeded in establishing its authority and in defending its philosophy during the first months of the NRA experience. In part, the Code Authority's success was due to the fact that the Recovery Administration itself was just beginning to take shape as an organization. While the NRA struggled with its staff problems, the Code Authority raced ahead, establishing procedures, defining terms, and in effect dominating the process of code administration. Another factor which helped the Code Authority strengthen its position was the lack of a clearly defined body of economic and organizational principles which could guide the Recovery Administration in its formative days. The NRA had to feel its way by hit and miss. As a result,

the rules of procedure were constantly changing, constantly dis-
rupting the activities of administrators from Johnson down to the
most insignificant clerk. Given these circumstances, it is little
wonder that many of the administrators came to depend upon the
Code Authority for its dependable personnel, experience, and
settled administrative procedure.

Initially the main focus of NRA activity was not upon administration, and this, too, helped the Code Authority. Johnson was
determined to bring all of American industry under NRA codes
as quickly as possible. For a time his wishes were met; during one
week, the first week of August, 1933, he received almost three
hundred new codes. Where the businessmen dragged their feet
they found themselves under a general code introduced by the
President's Re-employment Agreement.[1] Johnson's drive was so
successful that it kept the NRA from attending to the problems
of code administration while the first steps in applying Code No. 1
were being taken by the industry.[2]

Unconcerned about other industries or the broader national
problems of the recovery plan, the Cotton Textile Code Authority
was soon able to put its own house in order. By early August the
Authority had formed a series of small subcommittees to handle
its business. These subcommittees regularly reported to the Code
Authority, which met approximately once a month, unless there
was an emergency. Between these meetings the association leaders,
Sloan and Dorr, watched over the code and stayed in touch with
the Recovery Administration and other government agencies.[3]

Operating from this simple but smooth-working organization,
the Authority quickly dominated the sources of information about
their industry and the channels through which this information
might flow to the government. In accordance with one of the

[1] Executive Secretary of the Executive Council, Memo to the President,
August 8, 1933, in RG 44, Executive Council, NA.

[2] Hugh Johnson felt that the drive to get all of the industries under a code
would end about August 21; then would come a period in which the NRA
would "mobilize buying power"; after that second phase ended, around
September 15, he would start "the phase of disciplining these people . . .";
Special Industrial Recovery Board, Proceedings, August 21, 1933, RG 44, NA;
Schlesinger, *The Coming of the New Deal*, p. 119, is apparently mistaken in
his description of Johnson's concept of these phases.

[3] CTI, Minutes, CTIC, August 1, 1933, to May 15, 1934, in Dorr MSS.

code's provisions, the Authority continued to collect the sort of statistics that CTI had been gathering since 1927. Now, however, it was mandatory for all of the mills to submit this data. Regular reports were required upon such items as production, machine hours of operation, and stock on hand.[4]

Only the Authority had this information. No provision was made for transmitting the data to the government; and the Recovery Administration had no means of gathering its own figures.[5] Government officials had to ask the Authority for information upon which to judge the Authority's decisions and recommendations. This had been the case while the code was being drafted, and at that time the government officials had found it difficult to evaluate the industry's proposals. The same was true after the code was in operation.[6]

As long as the Authority controlled this information, it was the only organization which could effectively make decisions about the code's operations. The economics of production control, the effect of the government program on production costs, the crucial question of labor costs, and the extent to which mills were complying with the code's provisions: these problems could only be handled intelligently on the basis of relevant and up-to-date statistics. Only the Code Authority had these figures.

In a similar fashion the Authority took over the job of interpreting the code's provisions. Having already served as legislature in drafting the code, the Authority now became a judiciary which explained and elaborated the new industrial law. In reality the industry's representatives were forced into this position of strength because NRA was simply unprepared for the job. When the code was announced, manufacturers throughout the industry wanted to know what certain words meant and how particular

[4] CTI, Minutes, CTIC, September 13, 1933, NTA MSS.

[5] The Authority had apparently stopped the practice of making part of this information public; CTI, Minutes, CTIC, August 1, 1933, NTA MSS.

[6] This became an issue of considerable importance; businessmen began to refuse to report to any government agency, including the Department of Labor, on the grounds that they sent their data to the Code Authority; Special Industrial Recovery Board, Proceedings, August 14 and 28, 1933, RG 44; Executive Secretary, Memorandum to Members of the Executive Council, August 21, 1933, RG 44, Executive Council, NA; F. D. R., Memorandum for General Johnson, OF 466, RL; C. F. Roos, *NRA Economic Planning*, pp. 64–66.

provisions were to be interpreted.[7] Perplexed by a blizzard of questions, the NRA officials began to dump the requests—whether they came from management or labor—into the lap of the Code Authority.[8] In August the Authority took independent action to draft a set of standard interpretations of code provisions.[9] Similarly, the Authority began to pass down decisions in jurisdictional questions, bringing related industries (such as rayon weaving) under their code while excluding some businesses which it was decided should operate under a separate code. NRA approved all of these decisions about jurisdiction, and accepted them as amendments to the code.[10] Although the Authority's standard interpretations were never given this kind of official approval, NRA acquiesced in their use and never was able to produce a manual or guide to replace them. In effect the Authority's position was sustained.[11]

Even in the field of labor relations the trade association was able to seize a position of unusual power within NRA. First of the numerous labor problems to develop was the question of the "stretch-out." Limitations on the workweek would be of little avail if employers made each worker handle more machines, stretching out the labor. When this possibility had been raised in the hearings, Hugh Johnson had agreed to establish a special committee to study the situation.[12] The committee named by Johnson consisted of Robert W. Bruere as chairman, Benjamin Greer as the manufacturers' representative, and George L. Berry

[7] Letters of: Lester G. Wilson to C. B. Gudebrod, July 19, 1933; C. W. Metcalf to Flint Garrison, August 9, 1933; Godfrey Bloch to J. Foy Brown, August 12, 1933; G. Bloch to Atkins Manufacturing Company, August 12, 1933; C. W. Metcalf to M. A. Rosen, August 15, 1933; all in RG 9, 1807, 1809, 1824, NA.

[8] Letters of: W. L. Allen to L. Rodman, July 12, 1933; Elmer Gerrish to H. S. Johnson, July 27, 1933; A. R. Forbush to E. Gerrish, August 4, 1933; all three in RG 9, 1808 and 1809, NA.

[9] CTI, Minutes, CTIC, August 1, 1933, NTA MSS.

[10] CTI, Minutes, CTIC, August 15 and 23, 1933, NTA MSS; F. D. Roosevelt, Executive Orders, 1–2 through 1–5 and 1–7 through 1–11, in RG 9, NA; Letter of G. A. Sloan to Russell H. Leonard, December 28, 1933, in Sloan MSS.

[11] CTI, Minutes, CTIC, May 15, 1934, Dorr MSS; Letter of W. S. Nicholson to G. A. Sloan, February 8, 1934, in RG 9, 1812; Mr. Chisholm, Division of Review, Standard Work Sheet, in RG 9, 1809, NA.

[12] NRA, Hearing No. 1, June 27, 1933; Hugh Johnson had already begun to work on this problem before the hearing; CTI, Minutes, CTIC, June 16, 1933, in Dorr MSS.

as the spokesman for labor.[13] From the very beginning this committee was friendly to the manufacturers and hostile to the labor unions. Bruere felt that management in this industry had every right to be upset by an investigation held so soon after the associations had submitted the first code, a document containing magnanimous labor provisions. In Bruere's view it was essential that his committee convince the Code Authority that management was not about to be subjected to an "ex parte inquisition."[14] Even Berry was a moderate who was not inclined to challenge Bruere's pro-management bias.[15] The result was a superficial investigation of the stretch-out and an innocuous report; the manufacturers were left alone to settle the problem on a local basis.[16]

After the Bruere Committee took this tack, the manufacturers naturally supported a move to transform Bruere's group into a cotton textile national industrial relations board which would handle all labor problems arising under the code. When this was done, the Code Authority's position in labor matters was almost impregnable.[17] As one of Bruere's assistants explained: "I have been in the industry for years and years, and know how the manufacturer feels about a man snooping around from the Government. I was hoping to keep that condition from exhisting [sic] in the industry. I think Mr. Sloan takes this position."[18]

The best way to keep government agents from "snooping around"

[13] CTI, Minutes, CTIC, August 1, 1933; Letter of Robert W. Bruere et al. to H. S. Johnson, July 21, 1933, in RG 9, 1798, NA. Bruere was an author, teacher, and administrator who had previous experience in arbitrating labor-management differences and in studying industrial problems. Greer was a cotton manufacturer, and Berry was the president of the AF of L's International Pressmen's Union.

[14] Letter of R. W. B[ruere] to Alexander Sachs, July 15, 1933, in RG 9, 1814, NA.

[15] Letter of D. Comer to H. D. Warner, December 16, 1933, in Comer MSS; James A. Hodges, "The New Deal Labor Policy and the Southern Cotton Textile Industry, 1933–1941" (unpublished Ph.D. dissertation, Vanderbilt University, 1963), pp. 211 ff., takes a somewhat more charitable view of the Board's bias.

[16] R. W. Bruere et al. to H. S. Johnson, July 21, 1933, RG 9, 1798, NA; the report was accepted without objection by the Code Authority: CTI, Minutes, CTIC, August 1, 1933, Dorr MSS.

[17] NRA, Release No. 160, August 2, 1933, in RG 9, 1797; G. A. Sloan, Memorandum to All Cotton Mills, August 3, 1933, RG 9, 1799, NA.

[18] Telephone Conversation of John K. Watson with L. R. Gilbert, April 10, 1934, in RG 9, Cotton Textile National Industrial Relations Board (hereafter cited as CTNIRB), 4454, NA.

was to leave the job of investigating in the hands of the Code Authority. At the suggestion of the Cotton Textile National Industrial Relations Board, NRA decided to let the Authority investigate all complaints about violation of the labor provisions of the code.[19] When the decision was made, the Authority was certainly not prepared for the flood of complaints that came pouring into Washington.[20] Between August 12 and September 6 NRA received 641 complaints in regard to the labor provisions of the cotton textile code.[21] At first the complainants were merely referred to the Code Authority with a curt letter explaining that it was "in a position to give . . . a full ruling on any subject that [might] arise in connection with the Cotton Textile Code."[22] This meant that the laborer had to write to a representative of management in order to complain about management's violation of the code's provisions. After some reflection the Board decided that there was a chance that management might take hostile action against the complaining employee. So a new procedure was adopted: the Board sent a copy of each complaint to the Code Authority, after deleting the name of the complainant. Although this ruled out the possibility of retaliatory action by management, it made effective investigation of the complaint virtually impossible. All that the Authority knew was that an unnamed employee in a particular mill felt that he or she was not receiving the minimum wage or was being forced to work longer than forty hours a week or was being mistreated because of union membership.[23]

This left the unions in an extremely precarious position. They could complain about particular problems. But they did not have accurate and official information that would indicate whether violations of the labor provisions warranted a change in procedures. Even NRA officials did not have access to this in-

[19] L. R. Gilbert, Memorandum to J. H. Wooten (with enclosure), April 26, 1934, in RG 9, 1801; Letter of C. W. Metcalf to Charles O. Beals, August 12, 1933, in RG 9, 1810, NA.

[20] Letter of S. P. Munroe to G. Bloch, August 15, 1933, in RG 9, 1798; Letter of S. P. Munroe to R. W. Bruere, August 21, 1933; Letter of R. W. Bruere to S. P. Munroe, August 25, 1933; both in RG 9, CTNIRB, 4441; H. V. Bary, Memo to L. J. Martin, August 15, 1934, RG 9, 1801, NA.

[21] L. R. Gilbert, Memo to Cotton Textile National Industrial Relation [sic] Board, September 6, 1933, in RG 9, 1794, NA.

[22] Forbush to Gerrish, August 4, 1933, RG 9, 1809, NA.

[23] H. V. Bary, Memo to L. J. Martin, August 15, 1934, in RG 9, 1801, NA.

formation, unless, of course, they received it from the Code Authority.

In the vital area of prices and production, the Authority's suzerainty was almost absolute. In addition to its control of the statistical data essential to decision-making, the Authority took over the job of processing in the first instance all requests for exemptions from the machine-hour limitations. Each such request was a threat to the principle and practice of production control; at least that was the way the requests appeared to the Code Authority. There was almost no argument strong enough to persuade the Authority to relax the machine-hour limitations. The company which was forced to shut down in order to overhaul its machinery could not expect to run an extra shift to make up the time missed. Moving quickly and harshly, the Authority beat down all threats to the sanctity of its machine-hour provision. Control meant control.[24]

The Code Authority also consolidated its control of entry and expansion. On its own initiative it worked out regular procedures for registering all of the machinery in the industry and for granting permission to replace old machinery or to install new equipment. Monthly reports on machinery in use had to be submitted to the central office. Without official permission no mill was allowed to operate new equipment that was not installed to balance existing machinery or to replace outdated units. With Hugh Johnson's approval these procedures became official NRA policy in October, 1933.[25]

By the end of the summer, 1933, the Code Authority was deeply entrenched within NRA. Moving with speed and great skill, the industry's representatives had transformed a venture in business-government collaboration into an experiment with guild control. While the voices of labor, the consumer, and the NRA planners were still heard—faintly—it was the Code Authority which in fact dictated affairs in the industry.

[24] CTI, Minutes, CTIC, September 13, 1933; November 10 and 27, 1933; and December 11, 1933; all in NTA MSS. Initially the NRA heard the applications on first instance, but this practice was quickly changed as the Code Authority got rolling; Allen to Johnson, July 15, 1933, RG 9, 1808; Z. W. Carter, Division of Review, Standard Work Sheet, in RG 9, 1809, NA.

[25] CTI, Minutes, CTIC, September 13, 1933; Letter of Cotton Textile Industry Committee to H. S. Johnson, September 14, 1933, in Dorr MSS; General Hugh S. Johnson, Administrative Order 1–16B, September 29, 1933; Letter of P. B. Halstead to All Mills, October 2, 1933, in RG 9, 1801, NA.

By the fall of 1933 when Hugh Johnson's heated campaign to bring all industry under the NRA ended, the General had become intensely dedicated to the concept of industrial self-regulation. The trade associations, he felt, should do most of the work of administering the codes. Initially he had thought that NRA would emphasize government planning. Now his experience with cotton textiles and other major industries had persuaded him that the new agency's basic premise was the concept of a business-government partnership. Johnson was convinced that the code authorities could not be considered merely as representatives of the businessmen; in his view they were mysteriously transmogrified as they walked into the NRA offices. Instead of spokesmen for a particular form of business philosophy, they became exponents of the general will who sought what was best for the national economy.[26]

Johnson's concept of "guild government" had significant implications for the cotton textile code. So long as the General held to this philosophy, it would be difficult for him or his opponents to see what trade associations like CTI really did represent. Johnson could not understand, for instance, that the Institute's pre-NRA experience had included virtually no contact with organized labor. Where unions were involved, the association leaders had no particular ideology of their own; they tended to follow the wishes of their members. Their members' acceptance of Section 7(a) had been, at best, superficial. But it was hard for Johnson to see this. His opponents, on the other hand, were forced to view the Institute as nothing more than a mouthpiece for the members. Unable to recognize the peculiar middleman's role that the association played, they could not effectively exploit the organization's power and prestige. They rejected the trade association in the same absolute terms in which Johnson defended it.[27]

At the top of the Roosevelt Administration the struggle over Johnson's partnership principle was centered in the Special Industrial Recovery Board. Frances Perkins came to the Board meetings concerned about the labor provisions in the cotton textile

[26] Special Industrial Recovery Board, Proceedings, August 28, and September 11, 1933, RG 44, NA; also see Letter of C. W. Metcalf to Chesterfield Yarn Co., October 3, 1933, in RG 9, 1804, NA.

[27] Special Industrial Recovery Board, Proceedings, August 28 and September 11, 1933, RG 44, NA; Division Advisory Committee, Minutes, December 19, 1933, in RG 9, 7399, Research and Planning Division, Personal Files, Leon Henderson, NA.

code. Enforcement, she said, was a major problem which should not be left in the hands of the trade associations. Nor should these organizations become the sole agencies for collecting statistics; "I think we are in deep water if we allow trade associations to handle our statistics," Perkins told the Board.[28] Price-fixing was another major issue, and Secretary of Agriculture Wallace and his assistant secretary, Rexford Tugwell, joined Perkins in an assault upon price and production controls.[29]

Johnson left no doubt about his position on these matters. In regard to price-fixing he explained that

> . . . the purpose is to benefit these industries that have been de-graded—and they have been degraded by one step after another.
>
> Take the Cotton Textile Industry, for instance; that is one of them. I think many of these problems will be solved simply by what they call an open-price arrangement by which they report their prices. Every one of these industries is a little different and I know that in order to put a bottom under some of them we shall have to arrive at some formula. With some of them you have pretty nearly got to fix a minimum price. The purpose of the Act just goes out the window if you don't.[30]

According to Johnson the associations had to play a primary role in administering the codes. He was not going to let the NRA become "an investigating or inquisitorial body. I think the moment it does, the idea of self-government goes out the window; and the idea of self-government is the essential thing on which this is based."[31]

Johnson's confidence in self-regulation and production control was actually strengthened by the Board's queries. In the General's

[28] Special Industrial Recovery Board, Proceedings, August 14 and 28, September 6 and 18, 1933, in RG 44, NA.

[29] Special Industrial Recovery Board, Proceedings, August 14 and 28, September 6, October 2, 9, and 13, November 13, 20, and 27, December 12, 1933, RG 44, NA; Letters of Henry A. Wallace to the President, September 11, 12, and October 2, 1933, OF 1, RL; Executive Council, Minutes, August 15 and 29, 1933, RG 44, NA; Executive Secretary, Memo to Members of the Executive Council, August 21 and October 2, 1933, RG 44, Executive Council, NA.

[30] Special Industrial Recovery Board, Proceedings, August 14, 1933, RG 44, NA.

[31] Special Industrial Recovery Board, Proceedings, August 14 and 28, 1933, RG 44, NA; also see Letter of Donald Richberg to George W. Norris, December 18, 1933, RG 9, 581, Office Files of the General Counsel, NA.

peculiar view of the universe, questions such as these became part of a systematic campaign, a conspiracy, to drive him from the helm of NRA. There could be no effective dialogue over the recovery program. Johnson found it hard to talk directly to the issues. Opponents of any particular policy were in his view merely searchers after power—power that Johnson held.[32] He fought back against the Board.[33] Finally he persuaded Roosevelt to disband the Special Industrial Recovery Board, shifting its functions to the National Emergency Council. As Johnson withdrew to his lonely throne at the top of NRA, he proclaimed himself the champion of guild government and of associations like CTI.[34]

A more dangerous threat to the Code Authority's position of power came from within the Recovery Administration itself. As the smoke cleared after Johnson's initial campaign to draft codes, the NRA began to function more effectively. Some of the personnel problems were overcome. Lines of authority were established. Administrative procedures were outlined for the departments charged with overseeing the operation of the various codes. As this took place, a revolt against Johnson's concept of the recovery program began to develop at the lower levels of the agency. An intellectual elite emerged to lead the revolution, and a wave of discontent spread from the Research and Planning Division to the Legal Division and from there to the Consumer's Advisory Board.

The leaders of the revolt were economists. Men such as Victor von Szeliski and Leon Henderson began to question the whole idea of stabilization through price and production controls. They saw the many advantages of a competitive economy with its market system for solving problems without central planning. If the nation were going to have central planning, however, they felt that it should be guided by the government; only the government could provide disinterested planning which would serve the best interests of all the people. Why, they asked, should the businessmen or trade association officials be given this responsibility? What was the difference, they wanted to know, between monopolization

[32] Johnson had sufficient cause to be suspicious; see Wallace to the President, May 31 and September 7, 1933; Letter of H. S. Johnson to F. D. Roosevelt, August 23, 1933; F. D. Roosevelt, Memorandum to H. A. Wallace, August 29, 1933, OF 1; S. T. E[arly], Memo for the President, August 22, 1933, OF 466, and September 16, 1933, OF 15; all in RL.

[33] Special Industrial Recovery Board, Proceedings, June 26, 1933, through December 12, 1933, RG 44, NA.

[34] Schlesinger, *The Coming of the New Deal*, pp. 127–128.

in quest of inordinate profits and industrial self-regulation in quest of stability?[35]

In their efforts to expose the limitations of the NRA's program, the economists suffered from two major handicaps. First, they had no clear alternative to the existing policy. Lacking Keynesian tools of analysis, they were unable to prescribe a policy that would solve the nation's economic problems. In a few short years the necessary theory would be available, but in 1933, the NRA economists still thought and talked in terms of the economic doctrines of the 1920's.[36] The state of economic theory in 1933 also made it difficult for the economists to talk about anything except monopoly or pure competition. They were just acquiring the theoretical apparatus that would enable them to analyze market behavior which fell between pure competition and monopoly.[37] Until they had worked out these new ideas, however, they had a tendency to classify situations as either competitive or monopolistic. They rejected monopoly as a goal for public policy, but the other alternative seemed equally unpleasant. From 1929 to 1933, competition had been tried, and competition had provided no solution to the nation's basic economic problem. These limitations of the theoretical models that they were using weakened the economists' assault.[38]

[35] V. S. von Szeliski, Memo to Dr. Alexander Sachs, September 24, 1933, RG 44, Research and Planning Division, Personal Files of V. S. von Szeliski, 7415; Corwin D. Edwards, Memorandum to Divisional Administrator Whiteside, December 22, 1933, RG 9, National Industrial Recovery Board, General File–A. D. Whiteside; Charles F. Roos, Minutes of Meetings of Advisory Group of Industrial Economists, RG 9, Research and Planning Division, Personal Files, Robert H. Montgomery, 7396; letter of Leon Henderson to C. George Perreault, April 11, 1934; Leon Henderson, Memo to H. S. Johnson, May 14, 1934; both in RG 9, Research and Planning Division, Personal Files, Leon Henderson, 7399 and 7042, NA; Letter of M. W. W[atkins] to F. D. Roosevelt (with enclosures), March 3, 1934, OF 466, RL.

[36] The significant turning point is 1936, when John Maynard Keynes' *The General Theory of Employment, Interest and Money* (New York: Harcourt, Brace and Co., 1936), was published.

[37] Two path-breaking studies of this problem were first published in 1933: Edward Chamberlin, *The Theory of Monopolistic Competition* (Cambridge: Harvard University Press), and Joan Robinson, *The Economics of Imperfect Competition* (London: Macmillan and Co., Ltd.).

[38] This is clearly revealed in the memoranda that Myron W. Watkins sent first to Dexter M. Keezer of the Consumer's Advisory Board and then to F.D.R. Watkins gave the guild philosophy a good drubbing, but his suggestions about an alternative course were very weak; M. W. W[atkins] to F. D. Roosevelt (with enclosures), March 3, 1934, OF 466, RL.

They could nevertheless expose the shortcomings of the associative philosophy and of the regulations such as those incorporated in the cotton textile code. They could point out that the
Code Authority thought primarily in terms of higher prices without really exploring the relationship between prices and the volume of production. Machine-hour limitations and control of entry,
they said, did not encourage modernization; these regulations
were posited on a relatively static concept of the industry. Furthermore, the code's controls seemed to assure that prices would move
up as fast or faster than wages. Where, then, would increased
purchasing power come from under this regime?

When the economists joined hands with a coterie of NRA officials who had not abandoned the traditional reformer's suspicion
of businessmen and their representatives, the cotton textile code
and the entire concept of guild government were subjected to a
punishing cross fire. During the winter and the early spring of
1934, the anti-guild alliance grew stronger. Its members sought
to supplant business-government partnership with a form of
limited government planning in the areas of working conditions,
wages, and support for unionization. The leaders of this movement within NRA began to seek support from outside the Recovery Administration. They found several members of the Cabinet and other New Dealers who had similar doubts about the
recovery program. Their questions stirred up a violent struggle
over what the goals and guiding philosophy of the NRA should
be.[39]

Johnson shielded the cotton textile code from the discontent
bubbling up within NRA. When the Research and Planning

[39] Division Advisory Committee, Minutes, December 19, 1933, and List of
Recommendations Arising from Study of Open Prices, in RG 9, 7399 and
7401, Research and Planning Division, Personal Files, Leon Henderson;
Edwin B. George, Report on the Evolution of Trade Practice Policies, RG 9,
8159, Advisory Council; Max Kossoris, Memo to Victor von Szeliski, January
30, 1934, and Memo to Col. Montgomery, February 1, 1934, in RG 9, 7396,
Research and Planning Division, Personal Files, Robert H. Montgomery;
R. E. Watson, Hearings, Modification Proposal, April 2, 1934, RG 9, 7153,
Transcripts of Hearings; Mercer G. Johnston, Memo on Cotton Textile Code,
RG 9, 1819, NA; Frank C. Walker, Memo to Members of the Executive Coun-
cil, March 13, 1934, RG 44, Executive Council, NA; C. F. Roos, Memo to
Mr. Henderson, May 26, 1934, GR 61, RL; Schlesinger, *The Coming of the
New Deal,* pp. 128, 130–132, 135, 158–160; Roos, *NRA Economic Planning,*
pp. 72, 94–99.

Division was causing trouble or the Consumer's Advisory Board was complaining too much, the administrator simply bypassed them. This drove some of the discontented officials out of NRA; but enough stayed to keep the General and the Code Authority under constant pressure. When Leon Henderson, an economist who was one of the leaders of the opposition, became head of the Division of Research and Planning in early 1934, the battle became especially intense. Each month it became more difficult for the General to blunder ahead, ignoring arguments that neither he nor the Code Authority could answer.[40]

While Johnson was battling to protect his experiment with guild government, Sloan, Dorr, and the Code Authority were not sitting on the sidelines. They felt that everything turned on the success or failure of their program, and they fought extremely hard to hold NRA to its original course and to perfect their own code. After their system of subcommittees began working smoothly they established formal rules of procedure (January, 1934) for the Code Authority.[41] They continued to work out interpretations of the code's provisions and to prepare amendments to the code on points which were especially in need of clarification. Finally, in February, 1934, a special subcommittee was appointed "to review and codify all the interpretations of the Code Authority to date...." Although it was impossible to get official approval for these interpretations the Authority was assured by friendly NRA officials that formal sanction was unnecessary "as long as the Code Authority continue[d] to handle them with such efficiency and common sense."[42]

Considerable attention was also devoted to the problem of defining the code's jurisdiction. In order to prevent proliferation of conflicting regulations the Authority brought under the cotton

[40] NRA, Release No. 4254, April 6, 1934, RG 9, 7399, Research and Planning Division, Personal Files, Leon Henderson, NA; von Szeliski, Memo to L. Henderson, September 27, 1934, GR 61, RL; for Johnson's opinion of the economists see Special Industrial Recovery Board, Proceedings, September 11, 1933, RG 44, NA.

[41] Letter of P. B. Halstead to Members of the Cotton Textile Industry Committee, January 24, 1934, in Dorr MSS.

[42] CTI, Minutes, CTIC, February 1 and May 15, 1934, Dorr MSS; Nicholson to Sloan, February 8, 1934; Chisholm, Division of Review, Standard Work Sheet; both in RG 9, 1812 and 1809, NA.

textile code a number of subindustries such as silk throwing and textile finishing. In each case special arrangements had to be negotiated by Sloan and Dorr. Then, an executive order by President Roosevelt amended Code No. 1 so as to include the new group. For the most part the association leaders were able to handle these problems of classification and regulation with a minimum of fuss.[43]

In one instance, however, a major struggle over jurisdiction arose. This involved the tire manufacturers who had fought against the code at the public hearing. At that time they had been able to win from Hugh Johnson and the President a special ruling which stayed the application of the 40–40 regulation insofar as their captive cotton mills were concerned. Despite intense efforts to sway the administration, however, they had as yet been unable to place their mills under a separate, tire industry code. They nevertheless continued the fight to disentangle their mills from the cotton textile code.

During the fall and winter of 1933 the Rubber Manufacturers Association and the Cotton-Textile Institute put on a fine display of pressure-group politics over this issue. Each side was represented by astute association leaders: CTI by Dorr and Sloan; the Rubber Manufacturers by Newton D. Baker, who had been Secretary of War under Woodrow Wilson. Each side was able to exert considerable pressure on the Roosevelt Administration. In CTI's campaign the smaller tire manufacturing companies (which did not own cotton mills) were encouraged to complain to NRA that they would find it difficult to compete with the larger (meaning monopolistic) corporations if the cotton textile code were not applied to the captive mills. Since the smaller companies had to purchase their tire cord in the open market, this was a reasonable argument, especially if one were not interested in efficiency.[44] At any rate, it provided CTI with considerable outside support and

[43] CTI, Minutes, CTIC, August 1, 15, and 23, and September 13, 1933; February 1, 1934, NTA MSS; Philip A. Johnson, Interim Report on Hearing of Amendment, October 9, 1933, RG 9, 1796, NA; NRA, Release No. 1321, October 21, 1933, RG 9, 1809, NA; Sloan to H. S. Johnson, December 29 [?], 1933, Dorr MSS; CMANC, *Proc.*, XXVII (1933), 43–46; F. D. Roosevelt, Executive Order, 1–2 through 1–5 and 1–7 through 1–11, RG 9, NA.

[44] Sloan to H. S. Johnson, October 13, 1933; Letter of A. A. Garthwaite to H. S. Johnson, October 21, 1933; Letter of Alfred H. Branham to H. S. Johnson, October 25, 1933; Letter of M. J. Flynn to H. S. Johnson, October 28, 1933; all four in RG 9, 1805, NA.

some additional arguments to use against Baker and his association.[45] Heavy political artillery was wheeled into action: CTI's case was supported by Governor Joseph B. Ely of Massachusetts and by other politicians.[46] Finally CTI was able to persuade Secretary of Labor Perkins to intervene on its side.[47] This seems to have tipped the scales in the Institute's favor. Perkins' support swayed Johnson and President Roosevelt, and in December, 1933, they canceled the exemption that had been granted the tire manufacturers. CTI had won its case.[48]

With a magnificent disregard for consistency, the Code Authority resisted the encroachment of all other codes while it fought to apply its regulations to the tire-cord plants.[49] Responding to the incursions of hostile code authorities, CTI demanded simplicity and efficiency that could only be achieved by concentrating control under one code authority—theirs.[50] But Sloan and Dorr were not able to defend their turf against all comers. In a few cases they beat back the challenge; always they were able to delay action; but gradually the cotton mills became entangled in the regulations of a number of different NRA codes.[51]

These bitter jurisdictional spats were a natural by-product of guild government. Any attempt to impose rational controls upon an economic system had to meet and overcome the problems of

[45] Sloan to D. Comer, November 17, 1933, Comer MSS; also see G. A. Sloan, Memo to Dr. Wolman, November 2, 1933, RG 9, 1805, NA.

[46] Telegram of Governor Joseph B. Ely to Alexander Whiteside, October 20, 1933; Letter of A. L. Bulwinkle (House of Representatives) to H. S. Johnson, September 18, 1933; Letter of A. L. Bulwinkle to F. D. Roosevelt, September 22, 1933; R. W. Lea, Memo to A. D. Whiteside, October 5, 1933; Letter of Ibra C. Blackwood (Governor of South Carolina) to A. D. Whiteside, October 20, 1933; Letter of Edwin S. Smith (Commissioner of Labor and Industries, Boston, Mass.) to Alexander Whiteside, October 20, 1933; all in RG 9, 1805, 1807, NA.

[47] Turner W. Battle, Memo to Mr. McIntyre, November 17, 1933, OF 355, RL; Letter of Russell T. Fisher to H. S. Johnson (with enclosures), November 1, 1933, RG 9, 1805, NA.

[48] F. D. Roosevelt, Executive Order 1–26, December 4, 1933, RG 9, 1805, NA.

[49] King Cotton Weekly, May 3, 1934; CMAG, Report, XXXIV (1934), 77–78, 88–89; XXXV (1935), 94–95.

[50] Letter of F. S. Blanchard to C. Sterry Long, April 18, 1934, RG 9, 1798, NA.

[51] NRA, Hearing on the Cotton Converting Industry, June 29, 1934, RG 9, 7156, Transcripts of Hearings; NRA, Release No. 7756, September 12, 1934, RG 9, 1809, NA; King Cotton Weekly, September 14 and November 15, 1934.

defining, delineating, and imposing authority. This had presented problems when the service associations worked out systems for standardization of sales terms and contracts for the raw-cotton and cotton-goods trades. NRA was attempting to impose similar controls upon hundreds of different markets at the same time; it was forced to move quickly. The result was a confusing jumble of codes and rulings which left the cotton manufacturers sweating and swearing over endless reports and the association leaders struggling to shield their industry from the adverse effects of rationalization.

Particularly troublesome were the processing taxes imposed under the Agricultural Adjustment Act. Cotton mills paid a tax of five cents a pound on the cotton that they used; according to the AAA, compensating taxes were supposed to be levied on competing fibers and materials so that cotton mills would not be unduly handicapped by the tax. Such taxes were in fact levied on paper and jute products.[52] The Authority was, however, unable to arrange a satisfactory tax on certain synthetic fibers which were making deep inroads into the market for fine cotton yarns.[53] To management in cotton textiles it seemed obvious that AAA should levy a tax on rayon; but AAA found it difficult to determine exactly how much of rayon's advantage was due to the processing tax. NRA turned down the Code Authority's requests to equalize costs by raising wages for the rayon manufacturers. As the Recovery Administration pointed out, hourly wage rates in rayon would have to be increased by 36 per cent to achieve this goal, and such a large increase would stir up trouble in other industries where workers of comparable or greater skill would be getting far less. Each effort to correct an initial disparity would create new disparities. Each such change would involve the NRA and the AAA in an administrative dog fight, with charges and countercharges, hearings and masses of statistical data. From the NRA's viewpoint it was better to "season" the question by letting it sit on somebody's desk for a few months. This was a victory for the rayon manufacturers.[54]

[52] G. A. Sloan to W. J. Vereen, January 15, 1935, in Comer MSS.

[53] CTI, Minutes, CTIC, December 11, 1933, Dorr MSS; von Szeliski, Memo to L. Henderson, April 24, 1934, RG 9, Research and Planning Division, Personal Files, V. S. von Szeliski, NA.

[54] Ibid.; CTI, Memorandum, November 14, 1933, RG 9, 1811, NA; King Cotton Weekly, October 18 and 27, November 2 and 16, 1933, and May 24, 1934; ACMA, Proc., XXXVIII (1934), 53–54.

In major battles within the Recovery Administration, cotton textiles scored more wins than losses, but as the NRA developed, the Code Authority began to bog down in the kind of petty dispute that left everyone a loser. Relentlessly, the logic of control pushed the Authority into the tiniest nooks and crannies of the highly complex textile industry. As this happened, the Authority's meetings became longer and longer and more and more tedious. No one objected to discussions of the major problems such as what should be done about the tire-cord mills. But it was hard to be patient when the entire committee had to consider a question which involved only ten to twenty looms or a mill operating a few hundred spindles.[55] Steadily guild government became a more time-consuming and expensive business.[56]

Despite these problems the Authority managed to keep a tight grip on all labor questions arising under the code. There were objections from the unions, from Secretary Perkins, and from a number of NRA officials, but the trade association continued to process the letters which complained about violations of the code's labor provisions. Between August 12, 1933, and January 1, 1934, over 1,800 such complaints were received by the Industrial Relations Board and forwarded to CTI. A large number of the complaints were culled out on the grounds that they did not refer to matters covered by the code or were defective in some other way. CTI's investigators checked on the remaining letters by talking to the management involved and in some cases by inspecting the mill's records. Since the investigators did not have the names of complainants, however, the workers who were involved could not give a direct report to CTI's men. Naturally the

[55] Anderson to Sloan, May 19, 1934; Letter of T. M. Marchant to G. A. Sloan, May 23, 1934; Letter of B. B. Gossett to G. A. Sloan, May 29, 1934; all three in Comer MSS; Letter of G. A. Sloan to Harold Joy, September 14, 1933, in Sloan MSS.

[56] For an excellent example of this problem see the Case of the Southern Jacquard Weavers: Letters of: W. K. Gunter to A. B. Dickinson, July 12, 1933; A. C. Hill, Jr., to W. L. Allen, July 31, 1933; both in RG 9, 1812, NA; W. K. Gunter to A. C. Hill, Jr., August 22, 1933; Senator James F. Byrnes to B. W. Murray, September 16, 1933; Barton W. Murray to W. K. Gunter, September 18, 1933; J. W. Proctor to A. Henry Thurston, October 17, 1934; all four in RG 9, 1802, NA; CTI, Minutes, CTIC, January 16, 1933, and March 7, 1934, Dorr MSS; CTI, Minutes, CTIC, May 15 and June 19, 1934, NTA MSS; Anderson to Sloan, May 19, 1934, Comer MSS.

number of cases in which management was found to be at fault was miniscule.[57] Although the Institute filed reports on only one-half of the complaints, the Industrial Relations Board maintained unlimited confidence in the association and its investigators.[58]

With the Board and the Code Authority plugging the channels through which workers could air their grievances, pressure within the industry steadily mounted. In the South, management and labor were engaged in a savage battle over unionization. Encouraged by the New Deal's frank support for organized labor, the United Textile Workers pushed into the South in search of new members; one by-product of this organization drive was a wave of wildcat strikes which ripped through the southern Piedmont in late 1933 and early 1934. Most of these strikes were spontaneous and unplanned. Most of them were quickly (although painfully) broken by management. In the process both sides surrendered principle, sacrificed moderation, and preached and practiced violence. While any search for the original sin would be fruitless, it is obvious that management was fighting to deny workers the privileges guaranteed in Section 7(a) of the NIRA and in the industry's code. It is equally clear that the contestants were sadly mismatched. Throughout the South, management controlled and frequently owned the local community; the company store, the company house, and the company constable all were important weapons.[59] Even the state governments were seldom hesitant to use the militia in defense of the sacred rights of property—mill property. So the unions were beaten down; and the workers built up deep grievances against a system which gave lip service to unionization while it allowed management to destroy the unions.

[57] G. A. Sloan, "A Close-Up of the Cotton Code in Action," February 21, 1934; H. V. Bary, Memo to L. J. Martin, August 15, 1934; both in RG 9, 1905 and 1801, NA; James A. Hodges, "The New Deal Labor Policy," pp. 253–254.
[58] Ibid.; R. W. Bruere, Memo to W. H. Davis, December 5, 1933, RG 9, CTNIRB, 4441, NA; in January, 1934, Bruere did become concerned because the Institute had only two field agents in the entire South checking complaints; Letter of R. Bruere to Dr. Wolman, January 4, 1934, RG 9, 1799, NA.
[59] Letter of Chairman, CTIC, to H. S. Johnson and Report of Sub-Committee on Mill Villages, December 28, 1933, in Dorr MSS; also see: ACMA, Mill Stores Committee, and the Piedmont Textile Retail Stores Association, Report on the Cotton Mill Worker and His Needs, RG 9, 1808; Advisory Council, Memo to National Industrial Recovery Board, January 18, 1935, RG 9, 5, National Industrial Recovery Board, General File, Donald Richberg; both in NA.

By the summer of 1934 a storm was brewing in the South, but the Code Authority ignored the warnings.[60]

By that time it was apparent that the NRA's mechanism for settling strikes was as ineffective as its system for handling complaints. Under the National Industrial Relations Board a complex arrangement of local mill committees and state boards had been established to mediate disputes. Such organizations obviously favored management. By attempting to settle differences within the mill as the court of first instance, they kept union officials from the national offices out of the disputes; they also blocked the intervention of government employees who might be inclined to favor the workers or, at least, to be unbiased. The state boards appear to have been loaded in favor of the employers. The personnel and prejudices of the state boards varied a great deal, but even a cursory examination of their decisions indicates that in general they favored management. These decisions gave a narrow definition to the range of permissible activities on the part of striking employees. They tended to analyze each problem in terms of the individual mill and the individual worker, giving little or no consideration to the national situation which had prompted action on the part of labor in the South. This entire system reflected the strong bias of the Bruere Board; and so long as the Authority could keep the Board intact it seemed that the unions and employees could probably be kept under control.[61]

The Code Authority also repulsed the union and government forces which sought to re-open the code—particularly the minimum wage and forty-hour week provisions—for negotiation. In this particular dispute the industry's position was that the code had been drafted as an exercise in business-government partnership. It was a contract between the industry and the New Deal. Now that the contract was drawn it was impossible for one party to change the pact unilaterally. If the government wanted to write a new code and impose it upon the industry, the Authority said, that was the government's business. But the industry flatly refused to re-open negotiations and insisted that the Code Authority would not cooperate with the government if a new code were

[60] NRA, Decisions Issued by the State Cotton Textile Industrial Relations Boards, August 8, 1933, to August 8, 1934, RG 9, 1799, NA.

[61] *Ibid.;* James A. Hodges, "The New Deal Labor Policy," p. 225, points out that the Bruere Board was "very successful" in ending disputes but that union officials soon recognized "that the code was not helping union efforts. . . ."

written. Johnson was too dedicated to the principle of guild government to let that happen. Rather than destroy his sacred partnership principle, he backed off and refused to support the drive to cut the forty-hour week and to raise minimum wages.[62]

During its first eight months of experience with the code, the Authority's dominant position on labor matters was shaken only once. That happened in the spring of 1934, when the Compliance Division of the NRA, rather than the trade association itself, began to investigate complaints arising under Section 7(a)—that is, the complaints dealing directly with the workers' right to organize. The unions had long demanded this. They were now supported by those NRA officials who were disgusted with the partnership idea. Unfortunately, when the Compliance Division was given this job the NRA merely switched from a biased trade association to an inefficient government agency: the administrative machinery of the Division was so complex and slow moving that little could be accomplished in time to help the workers. Months after a strike was broken or a mill hand laid off, the Compliance Division might decide that the worker's rights had been violated. By that time, however, it was usually too late to help either the worker or the union.[63] As a result, labor's discontent grew, creating a potentially explosive situation.

In the eyes of the Code Authority, the labor question was of secondary importance. Far more significant was the problem of extending and perfecting the association's means of controlling production, prices, and profits. When the 40–40 limitation had first been proposed, the spokesmen for the industry recognized that this alone would probably not solve the industry's competitive problems. They clearly intended to supplement the machine-hour limitations.[64] For a time, however, that had proved unnecessary. While the code was being drafted the manufacturers had received a tremendous rush of orders. Buyers had fought to purchase goods before the projected wage increases and production

[62] Letter of C. M. Bakewell to H. S. Johnson (with enclosures), February 19, 1934, RG 9, 1813, NA.

[63] Letter of G. A. Sloan to executives under the Cotton Textile Code, January 28, 1935, RG 9, 4171, Textile Labor Relations Board, NA; William L. Pencke, Memorandum on a Code Violation, October 24, 1935, RG 9, 1794, NA.

[64] See the amendments to the code (especially number 3) submitted by the industry at the Hearing: NRA, Hearing No. 1, June 30, 1933, RG 9, 7152, Transcripts of Hearings, NA.

controls inflated prices. During this rush certain mills actually had experienced labor shortages; some of them had accused their competitors of enticing skilled workers away from their plants.[65]

The party was soon over. By fall, 1933, the industry was slumping back into its pre-code depression, with its problems actually compounded by the earlier rush of orders. As demand fell off, the customary cycle began: production held steady while new orders declined and inventories began to pile up at the mills. Despite the 40–40 limitation, the industry could still produce much more than the market would take at prices which included a "normal" profit. As early as October, 1933, the statistics from several of the groups indicated that trouble was coming. By late November prices were sagging badly and the Code Authority began to consider additional measures aimed at controlling the market.[66]

To supplement the 40–40 proviso the Authority allowed the product groups to experiment with direct means of stabilizing prices. Certain mills began to circulate a "suggested price list"; other groups openly tried to set minimum prices. In the latter case, lists of so-called average cost figures were circulated with the admonition that mills should not, under any circumstances, cut their prices below the total cost indicated in the list.[67]

This experiment with direct price-fixing proved, however, to be a brief interlude. Even within the groups which tried this, there were mixed feelings about such measures. Some of the manufacturers definitely opposed the use of price lists. Stiff resistance within NRA also persuaded the Authority to back off. With opposition to the whole idea of guild government mounting, the Authority found good cause to discard the price lists, putting its faith in less direct but more acceptable measures.[68]

[65] Kennedy, *Profits and Losses*, pp. 249–250; *King Cotton Weekly*, July 13, 1933; CMAG, *Report*, XXXIV (1934), 80. The manufacturers' margin on gray goods jumped from 9.7 cents in February, 1933, to 23.9 cents in July, 1933.

[66] *King Cotton Weekly*, October 6, 1933; NACM, *Trans.*, CXXXIII (1933), 92; Dorr, *Comment on Certain Phases of the Draft of N.R.A. Textile Industry Report*, March 20, 1936, Sloan MSS; CTI, Minutes, CTIC, November 10, 1933, NTA MSS.

[67] *King Cotton Weekly*, August 9, 1933; S. P. Munroe to Executives of Carded Yarn Mills, August 24, 1933, Comer MSS.

[68] S. P. Munroe, Memo to Executives of Carded Sales Yarn Mills, November 29, 1933, Comer MSS; CTI, Minutes, CTIC, November 27, 1933; CTI, Minutes of the Meeting of the Carded Yarn Sub-Committee, January 15, 1934, Dorr MSS. Significantly, management representing 60.8 per cent of the spindleage in this group voted for minimum prices, but 11.6 per cent objected and 27.6 per cent did not bother to vote.

Both the Authority and the NRA did, nevertheless, approve supplementary codes which gave certain product groups elaborate controls over the market transactions of their members. These special codes were passed by the fine-yarn and carded-yarn manufacturers. Under the carded-yarn code, the terms of sale were rigidly controlled. The discount that could be given for cash payments was stipulated; tolerances for goods were specified; there were special regulations on the form of compensation that each party to the contract could receive. Selling agents were required to register with the Code Authority. And only bona fide—that is, registered—selling agents were allowed to buy and sell carded yarn. These provisions were very similar to those in the code that this product group had adopted in the 1920's, only now the regulations were backed by the authority of federal law.[69]

Each of the supplementary codes attempted to eliminate the results of cutthroat competition without dealing directly with its cause. Terms of sale were standardized because buyers forced the manufacturers to give better terms as a form of price concession; tolerances were specified because buyers frequently rejected orders without good cause. The manufacturers had been complaining about practices such as these since the early 1900's; in fact the first such code had been drafted in 1907/1908 by the regional associations. Without effective production control, however, these NRA regulations could no more solve the manufacturer's problems than had the earlier voluntary programs.

Most of the attention of Sloan, Dorr, and the Authority was devoted to supplementing the 40–40 provision. What were needed, apparently, were short-term adjustments in the eighty-hour limit. This would enable the industry to prevent price declines in the face of seasonal changes in demand. At its meeting on November 27, 1933, the Code Authority designed the administrative machinery that it hoped would solve the problem. First, a general curtailment under which the mills could operate only 75 per cent

---

[69] On the carded yarn code see: Dorr to Sloan, September 26, 1933; Chairman, CTIC, to H. S. Johnson, December 15, 1933; letter of P. B. Halstead to All Mills, December 18, 1933; Letter of Frank E. Slack to G. A. Sloan, December 19, 1933; all four in Dorr MSS; H. S. Johnson, Administrative Order No. 1–31F, December 29, 1933, RG 9, NA. On the finishing code see: CTI, Minutes, CTIC, November 28, 1933, Dorr MSS; Sloan to H. S. Johnson, November 29, 1933; H. S. Johnson, NRA Release 2048, December 3, 1933; both in RG 9, 1816 and 1809, NA.

of the normal schedule was recommended. To provide for future "temporary changes in the limitation of hours of operation of productive machinery," the Authority proposed an arrangement by which the Code Authority "with the concurrence of the Government representatives on the same may hereafter, for periods of not more than ninety days, require a temporary shortening of the hours of such machine operation within any group. . . ." According to this proposal, action would only be taken after the Authority had received a recommendation from the officers of the product group involved. And these officers would only recommend a cut in production after they had "ascertained the sense of the group as to the specific recommendation." This was clearly to be an exercise in self-regulation.[70]

When the Code Authority's proposal arrived at NRA, the resistance to all forms of price and production control was just beginning to boil to the surface. After debating the issue for weeks, the Advisory Committee of the Research and Planning Division had decided that in all future codes the Division "should discourage provisions limiting machine hours and at the same time limitations in the increase of productive capacity in an industry." If the economists had their way, the days of guild control were numbered.[71]

But Hugh Johnson did not allow the recommendations of the economists to block his path. He simply bypassed the Research and Planning Division. Within a week Johnson had approved the blanket, 25 per cent curtailment for the entire industry as well as the new program for temporary reductions in the various product groups. He made it necessary for each curtailment order to pass through the NRA and to receive his approval, but the initiative rested with the trade association and its group organizations.[72] Victor von Szeliski of Research and Planning found out about the new arrangement when it was described in the newspapers—after Johnson had issued his orders.[73]

The Code Authority began to use its new powers almost immediately. During December and January most of the mills were

[70] CTI, Minutes, CTIC, November 27, 1933, Dorr MSS.

[71] Division Advisory Committee, Minutes, November 13, 1933, RG 9, 7399, Research and Planning Division, Personal Files, Leon Henderson, NA.

[72] H. S. Johnson, Press Release 2048, December 3, 1933, RG 9, 1809, NA; Sloan to H. S. Johnson, December 16, 1933, Dorr MSS.

[73] von Szeliski, Memo to Leon Henderson, September 27, 1934, GR 61, RL.

satisfied with the 25 per cent curtailment, but even this seemed inadequate for two of the product groups. The producers of fine cotton and carded yarns still were accumulating stock. So they requested and received permission to reduce production to a total of forty-eight hours a week.[74]

This brought up a new problem. If the curtailment were successful and prices responded to a sharp cut in production, mills making other products would obviously shift to cotton yarns so as to take advantage of the price rise. This would increase production in the very groups that needed a special cut in machine hours. The solution was obvious: it was necessary for the Authority to prevent a mill which manufactured narrow sheeting from shifting its spindles to carded yarn. Consequently the Authority (with Johnson's permission) notified the mills that during the temporary curtailments, machinery could not be shifted to any of the products enumerated in the special orders. This subsequently became standard procedure during each temporary curtailment. Pushed forward relentlessly, the Code Authority was weaving an increasingly elaborate network of regulations.[75]

Indeed, the Code Authority proved to be a strict taskmaster. Almost every request for an exemption from the reduced schedule was turned down. Where unusual circumstances such as government contracts were involved, the Authority was willing to make exceptions. But once a curtailment order had been approved by the group committee, by the Code Authority, and by the NRA, it was almost impossible to obtain an exemption. Although there were many requests for special treatment, hardly any of the mills challenged the Authority by simply ignoring the NRA orders. Most of the violations that the Authority investigated were the

[74] CTI, Minutes, CTIC, December 11, 1933, and January 16, 1934; Emergency Requirement as to Further Limitation of Hours of Machine Operation in Carded Yarn Group, December 15, 1933; Emergency Requirements as to Further Limitation of Hours of Machine Operation in the Fine Goods Group and Rayon Group, December 29, 1933; Paul B. Halstead, *Urgent Memorandum,* January 10, 1934; all three in Dorr MSS.

[75] CTI, Minutes, CTIC, November 27, 1933, and January 16, 1934, NTA MSS; Emergency Requirement in Carded Yarn Group, December 15, 1933, Dorr MSS; Emergency Requirements of Combed Thread Producers Group, January 12, 1934; Emergency Requirement in the Wide Bed Sheeting Group, January 23, 1934; both in RG 9, 1813, NA. This in turn made the definition of the group extremely important, as became obvious at the January 16 meeting of the Code Authority.

products of misunderstanding, and CTI was able to handle the situations informally.[76] In a few cases, reports of violations were passed on to the government; and in at least two instances court action was taken against mills which refused to conform to the emergency curtailment plan in December, 1933. These particular companies pleaded guilty to a criminal charge and paid fines totaling $2,250. In general, however, compliance was never a problem.[77]

Apparently the major difficulty was "timing." Curtailment orders were always issued after the damage was done. For one thing, the NRA's administrative machinery was slow—much slower than the Worth Street market. A curtailment proposal had to go through a group meeting, win the approval of the Code Authority, and then be accepted and promulgated by Hugh Johnson's office. By the time all of this had been done, prices were badly depressed and large inventories were hanging over the market.

Often the proposal was not even initiated by the product group until the situation was out of hand. This weakness was of course generic to the trade association itself. As the associations had shown during the 1920's, they could react to manifest problems but could not anticipate difficulties before they impinged directly and decisively upon a large majority of the members. By opting for self-regulation instead of central planning, CTI had ensured that this handicap would be built into its NRA program. Under these conditions the Authority was unable to prevent inventories from periodically building up to the point where the market was demoralized.[78]

Sloan and Dorr recognized by the summer of 1934 that prices could not be stabilized so long as the manufacturer's product groups had to initiate the decisions to cut production. They

[76] CTI, Minutes, CTIC, December 11 and 12, 1933; January 16, February 1, and March 4, 1934; all in NTA MSS; nevertheless, more violations of curtailment orders than of labor regulations were referred to the Administrator of NRA; this, I believe, gives a better indication of the Authority's relative interest in the two subjects than it does of the incidence of violation.

[77] NRA, Release No. 4683, April 27, 1934, RG 9, 1794, NA.

[78] CTI, Minutes, Carded Yarn Sub-Committee, January 15, 1934; CTI, Minutes, CTIC, January 16, 1934; Chairman, CTIC, to H. S. Johnson, January 19, 1934; A. C. Rearick, Notes of Meeting, February 1, 1934; all in Dorr MSS; at the meeting on February 1 it was decided to take no action on a particular curtailment proposal because of "insufficient support"; the vote in favor of the proposal was 49–34, with 17 not voting.

needed to give that responsibility to a person or persons who could keep in touch with the statistical reports and check any overproduction before it became serious. But that idea carried the association leaders onto dangerous ground: the experts who made these decisions might end up being government experts, and to the manufacturers that was an outcome to be avoided at any cost. Was it not better to limp along with 40–40 and the belated temporary curtailments than to allow Leon Henderson or Victor von Szeliski to run the industry?[79]

Although the machine-hour limitation was not working very well, the Code Authority fought bitterly against all attempts to eliminate production control from the code. In March, 1934, when Johnson at last reacted to the mounting pressure within NRA, Dorr and Sloan had to defend their position in a public conference that was held in Washington. Since the conference brought together some four thousand representatives from the different code authorities, very little was accomplished; but the meeting did focus attention on the touchy question of price-fixing. In addition to making public statements at this time, both Dorr and Sloan spent much of their time expounding and advocating the associative philosophy. At every opportunity they pointed out to Johnson and to others the absolute necessity of retaining production control in the NRA's program.[80]

A serious challenge came from within the industry itself. The Johnson & Johnson Company, refusing to give up its fight against the machine-hour limitation, continued to press the case for efficiency as opposed to stabilization. As it became known in Washington that there was a revolution brewing within the NRA, Johnson & Johnson was able to locate allies within Hugh Johnson's own camp. Russell E. Watson, who was counsel for the company, found many NRA officials sympathetic to his company's plea for competition. As Watson discovered, a clear majority of

[79] This line of analysis resulted that summer and fall in a move to find a more flexible system of production control; Letter of G. A. Sloan to Members of the Cotton Textile Code Authority, June 26, 1934; Chairman, CTIC, to H. S. Johnson, August 13, 1934; both in Dorr MSS.

[80] CTI, Minutes, CTIC, March 4, 1934, NTA MSS; also see: G. A. Sloan and W. Ray Bell, Statements, January 9, 1934; G. H. Dorr, Memorandum as to Complaints Against the Cotton Textile Industry, January 3, 1934; all in Dorr MSS; Letter of G. A. Sloan to R. Stevens, March 19, 1934, in Sloan MSS.

the officials in the Consumers' Advisory Board and the Research and Planning Division wanted to abandon the NRA's basic program of stabilization through associative self-regulation. After filing an official request for a new hearing on his company's case, Watson stayed in Washington for several months to woo these rebellious administrators. Finally, his company was granted a hearing (scheduled for April 2, 1934) on its request for a code amendment that would allow mills to operate four six-hour shifts a day, with a thirty-hour week for the mill hands.[81]

For CTI the hearing was a decisive showdown, and all of the Institute's considerable resources were marshaled for the battle. Letters in support of the Code Authority were gathered.[82] The Authority passed a formal resolution stating that it was "inalterably opposed" to the Johnson & Johnson proposal, which was characterized as being "subversive of the welfare of the industry and the public interest. . . ." George Sloan practically camped in Hugh Johnson's office. The members of the Code Authority felt, Sloan said, that this was an all-important battle; if they lost, they could not continue to cooperate with the NRA.[83]

At the hearing, both sides reiterated charges that were by now familiar to everyone involved. Speaking for Johnson & Johnson, Watson insisted that "the essential strength of our system of free competition has been its continuous, irresistible pressure for the lowering of production costs." The Code Authority countered by charging that Johnson & Johnson was a large company that wanted to drive smaller competitors out of business. Sloan attacked the petition on humanitarian grounds; it would, he said, encourage night work. On behalf of the code, G. Edward Buxton, a Rhode Island manufacturer, pointed out that the 40–40 provision was

[81] Watson to H. S. Johnson, September 9, 1933; R. E. Watson to Dr. Alexander Sachs, September 20, 1933; both in RG 9, 1803 and 1802, NA; letter of G. A. Sloan to B. B. Gossett, October 12, 1933, Comer MSS.

[82] Letter of John Cutter to F. D. Roosevelt, October 16, 1933; F.D.R., Memorandum for General Johnson, October 26, 1933; both in OF 258, RL; R. B. Pills, Sworn Statement, March 7, 1934; Letter of E. E. Groves to Fred M. Allen, March 15, 1934; Letter of A. E. Colby to Cotton Textile Institute, March 19, 1934; Letter of J. Earle Parker to G. A. Sloan, March 22, 1934, RG 9, 1802, NA.

[83] Letter of G. A. Sloan to Blackwell Smith, October 4, 1933; Sloan to H. S. Johnson, October 18, 1933; both in RG 9, 1815 and 1805, NA; CTI Minutes, CTIC, October 17, 1933; Letter of G. A. Sloan to A. D. Whiteside, November 1, 1933, Dorr MSS; G. A. Sloan, Memo for Mr. Comer, November 2, 1933, Comer MSS.

designed to benefit "the interest of labor, consumer and manufacturer alike. . . ."[84]

When the various divisions of NRA explicitly defined their positions on the proposal, there were some curious results. Only the Consumers' Advisory Board came down unequivocally on the side of Johnson & Johnson. Calling for an end to production control, the Board insisted that the company's request should be granted as the first move toward completely eliminating the 40–40 regulation.[85] By contrast the Research and Planning Division equivocated: while the Division favored the elimination of machine-hour limitations, it recognized that the industry had basic problems which could not be solved by accepting the proposed amendment. The report, which was written by von Szeliski, submitted a detailed analysis of the industry's economic structure and concluded that the government should help change that structure. According to von Szeliski, the government should (1) promote mergers in the industry, (2) remove the machine-hour limits while keeping the eight-hour shift, and (3) eliminate the AAA's processing tax. Although his memorandum included an excellent analysis of the limitations of a program built around production control, the alternatives proposed were beyond the NRA's grasp at that time. In regard to the matter at hand, Johnson & Johnson's request, the report concluded with a rather weak affirmative vote.[86]

A number of the NRA officers strongly supported the Code Authority. The assistant administrator who was in charge of the hearing voted against the company on the grounds that the small firms in the industry would be hurt by unrestricted competition.[87]

[84] NRA, Hearing on the Cotton Textile Industry, Modification Proposal, April 2, 1934, RG 9, 7153, Transcripts of Hearings, NA.

[85] Stuart F. Heinritz, Memo to Colonel R. W. Lea, April 7, 1934, RG 9, 1804, NA.

[86] V. S. von Szeliski, Analysis of Johnson and Johnson's Proposed Amendment to Cotton Textile Code, May 21, 1934 (3rd ed.), RG 9, 1806; also see Letter of Frederick P. Poole to Leon Henderson and Poole's Memorandum to Leon Henderson, March 27 and 30, 1934, in RG 9, 1808, NA. By this time von Szeliski had decided that oligopoly was a more reasonable goal than pure competition or monopolization; his analysis seems to have been influenced by the theoretical studies published in 1933; see note 37 in this chapter.

[87] Stuart F. Heinritz, Memo to Colonel R. W. Lea, April 7, 1934, in RG 9, 1804, NA.

The Industrial Advisory Board concluded that "the amendment proposed by Johnson & Johnson, if approved, will tend to promote monopolies, oppress and discriminate against small enterprises and contravene the intent of Title I of the N.I.R.A. It is the most blatantly selfish thing we have encountered in our experience with the N.R.A."[88] Even the Labor Advisory Board lined up with the Authority. Although William Green of the American Federation of Labor urged NRA to grant the exemption, the Labor Board was apparently swayed by the arguments of Francis J. Gorman, Vice-President of the United Textile Workers of America. Gorman took the position that in general the 40–40 provision should be upheld; he would like to see shorter hours and higher wages, he said, but he was "glad to see the 'graveyard shift' go." He felt, furthermore, that it was easier to enforce limits on the workweek when machine hours were also limited. Although Gorman concluded that the NRA might do well to try the setup that Johnson & Johnson proposed, his arguments actually favored the Code Authority.[89]

On May 10, 1934, General Johnson issued a final order which rejected Johnson & Johnson's request for an amendment. It was a clear-cut decision in favor of the associative philosophy.[90] With renewed confidence in the Roosevelt Administration and General Johnson, the Code Authority pushed ahead in its search for better methods of production control.

The search had to continue; paradoxically, the Code Authority seemed to have done everything that it had set out to accomplish except stabilize prices and profits. Prices had been raised and the manufacturer's margin widened; but concomitant increases in wages and other costs kept profits down. In 1933—due primarily to the spurt of orders which preceded the introduction of con-

[88] Carroll Burton, Memo re Proposed Amendment, April 2, 1934, in Sloan MSS.

[89] Letter of William Green to R. W. Lea, March 31, 1934; Francis J. Gorman, Statement at the Hearing on the Modification of the Code of Fair Competition for the Cotton Textile Industry, April 2, 1934; S. F. Heinritz, Memo to Colonel R. W. Lea, April 7, 1934; in RG 9, 1813, 1810, and 1804; even the Legal Division, normally an opponent of production control, lined up with the trade association; also see: Letter of C. L. Heyniger to Col. Lea, April 6, 1934; M. J. Harron, Memo to Col. R. W. Lea, April 7, 1934; Gustav Peck, Memo to General Johnson, April 24, 1934; all three in RG 9, 1804, NA.

[90] NRA, Release No. 4972, May 10, 1934, RG 9, 1797, NA; J. Cutter to F. D. Roosevelt, October 16, 1933, OF 258, RL.

trols—the industry had shown a net profit for the first time in four years. During 1934, however, profits dropped again, and 481 of the 918 companies in the industry operated at a net deficit. By the end of the year, total net income (after taxes) for the entire industry was only $3,704,000, a pitifully small figure in light of the capital invested and the number of workers employed. As these figures suggest, the Code Authority had not yet achieved its own primary objective.[91]

Still, there was some cause for optimism in the early summer of 1934. With Hugh Johnson's backing and the support of the majority of the mills, the Code Authority was confident that a flexible method for anticipating changes in demand could be introduced. The association leaders began to discuss this question with their friends in the Recovery Administration as soon as the Johnson & Johnson case was settled. This new form of control, Sloan and Dorr felt, would surely be the key to economic success.

[91] Backman and Gainsbrugh, *Economics of the Cotton Textile Industry,* p. 212.

Chapter XI

Crumbling Walls of the Condominium

Like the swift lightning that announces a summer storm, a series of bitter, wildcat strikes in the southern cotton mills presaged dark days for the condominium of guild and government. Throughout the summer of 1934 there were rumblings of labor discontent—thunder that could be heard all the way from the Potomac to the tiny mill villages of northern Alabama. Men were angry about the machinery for handling complaints. Disillusioned workers continued to complain about the stretch-out. Even though hourly rates were now high, mill hands who worked a short week grumbled about their pay checks. Seeing the sharp contrast between the new deal they had anticipated and the deal they got, the workers vented their disappointment by walking off the job. Most of the strikes were unsuccessful; but that merely added to the backlog of discontent that was building up in the industry.[1]

The Code Authority had helped to seed these storm clouds by requesting (in May) an industry-wide curtailment of 25 per cent for a twelve-week period during the summer. When this was done, the Institute's officers recognized that it was a dangerous move

[1] Letter of Frank E. Coffee (Atlanta Regional Labor Board) to Lloyd K. Garrison (Chairman, National Labor Board), August 9, 1934, RG 9, CTNIRB, 4441; Letter of Edwin S. Smith to Blackwell Smith, August 14, 1934, RG 9, 1797; John G. Winant *et al.*, Report of the Board of Inquiry, September 20, 1934, RG 9, 1817, NA; Lahne, *The Cotton Mill Worker*, pp. 225–226; NRA, Decisions Issued by the State Cotton Textile Industrial Relations Boards, August 8, 1933, to August 8, 1934, RG 9, 1799, NA; Hodges, "The New Deal Labor Policy," pp. 232, 261–263, 265.

but went ahead with their plans.[2] It was essential, they felt, to continue to experiment with the machine-hour limitations, despite the dangerous political situation. If the Authority waited too long to start cutting back, the entire market would be demoralized again. Rather than let that happen, the committee proceeded quietly in the hopes that public attention could be avoided, at least until Congress had adjourned.

But it was impossible to negotiate with NRA without stirring up public debate. Once the Authority's opponents found out about the new plan, they threw down the gauntlet. The United Textile Workers fought bitterly against this latest threat to the workers' paychecks. Thomas McMahon, the UTW's president, carried the fight into Congress. In a letter to Representative William Connery (author of a thirty-hour bill that was before Congress at that time), McMahon warned "that in the *Cotton Textile Industry* employing approximately a half million workers and scattered in all parts of the United States, information of a reliable nature has been called to our notice that immediately upon adjournment of Congress, a drastic curtailment program will be forced upon this industry by the Code Authority. This means that the workers will be deprived of their existing meagre wages."[3] This created a volatile situation. Hugh Johnson was becoming sensitive to congressional pressures and to the growing resentment against production control within the NRA; so he decided to stall this latest request for a cut in production by channeling it through the Research and Planning Division.[4]

The Code Authority threw everything into this fight. As Sloan and the manufacturers knew, Johnson was still basically a proponent of self-regulation and stabilization. They once again put their entire program on the line, demanding that the NRA either back them up or lose their support. They were unwilling to let political reasons cause a delay. Sloan pressed the issue, and on May 22 Johnson surrendered. He signed an order calling for temporary curtailment (25 per cent) during June and August of 1934.[5]

[2] CTI, Minutes, CTIC, May 14 and 15, 1934; Letter of A. C. Rearick to G. H. Dorr, May 19, 1934; both in Dorr MSS.

[3] Letter of Thomas F. McMahon to William Connery, May 18, 1934, RG 9, 1812, NA.

[4] Sloan to Anderson, May 29, 1934, Comer MSS.

[5] *Ibid.;* CTI, Minutes, CTIC, May 14 and 15, and June 19, 1934, Dorr MSS; Anderson to Sloan, May 25, 1934, Comer MSS; NRA, Release No. 5252, May 22, 1934, RG 9, 1810, NA.

Startled by Johnson's order, the United Textile Workers fought back. If they were unable to work out their problems within the NRA, they would fight for the workers' goals with a general textile strike. Although perfectly willing to negotiate, the UTW held the threat of a strike over Johnson's head.[6]

Hoping that they could work out a more satisfactory way of handling complaints under the code, a group of the UTW's organizers also met with Bruere (May 30). As before, however, they found Bruere unsympathetic; he asked for more time to do things the proper way. He pointed out to the disgruntled labor leaders that "the primary responsibility for making the codes work rests with the industries. They presented the codes and they are responsible for the enforcement of the codes in the first instance. When the codes are up for hearing everybody has a chance to make a comment." Bruere said that he believed in a cooperative approach to labor-management problems. The UTW, he felt, was operating on "a war basis,—workers on one side; employers on the other."[7]

At this conference the union officials seemed to jettison all hope that something might be accomplished through Bruere's National Industrial Relations Board. They could no longer be satisfied by demands for more time to study the problem. They had tried to cooperate, but their organizers were being fired. Their union was being pushed around by management. They wanted action.[8]

When they trooped into Johnson's office they found the General more cooperative than Bruere. Johnson wanted to head off the strike. His own position at the top of NRA was too shaky to withstand a major strike. As he knew, direct negotiation between the Code Authority and the United Textile Workers was impossible since the industry refused to recognize the UTW as a bona fide representative for the workers. So Johnson placed the UTW's men in one room and Sloan in another. Working his way back and forth from labor to management, the General finally drafted a settlement that was accepted by both sides. Under this agreement the UTW countermanded its strike order without relinquishing

[6] Letter of T. F. McMahon to H. Johnson, May 28, 1934; Winant *et al.*, Report of the Board of Inquiry, September 20, 1934, RG 9, 1815 and 1817, NA; Lahne, *The Cotton Mill Worker*, p. 225.

[7] NRA, Report of the Conference between Organizers of the United Textile Workers of America and Cotton Textile National Industrial Relations Board, May 30, 1934, RG 9, 1812, NA.

[8] *Ibid.*

its right to strike in the future. Labor's representation within NRA was strengthened, and provision was made for more labor spokesmen on the Bruere board. Meanwhile, the NRA was given a series of questions to study: the Recovery Administration was to determine whether the industry was able to pay higher wages; whether wage differentials for different skills had been maintained; and what machine-hour limitations would be essential if the industry were to meet the demand for textile products. It was assumed that these studies, when completed, would provide the basis for changes in the code.[9]

Although the Authority was angry over Johnson's decision to alter the code by changing the membership of the Industrial Relations Board, the settlement was recognized as a victory for management. Johnson had obviously not given the union any concessions that were not absolutely essential. At best the NRA studies would merely inaugurate another feud between the UTW and the Authority; there was no guarantee that the administration would heed the reports even if they indicated that changes were needed. On the other hand, the settlement included a provision recognizing the need for temporary curtailments to supplement the 40–40 regulation. This in effect acknowledged that the Authority's position on the curtailment order had been correct! No move had been made to recognize the UTW as a bargaining agent. Nothing was said about keeping weekly wages up when curtailment was in effect. The Institute's officers celebrated when they saw the final settlement.[10]

The festivities were premature.[11] Within a month the threat of a general textile strike again hung over the industry. Two of the research reports came in during June; one of them indicated that

[9] NRA, Final Terms of Settlement between NRA Administrator and Officials of the United Textile Workers, June 2, 1934, RG 9, 1812, NA.

[10] Ibid.; Letter of G. A. Sloan to L. DuPont, June 4, 1934, in Sloan MSS; Anderson to Sloan, June 4, 1934; ACMA, Report to Members, June 5, 1934; both in Cramer MSS; A. C. Rearick, Memorandum for Mr. Sloan, June 15, 1934; CTI, Minutes, CTIC, June 19, 1934; Sloan to H. S. Johnson, June 21, 1934; Draft of Letter to F. S. Blanchard, June 22, 1934; all four in Dorr MSS.

[11] Anderson to D. Comer, July 25, 1934, Cramer MSS; CTI, Minutes, CTIC, June 19, and August 3, 1934, Dorr MSS; NRA, Release No. 6382, July 11, 1934; Sloan to H. S. Johnson (with enclosure), July 19 and August 6, 1934; Blackwell Smith, Memo to Edwin S. Smith and Dr. Gustav Peck, August 8, 1934; Winant et al., Report of the Board of Inquiry, September 17, 1934; all five in RG 9, 1809, 1798, 1797, and 1817, NA.

management was in no position to grant wage increases in cotton textiles; the other concluded that "normal demand" did not warrant a further reduction in machine-hour limitations. Nevertheless, the industry went ahead with its temporary curtailment plan. As far as the union was concerned there seemed to be no change in labor-management relations at the local level. Increased union representation in NRA and in the labor board worked no miracles; the UTW announced that the strike was on again.[12]

This brought another burst of frenetic activity in Washington. There was a call for a joint conference between the UTW and the Code Authority, but the industry was unwilling to extend de facto recognition to the union by meeting in an open conference. Although the labor relations board held separate conferences with the two contestants, no settlement was reached. The strike was set for September 3.[13]

By this time the objectives of both sides were clearly stated, firmly established, and virtually non-negotiable. The union wanted recognition as a bargaining agent for the workers. The NRA must, the UTW said, create more effective and impartial means of handling complaints arising under the labor provisions of the code; management must accept the thirty-hour week without lowering the minimum weekly wages; the employers had to reinstate all workers who had been dismissed because of their union membership; and finally, there had to be a more satisfactory settlement of the stretch-out problem. On each of these points management's position was equally clear and adamantly maintained. The Authority demanded that the existing code be enforced. In effect this would mean that the union would not be officially recognized as a bargaining agent and that collective bargaining would be used only where the unions could force it upon management; wages and hours would remain unchanged; most of the complaint machinery would stay under the control of the Code Authority; and questions concerning the stretch-out would continue to be settled by government officials who felt that in any circumstances industry should be able to improve its efficiency by altering work loads.[14]

Management's chances of achieving these basic objectives were very good while the UTW's position was extremely weak. The

[12] *Ibid.;* NRA, Release No. 6140, June 29, 1934, RG 9, 1809, NA.
[13] Winant *et al.,* Report of the Board of Inquiry, September 17, 1934, NA.
[14] *Ibid.;* Lahne, *The Cotton Mill Worker,* pp. 225–226.

union barely had a foothold in the southern industry. Its finances were in bad shape and the central office was seldom able to exercise strong control over its locals. While the Roosevelt Administration was friendly to organized labor, the government definitely opposed the general textile strike. Such a strike would affect many other industries, threatening in fact the entire recovery program. It would embarrass an administration which had promised American labor a new deal under the NRA.[15]

Refusing to accept the government's or management's terms, the UTW—joined now by a rival union, the Textile Workers Union of America (TWUA)—went to war in September. Throughout the nation, particularly in the South, textile workers, employers, union organizers, police, and state militias fought bloody battles to determine how new the New Deal would be. Flying squadrons of union members dashed from town to town in the southern Piedmont, stirring up support for the general strike. As the union battle lines drew tight around the mills, violence became commonplace; reason and negotiation gave way to a reign of passion and power.[16]

George Sloan and the Institute coordinated management's offensive on the national level. In an effort to counter the unions' effective publicity CTI hired "some of the leading public relations men in America."[17] Throughout the South the state associations supported the Institute by mounting their own publicity campaigns aimed at presenting the manufacturer's philosophy.[18] Sloan used the radio to broadcast management's viewpoint of the strike. Throughout this campaign CTI drummed away at its two central points: labor had benefitted under the NRA; and the unions had no right to strike against the code since in effect they were striking against the federal government itself.[19]

In appealing for public support, Sloan and the Code Authority found it difficult to counter the adverse publicity that the southern mill owners were receiving in national magazines and leading

[15] Even Frances Perkins was not very happy with the union's strike committee: Frances Perkins, Memo to Colonel McIntyre, August 17, 1934, OF 407-B, RL.

[16] Lahne, *The Cotton Mill Worker*, pp. 226–229; Hodges, "The New Deal Labor Policy," pp. 279–282.

[17] G. A. Sloan to P. A. Redmond, October 9, 1934, in Comer MSS.

[18] CMASC, Minute Book, June 27, 1935; CMAG, *Report*, XXXV (1935), 99.

[19] CTI, Press Release, September 1, [1934]; CTI, Copy of Radio Address, September 4, 1934; both in Sloan MSS.

newspapers. It was impossible to disguise the fact that in the mill towns of the South, management held all of the trump cards.[20] When the police powers of local and state governments were brought into play they served management, not labor. Although the unions called for impartial federal troops, nothing was done. As plant after plant got back into production, management seemed to be on the verge of complete victory over the unions.[21]

By this time, however, Roosevelt was under increasing pressure to take action. The violence, the unions' renewed demands for intervention, and the disruption of the recovery program could not long be ignored. In an effort to settle the strike peacefully, FDR appointed a mediation board under the chairmanship of John G. Winant, ex-Governor of New Hampshire. The board was empowered to arbitrate any issues submitted to it by both parties. Promptly, the United Textile Workers agreed (with certain conditions) to arbitration of the central issues that had prompted the strike.[22] The employers refused arbitration. Arbitration threatened to bring under consideration the full range of union demands, and the Code Authority was not even prepared to discuss most of these points. Rejecting arbitration was a dangerous maneuver; but the Authority felt that the existing code was too strong a fortress to abandon for an open battle before Winant's committee.[23]

Despite being rejected by the employers, the arbitration board studied the problem and prepared a report (submitted on September 17, 1934) for the President. The report reassured the nervous members of the Code Authority. In regard to collective bargaining, the board decided that it was impossible, except on a plant-to-plant

[20] CMASC, Minute Book, September 12, 1934; Sloan to Redmond, October 9, 1934, Comer MSS.

[21] Telegram of Francis J. Gorman to Josiah W. Bailey, September 12, 1934; Letter of J. W. Bailey to F. D. Roosevelt, September 13, 1934 (also see copy in OF 407-B, RL); Letter of J. W. Bailey to B. B. Gossett, September 17, 1934; Letter of B. B. Gossett to W. D. Anderson, September 18, 1934; all four in Cramer MSS; CMASC, Minute Book, September 12, 1934; CMAG, Report, XXXV (1935), 96–98; Hodges, "The New Deal Labor Policy," pp. 284–285.

[22] Telegram of Stephen Early to M. H. McIntyre, September 6, 1934; Telegram of F. J. Gorman to F. D. Roosevelt, September 7 and 8, 1934, OF 407-B, RL; Letter of F. J. Gorman to Governor John G. Winant (with enclosure), September 9, 1934, RG 9, 4475, Winant Board, NA. Hugh Johnson was under considerable pressure at this time and he, too, could little afford a major strike: Letter of D. Richberg to M. H. McIntyre (with enclosure), September 5, 1934; Letter of Rexford Tugwell to F. D. Roosevelt, September 5, 1934; Unsigned Memorandum, September 13, 1934; all three in OF 466, RL.

[23] CTI, Minutes, CTIC, September 11 and 12, 1934, Dorr MSS.

basis; this virtually sealed the fate of the UTW's organization drive in the South. Also, the board could find no evidence indicating that wages or hours should be changed. The report suggested further government study of the problem, but that of course was merely a sop for the unions. The committee did find that in order to protect the workers' rights under Section 7(a), a new and permanent textile labor relations board had to be created. This board should handle all complaints in labor matters and, the report said, should have an adequate staff to do its own field work. No longer would CTI's field agents investigate labor problems. Winant's committee also decided that the stretch-out was a real problem. Work loads had been increased throughout the industry, the report said; it recommended that a special board be appointed to study this question and to develop means of controlling future changes in work loads.[24]

Using the Winant report, the NRA was able to reach a final settlement of the strike in late September. Negotiations over particular points continued for some weeks, but the basic terms were already charted in the report. The ensuing peace treaty gave little satisfaction to the United Textile Workers. Their immediate objectives of shorter hours, higher wages, and industry-wide collective bargaining were lost. Their drive for southern members was turned back, and the basic code was still intact.[25]

Events during the next few months made the employers' victory seem even more complete. The Federal Trade Commission and the Department of Labor filed reports on wages and hours in the industry; their findings merely corroborated the conclusions reached earlier by the Winant board. At that time, the reports said, the mills could not afford higher labor costs; and management had, for the most part, preserved the wage differentials that had existed for skilled labor before 1933. Both the FTC and the Department of Labor thus substantiated certain essential parts of the position the Authority had adopted from the very beginning.[26]

[24]Winant et al., Report of the Board of Inquiry, September 17, 1934, NA.
[25] Lahne, The Cotton Mill Worker, pp. 229–231; CMANC, Proc., XXVIII (1934), p. 30.
[26] U. S., Federal Trade Commission, Report on the Textile Industry in 1933 and 1934, Part I (Washington, 1935); U. S., Bureau of Labor Statistics, Textile Report, Part I (1935); both in RG 9, 1818, NA. For a different interpretation of the conclusions suggested by the reports see Hodges, "The New Deal Labor Policy," pp. 322–323.

The Authority was also able to regain its powerful administrative position on labor matters. As the union waited for the reports, CTI began once again to use its field agents to check compliance with the wage and hour provisions of the code. Complaints under Section 7(a) were handled by the new Textile Labor Relations Board. But quietly and skillfully Sloan and Dorr guided the Institute back into one of the defensive positions that had been lost in the settlement; seldom was the influence of the association leaders more obvious.[27]

Even the activities of the Textile Labor Relations Board provided little satisfaction for the UTW. In attempting to settle the problems arising from the strike, the Board found it very difficult to side with the employees. When a worker claimed that he or she had been fired because of union activity, for instance, the employers were usually prepared to cite instances of substandard work or other factors which they said brought about dismissal. Who was right? How was the Board to decide? And what was it to do when other workers had been hired to replace the mill hands who had been released? An order to re-employ the old hands would throw the new employees off the job. Although the Board apparently made every effort to give the unions and the workers a fair hearing, it was impossible to right all of the wrongs perpetrated during the strike.[28]

Although management could well consider the settlement a victory, the Code Authority had in reality lost a great deal in the strike. Some of these losses were immediate and obvious. One of

[27] If the problem had not been so serious the government's performance in this interlude would provide fine material for a bureaucratic comedy. Each time the situation was studied, the investigatory process had slipped back into CTI's hands. Letter of B. M. Squires to G. A. Sloan, October 7, 1934; Letter of Stanley I. Posner to S. P. Munroe, November 22, 1934; Letter of S. P. Munroe to J. J. Reinstein, January 18, 1935; L. J. Martin, Memo to Prentiss L. Coonley, February 5, 1935; all in RG 9, 1801, NA; Marion J. Harron, Memo to P. L. Coonley, December 11, 1934, RG 9, 1800, NA; M. J. Harron, Memo to Howard E. Wahrenbrock, February 12, 1935, RG 9, 1794, NA; Letter of Frank P. Douglass to Cotton-Textile Institute, December 27, 1934; Sloan, Memo to Mr. Comer, January 9, 1935; both in Comer MSS; Letter of Col. F. P. Douglass to G. A. Sloan, March 20, 1935, RG 9, 4171, Textile Labor Relations Board, NA; Hodges, "The New Deal Labor Policy," pp. 306–307.

[28] Textile Labor Relations Board, Decisions, September 26, 1934, to May 27, 1935, RG 9, NA; Letter of F. J. Gorman to G. A. Sloan, November 2, 1934, OF 355, RL; Lahne, The Cotton Mill Worker, p. 231.

the first casualties had been the Bruere Board; although its replacement could not solve all of labor's problems, the new Textile Labor Relations Board was inclined to favor organized labor. At least this Board had every intention of seeing that the workers received all of the rights guaranteed to them in the NIRA. The new apparatus for settling the stretch-out problem also weakened the position of the Code Authority. Under this system a special government committee was created to study the entire problem and to devise permanent means of regulating work loads. For the time being, all changes in work assignments were subject to government control. Mill hands who felt that their work loads were being increased could appeal to the district chairmen of the Textile Work Assignments Board.[29]

The Authority suffered other, less obvious, but serious losses as a result of the strike. A flaw in the partnership principle had been clearly revealed: despite Section 7(a), the industry would not accept and deal with organized labor in a forthright manner. So long as the Authority was merely another form of trade association, the unions were fated to play a subordinate role in the operation of the code.[30] Those NRA officials who had been attacking Johnson and the partnership concept now had additional evidence supporting their contention that the associations could not be expected to run their industries with the national interest in mind. The guild philosophy was, the officials said, a managerial ideology which offered little or nothing to the union organizations that the New Deal wanted to support. By dramatically exposing this blind spot in the associative philosophy, the general textile strike seriously weakened the alliance between CTI and the government. The strike also contributed to the downfall of General Johnson—the Code Authority's staunchest friend within the Roosevelt Administration.

[29] Letter of G. A. Sloan to the President of the United States (with enclosure), October 12, 1934; Letter of S. Clay Williams to the President, October 15, 1934; Letter of A. Henry Thurston to the National Industrial Recovery Board; all in RG 9, 1796, NA; Letter of G. H. Dorr to Robert Henry, December 8, 1934, Dorr MSS. The Final Report (May 13, 1935) of the Cotton Textile Work Assignment Board was very favorable to management.

[30] See, for instance, the Letter of L. Henderson to V. G. Iden, October 17, 1934, RG 9, 7397, Research and Planning Division, Personal Files, Leon Henderson, NA.

By the fall of 1934 Hugh Johnson was losing his grip on the NRA. Unable to cope single-handedly with the pressures of administering his sprawling agency and unwilling to delegate authority to his competent administrators, Johnson was headed toward a mental and physical collapse. When the pressures became too great—and they regularly did—he retired with a good bottle of whiskey. Johnson's drunks were like everything else about the General—just a little bit bigger than life. As the drinking bouts became more frequent and the NRA's internal problems became more acute, FDR found it impossible to avoid the conclusion suggested by Johnson's several opponents: the General had to go.[31]

As Johnson faltered, the forces attacking the recovery program from outside the administration stepped up their assault. During 1934 many Americans seem to have had second thoughts about the desirability of stabilization, cooperation, and associative self-regulation. Congressional leaders were concerned about the monopolistic powers that had been granted to the code authorities. Under pressure from Congress, a National Recovery Review Board was established to investigate the monopoly powers that had been granted in the codes. With Clarence Darrow leading the way, the Board very quickly discovered that NRA had spawned a giant nest of new and dangerous monopolies. Although Darrow's prosecution of NRA was unconvincing to those familiar with his methods of investigation, the Board's reports helped to erode the popular support that the Recovery Administration had once had.[32] Even many businessmen who had been cooperative began to see that their earlier fears had been well grounded: self-regulation was threatening to become government regulation. The partnership principle seemed to have been forgotten. In the fall of 1934 there was a steady chorus of voices calling for an end to guild government and the reign of General Johnson.[33]

[31] [Donald Richberg], *Outline of A Program, ca.* June 20, 1934; Richberg to McIntyre (with enclosure), September 5, 1934; Tugwell to F. D. R., September 5, 1934, OF 466, RL; Schlesinger, *The Coming of the New Deal,* pp. 154–157.

[32] *Ibid.,* pp. 132–134.

[33] Dorr to Anderson, November 2, 1934; Sloan to Dorr, November 19, 1934; both in Dorr MSS; Sloan to H. S. Johnson, December 11, 1933; Telegram of G. A. Sloan to Henry S. Dennison, n.d.; Letter of M. O. Maughan to the Members of the Executive Committee of the American Trade Association Executives, January 8, 1934; Letter of James W. Hook to G. A. Sloan, November 17, 1934; Letter of G. A. Sloan to J. W. Hook, November 23, 1934; all five in RG 9, 1824, NA; Letter of G. A. Sloan to Clarence Francis, December 6, 1934, in Sloan MSS.

By the time the textile strike broke out, Johnson and his concept of the recovery program were thus being shelled heavily from three sides. One attack came from within the NRA itself where the opponents of guild government were growing stronger each day. Another assault had been launched from within the President's coterie of advisers and cabinet officers. The third attack came from a combination of external critics in Congress, in business and labor organizations, and in the general public. Together these three columns pressed in on the General. By September, 1934, their campaign had achieved its objective; Johnson was at last forced to resign.

As soon as the General had withdrawn, FDR set out to reshape the Recovery Administration. For the first time the opponents of self-regulation were given a good chance to formulate their own program for economic recovery.[34]

To replace Johnson, Roosevelt appointed a five-member National Industrial Recovery Board (NIRB) which promptly set out to formulate a new set of policies for NRA. In the deliberations of the Board, the economic philosophy expounded by the Research and Planning Division, the ideas expressed by Leon Henderson, and the attitudes of the Consumers' Advisory Board weighed far more heavily than did the concepts of self-regulation advanced by the association leaders. As far as the majority of the Board was concerned the trade associations had had their day and had failed. The Board intended to chart a new course. After considerable discussion, most of the members of the NIRB agreed on a basic policy: the industrial codes should be stripped down until they included little more than minimum wages, maximum hours, a regulation eliminating child labor, and a section protecting union members and their organizations.[35]

The position taken by the NIRB fed the disillusionment that was growing within the industry. Many of the manufacturers were

[34] Letter of H. S. Johnson to the President, September 24, 1934; Letter of F. D. Roosevelt to H. S. Johnson, September 25, 1934; both in OF 466, RL. The manufacturers recognized that Johnson had protected them: Anderson to D. Comer, July 25, 1934, Cramer MSS.

[35] NRA, Agenda for National Industrial Recovery Board (hereafter cited as NIRB); NIRB, Minutes, May 13, 1935; both in RG 9, 8449, Central Records Section, NIRB; NRA, Policy Series No. 1, RG 9, 5, NIRB, General File, Donald Richberg; Letter of D. R. Richberg to E. P. Hoyle, May 14, 1935, RG 9, 581, Office Files of the General Counsel, NA; D. Richberg to the President (with enclosure), April 12, 1935, OF 466, RL.

becoming discouraged with their experiment in guild government. Seemingly endless bouts with regulatory trivia had exhausted the members of the Code Authority. There seemed to be no way to prevent the proliferation of controls. In the carded-yarn group, the very members who had demanded a detailed subcode that would tightly regulate their market had found the regulations too burdensome.[36] Even CTI's most ardent fans became disturbed. Given the most favorable interpretation possible, the statistics on the entire industry suggested that the code had protected some marginal firms (particularly in New England) and had prevented disastrous price declines. But that was all. According to the report filed by the Federal Trade Commission, the first year of code operation (1933) had been relatively profitable for cotton manufacturers; total net income (before taxes) for all of the corporations manufacturing cotton goods had been almost thirty-two million dollars. But in 1934 the industry slumped back; net income fell off to about eight and a half million dollars and the number of companies reporting no net income jumped from 288 to 481 (52 per cent of the companies filing returns). With over half of the industry operating at a deficit, guild government seemed hardly worth the effort.[37]

While reading the sad message from his balance sheet and preparing to fill out another report for the Code Authority, the manufacturer also found himself buried under a new wave of legislation. He had convinced himself that by cooperating with NRA he would block the passage of new regulatory measures. In 1934 this fantasy had been rudely crushed. With Congress considering a new and, to his mind, dangerous labor bill, a measure to regulate securities exchanges, and a new provision for unemployment insurance, the manufacturer felt that he had been betrayed. What had happened to the partnership principle, he asked. It seemed to him that the entire New Deal—like the NRA itself—was threatening to replace cooperation with strict government control.[38]

In the South the discontent was compounded by a growing

[36] G. A. Sloan to Sydney P. Cooper, July 3, 1934, Comer MSS.

[37] FTC, *Report on the Textile Industry, Part I;* also see Horace B. Drury's Report on Administration and Effects of Production and Capacity Control Provisions in NRA Codes, May 1, 1935, GR 61, RL.

[38] *King Cotton Weekly,* March 23 and 29, and April 5, 1934; ACMA, *Proc.,* XXXVIII (1934), 63–65, 82–83; Rearick to Sloan, April 11, 1934, Dorr MSS; Letter of C. D. Owen to P. B. Halstead, March 1, 1934, RG 9, 1808, NA.

undercurrent of sectional animosity. Softly the old sectional themes that had plagued CTI's pre-NRA experiences began to sound again. In 1933 the southern mill executives had been willing to sacrifice certain of their advantages in order to get a code drafted and into operation. North-South cost differentials had been sharply reduced and as a consequence, the New England industry had begun to recover. After making this sacrifice the southerners had seen their own dreams of happy prosperity under the Code Authority dashed. As they worried over their account books it became more and more difficult to choke back the feeling that they were being done in by their clever northern competitors.[39]

After the general strike in 1934, southern suspicions had begun to focus on CTI's leadership. Some felt that too much of the Code Authority's business had slipped into the hands of the association leaders. There were angry glances in the direction of George Sloan; there were suggestions that Sloan had listened more to the businessmen in New York and New England than he had to the southerners. Sloan was himself growing tired of the pressures exerted by his job. He had tried to resign in 1934, but when the general strike hit the industry he had stayed to guide the Code Authority through this crisis. In early 1935 Sloan submitted his final resignation as president of the Institute. On a temporary basis Dorr stepped in to head the association, but he did so with the understanding that the members would soon find a new president. As Sloan left the Institute there was fulsome praise for his long and energetic service to the cause of self-regulation; but quite a few of the southern manufacturers were happy to have the opportunity to replace Sloan with a man who they felt would pay more attention to their vital interests.[40]

It was thus necessary for the Institute and its leaders to contend simultaneously with the growing disillusionment in their own

[39] Letter of T. M. Marchant to W. D. Anderson, August 14, 1934; Letter of B. B. Gossett to E. H. Bennett, August 18, 1934; both in Cramer MSS; D. Comer to Sloan, February 4, 1935, Comer MSS.

[40] Letter of W. D. Anderson to Col. G. Edward Buxton, August 13, 1934; Letter of T. M. Marchant to S. W. Cramer, August 14, 1934; Letter of R. E. Henry to Col. W. D. Anderson, August 15, 1934; all three in Cramer MSS; *Charlotte Observer*, August 5, 1934; *New Bedford Mercury* (Massachusetts), August 13, 1934.

industry and the new ideas circulating at the top of the NRA. In its struggle with the NIRB, the Authority was strengthened by its record of effective code administration. Questions of compliance with code standards continued to be handled by the Authority. All of the complaints in regard to trade practice provisions, minimum wages, maximum hours, and child labor were investigated by CTI's field agents. Most of these questions were settled informally, with only a few cases being forwarded to the NRA for enforcement. For the most part the Authority encountered no serious problems in enforcing its regulations. After a full-scale investigation of one aspect of this question, the Bureau of Labor Statistics reported (January, 1935) that there had been "an overwhelming compliance" with the wage provisions of the code.[41]

There were of course major problems that the Authority was unable to solve. Wherever it tried to strengthen the industry's position by persuading other governmental agencies to alter their policies, it usually failed. The battle over the processing tax was a good example. CTI was unable to get any relief from the AAA's processing taxes on cotton and was stymied in its efforts to persuade the government to levy compensating taxes on competing fibers. In this case, administrative inertia was the association's enemy. Despite a fierce and relentless campaign, the Institute was defeated by the Department of Agriculture and by the associations representing producers who would be damaged by compensating taxes.[42]

The same situation existed in regard to imports. Although the NIRA had specifically stated that domestic manufacturers would be protected from foreign competition, CTI was unable to get the government to respond to its demands for higher duties on cotton goods. Each request for action aroused further study of the problem. The only product of the investigations was further delay. As the association's officers discovered, the principle of squatter's rights often explained more about the governmental process than did the principle of the lever.[43]

[41] Bureau of Labor Statistics, *Textile Report, Part I* (1935).
[42] G. H. Dorr, Release, March 28, 1935, RG 9, 1800, NA; *King Cotton Weekly,* August 2, 1934; March 28, April 4 and 10, and May 2, 1935; ACMA, *Proc.,* XXXIX (1935), 40–41.
[43] Letter of C. C. Frick to Charles G. Akin, April 10, 1935; Letter of L. C. Marshall to the President (with enclosure), April 1935; both in RG 9, 1810 and 1824, NA; ACMA, *Proc.,* XXXIX (1935), 35.

In administrative matters, however, the Code Authority was able to keep its house in good order. Although its codification of interpretations never received official sanction, the interpretations satisfied the manufacturers who were operating under the code. There was never any serious objection to the interpretations from either management or labor.[44] Similarly, the job of categorizing different companies was performed with a minimum of discomfort. By the end of 1934 most of these problems were being handled in a routine manner by the Institute's staff. CTI's excellent record of code administration helped to shield the Authority from the critics who were demanding wholesale changes in the codes.[45]

One of the points of attack was the make-up of the Code Authority itself. If the Authority were to represent anyone except management, its critics said, it had to include representatives of labor and of the consumers. This was an anathema to the Code Authority. How could they discuss their problems if they had a representative from the UTW sitting in their midst? It was unthinkable! They flatly rejected this proposal. There was a government representative on the Authority, they said, and he could protect the interests of labor and the consumer—if they needed further protection. As a compromise, the NRA appointed a labor adviser to the government representative and also began to make certain that the government official was present at all of the Authority's meetings. Aside from this, however, the committee's membership remained unchanged. The Consumers' Advisory Board was never given the special representation that it requested.[46]

A more bitter and far more decisive struggle was waged over production control. Even before Johnson left the Recovery Ad-

[44] Mary K. Bell, Memo to Mr. Rubinow, December 19, 1934; A. H. Thurston, Memorandum to N. B. Bond, January 18, 1935; J. L. Donovan, Memo to A. H. Thurston, February 19, 1935; all three in RG 9, 1812, and 1810, NA; CTI, Minutes, CTIC, February 26, 1935, Dorr MSS.

[45] This is well illustrated by the Authority's handling of the interpretations problem: Nicholson to Sloan, February 8, 1934; Chisholm, Division of Review, Standard Work Sheet; both in RG 9, 1812 and 1809, NA.

[46] CTI, Minutes, CTIC, June 19, 1934, NTA MSS; Advisory Council, Minutes, July 19, 20, and 24, 1934, RG 9, 8173, Advisory Council, NA; Henderson to Iden, October 17, 1934, RG 9, 7397, Research and Planning Division, Personal Files, Leon Henderson, NA; D. R. Richberg, Memo to the President, November 13, 1934; National Emergency Council, Minutes, November 13, 1934; both in RG 44, Appendix 7, NA; Sloan to Dorr, January 11, 1935, Dorr MSS.

ministration, the Consumers' Advisory Board began to engage in flanking maneuvers by voting approval of almost all requests for exemption from the machine-hour limitations. While approving the exemptions, Mercer Johnston, chairman of the Board, made it clear that he was using his vote to express opposition to the basic principle of production control. By constantly drumming away at the 40–40 regulation, the Board kept the Code Authority on the defensive.[47]

Every order that the Authority attempted to push through NRA was caught in the cross fire. This included the special amendments designed to provide regulations for subindustries which had originally been brought under the general code. Most of these amendments had been approved before Hugh Johnson resigned. A few, including the thread industry's code, were still pending when the NIRB took over. Without Johnson's help the Authority found it almost impossible to push the subcodes through the lower levels of the NRA. Only by stripping them of all provisions which even hinted at price and production control was the committee able to win final approval. In their truncated versions, however, the special codes were not worth all the trouble they had caused.[48]

On the Authority's other flank was Leon Henderson, who proposed a plan for inventory control as an alternative to the limit on machine-hours. Henderson's proposal would have enabled the more efficient producers to take a larger share of the market so long as they did not pile up large stocks of unsold goods. His plan

---

[47] NRA, Conference on the Cotton Textile Code, June 8, 1934, RG 9, 1804; NIRA, Conference on the Knitted Underwear Industry, June 8, 1934; Consumers' Advisory Board, Memo to A. H. Thurston, June 12, 1934; both in RG 9, 1800; Data on the Formulation and Administration of the Code of Fair Competition for the Cotton Textile Industry, RG 9, 1819; Advisory Council, Minutes, February 4, 1935, RG 9, 8173, Advisory Council; Mercer G. Johnston, Memo to A. H. Thurston, April 29 and May 14, 1935, RG 9, 1802 and 1800; all in NA.

[48] CTI, Minutes, CTIC, June 19, 1934; CTI, Code of Fair Trade Practices Governing the Cotton Thread Manufacturing Branch; Letter of Secretary, CTIC, to A. H. Thurston, March 14, 1935; all three in Dorr MSS; C. W. Metcalf to Major C. P. Wood, June 20, 1934; NRA, Amendment to Code of Fair Competition for the Cotton Textile Industry, July 17, 1934; both in RG 9, 1796, NA; Letter of C. W. Metcalf to J. P. Babcock, August 21, 1934, RG 9, 1797, NA; Letter of A. H. Thurston to F. S. Blanchard, February 4, 1935, RG 9, 1810, NA; Letter of W. H. Dillingham to A. Henry Thurston, February 15, 1935, RG 9, 1795, NA; N. T. Bartlett, Memo to M. D. Vincent, April 19, 1935, RG 9, 1796, NA.

would prevent burdensome inventories from periodically depressing the market, without, however, protecting the marginal firms from their more efficient competitors.[49]

The most direct attack upon production control continued to come from economist Victor von Szeliski of the Research and Planning Division. He took the position that "preservation of . . . high cost mills is really the sole achievement of the Cotton Textile Industry. The machine-hour restriction works by preventing the low cost manufacturer from manufacturing at low cost—preventing his goods from being put on the market in quantities. This results in a higher price than the consumers would otherwise pay and enables the high cost producers to hobble along. But the necessary sequel of this is lessened work opportunities for labor, labor unrest, slow movement of goods into consumers' hands." He suggested that the association would not adopt Henderson's inventory-control plan because it would not enable the trade group to counter the thrust of the low-cost producers. These efficient mills, he said, were not the ones that were piling up unsold inventories; the low-cost mills were simply producing as much as possible and selling all of it at the market price. Only through the machine-hour limitation or price control could the Authority prevent these low-cost mills from dominating the market.[50]

As always, the strength of von Szeliski's analysis rested in his penetrating critique of the associative philosophy; his weakness lay in his inability to propose viable alternatives to the policy he was demolishing. At one point he suggested that the economic system was automatically self-corrective; the best thing to do was to let the efficient producers drive the high-cost mills out of the market. As Dorr pointed out in rebuttal, the New Deal had rejected this laissez faire philosophy because it had been tried with unpleasant results. Another of von Szeliski's propositions would have involved a thoroughgoing reorganization of the industry. That, too, was unacceptable. The NIRB was hunting for a middle ground, someplace between this radical idea and the old laissez faire concept of

[49] Sloan to Anderson, May 29, 1934; Leavelle McCampbell, Suggestions and Data Submitted to Committee on Inventory Control, July 27, 1934; both in Comer MSS; CTI, Minutes, CTIC, June 19 and August 3, 1934, NTA MSS.

[50] V. S. von Szeliski, Analysis of the question: What wage rise, if any, is possible in the Cotton Textile Industry? July 7, 1934, RG 9, 7419, Research and Planning Division, General Files, V. S. von Szeliski, NA; V. S. von Szeliski, Report on the Cotton Textile Industry, August 16, 1934, RG 9, 1819, NA; von Szeliski, Memo to L. Henderson, August 4, 1934, GR 61, RL.

a self-correcting competitive economy. While the Board was influenced by von Szeliski's critique of production control, even Henderson was unwilling to accept either of the alternative courses proposed.

In its defense of production control, the Authority was helped by the fact that in the lower echelons of NRA there were still many businessmen sympathetic to their cause. While the titans in the NIRB grappled with the abstract questions of economic philosophy, these administrators helped the Institute perfect its programs. Although the resulting conflict between policy and practice did not go unnoticed, it proved to be very difficult to prevent.[51]

Despite the assistance of the NRA "businesscrats," the Code Authority and the association leaders spent more and more of their time defending their philosophy and practice of industrial control. In January, 1935, when the NIRB held hearings on various policy problems, spokesmen from the Institute presented an elaborate defense of their concept of production control. In numerous personal discussions with NRA officials, the association leaders argued and re-argued this question.[52]

Under the NIRB, it became necessary for CTI's officers to change their tactics somewhat. Their response to Leon Henderson's inventory-control plan was at first to reject the idea out of hand. Very quickly, however, they discovered that they could no longer end a discussion by threatening to walk out on the administration. Hugh Johnson was no longer there to protect them. It was necessary now to go through the motions of seriously considering this and all other suggestions. So the Authority took up Henderson's ideas and, in effect, studied them to death. Prolonged

[51] Letter of H. S. Johnson to Frances Perkins, June 1, 1934, RG 9, 7399, Research and Planning Division, Personal Files, Leon Henderson, NA; Advisory Council, Minutes, July 27 and November 16, 1934, RG 9, 8173, Advisory Council, NA; Letter of A. H. Thurston to the NIRB, March 1, 1935, RG 9, 1796, NA; there were also some advocates of the business outlook at the top of NRA: Letter of S. Clay Williams to Daniel C. Roper, August 15, 1934, OF 172, RL.

[52] G. A. Sloan, Report on the NRA and the New Congress, November 30, 1934; G. A. Sloan, Report on the Relationship of Industry to Government, November 2, 1934; Letter of G. A. Sloan to D. R. Richberg, February 3, 1935; all three in Sloan MSS; Letter of G. H. Dorr to S. P. Cooper, February 23, 1935, Dorr MSS; CMANC, *Proc.*, XXVIII (1934), 29; Schlesinger, *The Coming of the New Deal*, p. 160; Advisory Council, Minutes, February 6, 1935, RG 9, 8173, Advisory Council, NA.

consideration became the fate of all proposals which threatened the Authority's vital interests.

While endless discussion served well as a defensive tactic, such maneuvers provided no guarantee that in the future CTI's production-control plan would be secure. The National Industrial Recovery Act was due to expire in June, 1935. It was clear that the NIRB would have a great deal of influence on the Roosevelt Administration's decision about the future of NRA. And by early 1935 it was equally clear that the tide of opinion in the NIRB was running against the Code Authority. Codes under the next recovery agency would probably not contain stabilizing controls on prices and production. Regulations on entry would probably be abandoned. There would undoubtedly be codes that stipulated minimum wages and maximum hours and that prohibited child labor; but otherwise, the antitrust statutes would be back in force. Cotton manufacturers would once again be left to solve their problems in a market-oriented economy.

To forestall this fate, the Institute's leaders settled on a new strategy. No longer would they argue in abstract terms the need for production control by a central agency. Instead of debating the necessity of having stabilizing institutions such as the Code Authority in all industries, they would carve out a special niche for cotton textiles. By stressing the particular nature of their industry's structure and problems they would perhaps be able to keep their machine-hour limitations. Other industries had adopted this strategy with considerable success. The so-called natural resources industries—the oil producers for instance—had established their right to particular regulations and special privileges that could not be granted to all manufacturing industries. CTI hoped to do the same for cotton textiles.[53]

By using this new approach they could pull the teeth out of some of their opponents' strongest arguments. Production control would not have to be tied to national economic recovery. Even though their code would not spur recovery, it could be defended. By reference to the problems cotton textiles faced during the 1920's (when most other industries were enjoying large profits)

[53] Special Committee of the Advisory Council, December 20, 1934, RG 9, 8157, Advisory Council, General Correspondence, NA.

they would be able to justify measures that might not be applicable to the steel or automobile manufacturers. They would actually be able to use some of the studies of the Research and Planning Division to support their contention that cotton textiles had unique problems that warranted special treatment.

Goldthwaite H. Dorr played the major role in persuading the government to accept the Institute's new line of reasoning. After discussions with a wide range of NRA officials, Dorr began to make some headway. When Donald Richberg (the new chairman of the NIRB) drafted the antitrust rules for his proposed revision of NRA (April, 1935), he gave cotton textiles a special place in the bill. Although in general Richberg wanted to abandon self-regulation, he made a special exception for "provisions found necessary and proper in exceptional industries and in emergencies to prevent or to correct, under governmental control, a depression in a trade or industry resulting from production largely in excess of effective demand. . . ." Penciled in the margin was Richberg's explanation that this referred to such industries as cotton textiles.[54]

Using its classification as a special industry, the Code Authority was actually able to push through another improvement in the machinery for controlling production. Recognizing that the failure to act quickly had been the outstanding weakness of their programs thus far, the Code Authority had for some months been suggesting that new power be given to a "Planning and Research Committee." According to the proposal that had originally been submitted to Hugh Johnson, this Committee would be empowered to "study the situation *in advance* and formulate plans so that the Code Authority can set [out] to make them *immediately effective* as [the] occasion arises." The committee would be given permission to initiate cuts in production with a minimum of government supervision so long as the reduction did not exceed 15 per cent of the total number of machine-hours allowable under 40–40 during any six-month period. Orders issued by the committee had to be acted on by the Recovery Administration within a few days or they would automatically go into effect. Under this proposal, the Planning and Research Committee had the potential to become a true planning agency, an organization that could

---

[54] Telegram of D. R. Richberg to M. H. McIntyre, March 30, 1935; Richberg to the President (with enclosure), April 12, 1935; both in OF 466, RL.

avoid the pitfalls of self-regulation by anticipating difficulties and moving swiftly to prevent price declines.[55]

After the proposal had been presented to the NRA several times, the NIRB finally approved the plan on March 23, 1935.[56] By this time a committee from the NRA's Advisory Council had submitted a report favorable to this type of program so long as it was limited to special industries such as cotton textiles and so long as a "special committee of experts should be set up to help pass upon provisions of this sort." The project had been sifted through another committee and at last given formal approval by the NIRB.[57]

At the NRA's insistence the technical committee which would control production consisted of one government representative and three trade association officials. The Code Authority had merely suggested that it appoint three members. NRA insisted that there would be too much opportunity for conflict of interest if the members were themselves manufacturers. For such an important committee as this, they needed men who were not personally involved in the market operations they would be controlling. This was a belated but nonetheless significant decision. The NRA had at last recognized that the businessmen and the professional staff members of policy-shaping associations like the CTI were not identical. Special authority could be given to the association leaders; they could be granted power that could not be trusted in the hands of the businessman who had a vested interest in the decisions to be made. Never before had the semi-autonomous position of the policy-shaping association been granted such clear and positive recognition by the government.[58]

Dorr and his colleagues now had their best opportunity to stabilize the market. No longer were the association leaders constrained to bow to the principle of the concurrent majority. If they chose to

[55] Letter of G. A. Sloan to A. H. Thurston, August 13, 1934, Sloan MSS; P. L. Coonley, Memo to Blackwell Smith, August 27, 1934; Proposed Order to Provide a Means for Further Limitation on the Hours of Machine Operation; both in RG 9, 1815, NA.

[56] In its final form the plan provided for a maximum cut of 25 per cent of the hours or machines operated during the prior six months.

[57] Letter of CTIC to the NIRB, March 16, 1935, RG 9, 1798, NA; NIRB, Minutes, March 6, 21, and 23, 1935, RG 9, 8449, Central Record Section, NIRB, NA; NRA, Release No. 10689, March 26, 1935, RG 9, 1808, NA.

[58] NRA, Procedure under the Proposed Requirement of the Cotton Textile Industry Code Authority, March 24, 1935, RG 9, 1824, NA.

be bold, they could seize the helm. They could manipulate production—within the limits established—so as to anticipate surpluses and prevent price declines.

The association leaders were, however, under considerable pressure to score a quick success with the new program. Disillusionment within their own membership was growing. NRA was no longer in the safe hands of Hugh Johnson, and the unions and other opponents of the Recovery Administration were loudly and clearly voicing their discontent. In the weeks since the general textile strike, the condominium of guild and government had seemed to be crumbling before the onslaught of its enemies.[59] For the time, CTI's leaders had been able to build a new fortress in which to continue their efforts to stabilize the industry; but it was very clear that time was growing short.

[59] Ellis W. Hawley's study *The New Deal and the Problem of Monopoly* (Princeton: Princeton University Press, 1966) was published after my manuscript was completed; for the most part, however, our conclusions about the evolution of the NRA are similar.

Gastonia, North Carolina: Spring 1937

Gastonia could afford a bit of optimism in the spring of 1937. Things were looking better in the southern Piedmont, particularly in the textile towns. Gastonia was one of these. Its fortunes depended upon the cotton mills which were scattered throughout the stream-cut countryside of Gaston County. When the mills prospered, Gastonia was a happy city. But for the last ten years there had been precious little cause for cheer. Intense competition had slashed prices and profits, choking off Gastonia's income.

By the spring of 1937 the outlook was improved. Prices for the cotton yarns that were Gastonia's major product had been steadily climbing. The manufacturer's margin was larger than it had been since the first days of the New Deal. Employment was creeping upward. The entire industry seemed at last to be recovering from a depression that had destroyed much of Gastonia's northern competition.

Blended with this optimism was a strain of caution that had not been present in an earlier day. For management and the city fathers there was labor unrest to worry about. The scars of recent struggles had barely healed, and now another battle was about to start. A new union, the Congress of Industrial Organizations, was about to launch an organization drive in the South. Judging from the performance of the CIO in the North, Gastonia was in for a tough fight.

The CIO was merely one of the many new organizations which impinged on Gastonia's fortunes. There was a WPA and an AAA and a TVA and a CCC, to mention only a few. There was even an SEC which periodically issued statements about inflation and the threat of another financial panic. It was all rather disconcerting.

Even more disturbing was the threat of competition from the mills of the deep South and the fast-growing Japanese industry. Gastonia's past success had been a product of stiff price competition, but now there seemed to be much to lose and little to gain from cutthroat competition. Wishing to keep what it had, Gastonia was interested in stability as well as profitable operations. Cooperation was an essential element in the new age of organizations, and the city was attuned to group, not individual, action. While Gastonia's spring theme was full of recovery and hope, the triad of stabilization, cooperation, and control sounded throughout the song.

Chapter XII

New Perspectives

Between March, 1935, and the spring of 1937, the Cotton-Textile Institute and American public policy on business both experienced a series of significant changes. In May, 1935, the National Industrial Recovery Act was declared unconstitutional by the Supreme Court. After this decision the Roosevelt Administration decided not to revive the condominium of guild and government. Suddenly and swiftly CTI fell from the position of power that it occupied when the recovery administration granted to the association leaders a limited prerogative to control the production of cotton goods (March, 1935).

With the demise of the NRA, the alliance between the trade associations and the government reverted to its earlier, pre-New Deal form. The associations, including CTI, continued to co-operate with the federal government; in a wide variety of activities the trade organizations and the government still shared the same goals. But public policy on competition slipped back into its traditional American stance. A vigorous antitrust campaign was inaugurated to atone for the sins of the NIRA, and loose combinations in restraint of trade were once again prosecuted with vigor.

This shift in public policy had an important effect upon the trade association movement in cotton textiles. The associations did not wither away. But insofar as a movement involves a series of interrelated organizational and ideological changes which advance along a certain course, toward a certain objective, the trade association movement was interrupted by the death of the NRA. From the post-Civil War years through 1935, the trade institutions in this industry had steadily evolved into more formidable and autonomous organizations. Gradually they had developed better leaders and a more elaborate cooperative ideology. With the end of the guild-government alliance under NRA, however, this particular line of development stopped. By 1937 it was clear that in America the trade association was not fated to play the significant role that it had found in the industrial systems of Germany and England.

An indication of what the future held for CTI came immediately after the NIRB gave to the association leaders the power to implement flexible production controls. At this moment the trade organization and its leaders stood before a crucial threshold. By quickly and forcefully exercising the independent power that they had been granted they might well have been able at last to stabilize prices and profits in the industry. But the association leaders failed to accept this challenge; they chose to be bound by the majority opinion of the product groups they were trying to regulate. As before, special curtailment orders were not issued until they had been approved by the manufacturers themselves. In effect this shackled the special technical committee of association officers to the same voluntary system of production control that had failed with dismal regularity since 1927—since the 1880's for that matter. This became clear shortly after the committee was organized. When demand began to slacken and prices to drop, the committee projected a cut in production. The proposal was swiftly relayed to the product groups. But there it stopped. Only three groups (of the nine that even bothered to express an opinion on the matter) took advantage of the proposed 25 per cent cut in output. The problem was not yet overwhelming and unavoidable—conditions which had to exist before a majority decision would be reached. With the help of a new gimmick the potentialities of self-regulation had again been explored; the results were depressing.[1]

The Code Authority's failure to exploit fully the potentialities of the technical committee was extremely important. When the government had decided on the membership of the committee,

[1] Letter of Robert Amory to All Manufacturers of Cotton and Part Wool Blankets, March 27, 1935; Letters of P. B. Halstead to James P. Davis, April 30 and May 2, 1935; J. P. Davis, Memorandum to P. L. Coonley, May 4, 1935; all in RG 9, 1808, NA.

it had officially recognized the fact that the association leaders were not exactly the same as the businessmen whom they represented. But CTI's leaders had been unwilling to push ahead from that point, unwilling to make full use of their independence. By May, 1935, they had missed the main chance. CTI was not to become an autonomous economic institution along the lines of some of the German cartels; nothing short of that, however, could make the Code Authority's system of production control successful. The association had already shown that the middle ground between tight control (which anticipated declines) and unrestrained competition was untenable.

By May, 1935, it was manifest that the Code Authority had not achieved its basic economic objective. As Tables 13–17 illustrate, the NRA had temporarily arrested the decline of the New England industry. The number of active spindles in New England mills had actually increased in 1934. These figures show that the code was protecting certain marginal northern producers who otherwise would have been squeezed out of the industry. Undoubtedly, the code had improved conditions for the workers. In 1934, employment in the industry had increased; the average workweek had been cut; average hourly wages had been raised. Still, from the point of view of the trade association, the most important statistics, those on total profits for the industry, indicated that the code was not able to restore profitable operating conditions for most of the mills. While the industry came out of the red in 1933, during the next year the total income slumped to $3,724,000. Over half of the firms manufacturing cotton recorded a net deficit in 1934, and by early 1935 many of the manufacturers were certain that NRA was not worth the trouble it took to administer the program.

TABLE 13

CAPACITY, COTTON TEXTILES, 1933–1935

	1933	1934	1935
Active spindles			
U.S.	26,894,860	27,742,462	26,700,946
New England	8,205,352	8,457,362	7,763,038
South	17,928,934	18,511,156	18,211,994
all other	760,574	773,944	725,914

NOTE: The data on capacity is from U. S., Bureau of the Census, *Bulletin 179, Cotton Production and Distribution, Season of 1941–42* (Washington, 1942), p. 31.

TABLE 14

PRODUCTION, COTTON TEXTILES, 1933–1935

	1933	1934	1935
Cotton consumed (bales)			
U.S.	6,137,395	5,700,253	5,360,867
New England	884,044	985,398	818,191
South	5,086,573	4,550,037	4,305,950
all other	166,778	164,818	236,726
Spindle hours			
U.S.	85,265,000	80,419,000	72,526,000
New England	17,231,000	19,290,000	16,245,000
South	66,366,000	59,291,000	54,642,000
all other	1,667,000	1,839,000	1,639,000

NOTE: All of the figures on production are for cotton years; the South includes all of the cotton-growing states; and the bales are in running bales; U. S., Bureau of the Census, *Bulletin 179*, p. 31. The figures on spindle hours are from U. S., Department of Commerce, *Statistical Abstract of the United States, 1936* (Washington, 1936), p. 785.

TABLE 15

PRICES AND MARGINS, COTTON TEXTILES, 1933–1935

	1933	1934	1935
Average cloth prices (¢/lb.)	17.52	29.13	28.72
Average manufacturers' margin (¢/lb.)	10.07	13.95	11.83

NOTE: The information on prices and margins comes from Backman and Gainsbrugh, *Economics of the Cotton Textile Industry*, pp. 183–184.

TABLE 16

PROFITS, COTTON TEXTILES, 1933–1935

	1933	1934	1935
Net income	$25,011,000	$3,724,000	−$12,701,000
Profits (selected firms)			
North	$2,728,000	−$2,149,000	−$4,019,000
South	$25,369,000	$18,911,000	$8,366,000
Ratio of profits to receipts			
North	2.06%	−1.43%	−2.39%
South	8.65%	5.42%	2.16%
Ratio of profits to net worth			
North	1.59%	−1.37%	−2.69%
South	7.43%	5.52%	2.50%

NOTE: The income statistics can be found in U. S., Bureau of Internal Revenue, *Statistics of Income, 1933*, p. 155; *Statistics of Income, 1934*, Part II, p. 61; *Statistics of Income, 1935*, Part II, p. 35. The source and the nature of the information on profits is described in the notes to Tables 1–4, Chapter V.

TABLE 17

LABOR, COTTON TEXTILES, 1933–1935

	1933	1934	1935
Average number of wage earners..........	379,445	393,100	369,062
Average number of weekly hours..........	41.4	33.2	34.6
Real hourly earnings (¢)................	30.0	49.5	38.3
Real weekly earnings ($)................	$12.51	$13.15	$13.31

NOTE: The above data can be found in Backman and Gainsbrugh, *Economics of the Cotton Textile Industry*, p. 207.

Discouragement was thus already undermining CTI's authority when on May 27, 1935, the Supreme Court struck down the NIRA. The Schechter decision rudely disrupted the alliance between guild and government. In a sense, the Court's decision raised the political price of continuing the NRA experiment higher than the Roosevelt Administration wanted to bid. Within the administration there was already a strong faction which was calling upon the President to abandon his efforts to work with the business community; the young men who sat at the feet of Justice Brandeis of the Supreme Court and Professor Felix Frankfurter of the Harvard Law School were determined to destroy the condominium which was sheltering business associations from the antitrust laws. Other New Dealers were beginning to look to federal fiscal policy as the only means of spurring economic recovery. These opponents of guild government joined the NRA economists who had already been crying out against the associative philosophy for over a year. Together these groups called upon the President to forego the task of creating a new Recovery Administration.[2]

While many businessmen and association officers wanted the NRA restored, the devotees of competition and the business opponents of any sort of involvement with the government had grown more numerous since 1933. The sharp edge of the depression had been blunted; no longer did it appear that America's capitalistic system was on the verge of collapse. In the meantime the experience with the NRA had been discouraging. After the businessmen had entered a partnership with the government, the Roosevelt Administration had changed the terms of the "con-

[2] Schlesinger, *The Coming of the New Deal*, pp. 165–167; Leuchtenburg, *Franklin D. Roosevelt and the New Deal, 1932–1940*, pp. 145–150.

tract." By 1935 it appeared that there would be no end to the new regulations that the federal government would adopt. With its opponents in politics and business growing stronger and its supporters hard pressed to show how the associations had actually contributed anything to economic recovery, guild government was allowed to die a quiet death after the Schechter decision.

In effect the Roosevelt Administration reverted to the traditional and moderate American policy on stability-oriented economic institutions. The federal government ostentatiously cracked the antitrust whip while condoning oligopoly. It was possible to pretend that oligopolistic competition was competition in the old sense of the word. One could not do this with a system built around associations. As the NRA experience had shown, the cartel required an ideological commitment to stability and control which most Americans were not prepared to make on a permanent basis. Furthermore, oligopoly offered technological and economic benefits that the trade groups could never match. As a result the New Deal took back the government authority and approval that it had given to the associations in 1933.

CTI was not yet ready to accept that fate. Dorr and the members of the Code Authority attempted to maintain the code standards in regard to wages, 40–40, and child labor on a voluntary basis. They felt that there was still a chance that the Roosevelt Administration would press for a new recovery measure, one that the Supreme Court would uphold. Besides, the only alternative was to admit a final and crushing defeat.[3]

Initially CTI was able to keep the mills toeing the line. According to the Institute's careful surveys, at the end of the summer of 1935 over 90 per cent of the companies were still adhering to the NRA standards. There were some mills which adopted three-shift operations the moment the NIRA was declared unconstitutional, but this was the exception—at first.[4]

Then slowly CTI's magnificent structure of ideas and coopera-

[3] G. H. Dorr, Memorandum to the Members of the Board of Directors, July 3, 1935, Comer MSS; CTI, Minutes, Executive Committee, December 4, 1935, Dorr MSS.

[4] S. P. Munroe, Memo to All Cotton Spinning and Weaving Mills, September 23, 1935, in Comer MSS.

tive programs began to crumble. By November, 1935, rumors were spreading throughout the industry: mill x had gone to the third shift; mill y was said to be running machinery during the noon-time break; mill z had cut wages, again. CTI fought to hold the line.[5] Indeed the outstanding thing is that the Institute did not officially abandon the effort until the fall of 1936. By the time this action was taken, however, it was obvious that the association was not going to be able to put over a program comparable to the night-work plan. That road had been traveled once, and too many of the manufacturers now felt that another trip through the same countryside would be fruitless.[6] Some managers became enthusiastic about forming small open-price associations. Other executives revived the old plan for a joint selling agency that would effectively eliminate competition among the members, a la Appalachian Coals. But in the meantime they withdrew their allegiance from CTI's economic programs.[7]

In the aftermath of NRA, the Institute actually became a different form of trade organization. By 1937 its major function was to provide the mills with political representation in Washington. The association had proved its ability as a political representative and organizational middleman. With more New Deal regulations piling up each month, the mills recognized that they could not afford to lose this service. But they also saw that stabilizing the industry's market could no longer be the major goal of the association. Having exhausted the possibilities of using the association as an alternative to oligopoly, many of the manufacturers seemed resigned to waiting until competition or combination would solve their economic problems.

With this change in functions came significant changes in the organization. CTI's income was cut and its bureaucratic structure pared down. Leadership of the trade association was now placed in the hands of men who closely resembled the staff officers of the regional groups. No longer were the manufacturers eclipsed

[5] G. H. Dorr, Memo to the Mills, August 30, 1935, Comer MSS; *King Cotton Weekly*, October 17, November 20 and 27, 1935.

[6] Letter of Robert West to D. Comer, May 8, 1936; CTI, Minutes, Executive Committee, June 16, 1936, Comer MSS.

[7] Charles M. Sears, Report on the Manufacture and Distribution of Print Cloth, February 1936, RG 9, 1808, NA; Letter of Bragg Comer to D. Comer, September 3, 1936, in Comer MSS; CTI, Memorandum on a Central Sales Agency, January 6, 1939, Dorr MSS.

by leaders of the stature of Walker D. Hines, George A. Sloan, and Goldthwaite H. Dorr.[8]

In effect CTI became a kind of national service association. After 1937 its leadership and functions were much like those of the regional groups, NACM and the American Association. Like the regional organizations, the Institute provided a wide variety of cooperative programs attuned to the industry's institutional environment. The demands of pressure-group politics, the opportunities to cooperate with the government in technical programs, and the need for an organizational spokesman assured the future for a strong, well-financed national association. CTI simply reverted to an earlier form—one which was in fact more common throughout American industry than the policy-shaping association. In doing so, only the developments of the ten years between 1925 and 1935 were overturned. The entire trade association movement, a seventy-year history of institutional and ideological changes, was not by any means reversed.

The transformation of CTI did come about abruptly, but given the nature of the association and of the NRA experience, this sudden change was understandable. CTI was originally founded upon the single premise that a powerful association could stabilize the cotton textile market. By 1933, after extensive experimentation with relatively non-coercive programs, the central premise had been amended; in its new form it stated that an association armed with government authority could stabilize the market. After the NRA collapsed, however, this proposition was no longer tenable. The policy-shaping association had to be abandoned.

In terms of the industry's future and of the national economy there can be little doubt that this was a desirable change. To make their programs effective, associations like CTI were relentlessly driven toward complete control of their respective industries. The objective of this control was stability, and so long as the associations were dominant, forces pressing for growth and change were, and would have continued to be, suppressed. The vitality of

[8] Letter of T. H. Webb to G. H. Dorr, March 26, 1936; CTI, Minutes, Board of Directors, October 27, 1937; CTI, Minutes, Executive Committee, November 16, 1938; all three in Dorr MSS; letter of Charles K. Everett to D. Comer, April 14, 1936; Letter of Claudius T. Murchison to D. Comer, July 30, 1936; Dorr to D. Comer, June 9, 1936; CTI, Income for Year Ended September 30, 1936; CTI, Budget for Year Ending September 30, 1937; all five in Comer MSS.

the national economy depends in large part upon innovation, and the policy-shaping association and the entrepreneur were natural enemies.

Compared with the large firm and an oligopolistic industrial structure, the associative system was a poor method of adjusting to the demands of a mature economy. While the associations and big business both sought to stabilize prices and profits, the giant firm could do this while retaining many of the benefits of a competitive system. Furthermore, large-scale production in the modern firm enabled businessmen to achieve efficiencies of scale and to conduct research and development programs which were beyond the grasp of the trade associations. America thus struck a compromise between competition and cooperation, a compromise that was economically and socially preferable to the guild-government condominium.

Seen from the vantage point of 1937, the three stages of the association movement in cotton textiles emerge very clearly. From the end of the Civil War to the turn of the century, dinner-club associations handled the business of interfirm relations in the industry. These rudimentary organizations were weak in terms of ideology, leadership, and administrative techniques; this type of association had virtually no identity or existence apart from its members. With some few exceptions the dinner-club associations demanded very little from the manufacturers and offered only a limited number of services in return. Their major function was to provide a meeting ground for the businessmen, an opportunity for discussion of technological, political, or economic developments within and without the industry. When the talks led to action, the manufacturers acted in the name of the associations.

In the early years of the twentieth century a different form of trade group, the service association, emerged. In cotton textiles the regional service associations and ancillary groups were characterized by the beginnings of a bureaucracy and by systematic political and economic programs. This type of trade organization replaced the *ad hoc* policies of the nineteenth-century groups with long-range programs aimed at achieving on a continuing basis the associative objectives of stabilization, cooperation, and control. Professional officers gave the service associations effective and steady leadership. In this stage of the association movement a working alliance between the government and the trade groups began to take shape. During and after the First World War the association and government bureaucracies discovered that they had many things in common, including most prominently, an interest in industrial stability and in the rationalization of economic activity.

In the 1920's a third type of trade group, the policy-shaping association, began to develop. This particular form of trade association was distinguished by outstanding leaders, a well-defined and carefully articulated ideology, and formidable cooperative programs. It was a semi-autonomous economic institution with an identity clearly distinguished from its members. In seeking to implement associative values, it impinged forcefully upon individual manufacturers, members, and non-members alike. As the Cotton-Textile Institute's programs evolved, the association steadily increased the pressure exerted on the manufacturers; the network of controls and cooperative programs became more elaborate and more forceful; yet, the quest for stability was fruitless. Although CTI carefully nurtured industry-wide, cooperative norms and was able to achieve significant changes in the industry's managerial philosophy, the association's voluntary programs failed to stabilize production, prices, or profits.

Under CTI's leadership a tight alliance between the association and the government was created. After a successful campaign to transform public policy, the Institute experimented for two years with guild government as a means of preventing cutthroat competition. By 1935 this effort had also failed. When the government abandoned the NRA, the association was left to struggle once more with the problems of voluntary self-regulation. Unwilling to do that again, the members revamped the organization, transforming it into a national service association.

While the focus of this study has been upon the association movement in the cotton textile industry, enough information exists to support the hypothesis that the associations in most manufacturing industries passed through the first two stages, and many experienced the third. Dinner-club associations were a common feature of the nineteenth-century American economy. Service associations became so widespread in the years after 1900 that scholars began to identify them as products of a general trade association movement.[9] A number of industries also developed policy-shaping associations. These stages might then be used to categorize the entire association movement: The nineteenth century—a single period characterized by dinner-club associations; the years from 1900 through about 1925—dominated by service associations;[10] the period from 1925 to 1935—highlighted by the emergence of policy-shaping associations and the association-government alliance; in the aftermath of the NRA—the revitalization of the service associations.[11]

All of these organizations were products of a rapidly changing environment, and they in turn influenced their surroundings in numerous ways. One cannot identify the "real core of the trade association movement" in terms of a simple goal such as the elimination of "free competition."[12] Although the search for stability was an important element in the movement, it was only one aspect of a complex phenomenon. The dinner-club associations, for instance, helped the manufacturers preserve their considerable influence upon state and national politics. They contributed to the exchange of technical information, thus helping to shape the industry's technological progress.

Far more impressive were the accomplishments of the service associations. Under their guidance several new systems of rational control were developed. Although never able to match the bureaucracies of big business, the service associations standardized products, testing methods, and cotton contracts. As organizational middlemen and political representatives they helped the manufacturer cope with the wave of organizations which sprang up in modern America; to some extent they made it possible for

[9] I. L. Sharfman, "The Trade Association Movement," *American Economic Review*, XVI, No. 1 (March 1926), 203–218.

[10] According to Burns, *The Decline of Competition*, p. 45, the movement "lost influence during the decade from 1920 to 1930," but all of my evidence indicates that the contrary was true; see Cochran and Miller, *The Age of Enterprise*, pp. 304–305, for a sounder generalization.

[11] For some different attempts at periodization see: Joseph H. Foth, *Trade Associations* (New York: Ronald Press, 1930), pp. 4–5; Myron W. Watkins, "Trade Associations," *Encyclopedia of the Social Sciences* (New York, 1934), XIV, 674–675; Dudley F. Pegrum, *Public Regulation of Business* (Homewood, Illinois: Richard D. Irwin, Inc., 1959), pp. 119–120.

[12] Whitney, *Trade Associations*, p. 38.

businessmen to counter or at least to dampen the thrust of progressive reform. By adopting the systematic techniques called for by twentieth-century pressure-group politics, they enabled manufacturers to reap the full advantages of the counterreformation of the 1920's.

Of all the associations, the Cotton-Textile Institute was most effective in shaping its own historical context. Within the industry, CTI was able to spread the cooperative ideology and to formulate and implement relatively complex systems of control. With its association leaders acting as intellectual brokers between industry and government (and society in general), CTI arranged programs which altered the content of business behavior and public policy. In the matter of social control of working conditions, the Institute's leaders softened the harsh laissez faire philosophy that the industralists had inherited from the previous generation. Through "emergency" curtailments and the night-work plan the Institute modified the nation's antitrust policy.

Finally, in the early 1930's, the association played a leading role in the development of a new federal policy on competition. The NRA episode revealed the policy-shaping association at its best. From the beginning of the drive for a new antitrust policy until the Schechter decision, CTI's leaders mediated between the businessmen and the government in order to achieve a series of vital compromises. These compromises kept the alliance of guild and government intact and frequently exerted a decisive influence upon the recovery program. CTI's activities during the first days of the NRA helped to ensure that the program would be built around the concept of business-government partnership and not government regulation. Once this concept was established, the Code Authority, representing cotton textiles, fought a skillful and effective battle which made it difficult to abandon the partnership principle.

The entire NRA experiment can only be understood when seen against the background of the general association movement, a development in which CTI and many other trade groups took part. Like other aspects of the New Deal, the Recovery Administration was in large part a product of institutions and assumptions created long before 1933. If the associative ideology had not been formulated and spread during the years before F.D.R. took office, the traditional antitrust policy would never have been abandoned.

If powerful national trade organizations had not emerged in cotton textiles and other industries, if a strong alliance between these organizations and government agencies had not been formed in the 1920's, the recovery program would never have been entrusted to guild government.

In turn the association movement itself was only one aspect of modern America's organizational revolution. The institutional framework of our entire society was changing to meet the needs of a mature, urban-industrial system. New organizations in government and business, in agriculture and labor brought forth new elites and a variety of new ideologies. Many of the members of these elites were organization men like CTI's association leaders or the bureaucrats of the service associations. Most of the philosophies stressed the need for security, for cooperation, for control; in the words of David Riesman these ideologies provided "other-directed" value systems which were in sharp contrast to the "inner-directed" and more individualistic values of the previous century.[13]

In many ways twentieth-century America was a new society, and the institutional approach, which does so much to illuminate this particular phase of our politico-economic history, should help us to understand other aspects of the progressive period, the 1920's, and the New Deal. Indeed, the shifting patterns of organizational development and action may someday provide a historical synthesis which will avoid some of the pitfalls of progressive or reform history. Some of the bright color of reform history will be lost by the adoption of an institutional context. But we may thus achieve a better understanding of the forces, such as the association movement, which have shaped modern America.

[13] David Riesman, *The Lonely Crowd* (New Haven: Yale University Press, 1950).

BIBLIOGRAPHY

The major problem of the historian who is interested in the modern trade association movement is to find sufficient material, particularly manuscripts, upon which to base his study. Many of the associations have apparently retained only their current records or working files; few of the groups have been willing to open for study even those records which they have kept; hardly any associations have placed their out-of-date files in university or public archives. The reluctance to keep records or to open them for scholarly use is a product of several different factors. For one thing, the associations have been fearful of prosecution under the antitrust laws; correspondence which is saved is correspondence which can be subpoenaed—and there is no statute of limitations on antitrust violations. Another consideration has been the association's special relationship with its members: the trade group provides professional services for members who are, in a sense, clients; some association officers have been fearful that by opening their records they would violate the confidence which is a vital element in this relationship. A third factor is the opposition which many business associations have mounted against liberal or progressive reforms. Rather than try to explain to the public or to historians (who have tended to be reform oriented) why they opposed these measures, the associations have preferred to leave the historical record blank. Furthermore, many normal association functions—lobbying, for instance, or opposition to union organizations—have in the past half-century been tolerated but not approved of by the general public. In the circumstances association officers have preferred obscurity to what they feel certain would be an historical exposé.

Consequently, a major part of my research efforts had to be directed toward locating and opening for examination the manuscripts which would enable me to study the changing strategy and tactics of the regional and national associations in this industry. The following collections were the fruits of that research.

I. Manuscript Collections

A. **Donald Comer MSS:**   The late Donald Comer, of Birmingham, Alabama, made available for my research project his personal and company letter files. Mr. Comer was president of Avondale Mills, one of the largest producers of cotton textiles in the South. He had been a president of the American Cotton Manufacturers Association, a member of the Board of Directors and the Executive Committee of the Cotton-Textile Institute, and a member of the Cotton Textile Industry Code Authority under the NRA. When I began working on these materials they were stored in the attic of the Avondale Mills in Birmingham; since that time the records have been donated to the Baker Library, Harvard University, where they are now available for scholarly research. The records are voluminous (approximately 120 file drawers) and very complete; Mr. Comer seems to have kept almost all of his incoming mail and carbon copies of his own letters. Particularly valuable to me were the letters and reports from the various associations to which he and Avondale Mills belonged. Also useful were the letters from other southern manufacturers, explaining their feelings about current associative or governmental policies. Most of the records now at the Baker Library are drawn from the years 1922 through 1937.

B. **Goldthwaite H. Dorr MSS:**   Equally valuable were the private papers of Goldthwaite H. Dorr, who was a legal adviser to the Cotton-Textile Institute, a partner and close personal friend of Walker D. Hines, and, for a brief period, president of CTI. Mr. Dorr has kept a large number of records from the period 1927 through 1937, and he very kindly allowed me unrestricted use of these papers. Especially informative were the detailed discussions in memoranda and letters of the Institute's policies. In some cases Mr. Dorr had preserved various drafts of the memoranda that he and Hines exchanged, so I was able to study the manner in which their ideas took shape, as well as the final product of their deliberations. While I was working on these records Mr. Dorr and Mr. John K. Watson gave me considerable assistance, and I am very grateful for the many courtesies that they and their staff extended to me.

C. **Northern Textile Association MSS:**   Of the various organizations which I studied, only the Northern Textile Association, which has replaced the National Association of Cotton Manufacturers as spokesman for the New England industry, has retained a substantial amount of material pertaining to events before 1940. William F. Sullivan graciously allowed me to make full and unrestricted use of these papers; Jessie E. Vint and Josephine A. Loughry helped me to dig out the records which were in the Association's office in Boston. The papers included minute books, scattered correspondence, newspaper clippings, copies of the bulletins issued by the Arkwright Club and by the National Association, and some memoranda written by the Association's officers. The bulk of these records concerned developments in the twentieth century, particularly during the 1930's; even NTA has very few papers left from the nineteenth century.

D. George A. Sloan MSS: Mrs. H. Bartow Farr of Greenwich, Connecticut, very kindly allowed me to look at the remaining personal records of the late George A. Sloan. In addition to books of clippings and copies of Mr. Sloan's articles, these papers included some valuable correspondence relating to the Cotton-Textile Institute and to the operations of the Code Authority under the NRA. While the Sloan MSS were neither so voluminous nor so complete as those in the Comer and Dorr collections, they provided me with some valuable insights into George Sloan's philosophy and his manner of handling CTI's problems. Since I examined these papers they have been given to the Wisconsin Historical Society and in the future should be available to other scholars.

E. Stuart W. Cramer MSS: It is indeed unfortunate that the bulk of the late Stuart W. Cramer's papers were destroyed a few months before I was able to contact his son and daughter. This is particularly disconcerting because Cramer was very influential in trade association activities in the southern industry. He was president of the Cramerton Mills in North Carolina, was at one time president of the American Cotton Manufacturers Association, and was an industry representative in a variety of government agencies. He maintained extensive contacts with political leaders in North Carolina and throughout the nation. Judging from the few papers that remain, the letter files which were burned would have been a mine of valuable information for students of the New South. Mrs. James R. Angell and George B. Cramer kindly allowed me to find and to examine those papers which were not burned; they also gave me invaluable assistance in obtaining the major collections upon which my book is based.

F. Other Private Collections: Among the other manuscript sources which proved valuable to me were the records at the office of the Cotton Manufacturers Association of South Carolina, Columbia, S. C. Mr. John Cauthen, executive-secretary of the organization, allowed me to read the Association's minute book, January 2, 1930, through October 13, 1936. I also located some materials at the headquarters of the Association of Cotton Textile Merchants of New York (New York City), at the central office of the Chamber of Commerce of the United States (Washington, D. C.), and at the New York office of the National Association of Manufacturers. Mr. William M. McLaurine (Charlotte, N. C.) provided me with his personal copies of the *A.C.M.A. Gazette* for the years 1925–30; this was the newsletter published for the members of the American Cotton Manufacturers Association. Mr. C. C. Dawson (executive-secretary of the Southern Combed Yarn Spinners Association in Gastonia, N. C.) allowed me to examine his file of the *King Cotton Weekly,* a newsletter sent to the members of the Gaston County Textile Manufacturers Association during the 1930's. A number of unpublished materials are scattered among the books in the library of the American Textile Manufacturers Institute (this association replaced CTI and ACMA, and later combined with the New York merchants' association) in Charlotte, N. C. Mr. F. S. Love, who is executive-secretary of the group, gave me permission to look through the library; he also helped me to arrange interviews with some of the members of his organization. Mr. Hunter Marshall and Mr. Thomas Ingram allowed me to use the records that they have kept in the library of the North Carolina Textile Manufacturers Association, Charlotte, N. C.

G. **Public Manuscript Collections:** A number of manuscript collections already in libraries and archives proved valuable; these included the following:

The Baker Library, Harvard University. In a sometimes futile search for references to trade groups, I consulted the records of the following companies: the Amoskeag Manufacturing Company; the Boston Manufacturing Company; the Dwight Manufacturing Company; the Hamilton Manufacturing Company; the Lawrence Manufacturing Company; the Lyman Mills; the Nashua Manufacturing Company; the Naumkeag Steam Cotton Manufacturing Company; the Pepperell Manufacturing Company; the Slater Companies; the Whitin Machine Works.

The National Archives, Washington, D. C. I used the Records of the National Recovery Administration (Record Group 9); the Records of the Executive Office (RG 44); the Records of the War Industries Board (RG 61); the General Records of the Department of Commerce (RG 40); and the General Records of the Department of Justice (RG 60).

The Franklin D. Roosevelt Library, Hyde Park, New York.

The Manuscripts Division of the Library of Congress. I examined certain of the papers of Donald R. Richberg and of Henry Laurens Dawes.

The Massachusetts Historical Society in Boston. I consulted the relevant sections of the Edward Atkinson Papers, the John Davis Long Papers, and the papers of Edward Stanwood.

The Robert Wagner MSS, Georgetown University. Professor Joseph J. Huthmacher allowed me to examine these papers and assisted me while I was working at the University.

The Southern Historical Collection, Chapel Hill, N. C. Here I examined (with very little success) the Daniel A. Tompkins MSS, and the papers of Braxton Bragg Comer, who was Donald Comer's father and the founder of Avondale Mills, Birmingham, Alabama.

The Fall River Historical Society, Fall River, Massachusetts.

II. Trade Association Proceedings and Transactions.

The American Cotton Manufacturers Association, *Proceedings.* 1904–1936.
The Cotton Manufacturers Association of Georgia. *Report.* 1924–1936.
The Cotton Manufacturers Association of North Carolina, *Proceedings.* 1915–1936.
The Cotton-Textile Institute. *Annual Reports.* 1927–1932.
The National Association of Cotton Manufacturers. *Transactions.* 1906–1942.
————. *Yearbook.* 1924, 1926, 1927, and 1929.
The New England Cotton Manufacturers' Association. *Proceedings.* 1866–1894.
    (in the footnotes I listed these as *Transactions* to avoid confusion).
————. *Transactions.* 1894–1905.

The Southern Cotton Spinners' Association. *Constitution and By-Laws, 1900.* Charlotte, N. C.: Queen City Printing Company, 1900.
———. *Proceedings.* 1901–1903.

III. Trade Association Pamphlets and other Miscellaneous Publications.

The American Cotton Manufacturers Association. *American Cotton Manufacturers Association: A Clearing House for Southern Mill Problems.* Charlotte, N. C.: Queen City Printing Co., *ca.* 1927.
———. *An Adequate Tariff on Jute and Jute Products Necessary for South's Economic Safety: Some Reasons Why.* Charlotte, N. C., 1932.
———. *Brief of Committee, American Cotton Manufacturers Association, Presented to U.S. Senate Committee on Agriculture and Forestry, Washington, D. C., January 27–30, 1933.*
———. *Conditions in Cotton Textile Industry.* Washington, D. C., May 2, 1935.
———. *The Cotton Mill Worker and His Needs. ca.* 1935.
———. *Lest We Forget.* 1947.
———. *Shall Unfair Freight Rates Kill Southern Industry?* Atlanta, Ga.: Ivan Allen-Marshall Co., *ca.* 1934.
———. *Southern Village Costs and Wage Study.* Charlotte, N. C., 1935.
———. *A Tax Study of New England Cotton Textile Mills for Years 1930 to 1933, Inclusive.* Charlotte, N. C., 1934.
———. *A Tax Study of Southern and Eastern Cotton Textile Mills for Years 1920 to 1930, Inclusive.* Charlotte, N. C., 1930.
Arkwright Club. *By-Laws of the Arkwright Club and List of Officers and Members, Together with a Brief Account of Its Origin and a Complete List of Present and Past Members.* Boston, 1924.
The Association of Cotton Textile Merchants of New York. *Twenty-Five Years, 1918–1943.* New York, 1944.
———. *Worth Street Rules.* New York: John G. Mohair, 1936.
The Cotton-Textile Institute. *Analysis of Some Features of Our Cotton Textile Export Situation.* New York, 1929.
———. *The Base Period Problem of the Cotton-Textile Industry.*
———. *Certificate of Incorporation and By-Laws of the Cotton-Textile Institute, Inc.* 1926 edition.
———. *Cotton Facts and Figures: Statistical and Economic Material Relating to the Cotton Textile Industry.* New York, 1938.
———. *The Cotton Textile Industry Committee and the Cotton-Textile Institute.* 1935.
———. *In the Matter of Proposed Standardized Depreciation Rates for the Cotton Textile Industry.* New York, 1930.
———. *An Outline of Bases to be Used in Predetermining Costs for Guidance as to Sales Policies.* New York, 1928.
———. *Promoting Stabilization through Keeping Production in Balance with Demand.* New York, 1931.
———. *Senate Investigation: Steps taken by the industry . . . to bring the production of cotton in line with the demand therefor.*

———. *Special Report on Extending Uses of Cotton.* New York, 1929.

National Association of Cotton Manufacturers. *A Brief Fireside Biography of the National Association of Cotton Manufacturers.* 1954.

———. *Early History of the Association.*

———. *New England Mills Liquidated or Moved, 1924–1949.* 1950.

———. *New England Terms for Buying and Selling Cotton.* 1911 and 1917.

———. *Shall Freight Rates Be Based on Economics or Politics?* Boston, *ca.* 1935.

The New England Cotton Manufacturers' Association. *Statistics of Cotton Manufacturers in New England, 1866; Together with the Constitution and List of Members.*

IV. Books

Backman, Jules, and Gainsbrugh, M. R. *Economics of the Cotton Textile Industry.* New York: National Industrial Conference Board, 1946.

Bailyn, Bernard. *The New England Merchants in the Seventeenth Century.* Cambridge: Harvard University Press, 1955.

Baker, Richard C. *The Tariff Under Roosevelt and Taft.* Hastings, Nebraska: Democrat Printing Co., 1941.

Bishop, J. Leander. *A History of American Manufactures from 1608 to 1860.* 2 vols. Philadelphia: Edward Young & Co., 1864.

Blicksilver, Jack. *Cotton Manufacturing in the Southeast: An Historical Analysis.* Atlanta: Bulletin No. 5 of the Bureau of Business and Economic Research, School of Business Administration, Georgia State College of Business Administration, 1959.

Bonnett, Clarence E. *Employers' Associations in the United States.* New York: The Macmillan Co., 1922.

———. *History of Employers' Associations in the United States.* New York: Vantage Press, 1956.

Boston Chamber of Commerce, New England Industrial Surveys. *The Cotton Manufacturing Industry of New England.* Boston, 1926.

Boulding, Kenneth E. *The Organizational Revolution.* New York: Harper & Brothers, 1953.

Bradley, Joseph F. *The Role of Trade Associations and Professional Business Societies in America.* University Park, Pennsylvania: Pennsylvania State University Press, 1965.

Brady, Robert A. *Business as a System of Power.* New York: Columbia University Press, 1943.

Brown, John H. (ed.) *Lamb's Textile Industries of the United States.* 2 vols. Boston: James H. Lamb Company, 1911.

Burgy, J. Herbert. *The New England Cotton Textile Industry.* Baltimore: Waverly Press, Inc., 1932.

Burns, Arthur R. *The Decline of Competition.* New York: McGraw-Hill Book Company, Inc., 1936.

Chamberlin, Edward H. *The Theory of Monopolistic Competition.* Cambridge: Harvard University Press, 1950 edition.

Chandler, Alfred D., Jr. *Strategy and Structure: Chapters in the History of the Industrial Enterprise.* Cambridge: Massachusetts Institute of Technology Press, 1962.

Clark, J. Maurice. *Studies in the Economics of Overhead Costs*. Chicago: University of Chicago Press, 1923.

Clark, Victor S. *History of Manufactures in the United States from 1607 to 1914*. 2 vols. Washington, D. C.: Carnegie Institution of Washington, 1916–1928.

Cochran, Thomas C. *The American Business System*. New York: Harper edition, 1962.

Cochran, Thomas C., and Miller, William. *The Age of Enterprise*. New York: The Macmillan Co., 1942.

Cole, Arthur H. *The American Wool Manufacture*. 2 vols. Cambridge: Harvard University Press, 1926.

Commons, John R., *et al*. *History of Labor in the United States*, II. New York: Macmillan Co., 1918.

Conference on Price Research of the National Bureau of Economic Research. *Textile Markets, Their Structure in Relation to Price Research*. New York: National Bureau of Economic Research, 1939.

Copeland, Melvin T. *The Cotton Manufacturing Industry of the United States*. Cambridge: Harvard University Press, 1912.

Copeland, Melvin T., and Learned, Edmund P. *Merchandising of Cotton Textiles*. Cambridge: Harvard University, Graduate School of Business Administration, Division of Research, Business Research Studies, No. 1, 1933.

Cox, Reavis. *The Marketing of Textiles*. Washington, D. C.: The Textile Foundation, 1938.

Daugherty, Carroll R., *et al*. *The Economics of the Iron and Steel Industry*. 2 vols. New York: McGraw-Hill, Inc., 1937.

Davis, Hiram S., *et al*. *Vertical Integration in the Textile Industries*. Washington: The Textile Foundation, 1938.

Davis, John P. *Corporations*, II. New York: Putnam (Capricorn Books Edition), 1961.

Davis, Pearce. *The Development of the American Glass Industry*. Cambridge: Harvard University Press, 1949.

Davison Publishing Company, *Davison's Textile Blue Book*. New York, 1916–1936.

Dearing, C. L., *et al*. *The ABC of the NRA*. Washington, D. C.: The Brookings Institution, 1934.

Dewing, Arthur S. *Corporate Promotions and Reorganizations*. Cambridge: Harvard University Press, 1914.

Dimock, Marshall E. *Business and Government*. New York: Henry Holt and Co., 1949.

Donald, William J. A. *Trade Associations*. New York: McGraw-Hill Book Co., Inc., 1933.

Eddy, Arthur J. *The New Competition*. New York: D. Appleton and Co., 1912.

Ehrmann, Henry W. *Organized Business in France*. Princeton: Princeton University Press, 1957.

Faulkner, Harold U. *The Decline of Laissez Faire, 1897–1917*. New York: Rinehart & Co., 1951.

Fine, Sidney. *The Automobile under the Blue Eagle*. Ann Arbor: University of Michigan Press, 1963.

———. *Laissez Faire and the General-Welfare State*. Ann Arbor: University of Michigan Press, 1956.

Fitzpatrick, F. Stuart. *A Study of Business Men's Associations*. Olean, New York: Olean Times Publishing Company Press, 1925.

Fogel, Robert W. *Railroads and American Economic Growth*. Baltimore: Johns Hopkins Press, 1964.

Foth, Joseph H. *Trade Associations*. New York: Ronald Press Co., 1930.

Galbraith, John K. *American Capitalism*. Boston: Houghton Mifflin Co., 1956.

———. *The Great Crash, 1929*. Boston: Houghton Mifflin Co., 1961.

Gibb, George S. *The Saco-Lowell Shops*. Cambridge: Harvard University Press, 1950.

Goldman, Eric. *Rendezvous with Destiny*. New York: Random House, 1952.

Hamerow, Theodore S. *Restoration, Revolution, Reaction: Economics and Politics in Germany, 1815–1871*. Princeton: Princeton University Press, 1958.

Handler, Milton (ed.). *The Federal Anti-Trust Laws*. Chicago: Commerce Clearing House, 1932.

Harris, Seymour E. *The Economics of New England*. Cambridge: Harvard University Press, 1952.

———. *Twenty Years of Federal Reserve Policy*, I. Cambridge: Harvard University Press, 1933.

Hawley, Ellis W. *The New Deal and the Problem of Monopoly*. Princeton: Princeton University Press, 1966.

Hays, Samuel P. *The Response to Industrialism, 1885–1914*. Chicago: University of Chicago Press, 1957.

Heckscher, Eli F. *Mercantilism*. 2 vols. Translated by Mendel Shapiro. London: G. Allen and Unwin, Ltd., 1934.

Herring, E. Pendleton. *Group Representation Before Congress*. Baltimore: Johns Hopkins Press, 1929.

Hicks, John D. *Republican Ascendancy, 1921–1933*. New York: Harper & Brothers, 1960.

Hidy, Ralph W. and Muriel. *Pioneering in Big Business, 1882–1911*. New York: Harper, 1955.

Hofstadter, Richard. *The Age of Reform*. New York: Vintage Books Edition, 1955.

Hoover, Calvin B., and Ratchford, B. U. *Economic Resources and Policies of the South*. New York: The Macmillan Co., 1951.

Hoover, Herbert. *The Memoirs of Herbert Hoover*, II. New York: Macmillan, 1952.

Ickes, Harold L. *The Secret Diary of Harold L. Ickes:—The First Thousand Days*. New York: Simon and Schuster, 1953.

Johnson, Hugh S. *The Blue Eagle From Egg to Earth*. Garden City, New York: Doubleday, Doran & Co., 1935.

Jones, Eliot. *The Trust Problem in the United States*. New York: The Macmillan Co., 1921.

Jones, Franklin D. *Trade Association Activities and the Law*. New York: McGraw-Hill Book Co., Inc., 1922.

Kennedy, Stephen Jay. *Profits and Losses in Textiles*. New York: Harper & Brothers Publishers, 1936.

Key, V. O., Jr. *Politics, Parties, and Pressure Groups*. New York: Thomas Y. Crowell Co., 1948.

Keynes, John Maynard. *The General Theory of Employment, Interest and Money*. New York: Harcourt, Brace, and Co., 1936.

Kirkland, Edward C. *Business in the Gilded Age*. Madison: University of Wisconsin Press, 1952.

————. *Dream and Thought in the Business Community, 1860–1900*. Ithaca: Cornell University Press, 1956.

————. *Industry Comes of Age: Business, Labor, and Public Policy, 1860–1897*. New York: Holt, Rinehart and Winston, 1961.

Kirsh, Benjamin S. *Trade Associations, the Legal Aspects*. New York: Central Book Co., 1928.

Knowlton, Evelyn H. *Pepperell's Progress*. Cambridge: Harvard University Press, 1948.

Kolko, Gabriel. *The Triumph of Conservatism*. New York: The Free Press of Glencoe, 1963.

Lahne, Herbert J. *The Cotton Mill Worker*. New York: Farrar & Rinehart, Inc., 1944.

Lamb, George P., and Kittelle, Sumner S. *Trade Association Law and Practice*. Boston: Little, Brown and Co., 1956.

Latham, Earl. *The Group Basis of Politics*. Ithaca: Cornell University Press, 1952.

Latimer, Murray W., and Copeland, Melvin T. *Distribution of Textiles*. Cambridge: Harvard University, Graduate School of Business Administration, Bureau of Business Research, Bulletin No. 56, 1926.

Lecht, Leonard A. *Experience Under Railway Labor Legislation*. New York: Columbia University Press, 1954.

Lemert, Ben F. *The Cotton Textile Industry of the Southern Appalachian Piedmont*. Chapel Hill: University of North Carolina Press, 1933.

Leuchtenburg, William E. *Franklin D. Roosevelt and the New Deal, 1932–1940*. New York: Harper & Row, 1963.

Lindahl, Martin L., and Carter, William A. *Corporate Concentration and Public Policy*. Englewood Cliffs, N. J.: Prentice-Hall, Inc., 1959.

Loescher, Samuel M. *Imperfect Collusion in the Cement Industry*. Cambridge: Harvard University Press, 1959.

Lorwin, Lewis L., and Wubnig, Arthur. *Labor Relations Boards*. Washington, D. C.: The Brookings Institution, 1935.

Lott, Davis Newton (ed.). *The Inaugural Addresses of the American Presidents from Washington to Kennedy*. New York: Holt, Rinehart and Winston, 1961.

Lyon, Leverett S., and Abramson, Victor. *The Economics of Open Price Systems*. Washington, D. C.: The Brookings Institution, 1936.

Lyon, Leverett S., et al. *The National Recovery Administration*. Washington, D. C.: The Brookings Institution, 1935.

Mason, Edward S. (ed.). *The Corporation in Modern Society*. Cambridge: Harvard University Press, 1959.

McCloskey, Robert G. *American Conservatism in the Age of Enterprise*. Cambridge: Harvard University Press, 1951.

Michl, H. E. *The Textile Industries*. Washington, D. C.: The Textile Foundation, 1938.

Miller, William (ed.). *Men in Business.* New York: Harper & Row edition, 1962.

Mitchell, Broadus. *Depression Decade.* New York: Holt, Rinehart and Winston, 1962.

——. *The Rise of Cotton Mills in the South.* Baltimore: The Johns Hopkins Press, 1921.

Mitchell, Broadus, and Mitchell, George S. *The Industrial Revolution in the South.* Baltimore: The Johns Hopkins Press, 1930.

Mitchell, George S. *Textile Unionism in the South.* Chapel Hill: University of North Carolina Press, 1931.

Morris, Richard B. *Government and Labor in Early America.* New York: Columbia University Press, 1946.

Mowry, George E. *The Era of Theodore Roosevelt.* New York: Harper, 1958.

Murchison, Claudius T. *King Cotton Is Sick.* Chapel Hill: University of North Carolina Press, 1930.

National Industrial Conference Board. *Trade Associations, Their Economic Significance and Legal Status.* New York, 1925.

Navin, Thomas R. *The Whitin Machine Works Since 1831.* Cambridge: Harvard University Press, 1950.

Naylor, Emmett H. *Trade Associations.* New York: The Ronald Press Co., 1921.

Nelson, Milton N. *Open Price Associations.* Urbana: University of Illinois Press, 1923.

Pearce, Charles A. *NRA Trade Practice Programs.* New York: Columbia University Press, 1939.

Pegrum, Dudley F. *Public Regulation of Business.* Homewood, Illinois: Richard D. Irwin, Inc., 1959.

Perkins, Frances. *The Roosevelt I Knew.* New York: The Viking Press, 1946.

Pope, Liston. *Millhands and Preachers: A Study of Gastonia.* New Haven: Yale University Press, 1942.

Price, William H. *The English Patents of Monopoly.* Boston: Houghton Mifflin, 1906.

Prothro, James W. *The Dollar Decade: Business Ideas in the 1920's.* Baton Rouge: Louisiana State University Press, 1954.

Richberg, Donald. *My Hero.* New York: G. P. Putnam's Sons, 1954.

Riesman, David. *The Lonely Crowd.* New Haven: Yale University Press, 1950.

Ripley, William Z. (ed.). *Trusts, Pools and Corporations.* Boston: Ginn and Company, 1916.

Robinson, Joan. *The Economics of Imperfect Competition.* London: Macmillan and Co., Ltd., 1946 edition.

Roos, Charles F. *NRA Economic Planning.* Bloomington, Indiana: The Principia Press, 1937.

Rostow, W. W. *The Stages of Economic Growth.* Cambridge: The Cambridge University Press, 1960.

Saluotos, Theodore. *Farmer Movements in the South, 1865–1933.* Berkeley, California: University of California Press, 1960.

Schattschneider, E. E. *Politics, Pressures, and the Tariff.* New York: Prentice-Hall Inc., 1935.

Schlesinger, Arthur M., Jr. *The Coming of the New Deal.* Boston: Houghton Mifflin, 1958.

————. *The Crisis of the Old Order, 1919–1933*. Boston: Houghton Mifflin Co., 1957.

————. *The Politics of Upheaval*. Boston: Houghton Mifflin, 1960.

Schumpeter, Joseph A. *Capitalism, Socialism, and Democracy*. New York: Harper & Brothers Publishers, 1950.

————. *The Theory of Economic Development*. Translated by Redvers Opie. New York: Oxford University Press, 1961.

Seager, Henry R., and Gulick, Charles A., Jr. *Trust and Corporation Problems*. New York: Harper & Brothers, 1929.

Separk, Joseph H. *Gastonia and Gaston County North Carolina, 1846–1949*. Gastonia, N. C., 1949.

Smith, Adam. *The Wealth of Nations*. New York: Modern Library Edition, 1937.

Smith, Robert S. *Mill on the Dan: A History of Dan River Mills, 1882–1950*. Durham, N. C.: Duke University Press, 1960.

Smith, Thomas R. *The Cotton Textile Industry of Fall River, Massachusetts*. New York: King's Crown Press, 1944.

Soule, George. *Prosperity Decade*. New York: Rinehart & Co., 1947.

Steigerwalt, Albert K. *The National Association of Manufacturers, 1895–1914*. Grand Rapids, Michigan: The University of Michigan, Bureau of Business Research, Graduate School of Business Administration, 1964.

Stocking, George W., and Watkins, Myron W. *Monopoly and Free Enterprise*. New York: The Twentieth Century Fund, 1951.

Summers, Festus P. *William L. Wilson and Tariff Reform*. New Brunswick, N. J.: Rutgers University Press, 1953.

Supple, Barry E. (ed.). *The Experience of Economic Growth*. New York: Random House, 1963.

Sutton, Francis X., *et al. The American Business Creed*. Cambridge: Harvard University Press, 1956.

Swope, Gerard. *The Swope Plan, Details, Criticisms, Analysis*. Edited by Frederick J. George. New York: The Business Bourse, 1931.

Taft, Philip. *The A. F. of L. in the Time of Gompers*. New York: Harper, 1959.

Taussig, Frank W. *Some Aspects of the Tariff Question*. Cambridge: Harvard University Press, 1915.

————. *The Tariff History of the United States*. 7th ed. revised. New York: The Knickerbocker Press, 1923.

Taylor, George R. *The Transportation Revolution*. New York: Holt, Rinehart and Winston, 1951.

Thompson, Holland. *From the Cotton Field to the Cotton Mill: A Study of the Industrial Transformation in North Carolina*. New York: The Macmillan Co., 1906.

Thorelli, Hans B. *The Federal Antitrust Policy*. Baltimore: The Johns Hopkins Press, 1955.

Tocqueville, Alexis de. *Democracy in America*. Phillips Bradley ed., 2 vols. New York: Alfred A. Knopf, 1945.

Ulman, Lloyd. *The Rise of the National Trade Union*. Cambridge: Harvard University Press, 1955.

Unwin, George. *Industrial Organization in the Sixteenth and Seventeenth Centuries*. Oxford: Clarendon Press, 1904.

Ware, Caroline F. *The Early New England Cotton Manufacture*. Boston: Houghton Mifflin Co., 1931.

Whitney, Simon N. *Antitrust Policies*. 2 vols. New York: The Twentieth Century Fund, 1958.

————. *Trade Associations and Industrial Control*. New York: Central Book Company, 1934.

Wiebe, Robert H. *Businessmen and Reform: A Study of the Progressive Movement*. Cambridge: Harvard University Press, 1962.

Wike, J. Roffe. *The Pennsylvania Manufacturers' Association*. Philadelphia: University of Pennsylvania Press, 1960.

Wilbur, Ray L., and Hyde, Arthur M. *The Hoover Policies*. New York: C. Scribner's Sons, 1937.

Wilcox, Clair. *Public Policies Toward Business*. Chicago: Richard D. Irwin, Inc., 1955.

Wilhelm, Dwight M. *A History of the Cotton Textile Industry of Alabama, 1809 to 1950*. Montgomery, 1950.

Williamson, Harold F. *Edward Atkinson*. Boston: Old Corner Book Store, Inc., 1934.

Williamson, Harold F. (ed.). *The Growth of the American Economy*. Englewood Cliffs, N. J.: Prentice-Hall, Inc., 1959.

Williamson, Harold F., and Daum, Arnold R. *The American Petroleum Industry: The Age of Illumination, 1859–1899*. Evanston, Illinois: Northwestern University Press, 1959.

Wolfbein, Seymour L. *The Decline of a Cotton Textile City; A Study of New Bedford*. New York: Columbia University Press, 1944.

Wolman, Leo. *The Growth of American Trade Unions, 1880–1923*. New York: National Bureau of Economic Research, 1924.

Woodward, C. Vann. *Origins of the New South, 1877–1913*. Baton Rouge: Louisiana State University Press, 1951.

Zeller, Belle. *Pressure Politics in New York*. New York: Prentice-Hall, Inc., 1937.

V. Articles.

Brandeis, Elisabeth. "Labor Legislation," *History of Labor in the United States, 1896–1932*, edited by John R. Commons, IV, 399–697.

Chandler, Alfred D., Jr. "The Beginnings of 'Big Business' in American Industry," *Business History Review*, XXXIII, No. 1 (1959), 1–31.

Chen, Chen-Han. "Regional Differences in Costs and Productivity in the American Cotton Manufacturing Industry, 1880–1910," *Quarterly Journal of Economics*, LV, No. 4 (1940–41), 533–566.

Dale, Ernest, and Meloy, Charles. "Hamilton MacFarland Barksdale and the DuPont Contributions to Systematic Management," *Business History Review*, XXXVI, No. 2 (1962), 127–152.

Edwards, James D. "Public Accounting in the United States from 1913 to 1928," *Business History Review*, XXXII, No. 1 (1958), 74–101.

Everett, Charles K. "Cotton Consumption in the United States," *The Annals* (American Academy of Political and Social Science, September, 1937), pp. 34–48.

Fine, Sidney. "President Roosevelt and the Automobile Code," *The Mississippi Valley Historical Review*, XLV, No. 1 (1958), 23–50.

Fishbein, Meyer H. "The Trucking Industry and the National Recovery Administration," *Social Forces*, XXXIV, No. 2 (1955), 171–179.

Gable, Richard W. "Birth of an Employers' Association," *Business History Review*, XXXIII, No. 4 (1959), 535–545.

Griffin, Richard W. "The Augusta (Georgia) Manufacturing Company in Peace, War, and Reconstruction, 1847–1877," *Business History Review*, XXXII, No. 1 (1958), 60–73.

Hammond, Seth. "Location Theory and the Cotton Industry," *The Journal of Economic History, Supplement* (December, 1942), 101–117.

Hibbert, A. B. "The Economic Policies of Towns," *The Cambridge Economic History of Europe*, edited by M. M. Poston *et al.* (3 vols.; Cambridge: The Cambridge University Press, 1963), III, 157–229.

Hines, Walker D. "Textile Industry and the Anti-Trust Laws," *Southern Textile Bulletin*, XLI, No. 16 (1931), 5, 8–9; No. 17 (1931), 10, 23–25.

Kendall, Henry P. "Cotton Textiles First," *Survey Graphic*, XXII, No. 9 (1933), 443–448.

———. "What Can Management Do to Increase Security," *The Annals* (American Academy of Political and Social Science, March, 1931), pp. 138–142.

Lescohier, Don D. "Working Conditions," *History of Labor in the United States, 1896–1932*, edited by John R. Commons (4 vols.; New York: Macmillan, 1918), III, 1–396.

Lester, Richard A. "Effectiveness of Factory Labor, North-South Comparisons," *Journal of Political Economy*, LIV, No. 1 (1946), 60–75.

———. "Trends in Southern Wage Differentials Since 1890," *The Southern Economic Journal*, XI, No. 4 (1945), 317–344.

Litterer, Joseph A. "Systematic Management: The Search for Order and Integration," *Business History Review*, XXXV, No. 4 (1961), 461–476.

Lively, Robert A. "The South and Freight Rates," *Journal of Southern History*, XIV, No. 3 (1948), 357–384.

Main, Charles T., and Gunby, Frank M. "The Cotton Textile Industry," *Mechanical Engineering*, XLVIII, No. 10 (1926), 999–1004.

Marburg, Theodore F. "Government and Business in Germany," *Business History Review*, XXXVIII, No. 1 (1964), 78–101.

Markham, Jesse W. "Regional Labor Productivity in the Textile Industry," *American Economic Review*, XXXIII, No. 1 (1943), 110–115.

———. "Some Comments Upon the North-South Wage Differential," *The Southern Economic Journal*, XVI, No. 3 (1950), 279–283.

Mead, Edward S. "Cotton-Textile Institute," *The Annalist* (October 4, 1929), 637–638.

Murchison, Claudius T. "Requisites of Stabilization in the Cotton Textile Industry," *American Economic Review*, XXIII, No. 1 (1933), 71–80.

———. "Southern Textile Manufacturing," *The Annals* (American Academy of Political and Social Science, January, 1931), pp. 36–39.

Naylor, Emmett H. "History of Trade Associations in America," *Trade Association Activities* (U. S. Department of Commerce [Washington, D. C., 1923,]), pp. 301–307.

Nelson, Milton N. "Effect of Open Price Associations on Competition and Prices," *American Economic Review*, XIII, No. 2 (1923), 258–275.

Osborne, George G. "The Development of the Cotton Textile Industry of the

United States from 1920 to 1930." *The Journal of the Textile Institute,* XXVII, No. 1 (1936), 4–21, and No. 2 (1936), 30–38.

"Playboy of the Textile World," *Fortune,* XLI, No. 1 (1950), 66–69.

Potter, David M. "The Historical Development of Eastern-Southern Freight Rate Relationships," *Law and Contemporary Problems* (Summer, 1947), pp. 416–448.

Reynolds, Lloyd G. "Cutthroat Competition," *American Economic Review,* XXX, No. 4 (1940), 736–747.

Roover, R. de. "The Organization of Trade," *The Cambridge Economic History of Europe,* edited by M. M. Poston *et al.* (3 vols.; Cambridge: The Cambridge University Press, 1963), III, 42–118.

Sanford and Kelley. *Fall River, Mass.: Statistics Relating to its Cotton Manufacturing Corporations for the year 1923* (1924).

Silver, James W. "The Hardwood Producers Come of Age," *Journal of Southern History,* XXIII, No. 4 (1957), 427–453.

Sloan, George A. "How the Oldest Code is Working," *Nation's Business,* XXII, No. 2 (1934), 17–18, 65.

———. "Someone Had to Pioneer," *Dress Fabrics,* XII, No. 9 (1933), 15, 22.

Soltow, James H. "Small City Industrialists in the Age of Organization," *Business History Review,* XXXIII, No. 2 (1959), 178–189.

Stephenson, Francis M., *et al.* "The North-South Differential—A Different View," *Southern Economic Journal,* XV, No. 2 (1948), 184–190.

Stevens, William H. S. "A Classification of Pools and Associations Based on American Experience," *American Economic Review,* III, No. 3 (1913), 545–575.

Thrupp, Sylvia L. "The Gilds," *The Cambridge Economic History of Europe,* edited by M. M. Poston *et al.* (3 vols.; Cambridge: The Cambridge University Press, 1963), III, 230–280.

Tosdal, H. R. "Open-Price Associations," *American Economic Review,* VII, No. 2 (1917), 331–352.

Trask, Roger R. "The United States and Turkish Nationalism," *Business History Review,* XXXVIII, No. 1 (1964), 58–77.

Watkins, Myron W. "Trade Associations," *Encyclopaedia of the Social Sciences,* XIV, 670–676.

Whitney, Simon. "Competition Under Secret and Open Prices," *Econometrica,* III, No. 1 (1935), 40–65.

VI. Newspapers and Trade Journals

Atlanta Constitution

Augusta Chronicle

Birmingham Age Herald

Boston Transcript

Charlotte Observer

Commercial and Financial Chronicle

Concord Tribune

Daily News Record

Fall River Daily Globe

Gastonia Gazette

Nashville Tennessean
New Bedford Mercury
New Bedford Standard
New York Evening Telegram
New York Journal of Commerce and Commercial Bulletin
New York Times
Textile Manufacturers Journal
Textile Record of America
Textile World
United States Daily

VII. Government Documents and Reports

Massachusetts, Bureau of Statistics of Labor. *Cotton Manufactures in Massachusetts and the Southern States.* 1905.
Massachusetts, Department of Labor and Industries. *A Record of Cotton Mills in Massachusetts Which Went Out of Existence During the Period 1921–1934, Inclusive.* 1935.
———. *The Report of the Special Investigation into Conditions in the Textile Industry in Massachusetts and the Southern States.* 1924.
U. S. Attorney General. *Annual Report of the Attorney General of the United States.* 1923–1926.
U. S. Bureau of the Census. *Bulletin No. 134, Cotton Production and Distribution.* 1916.
———. *Bulletin No. 179, Cotton Production and Distribution.* 1942.
———. *Fourteenth Census of the United States: 1920. Manufactures, 1919, Reports for Selected Industries,* X.
———. *Historical Statistics of the United States, Colonial Times to 1957.* 1960.
———. *Statistical Abstract of the United States, 1920–1936.* Washington, D. C., 1921–1936.
———. *Thirteenth Census of the United States: 1909. Manufactures,* X.
———. *Twelfth Census of the United States: 1900. Manufactures, Textiles.* 1902.
U. S. Bureau of Internal Revenue, Excess Profits Tax Council. *The Cotton Textile Industry: An Economic Analysis of the Industry With Reference to the Investigation of Claims for Relief Under Section 722 of the Internal Revenue Code.* 1948.
———. *Statistics of Income, 1916–1935.*
U. S. Congress. *Biographical Directory of the American Congress, 1774–1927.* 1928.
U. S. *Congressional Record.*
U. S. Department of Commerce. *Annual Report of the Secretary of Commerce.* 1922–1926.
———. *Industrial Structure of New England.* Domestic Commerce Series No. 28, 1930.
———. *Trade Association Activities.* 1923 and 1927.

———. *Trade and Professional Associations of the United States.* Industrial Series No. 3, 1942.

U. S. Department of Labor, Bureau of Labor Statistics. *History of Labor Legislation for Women in Three States.* Prepared by Clara Mortenson Byer. Bulletin 66 of the Women's Bureau, 1929.

———. *Textile Report, Part I. Wage Rates and Weekly Earnings in the Cotton Textile Industry.* 1935.

U. S. Federal Trade Commission. *Open-Price Trade Associations.* Senate Doc. 226, 70th Cong., 2nd Sess., 1929.

———. *Report of the U. S. Federal Trade Commission on Combed Cotton Yarns.* 1921.

U. S. House of Representatives. *Executive Document No. 21, Labor in Europe and America,* 44th Cong., 1st Sess., 1876.

———. *House Document No. 643, Cotton Manufactures,* 2 vols. 62nd Cong., 2nd Sess., 1912.

U. S. National Recovery Administration, Division of Industrial Economics. *History of the Code of Fair Competition for the Cotton Textile Industry.*

———. Division of Review. *The Content of NIRA Administrative Legislation, Part F: A Type Case: The Cotton Textile Code.* 1936.

———. Research and Planning Division. *Hours, Wages, and Employment Under the Codes.* 1935.

U. S. Senate. *Senate Document No. 126, The Cotton Textile Industry.* 74th Cong., 1st Sess., 1935.

U. S. Temporary National Economic Committee. *Antitrust in Action.* By Walton Hamilton and Irene Till. Monograph No. 16, 1940.

———. *Competition and Monopoly in American Industry.* By Clair Wilcox. Monograph No. 21, 1940.

———. *The Structure of Industry,* Part IV, "The History of Concentration in Seven Industries," pp. 235–264. By Willard L. Thorp and Grace W. Knott. Monograph No. 27, 1941.

———. *A Study of the Construction and Enforcement of the Federal Antitrust Laws.* By Milton Handler. Monograph No. 38, 1941.

———. *Trade Association Survey.* Prepared by Charles A. Pearce. Monograph No. 18, 1941.

VIII. Legal Citations

American Column & Lumber Company v. *U. S.* 257 U. S. 410. 1921.

Appalachian Coals, Inc., et al. v. *U. S.* 288 U. S. 344, 356–364, 372–374, 377. 1933.

Cement Manufacturers' Protective Association v. *United States.* 268 U. S. 588. 1925.

Central Ohio Salt Co. v. *Guthrie.* 35 Ohio St., 666. 1880.

Maple Flooring Manufacturers' Association v. *United States.* 268 U. S. 563, 582–583.

New State Ice Co. v. *Liebmann.* 285 U. S. 307. 1932.

United States v. *American Linseed Oil Co.* 262 U. S. 390. 1923.

United States v. *E. C. Knight Co., et al.* 156 U. S. 1, 15 Sup. Ct. 249. 1895.

United States v. *Patten.* 226 U. S. 525. 1913.

United States v. *U. S. Steel Corporation, et al.* 251 U. S. 446, 447. 1920.

IX. Unpublished Theses and Dissertations

Brown, Harry J. "The National Association of Wool Manufacturers." Ph.D. dissertation, Cornell University, 1947.

Chen, Chen-Han. "The Location of the Cotton-Manufacturing Industry in the United States, 1880–1910." Ph.D. dissertation, Harvard University, 1940.

Clay, Howard B. "Daniel Augustus Tompkins: An American Bourbon." Ph.D. dissertation, University of North Carolina, 1951.

Donald, Gordon, Jr. "The Depression in Cotton Textiles, 1924 to 1940." Ph.D. dissertation, University of Chicago, 1951.

Fraunberger, R. C. "Lumber Trade Associations." M.A. Thesis, Temple University, 1951.

Gies, Thomas G. "The Effect of Trade Associations upon Competition in Selected Industries." Ph.D. dissertation, University of Michigan, 1952.

Hammond, Seth. "The Cotton Industry of This Century (and its immediate antecedents)." Ph.D. dissertation, Harvard University, 1941.

Hickman, Bert G., Jr. "Cyclical Fluctuations in the Cotton Textile Industry." Ph.D. dissertation, University of California, 1947.

Himmelberg, Robert F. "Relaxation of the Federal Anti-Trust Policy as a Goal of the Business Community During the Period 1918–1933." Ph.D. dissertation, Pennsylvania State University, 1963.

Hodges, James A. "The New Deal Labor Policy and the Southern Cotton Textile Industry, 1933–1941." Ph.D. dissertation, Vanderbilt University, 1963.

Keith, Edward G. "Financial History of Two Textile Towns: A Study of Lowell and Fall River." Ph.D. dissertation, Harvard University, 1936.

Lamb, Robert K. "The Development of Entrepreneurship in Fall River: 1813–1859." Ph.D. dissertation, Harvard University, 1935.

Shen, Tsung-yuen. "A Quantitative Study of Production in the American Textile Industry, 1840–1940." Ph.D. dissertation, Yale University, 1956.

Siniavsky, Boris M. "The Cotton-Textile Institute, Inc., a Stabilizing Agency in the Cotton Textile Industry." M.A. thesis, University of North Carolina, 1931.

Stelzer, Irwin M. "The Cotton Textile Industry." Ph.D. dissertation, Cornell University, 1954.

Williamson, Gustavus G. "Cotton Manufacturing in South Carolina, 1865–1892." Ph.D. dissertation, Johns Hopkins University, 1954.

X. Personal Interviews

Cason J. Callaway. November 6, 1958.

Charles A. Cannon. March 6, 1959.

Donald Comer. November 3, 1958.

Goldthwaite H. Dorr. July 20, 1959, and August 31, 1961.

William M. McLaurine. October 24 and 28, 1958.

Hunter Marshall. August 15, 1958, and October 27, 1958.

Index

COMPETITION AND COOPERATION:
The Emergence of a National Trade Association

by Louis Galambos

designer : Edward King
typesetter : Monotype Composition Company, Inc.
typefaces : Baskerville (text) and Cloister Bold (display)
printer : John D. Lucas Printing Company
paper : Warrens "1854"
binder : Moore & Co., Inc.
cover material : Columbia Riverside RL-1988